De

A CALENDAR OF MURDER

MICHAEL JOSEPH BOOKS ON
LIVE ISSUES

Series editors H. L. Beales   O. R. McGregor

A Calendar of Murder

CRIMINAL HOMICIDE IN ENGLAND SINCE 1957

TERENCE MORRIS *and* LOUIS BLOM-COOPER

London
MICHAEL JOSEPH

First published by
MICHAEL JOSEPH LTD
26, Bloomsbury Street,
London, W.C.1
1964

MADE AND PRINTED IN GREAT BRITAIN
BY CHARLES BIRCHALL & SONS, LTD.,
LIVERPOOL AND LONDON

To

Sir Ernest Gowers, G.C.B., G.B.E.,
Chairman of the Royal Commission on Capital Punishment
1949-1953
whose report ranks as one of the great social documents of our
age, and whose recommendations have been—to the country's
detriment—spurned by the legislature

CONTENTS

INTRODUCTION

THIS BOOK is not a polemical contribution to the debate on capital punishment. Its principal aim is to provide those who wish seriously to contribute to this continuing debate with the kind of basic and comprehensive evidence which has simply never been available before. Celebrated cases of murder have indeed been written about at length—some of them *ad nauseam*—while many others, less spectacular, have escaped the attention of the British public as a whole. But any discussion about the nature of murder or the character of murderers must, if it is to be valid, take into account all instances of the crime, many of which are lacking in any newsworthy quality.

We have therefore provided the reader with thumb-nail sketches of all the 764 men and women who between 21 March 1957 and 31 December 1962 stood in the docks of the Assize Courts of England and Wales indicted for murder, whatever were the results of those proceedings. The vignettes are to be regarded as nothing more than the raw material of the situational factors at work whenever there is a homicide; since the sketches are largely distilled from what is revealed to the courts they contain little or no material pertaining to the social or medical backgrounds of the actors in the homicidal situation, the evidence of which remains either locked away from public scrutiny or unrevealed even to the authorities. Apart from their intrinsic quality of indicating broadly the nature of the individual homicides, the sketches provide complete information on the judicial disposal of every case. This book then is a calendar—not an anatomy or encyclopaedia—of murder since the Homicide Act 1957.

We chose for our study the point at which an accused is indicted for murder, since this moment provides probably the most accurate measure of the number of persons who may reasonably have been suspected of unlawful homicide. It has two distinct advantages: first, the initial definition of murder by the police may be significantly changed before the suspect (if, as many do, he has not already committed suicide) stands trial; secondly, it avoids the bias inherent in looking at cases in which the courts have made their final judgment, for the judicial process produces a whole series of factors—the actions of juries, the technicalities of law and the modifications resulting from appeal—which may well distort the original commonsense picture.

The thumb-nail sketches are also designed to provide information in one area in which knowledge has been conspicuously lacking, namely, about the victims of homicide. There are few crimes, apart from homicide, where the relationship between offender and offended is more crucial. Moreover, the role of the victim in those circumstances where his actions have contributed to his own death cannot be ignored. What we have attempted to do is to include certain basic data—the ages, occupations and relationships of accused and victim, as well as the circumstances of the offence—together with the details of the judicial process and, wherever relevant, legal or other commentary. There is noticeably a paucity of information about any previous criminal activities on the part of either actor in the murder situation. Because the sentences for murder are mandatory, evidence of previous convictions is not relevant to the sentencing process. In other crimes where the court has a discretion, evidence as to previous convictions forms a vital part of that process.

It might seem that knowledge of the previous criminal careers of the victims of murder is wholly irrelevant and in any case conflicts with the mantle of innocence with which the victims of murder are almost invariably shrouded. But if the question of victim-precipitation is an important issue—as we think it is—then to study the character of the victim is equally important. Another less serious omission is the lack of follow-up material on the individual cases, but this is inevitable since publicity is not usually given to the subsequent history of those who have passed out of the judicial process into the penal or mental health systems. We are not aware, for example, of any person, sentenced to life imprisonment since the Homicide Act 1957 either for non-capital murder or as a result of a commutation of the death penalty, having been released on licence; it is unlikely that there have been any as yet.

Where the courts have made hospital orders under the Mental Health Act 1959 in respect of those persons who successfully pleaded diminished responsibility, we have generally been unable to indicate whether the patient has been discharged from mental hospital—it will have occurred only in those cases where no restriction order was attached by the court to the hospital order. A number of accused, who did successfully plead diminished responsibility and who were sentenced to terms of imprisonment, have been transferred to Broadmoor by the Home Secretary; where this has been done, and this information has come to our notice, we have recorded the fact. There have in fact been three women and two men committed to Broadmoor since 1957 who have been discharged. For obvious reasons, it is not thought fit to make these names known. Some other Broadmoor patients, included in this calendar of murder, have been transferred to ordinary mental hospitals and may possibly have been discharged from there.

No one needs to be reminded of the relevance of an accused's previous criminal record. Yet this information has on the whole rarely been forthcoming. It is ruthlessly excluded from the trial process—the case of Hanratty (1962) was a rare instance where the accused's criminal record provided part of his defence to murder. And after the mandatory sentence is passed the executive is not unnaturally reticent about revealing it. Where we have known of a killer's previous criminal record the fact has been noted, but readers must regard the thumb-nail sketches as being, in this important respect, significantly defective.

The emphasis in what has been written on the subject of homicide in this country has been directed almost exclusively to the issue of the death penalty—and most of it has come from the abolitionist camp. What we have tried to do is to comment more broadly on a range of issues touching on the subject of homicide from both the legal and sociological viewpoints. The reader must make up his own mind to what extent he agrees or disagrees with what we have to say. In these chapters we have been deliberately selective, but we are confident that any conclusions we may have drawn can be verified by reference to the thumb-nail sketches.

If the contribution by the Home Office to the research for this book was small in proportion, it was vital. Through Mr. Francis Graham-Harrison of the Home Office we were supplied with the lists of persons indicted before the various Assize Courts. On the basis of these lists, Mr. Gerald Levens, Miss Audrey Sander and Mr. Anthony Simpson, at various stages of our work, foraged among cuttings of newspapers—frequently obscure and even on occasions excessively parochial—to extract the vital information.

Much of the material was fortunately already collected in the library of the Howard League for Penal Reform, and we are grateful to both Mr. Hugh Klare and Mrs. Elizabeth Howard for ready access to this invaluable source material.

Thankless though the task is, the work of typing a manuscript—and ours must have been as scruffy and chaotic a manuscript as any typist has encountered—is always invaluable. We are particularly thankful that our two amanuenses, Mrs. A. Witts and Miss Grace Dobie, performed the task of restoring order out of chaos so that the book could go to the publishers in such fine fettle.

Temple   T.P.M.
September 1963   L.J.B.-C.

GLOSSARY

Gowers Commission	Royal Commission on Capital Punishment (1949-1953)
Atkin Committee	Departmental Committee on Insanity and Crime (1922-1923)
L.C.	Lord Chancellor
C.J. (or L.C.J.)	Chief Justice (or Lord Chief Justice)
C.C.A.	Court of Criminal Appeal
Smith J.	Mr. Justice Smith
Smith and Jones JJ.	Mr. Justice Smith and Mr. Justice Jones
L.Q.R.	Law Quarterly Review
M.L.R.	Modern Law Review
(1884) 14 Q.B.D.	Official Law Reports from 1875 to 1890, Queen's Bench Division
[1957] 2 Q.B.	Official Law Reports since 1891, Queen's Bench Division
[1957] A.C.	Official Law Reports since 1891, Appeal Cases (decisions of the House of Lords)
[1957] 1 W.L.R.	Weekly Law Reports
(1957) 41 Cr.App.R.	Criminal Appeal Reports since creation of Court of Criminal Appeal in 1907
(1957) 101 S.J.	Solicitors' Journal
[1957] Crim.L.R.	Criminal Law Review
[1957] 2 All E.R.	All England Reports
1946 J.C.	Justiciary Cases (Scottish Law Reports)
1958 S.L.T. 167	Scots Law Times
(1959) 98 C.L.R.	Commonwealth Law Reports (Reports of cases in the Australian High Court)
[1957] N.Z.L.R.	New Zealand Law Reports

[1951] 1. W.W.R.(N.S)	Western Weekly Reports (New Series)—law reports of courts of Western Canadian provinces
1959 (3) S.A.	South African Law Reports
214 F. 862 (D.C.Cir. 2d 1954)	Federal Reporter—series of American law reports of Federal Courts
171 F.Supp.474	Federal Supplement—another series of American law reports
R. v. Smith	Regina (or Rex) versus Smith
D.P.P. v. Smith	Director of Public Prosecutions versus Smith.

All persons charged on indictment with capital or non-capital murder are tried either at the Central Criminal Court (Old Bailey) —generally for crimes committed in the London area—or at one of the Assize towns.

All appeals come to the Court of Criminal Appeal presided over by the Lord Chief Justice (and staffed by all the judges of the Queen's Bench Division); the Court normally consists of three judges, but exceptionally may consist of five. Any person convicted of capital murder has an unqualified right of appeal; all other convicted persons have a right of appeal on a point of law but otherwise an appeal against conviction and/or sentence requires the leave either of the single judge or of the Court of Criminal Appeal. Until the Administration of Justice Act 1960, appeals to the House of Lords could be taken at the instance of either accused or prosecution only with the Attorney-General's *fiat*. As a result of the 1960 Act the power to grant leave to appeal to the House of Lords was transferred to the courts. If the Court of Criminal Appeal certifies that the case raises a point of law of general public importance, then that Court or the House of Lords itself can grant leave to appeal.

Any reference to sections in an unnamed Act of Parliament to the Homicide Act 1957 (the section most commonly quoted is section 2 which provides for the defence of diminished responsibility).

TYPES OF SENTENCE

Mandatory sentences

    Capital murder: death

    Non-capital murder: life imprisonment.

Anyone convicted of capital murder who is under 18 at the time of the killing is automatically detained during Her Majesty's pleasure (H.M.P.) under section 53(1) of the Children and Young Persons Act 1933. Similarly, both those who are found insane and unfit to plead and those found guilty but insane are automatically ordered to be detained during Her Majesty's pleasure and committed to Broadmoor or other State mental institution.

Alternative discretionary sentences for other forms of criminal homicide

1. Absolute discharge.
2. Probation, with or without condition that the probationer undergoes a period of mental treatment which must be limited to a maximum of 12 months (section 4 of the Criminal Justice Act 1948).
3. Hospital order (since Part V of the Mental Health Act 1959 came into force on 1 November 1960), with or without restrictions on the patient's discharge.
   1. Without any restrictions: section 60 of the Mental Health Act 1959
   2. With restrictions of limited or unlimited duration: section 65 of the Mental Health Act 1959
4. Imprisonment—the maximum in the case of all forms of manslaughter is life imprisonment.
5. Usual alternatives for young persons.

CASES

1957

Accused   *Victim*

Yusuf Haji Awad   Donald Clifford Rees

Awad (29), a Somali, was attacked by Rees (age not reported) and six others in the street; Rees hit him on the head with a bottle, and one of the others produced a clasp-knife. Awad grabbed the knife from him, opened it and showed it to the group in order to frighten them off. Cooze, the owner of the knife, attacked Awad and was wounded; then, as Rees tried to hit Awad again, he was stabbed. Rees died 10 days later.

Awad pleaded self-defence and was found *not guilty at Glamorgan Assizes, 10.4.1957*. The prosecution offered no evidence on a further charge of wounding Cooze with intent to commit grievous bodily harm.

Kenneth Barlow   Betty Barlow

Barlow (38), a male nurse, was charged with the non-capital murder of his second wife (30), who was 2 months pregnant, by drowning her in the bath when she was in a coma induced by injection(s) of insulin. (His first wife died a year before of natural causes, although doctors could not state the precise cause of death).

Prosecution alleged that, as a male nurse, Barlow had the opportunity to obtain supplies of insulin and that some time in the past he had mentioned to an acquaintance that "you can commit a perfect murder with insulin—it leaves no trace". (This statement he denied). Barlow admitted that both he and his wife were anxious to abort the coming child (though she was keener than he was since she was afraid for her health) and that he had stolen quantities of ergometrine from the hospital and administered injections of it to his wife, since he believed that this would be effective, taking care not to give too large doses.

Much evidence of a highly scientific nature was put forward at the trial at Leeds Assizes (where the prosecution was led by the

1

Solicitor-General). For example, with the aid of a magnifying glass several puncture marks were found on the wife's buttocks and the presence of insulin was detected in her body. Although it was established that ergometrine could not have had the effects which resulted in the death of Mrs. Barlow and her condition prior to it, defence questioned Crown evidence (based upon weeks of experiment and research) regarding the presence of insulin in the body. Testimony was presented of Barlow being a "devoted husband", and of the pair being extremely happy together at all times.

Motive was never firmly established, though it was suggested by the prosecution that when Barlow's attempts to abort his wife had failed he decided that the only way to kill the child was to kill the mother as well. It was suggested that she would allow him to inject her with insulin quite willingly, thinking it was ergometrine.

Barlow *was convicted of non-capital murder at Leeds Assizes, 13.12.1957, and sentenced to life imprisonment.*

Application for leave to appeal was refused, 24.3.1958.

Alfred Barnes   James William Forbes

Barnes (32) was in Preston prison serving his first sentence—9 months for shopbreaking—and was due for release in 12 days, having earned full remission. After a quarrel with another prisoner over tobacco, a fist fight developed between the two, and Forbes (22) died.

Barnes pleaded *not guilty to non-capital murder, but guilty to manslaughter*—This was accepted by the prosecution.

Sentenced to 3 years' imprisonment at Lancaster Assizes, 22.10.1957.

Victor Tony Bassett   Jennifer Bassett

Bassett (24) *was acquitted at Bedford Assizes, 10.10.1957,* of murdering his daughter (7 weeks), six years previously. It was alleged by the prosecution that he suffocated the child by putting a pillow over her face as she was sleeping between him and his wife in bed. At the time, the wife was aged 17, and Bassett was 18; she left him in 1954, and in 1957 told the police that he had deliberately killed the child because they could not afford to keep her.

Bassett admitted to the police that he had killed the child (though this was probably an attempt to get his wife to return to him some-how) but later retracted this statement.

Thomas Bennett   Annie Waters

Bennett (73), retired machinist, *found unfit to plead at Old Bailey, 10.5.1957,* on a charge of non-capital murder of his old neighbour (77). *Detained during H.M.P.*

Bennett was a widower living with his son. Mrs. Waters, who was said to have been very kind to Bennett, was killed with a hammer. Bennett made a statement to the police admitting the killing. He said he woke up with a headache feeling depressed and worried; he then visited Mrs. Waters twice, and on the second occasion asked her for some aspirins. "After this I remembered a continual talking to her . . . I think I can recollect something came over me and I'm almost certain I struck her [twice]". He later caught a train from Surbiton to Salisbury where he gave himself up. Bennett stated that he had recently been behaving very abnormally at home and was under observation in hospital.

Henry Beynon   Catharine Jane Beynon

Beynon (60), an unemployed labourer, was accused of murdering his wife (age not reported) and then attempting suicide. Doctors said that he suffered from senile dementia. He could not under-stand questions, instruct counsel or follow any evidence.

At Cardiff Assizes, he was found insane and unfit to plead on charge of non-capital murder, 3.4.1957. H.M.P.

[Authors' note: This case raised an important point of law ([1957] 2.Q.B.111). Mr. Justice Byrne refused to follow an earlier decision of Mr. Justice (now Lord) Devlin, holding that the law had always been that an insane person who was unfit to plead could not be tried. If the Court was aware of the fact that there was a pre-liminary issue whether the accused was insane, so that he was unfit to be tried, it was the Court's duty to see that that issue was dealt with before the issue of guilt or innocence, even though no applica-tion had been made by either prosecution or defence. In R. v. Roberts ([1954] 2.Q.B.329) Mr. Justice Devlin refused to try the preliminary issue of the fitness to plead of the accused (a deaf mute) whereupon the prosecution offered no evidence, and, on the Judge's direction, the jury found the accused not guilty. The majority of the Criminal Law Revision Committee, in its Third Report, Criminal Procedure (Insanity) by a majority recommended that the issue of an accused's unfitness to plead at his trial should be postponed from the moment of arraignment, but only up to the closing of the prosecution's case.

Ronald Boocock   Arthur Bairstow

Boocock (15), a warehouse boy, was alleged to have beaten Bairstow (19) to death, with blows, kicks etc.; outside a public house in Bradford during a fight between rival gangs of youths. Both had been drinking fairly heavily. Boocock had no previous convictions of any kind; it was stated that he had not had a decent home life.

Plea of not guilty to charge of non-capital murder but guilty to manslaughter was accepted at Leeds Assizes, 16.12.1957. Sentenced to be detained for a period not exceeding 5 years under section 53(2) of the Children and Young Persons Act 1933.

Pamela Bourne   Raymond Maurice Mezzone

Jealous of her married lover (29) who, although he had discarded her, still wanted custody of the child she had had by him, a young wife (19) took a knife from her bag and stabbed him as she was quarrelling with him and his wife outside their home.

She was acquitted of non-capital murder but *convicted of manslaughter and sentenced to 7 years' imprisonment at Birmingham Assizes, 16.7.1957.*

Elizabeth Bowron   Betty Floretta Bowron

A wife (48) of a commercial traveller charged with non-capital murder of her daughter (6). Accused, who had a personal and family history of mental illness (suffered from delusions; had attempted suicide 3 times prior to the murder), was alleged to have said later, "Nobody wants us. We have both got T.B. Betty had been spitting blood this afternoon. I just squeezed her throat and stuck the knife into her". Afterwards, accused attempted suicide by stabbing herself in the neck and taking an overdose of aspirins.

Doctor at the trial stated that there was no evidence of the child having had T.B. Accused apparently considered the act a mercy-killing. She had had eight children and, including Betty, six of them had died in tragic circumstances in one way or another.

Found guilty but insane at Warwick Assizes, 27.11.1957, and ordered to be detained as a patient at Broadmoor.

George Briers   John Topping

There were constant quarrels between Briers (17) and his stepfather (58). During one such altercation, after Topping had come home drunk, Briers went upstairs and sat down on his bed in despair. He heard a thud and thought Topping was striking his mother. He suddenly loaded his shotgun, which he kept for shooting wild pigeons, came downstairs and "just felt myself pulling the trigger".

When charged with capital murder, Briers said he had had no intention to kill, but had acted under provocation. Acquitted, *but convicted of manslaughter under section 3 and sentenced to 7 years' imprisonment at Liverpool Crown Court, 8.11.1957.*

Joan Burns   Helen Lynne Burns
                                                 Valerie Grace Burns

Mother (28) with history of mental illness (had spent 6 months as a patient in a mental hospital), *found unfit to plead at Newcastle Assizes, 8.10.1957,* when charged with the murder by drowning of her two daughters (4 years and 10 weeks). Attempted suicide afterwards. *H.M.P.*

George Harry Burnett   Ernest Horne
                                                 George Hoult

Burnett (22), unemployed colliery worker, went to pay his rent to the landlord, Horne (55), of the lodging-house where he was staying. Hoult (58) who was in the room, attacked him—for no apparent reason; Burnett took a stool, which Horne had picked up, and hit Hoult with it; he then turned round and hit his landlord with it because he thought he was also going to attack him.

The jury found him not guilty of either murder or manslaughter in the case of Hoult; he had acted in legitimate self-defence. He was convicted of manslaughter in respect of Horne, the jury finding that his action was the result of provocation. *Sentenced to 3 years' imprisonment at Sheffield Assizes, 25.11.1957.*

Shirley Campbell   Susan Pickles

Campbell (21), a coloured mill-girl, was alleged to have strangled on impulse the baby of 16 months whom she was minding for its parents, when the baby's crying interrupted a radio programme to which accused was listening. Campbell also claimed that she had lent the baby's mother both money and clothes which had never been returned, so had killed the baby to spite the mother.

Defence (for the first time since the passing of the Homicide Act 1957), invoked section 2 of the Act, and offered evidence of Campbell's abnormally low intelligence coupled with a "very deep-seated mental conflict associated with her colour", and a gross personality defect of a psychopathic nature.

Found not guilty of non-capital murder, but convicted of manslaughter under section 2, and sentenced to life imprisonment at Leeds Assizes, 26.4.1957.

David James Carter   Doreen Carter

Carter (30) was accused of the non-capital murder by manual strangulation of his wife (24) at their home. It was alleged that he had become very suspicious of her having an affair with a neighbour, for which there was some evidence, and that recently she had refused to have sexual relations with him (the accused). After the wife had insulted him and hit him, Carter lost his head and killed her.

Found not guilty of non-capital murder but guilty of manslaughter, the jury adding a plea for leniency. Oxford Assizes, 9.5.1957. 3 years' imprisonment.

John Thomas Daley   Anne Daley
                                     Eamon Daley

His estranged wife's (39) "adulterous association" with a barman led Daley (35) to pick up a knife and stab her violently after a quarrel. He then strangled his baby son (7 months) in case his crying attracted attention.

Found guilty of manslaughter by reason of provocation on the first charge and guilty of non-capital murder on the second. Sentenced to life imprisonment on the second conviction. No sentence passed on the conviction relating to the first. Birmingham Assizes, 12.7.1957.

Mary Dayson   Robert Dayson

Mrs. Dayson (23) decided to gas herself when distraught with worry over financial difficulties and in a severe depression following the birth of her second child, Edward (11 months at the time); she was also on bad terms with her husband. She decided also to gas her son, Robert (2½), since she was afraid to leave him alone with no-one to care properly for him. She was found unconscious at their home; the boy was dead.

Pleaded not guilty to non-capital murder, *but guilty to manslaughter on grounds of diminished responsibility at Stafford Assizes, 28.11.1957; she was put on probation,* with the condition that she undergo hospital treatment, under section 4 of the Criminal Justice Act 1948.

George Kelly Dinsdale   Henry Smith

Dinsdale (26), an unemployed seaman, stabbed Smith (33) when the latter, who had become very friendly with accused's former mistress, attacked him in the yard of her house after Dinsdale had been found hiding in the coal shed. Accused had become very jealous of Smith and had continued to follow the woman after she had taken up with Smith.

Found not guilty of non-capital murder, *but guilty of manslaughter and sentenced to 10 years' imprisonment. Leeds Assizes, 26.7.1957.*

Richard Dobb   Rachel Enser

Dobb (43), a warehouseman, did not meet with very favourable response when he pressed his attentions upon Mrs. Enser's daughter. She found his behaviour rather eccentric. He broke into their home and viciously attacked Mrs. Enser (67) with a knife and a razor blade—as she lay in bed, cutting her throat and finally stabbing her. He was evidently under the impression that the daughter was being cold towards him as a result of pressure from her mother.

He pleaded diminished responsibility at his trial at *Nottingham Assizes;* defence counsel claimed he was suffering from mental abnormality as a result of privations endured in a Japanese prisoner-of-war camp. This evidence was rebutted by the prosecution but he was *convicted of manslaughter under section 2, and sentenced to 15 years' imprisonment, 20.11.1957.*

William John Dodds   Charles Barrett

Dodds (50), an assistant school-caretaker, was charged with the non-capital murder of the resident caretaker (67) by battering him to death with a sandbag and a shovel during a fight in the school basement. The fight had arisen from a quarrel over Barrett's piling of work on to his assistant. After the death, accused made up long false stories about "masked attackers".

Defence based upon provocation on the grounds that Dodds was provoked by Barrett's words and conduct.

Convicted of non-capital murder and sentenced to life imprisonment at Lewes Assizes, 17.12.1957.

Desmond Dodshon   Lucy Dodshon

Dodshon (34) *was found insane and unfit to plead at Durham Assizes, 30.5.1957,* to the charge of stabbing his mother (56) at their home with a carving knife.

No specific details reported as to nature of his mental disorder, nor as to possible reason(s) for the crime. *H.M.P.*

Jan Dorosiewicz   Victor Bottono

Dorosiewicz (35), of Polish origin, was *found insane and unfit to plead at Old Bailey, 4.12.1957,* on a charge of non-capital murder. *H.M.P.* Dorosiewicz had been a patient in a mental hospital since 1942. He had a quarrel with another patient, Bottono, over a brush in the garden, which Dorosiewicz claimed was his. In the ensuing fight Bottono was killed.

Dorosiewicz had been violent on earlier occasions and in 1952 had as a result undergone a lobotomy. In 1956 he had so improved that he was regarded as a voluntary patient; soon after, however, following another fight, he was returned to a closed ward where the killing of Bottono took place. All the doctors agreed that Dorosiewicz was M'Naghten mad.

Ronald Patrick Dunbar   Selina Mewes

Dunbar (24), labourer, broke into the house of the victim, a semi-recluse (82), in order to rob her; he killed her, it was alleged, with blows on the head from a bottle when she woke up and recognised him. It was the second time he had broken into the house within a week. Accused gave himself up to the police.

Defence based upon section 2, and offered evidence that Dunbar was an "inadequate psychopath" with a long history of instability. Prosecution produced medical evidence to rebut this.

Convicted of capital murder and sentenced to death at Newcastle Assizes, 16.5.1957.

Appeal made to Court of Criminal Appeal ([1958] 1 Q.B.1) on grounds that Mr. Justice Ashworth had not given sufficient direction to the jury on the meaning of word "proof" in "onus of proof" (relating to diminished responsibility). Appeal court adjourned and reconvened before full court of 5 judges.

[Authors' note: Abolitionists almost decided to challenge in the courts the propriety of reconstituting the court where, in the original court there had been a majority for allowing the appeal. In the event the move proved unnecessary.]

Appeal successful, 5.7.1957. The Lord Chief Justice (Lord Goddard) ruled that the trial Judge should have pointed out to the jury that the onus of proof on the defence, when they entered a plea of diminished responsibility, was not as heavy as the onus of proof on the prosecution when they alleged murder. If the jury had been given the proper direction it was highly likely that it would still have returned the verdict it did; but in a matter which made the difference between a capital sentence and one of imprisonment, it would be impossible for the court to say there was no miscarriage of justice.

Conviction reduced to manslaughter under section 2, and Dunbar sentenced to life imprisonment.

Horace Henry Edwards   Alan Warren

Edwards (36), bench-hand, *pleaded guilty at Old Bailey, 25.10.1957, to the murder* of a boy (7) whose naked body, sexually assaulted, was found on a building site. He was alleged to have enticed the boy on to the site and to have suffocated him in his attempt to stop the boy crying. After death, Edwards stripped the boy and scraped the front of his body with a bunch of keys, causing long scratches. The murder was said to have preyed on his mind and he was some time later found by his sister-in-law with his head in a gas oven at his home.

Sentenced to life imprisonment.

Derrick Edwardson   Edwina Taylor

Edwardson (31), a factory labourer, *pleaded guilty at the Old Bailey to the non-capital murder* of a girl Edwina Taylor (4). It was alleged that he had enticed her to his flat in Upper Norwood, and there battered and strangled her with the intention of raping her after death. When he had killed her, however, he suffered remorse and did not interfere with her. He hid her body in the coal-cellar of his house and ran away, but surrendered to the police a week or so later. Edwardson had eight previous convictions for indecent assaults on young girls, indecent exposure, larceny, being in possession of housebreaking implements, etc., etc. and had been a patient in a mental hospital.

Sentenced to life imprisonment, 25.10.1957.

[Authors' note: The sombre theme of child murder is disturbingly used by Duerrenmatt in his play, *The Pledge*: see MacDonald, *The Murderer and his Victim*, p. 383. At the time of Edwardson's arrest a hostile crowd outside Gypsy Hill Police Station (Upper Norwood, London) stoned the police van which the crowd believed (erroneously) was conveying Edwardson to prison.]

John William Elms   Ethel Elms

Elms (44), a lorry driver, battered his wife (54) to death in the bathroom of their Bristol home during the course of a minor quarrel. She received 16 fractures of the skull with an unidentified "blunt instrument".

Defence pleaded diminished responsibility. There was a long history of mental disorder, and Elms was said to be suffering from minor forms of epilepsy and had "black-outs". Doctors for both the prosecution and the defence agreed that he was a psychopath, and medical evidence called by the Crown to rebut the defence seemed only to support it. In spite of this, however, the defence plea failed and Elms was *convicted of non-capital murder and sentenced to life imprisonment at Bristol Assizes, 25.6.1957.*

Elms had many convictions for larceny etc., resulting in his having been put on probation and subsequently sentenced both to Borstal training and imprisonment.

Harry Epstine   Lilian Davies

Epstine (45) had a long family—and personal—history of mental illness; had been a certified patient since May 1955, suffering from chronic schizophrenia. Absconded from an "open-ward" hospital, bought a knife, met Davies (42), a ward-maid in a maternity hospital, and went drinking with her. Took her home and stabbed her in the driveway of her hospital.

Following arrest, his condition worsened. *Found unfit to plead on charge of non-capital murder at Birmingham Assizes, 22.7.1957. H.M.P.*

Dennis Fenton

Greta Fenton
Sandra Fenton

Prosecution alleged that Fenton (46), a commercial traveller, strangled with his hands his wife and daughter (13) at their home. Defence entered plea of manslaughter on grounds of diminished responsibility, and offered evidence that Fenton, suffering from severe pains in the head and stomach, and believing that he and his wife were suffering from cancer, concluded a suicide pact with her. He killed the daughter first, then his wife; his attempted suicide in a gas oven was interrupted by visitors. Prosecution alleged that both victims had multiple injuries, indicating a fairly violent struggle.

He was found guilty of non-capital murder of his daughter. Sentenced to life imprisonment. The two charges of non-capital murder of his wife and of attempted suicide were left on the file. Stafford Assizes, 28.11.1957.

Frederick Samuel Foxall

Cyril Hassall

After drinking, Foxall (32), a greengrocer, was involved in a fight (not with the victim) outside a public house. The fight ceased, and he and his opponent walked towards the latter's home. Hassall (31) followed behind and chased Foxall when the accused ran towards his own home nearby. Foxall returned from his house, went up to him and stabbed him in the stomach with a carving knife. He immediately telephoned the police and confessed.

Defence pleaded provocation. Accused had allegedly no recollection of stabbing victim, nor any intention of murdering him. Not guilty on charge of non-capital murder but *guilty of manslaughter and sentenced to 4 years' imprisonment at Birmingham Assizes, 26.7.1957.*

Albert Richard Frith

Maria Chesson

Frith (37), an unemployed machinist, beat his mother (59) to death with a flat iron at their home and then ran away. They had been quarrelling about his eccentric habits of going for long walks and sleeping out in the open (mother refused to buy him any more pairs of shoes). Frith was found in the streets by a policeman who noticed excessively down-at-heel shoes.

Mental abnormality (schizophrenia) was present, sufficient to amount to diminished responsibility and he was *convicted at the Old Bailey, 29.10.1957, of manslaughter under section 2. Sentenced to 7 years' imprisonment. Transferred to Broadmoor, 23.12.1957, under section 2 of the Criminal Lunatics Act 1884.*

Harry Gent   Brian Bernard Gent

Gent (46), watchmaker, gassed his son (10 months) in his cot at their home after a quarrel with his wife. He had been drinking heavily.

He was said to have been very fond of the child, and a doctor at his trial claimed that he had killed the baby precisely *because* he loved it so much, and was afraid of anyone else having custody over it. Gent's plea of diminished responsibility was supported by his history of mental disorder (had been 3 times a mental patient); he was said to be suffering from paranoid delusions.

Found *guilty of manslaughter under section 2, at Liverpool Crown Court, 11.11.1957. Sentenced to 10 years' imprisonment.*

[Authors' note: This is a curious example of the violent disturbance of the parental relationship which, contrary to popular belief, accounts for such a large proportion of child murders (75 per cent of all child victims are killed by parents or older relatives). See also Bastian (1958) and Whitehead (1957).]

Elias Georgiou   Dr. John Pulfer

Georgiou (25), a Cypriot, was alleged to have stabbed Dr. Pulfer (54) in his surgery at Colindale after the doctor had given him advice which "was against our religion".

No specific details reported as to mental state, but *found unfit to plead. Old Bailey, 8.5.1957. H.M.P.*

Clara Gray   Cyril Gray

Found unfit to plead at Birmingham Assizes, 22.7.1957, on a charge of non-capital murder at the caravan home of her husband (58), a Ministry of Supply Inspector and former test pilot. Victim was battered to death with an iron saucepan.

Evidence of accused's paraphrenia—chronic delusional insanity. Accused (66) apparently had no memory of the killing. *H.M.P.*

Ronald H. J. Griffin   Dorothy Griffin

When his wife (45) kept on nagging at him to get a job, Griffin, (41), unemployed, picked up a coal-hammer and beat her to death.

At his trial at *Bristol Assizes, 19.11.1957, his plea of not guilty to murder but guilty to manslaughter (on grounds of diminished responsibility)* was accepted by the Crown, which also called medical evidence of Griffin's mental abnormality (melancholia, with delusions). The defence supported this evidence. Griffin had previously attempted suicide and had been a patient in a mental hospital in 1956. He was described as "mentally very sick".

Sentenced to 7 years' imprisonment.

Thomas James Harding   Veronica Chen

Harding (36), a coloured Liverpool barman, was alleged by the Crown to have beaten his mistress at their home when she arrived home late one night "rotten drunk" and refused to tell him where she had been. She died next day.

Harding admitted the facts but denied any intention to cause bodily harm. He was *acquitted of non-capital murder at Liverpool Crown Court, 6.11.1957* and discharged.

[Authors' note: He is believed to have made legal history by being the first man to be allowed bail in any English court on a charge of murder.]

Louie Harmon   Kenneth Harmon

Mrs. Harmon (46) *was sentenced to life imprisonment at Stafford Assizes, 6.12.1957, when convicted of manslaughter (on grounds of diminished responsibility)* of her son (16).

The boy had lost a finger in an accident earlier in the year, and had become depressed and downhearted. The mother became convinced that there was no improvement and that there was something wrong with his mental condition. She became worried and could not sleep, and eventually gassed the boy attempting to kill herself at the same time.

There was medical evidence that she had suffered from delusions and obsessional neuroses.

Francis Charles Harrison   Doris Harrison

Harrison (36), a progress chaser, was found guilty of the non-capital murder of his wife (31) by striking her on the head with an axe. He hid the body in a cupboard at home before it was discovered by police 2½ months later.

Defence offered evidence of accused's "hysterical personality" in a submission for a verdict of manslaughter on grounds of diminished responsibility. Prosecution's evidence of (a) wife's continual nagging; and (b) accused's association with another woman, together established sufficient motive. Jury decided that Harrison's "mental abnormality" was insufficient to bring him within section 2.

Sentenced to life imprisonment on conviction of non-capital murder; Old Bailey, 18.9.1957.

George Robert Harrison   Gwendoline Jones

Harrison (50) was accused of the murder by stabbing of the married woman (41) with whom he had been living.

Prosecution claimed that Harrison and Jones had had violent quarrels in public during the previous weeks and that accused was worried over mounting bills. Alleged that Jones had led Harrison a "merry dance" and had been going out with other men. Discounted the defence's plea that the killing had been an accident. Harrison maintained throughout that he did not realise he was carrying a knife in his hand as he raised his arms to reason with Jones during a quarrel at their home.

Some evidence offered (not denied by prosecution) that Harrison suffered from epileptic attacks.

Convicted of non-capital murder and sentenced to life imprisonment at Wiltshire Assizes, 9.5.1957.

Peter Frederick Hirst   Fred Littlewood

Hirst (23), a painter and decorator, *pleaded guilty* to the murder by shooting of his neighbour (47). There was no apparent motive, but some indications as to accused suffering from acute depression and persecution complex. No attempt, however, to enter plea of diminished responsibility.

Hirst was *sentenced to death at Leeds Assizes*, 27.3.1957, the first such sentence under the Act which came into force on 21.3.1957— but *reprieved by the Home Secretary, 9.4.1957. Life imprisonment.*

John Frederick Hodges   Kenneth Cooper

Hodges (25), a fun-fair attendant, had given a coloured U.S.

Airman, Cooper (21) £2 in order to buy him (Hodges) some American cigarettes. When he did not receive the cigarettes, he bought a sheath-knife so that he could frighten Cooper into returning the money, but "did not intend to harm him". In a fist-fight at the fairground, Hodges stabbed Cooper in the stomach, but later claimed he had no memory of having done so.

Jury returned after 2½ hours unable to agree. They were sent out again and returned, after a further 20 minutes, with a *verdict of not guilty of non-capital murder, but guilty of manslaughter. Sentenced to 10 years' imprisonment at the Old Bailey, 19.9.1957.*

Antol Horvath   Frank Alan Bentley

Horvath (25), a Hungarian refugee, was befriended by Bentley (30) and his wife when he fled to this country. They gave him free accommodation, lent him tools and money. Horvath was *convicted* of breaking into their home at night and of beating Bentley un-conscious in his bed with an axe which was normally kept in the coal shed. Bentley died later from his injuries. Mrs. Bentley was also similarly attacked at the same time; the charge of attempted murder of her was not proceeded with. Accused apparently stole Bentley's bicycle for escape.

Defence was based partly upon the possibility of Horvath suffer-ing from bouts of automatism as a result of (a) injuries sustained in an air-crash (Horvath was previously an officer in Hungarian Air Force); and (b) hearing the news of his brother's torture during the Hungarian Revolution.

No mention of possible motive was made by the prosecution, and Crown evidence was largely circumstantial. Jury was out for 3 hours, before returning a verdict of *guilty of non-capital murder.*

Sentenced to life imprisonment at Lincolnshire Assizes, 1.11.1957.

Dennis Howard   David Keasey

Howard (24), unemployed, was charged with the capital murder of Keasey (24) in the latter's outfitter's shop in Wolverhampton after a struggle during his attempt to rob the shop's till. Keasey was shot in the back by a Mauser automatic which Howard was carry-ing. ". . . it could not be disputed that it was a planned killing" (Lord Goddard C.J. in the C.C.A.).

Defence based upon "accidental killing" and lack of intention to use the gun (six revolvers were found by the police at accused's home). Judge said, in summing up: "It would be utterly wrong for you (the jury) to return a verdict of manslaughter just because you do not like the sound of murder. Justice could not be done in this country if juries were looking over their shoulders wondering what the result of their verdict might be".

Howard was convicted of capital murder and sentenced to death by Mr. Justice Hinchcliffe at Worcester Assizes, 18.10.1957.

Appeal to the Court of Criminal Appeal, 19.11.1957, on grounds that a suggestion, in a question by the prosecution, that Howard had been concerned in a previous incident in which a firearm was carried might have prejudiced the jury. *Appeal dismissed,* (1957) 42 Cr. App.R. 23. In the course of its judgment, the Court of Criminal Appeal ruled that it was undesirable that the report of the Crown psychiatrist, who had examined the accused while on remand in prison, should be given either to the prosecution or defence counsel, unless the question of the accused's insanity was to be raised at the trial.

Executed at Birmingham Prison, 4.12.1957.

John Percival Ingham   Louise Kate Ingham

Ingham (71), a retired retail manager, had previously been very ill for 2 months; he battered his wife (same age) to death with a coal hammer when he realised that she was growing seriously deaf and would have to enter hospital for a serious operation. Motive apparently a mercy-killing.

Found unfit to plead on a charge of non-capital murder at Liverpool Crown Court, 5.6.1957. H.M.P.

Ronald Alfred Keates (See: William Pickering)

Christopher Kelson   Stanley Jones

As Kelson (29) approached Jones (23) intending to "have it out" with him about his association with Kelson's wife, Jones put up his hands and Kelson thought he was going to fight. In fact, a fight then broke out during which Jones sustained a serious beating and died from his injuries. There had been a fight between them on an earlier occasion.

Kelson pleaded *not guilty to murder but guilty to manslaughter at Somerset Assizes, 16.10.1957;* this plea was accepted by the prosecution and he was *sentenced to 3 years' imprisonment.*

Jeffrey David Layland   Trevor Buck

Layland (26), a wood merchant, *found guilty but insane of the non-capital murder* of his stepson (13 months).

Evidence presented of accused's hysteria superimposed upon a low degree of intelligence. The question of Layland being certified had come up just previously to the crime.

After a bout of drinking (though not very heavy), Layland came home late, took the child from its cot and swung it violently by its ankles against the floor, wall or door, causing it severe injuries from which it later died. He then took the child upstairs and threw it on its mother's bed, saying "Here it is". Layland then collapsed and became incapable. Later he had no memory of what had happened in this or in other fits. Some evidence of his being otherwise a good and kind father to the child.

Ordered to be detained during H.M.P., Broadmoor. Worcester Assizes, 21.10.1957.

Archibald Anthony McBride   Donald McIntyre

McBride (22), a seaman, killed a fellow seaman (age not reported) in a fight, involving others as well, on board m.v. *Crane* while it was in a French port.

Evidence was given to suggest that McBride had acted in self-defence, and at his trial at the *Old Bailey, 22.5.1957, he was acquitted and discharged.*

Robert Mackintosh   Agnes Mackintosh

Mackintosh (68), an electrical fitter, battered his wife (73) to death with a butcher's cleaver, then gave himself up to the police. Medical evidence was given that he was suffering from a severe mental depression, probably induced by his belief that his wife's illness was cancer. He had not slept for 14 days and had had little to eat. Defence did not dispute the facts of the crime as presented by the prosecution and the Crown did not rebut defence medical evidence. Mackintosh was found *guilty but insane at Hampshire Assizes, 6.12.1957, and ordered to be detained during H.M.P. as a Broadmoor patient.*

Bernard James McParland   Terrence Charles King

McParland (35), a salesman, stabbed a man, who had been a New

2

Zealand boxing champion, during a fight at the house where they both lived, after a quarrel over the decorations which King (24) had done in the accused's flat. There seemed to be some element of provocation involved. McParland was *found guilty of manslaughter at the Old Bailey, 24.10.1957.*

Sentenced to 3 years' imprisonment.

Franklyn McPherson   Alexander Sinclair

When Sinclair (36), a Jamaican, known as a violent man, bullied the accused (32), labourer (also Jamaican), and paid unwelcome attentions to his sister over a long period of time, McPherson went out and bought a shotgun and cartridges. He sawed off the barrel, hid the gun in his coat, and the next day when Sinclair shouted offensively to him in the street, McPherson shot at him 4 times from close range.

Defence pleaded provocation (section 3) but McPherson was *found guilty of capital murder and sentenced to death, Nottingham Assizes, 28.6.1957.*

Appeal to Court of Criminal Appeal was successful on grounds of Judge's failure to direct the jury on the onus of proof regarding "provocation". *Conviction reduced to manslaughter and sentenced to 12 years' imprisonment, 23.7.1957.* [1957] *Crim. L.R.618.*

Vincent McTair   Merle Elaine Denniston

McTair (30), a West Indian, found that he was unable to get engaged to his girl-friend (also Jamaican (20)) when her mother informed him that she was already engaged to a man in the West Indies. He was alleged to have taken a knife and cut her throat, and then attempted suicide.

Since the indictment was signed before March 21, McTair's *conviction (upon a plea of "Guilty") carried the death sentence, Birmingham Assizes, 25.3.1957; the Home Secretary recommended a reprieve and McTair's sentence was commuted to life imprisonment.*

John Charles Martin   Piers St. Clair Willett

Martin (45), sales representative, took along a shotgun when he went to the house of his brother-in-law, Willett (52), in order to plead with his wife (who worked there as housekeeper) to return and live with him. His apparent intention was to commit suicide if she refused, However, an accident occurred with the defective gun. Willett was shot twice, and Martin shot himself, although not seriously.

Martin was *acquitted on the capital murder charge but convicted of manslaughter, Chester Assizes, 4.6.1957.* Martin was *bound over for two years*, since the judge considered that he had already suffered enough in spending 4 months in prison awaiting trial.

Victor Orford Masters   Esme Masters

Masters (38), a company director, offered a defence of "accident" against the charge of non-capital murder of his wife (35) who had been associating with another man. After the wife arrived home late one night, there was a violent quarrel and accused was punched and fell to the floor, knocking open a cupboard from which fell a knife. He "made pushes towards (his) wife" not knowing that he was grasping the knife.

Although defence not based upon provocation, it would seem that the wife's attitude of irresponsibility towards her family and her behaviour on the night in question might have played some part in the jury's finding of *not guilty of both murder and manslaughter, Surrey Assizes, 3.7.1957.*

Mary Morgan   David George Morgan

Mary Morgan (37), a frail housewife, was alleged by the prosecution to have poisoned her husband (74) by administering an overdose of drugs. He was frequently drunk and constantly bullied and assaulted her.

Although there was evidence of accused's low intelligence, his mental age being 10, and of a family history of abnormality, defence denied the charge and claimed that the drugs were self-administered by the victim when he was drunk.

Accused was acquitted at Glamorgan Assizes, 2.4.1957.

Kenneth Anthony Morris   Kenneth Michael Dodge

Morris (31), a scrap dealer, was alleged to have pushed Dodge (18) over a balcony during a quarrel which led to a fight at a dance at Louth Town Hall (Lincolnshire). Dodge fell 15 feet on to stone steps and later died from a fractured skull.

Morris originally charged with manslaughter, but Magistrates'

decision was that "on the evidence here today we have no alternative but to commit you on a charge of non-capital murder". At
Assize hearing, Judge called the incident a "quite unprovoked and
unnecessary attack".

After retirement of 2½ hours the jurors were unable to agree. Told
to try again, they returned after a further hour, and *convicted
Morris of manslaughter. Sentenced to 6 years' imprisonment at
Birmingham Assizes, 13.12.1957.*

Munuswamy   Latiff Khan

Munuswamy (43), an Indian seaman, the only Christian in an
otherwise Muslim ship, murdered the chief steward (age not
reported) of the m.v. *Westbank*, while it was on the high seas.
Quarrels and bad feelings had resulted from the religious situation
among the crew and matters reached a crisis when Munuswamy
and Khan quarrelled over breakfast. Khan was shortly afterwards
found in his cabin with serious head wounds, caused by a spanner,
and parts of his body had been mutilated with a knife—injuries
from which he later died.

Munuswamy was *convicted at the Old Bailey of non-capital murder and sentenced to life imprisonment, 23.9.1957.*

Marian Muzyka   Anne Muzyka

Muzyka (31), a Polish colliery-worker, became convinced that his
wife (26) was plotting to poison him. On an impulse he stabbed her
frenziedly with a breadknife at their home. Suffering from paranoid
delusions.
Found insane and unfit to plead at Leeds Assizes, 18.5.1957. H.M.P.

Patrick Myers   Anne Myers
Catherine Myers

The two parents, Patrick (29) and Catherine (23), were committed
for trial on a coroner's warrant on a charge of murdering their
daughter (20 months), whose wasted body was found in a box at
their home.

It was alleged that the child, who from birth had suffered from
hydrocephalus, a condition which made her very backward mentally and would cause her to have convulsive fits, had wasted away
and that her dead body had been hidden in a box by the mother, a

woman of low intelligence, who feared that she would be accused of not caring for her daughter.

The parents' plea of not guilty to the murder charges and to the charges of manslaughter was accepted by the court at Bedford Assizes, 10.5.1957. They both pleaded guilty to wilful neglect and were sentenced, Patrick Myers to *6 months' imprisonment*, and Catherine Myers to *12 months' imprisonment*.

Cyril Nightingale   Stanley Jackson

Nightingale (31), painter, stabbed, in a street fight, the husband of the woman with whom he was living; Jackson (36) wanted his wife to come back with him.

It was stated that Jackson had been the aggressor in the fight; Nightingale was *convicted of manslaughter at Manchester Crown Court, 21.12.1957; sentenced to 5 years' imprisonment.*

Horace Nixon   Grace Nixon

Nixon (41), engineering machinist, strangled his wife (46) at their home during a quarrel. He was alleged to have taken her stockings off and tied them around her neck.

At Leeds Assizes, 16.7.1957, he was found unfit to plead and ordered to be detained H.M.P. A doctor said Nixon suffered from a paranoid state which led him to have delusions about his wife's infidelity. He had based these upon misinterpretations of the most trivial sayings and events.

Herbert Ogle   Christopher Ogle

Ogle (38), electrician, visited his estranged wife's house with the intention of a mock suicide attempt (using chloroform and sleeping tablets) in front of her in order to win her back. But "things did not quite work out as I had planned". He burst into bedroom to see his son Christopher (11 months), locked the door and the boy began to cry, so he held a chloroform-soaked handkerchief under his nose. Then staged a suicide attempt and fell unconscious himself. Son found dead.

Accused when charged with non-capital murder offered a defence of diminished responsibility. He was said to come "of bad stock . . . his subsequent treatment in various homes tended to prevent his overcoming the disadvantages he was born with". Jury, however, *returned a verdict of simple manslaughter.*

Sentenced to 3 years' imprisonment at the Old Bailey, 23.7.1957.

John Henry Oliver   Rosetta Oliver

Oliver (44), formerly owner of a grocery shop, was alleged to have strangled, with an electric-light cord, his wife (46) in the bathroom of their home in Exeter. Oliver then moved the body to the bedroom, later telling a friend he had found it when returning home at 11.50 a.m. from public house. Motive not established, though prosecution claimed (a) after her death, Oliver took a roll of notes from wife's bag; (b) Oliver did not want to emigrate to Canada as he and his wife had planned to do. No evidence of any great disagreement between accused and his wife.

Trial at Devon Assizes stopped by Mr. Justice Salmon when inaccurate reports of proceedings appeared in the national press. *Resumed at the Old Bailey, 16.12.1957.*

[Authors' note: since the inaccurate reports were in national and not provincial newspapers it is a little difficult to understand how a mere change of venue for the trial could alleviate any prejudicial effect of such publicity.]

Convicted of non-capital murder and sentenced to life imprisonment, 19.12.1957.

Vilis Ozolins   Janis Abolins

Ozolins (35), Latvian refugee (cabinet maker), was alleged to have murdered Abolins (32), also a Latvian, by luring him to his garage where he hit him, rendering him unconscious, and then ran his car over him. Prosecution claimed he then took the body in the car and dumped it in a lonely country lane on Dartford Heath in an attempt to make it resemble a road accident. It was stated that Abolins had recently become very friendly with Ozolins' former mistress, and that the accused was very jealous. Bloodstains similar to victim's blood-group were found in accused's car.

Defence claimed that accused had lent his car to another Latvian friend for a couple of hours on the night of the murder. Accused had reason to believe that this latter man was a Soviet agent and that he (accused) had been "framed" for his anti-Communist resistance during the war. The "missing witness" was not traced.

Convicted of non-capital murder and sentenced to life imprisonment at the Old Bailey, 10.7.1957.

William Pickering   Michael James Cutting
Ronald Alfred Keates

Pickering (32), motor technician and previously an army sergeant,
and Keates (21), army corporal, were out walking on Whit Sunday
with Pickering's family across some fields near Northampton when
Pickering's grandmother reported seeing a "Peeping-Tom" in the
bushes. Cutting (21) was in fact pigeon-shooting. Cutting was
reported to have brought his gun round towards Pickering who,
in "self-defence", attempted to disarm him and in so doing beat
him about the head with the gun. Victim died some days later from
injuries.

Pickering and Keates failed to report the incident to the police,
were both charged with non-capital murder.

No evidence was offered against either on these charges. *Keates
acquitted and discharged. Pickering pleaded guilty to manslaughter
and was bound over in the sum of £5. Northampton Assizes,
16.10.1957.*

Didimo Quaresima   Robert Owen Bishop

Quaresima (25), an Italian nursery-hand, was alleged to have
killed by battering with part of a pipe wrench, on a river towpath,
the husband (25) of the young married woman with whom he was
associating. Prosecution claimed that accused wanted her to
divorce her husband and go with him (Quaresima) to Italy.

*Convicted of non-capital murder and sentenced to life imprison-
ment at Herts Assizes, 10.10.1957.*

*Application for leave to appeal was refused by Court of Criminal
Appeal, 13.12.1957.*

Gordon William Robinson   John Arthur Roebuck

Prosecution claimed that Robinson (27), a storekeeper, suffocated with a piece of towelling John Roebuck, a schoolboy (14)
during the course of, or after, committing an indecent offence in his
car. Roebuck's body was discovered lying in the car after the
accused went off to get a can of petrol. Robinson appeared not to
know that the boy was dead.

Defence pleaded diminished responsibility, in that the accused
was suffering from an attack of epilepsy at the time of the offence
such as substantially to impair his mental responsibility. Had
suffered further fits while in custody.

Plea rejected. *Convicted of non-capital murder and sentenced to life imprisonment at Nottingham Assizes, 25.6.1957.*

George Frederick Robinson-Brannon   William Henry Robinson

Robinson-Brannon (20), an unemployed clerk, pleaded defence of provocation on the charge of murdering his father (70). He alleged that father made a remark concerning possible homosexual friendship which he (accused) had with another man and, in addition, demanded £3.5.0 for board and lodging even though accused was out of work. Submitted that father struck him with a strap and that the killing, by manual strangulation, was a sudden act of violence done on the spur of the moment. Afterwards, hid the body in a bedroom closet which he nailed up. Accused was then alleged to have tried to obtain money, with forged signatures, which his father had invested in Halifax Building Society and continued to draw his retirement pension.

Convicted of non-capital murder at Leeds Assizes, 12.12.1957, and sentenced to life imprisonment.

Teodor Romaniuk   Clarice Romaniuk

Romaniuk (30), a Ukrainian bus conductor in Nottingham, was alleged to have stabbed his wife (25) at their home. The wife had been living and going out with coloured men and was 3 months pregnant by one of them. Three times Romaniuk allowed his wife to return and forgave her. On the fourth occasion, after an argument about £25 which he had given her to buy clothes, he threatened to leave her. He said that she then attacked him with a knife, but he somehow snatched it from her and stabbed her in the throat. He immediately confessed to the police.

Defence entered a successful plea for a *verdict of manslaughter under provocation. Sentenced to 5 years' imprisonment at Nottingham Assizes, 21.11.1957.*

David Patrick Rooney   Thomas Rooney

Rooney (16) was accused of shooting his father (46) at their home in Coventry. It was alleged that the father, who had at some time been a voluntary patient at a mental hospital, ruled in a reign of terror at home and was constantly being violent, insulting towards accused, his mother and brother. When brother twice left home, father became more antagonistic towards David; mother had left home no less than six times owing to ill-treatment. Although family had moved about 16 times (at the instigation of the father) and consequently accused had attended 6 different schools, his standard of academic work was high and he had won a scholarship to a grammar school. He had recently taken up an apprenticeship with an upholsterer who gave him an excellent character.

Accused was alleged to have shot his father with a shotgun after a quarrel. Although this was admitted by defence to have been a deliberate act, the judge agreed to accept plea of not guilty of murder but guilty of manslaughter because Rooney had probably been "subjected over a considerable period to a good deal of provocation".

Convicted of manslaughter and sentenced to 5 years' imprisonment, Warwick Assizes, 27.11.1957.

Pamela Ross   Raymond Ross

Mrs. Ross (29) was found *unfit to plead at Durham Assizes, 23.10.1957,* on a charge of murdering her son (18 months), by gassing him in his pram and then drowning him "to make sure he was not suffering".

Prosecution offered evidence of paranoid schizophrenia. Accused thought she had caught a disease from a neighbour via a tea-cup, and that she had passed this disease on to her children. She therefore decided on a "mercy killing" of all her 5 children but couldn't bring herself to continue after she had killed one.

Robert Rundell   Sarah Ann Brown

Rundell (60), a general foreman, strangled the woman (50-55) with whom he had been associating, with a belt, after a quarrel at her home. He took 23 aspirins and tried to gas himself.

He was said to suffer from bad headaches which had recently become worse; he had one such attack on the day of the incident. Since arrest, the coal-gas poisoning had affected his memory and he had become morbidly depressed. Though not reported as such, his conviction at *Kent Assizes, 2.12.1957, of manslaughter* would appear to have been on *grounds of diminished responsibility* for the above reasons.

Sentenced to 10 years' imprisonment.

John Alfred Shadbolt   Edna Shadbolt

Shadbolt (34), a toolmaker, was *acquitted at the Old Bailey of non-capital murder* of his wife (34). He had always been a "model husband" and "had devoted (his) whole life . . . to the welfare of (his) wife" whose health had deteriorated due to an incurable nervous disease which affected the brain and produced paralysis, resulting in her being in a very severe state of depression. When she attempted to stab accused with a carving knife, he lost his head and strangled her, though he could not later remember his actions.

Convicted of manslaughter, under section 3, 25.6.1957; the Judge, after the jury had recommended mercy, granted an absolute discharge.

Kenneth Sharley   Jean Saxton

Sharley (25), a dairyman, strangled his fiancée (22) as she slept with him at his home. Both prosecution and defence admitted there was no apparent motive to this crime, although accused was evidently in a severe state of depression which had been present for some while (had attempted suicide in 1956) and which had led him to feel that he could never make his fiancée really happy.

Defence plea of not guilty to non-capital murder but guilty to manslaughter under section 2 (for above reasons) was accepted by the prosecution.

Convicted of manslaughter under section 2 at Nottingham Assizes, 25.6.1957, and sentenced to 14 years' imprisonment.

Alfred Sharratt   Rose Sharratt

Sharratt, a railway worker (36), *acquitted of non-capital murder of* his mother (69). Prosecution alleged that Sharratt beat his mother, who was very small and frail, and who died subsequently from pneumonia caused by a broken arm. Before death, victim made a statement that accused had hit her. Sharratt was also cleared on a charge of causing grievous bodily harm.

Stafford Assizes, 3.7.1957.

Anthony Simpson   Joyce Simpson

Simpson (37), a fitter, strangled his wife (30) at their home after she had constantly nagged him, threatened to leave him and assaulted him. He felt her behaviour and attitude was prejudicial to the welfare of their 5 children but he refused to give her the divorce she wanted. After keeping him awake all night with her nagging, he suddenly lost control of himself and strangled her.

Simpson was *acquitted of murder but found guilty of manslaughter on grounds of provocation, and sentenced to 5 years' imprisonment at the Old Bailey, 23.9.1957.*

[Authors' note: One of the first cases under section 3 of the 1957 Act where things *said* as well as things *done* constituted provocation in law. ([1957] Crim.L.R.815).]

Darshan Singh   Joyce Stanton

Singh (28), a Sikh labourer, was accused of the murder by manual strangulation of the woman (about 30) with whom he had been living for some years and who was the mother of his 2 illegitimate children. Her body was found, minus shoes, in a small Leicester park. A few hours before her death, victim had served Singh with a bastardy summons relating to the second of their children, who had been born a month previously. It was also alleged that she had threatened to leave the accused in order to go and live with another Indian. Leaves belonging to a rare Swedish tree growing in the park were found in accused's bedroom and identical grass was found in his trouser turn-up. Singh simply denied the charge and stated his innocence.

Convicted of non-capital murder and sentenced to life imprisonment at Nottingham Assizes, 19.11.1957.

Application for leave to appeal refused by the C.C.A.

Dilbagh Singh   Sohan Singh

Singh (23), and Indian labourer, stabbed another Indian (27) during a brawl outside a public house in Derby. It was alleged that the victim had, a few days previously, slept with the prostitute with whom the accused was living; after some drinks, a fight developed in the street as a result of this, between several Indians, during which Sohan Singh was killed. The defence alleged that Sohan Singh drew a knife and attacked Dilbagh, who pulled out his own knife in self-defence and stabbed him 5 or 6 times. It was stated to be a religious custom for certain Indians to carry knives with them.

Jury at Derbyshire Assizes, 12.11.1957, found Dilbagh Singh guilty of non-capital murder, adding a strong recommendation for mercy. Sentenced to life imprisonment.

Harry Smith   Dorothy Hendley

Smith (61), a labourer, struggled with a prostitute (45) whom he
had taken on to Doncaster racecourse after she had said something
objectionable to him. Partly by accident, she was strangled (vagal
inhibition) and Smith gave himself up to the police straight away.

*At Sheffield Assizes, 26.11.1957, he was acquitted of non-capital
murder but convicted of manslaughter and sentenced to 7 years'
imprisonment.*

Roy Speake   Stephen Hince

Speake (20), a roadman, committed an indecent assault upon a
boy (4½) and then, when the boy threatened to tell his father, half-
strangled him, finally beating the boy to death with a brick.

The defence entered a plea of diminished responsibility; four
doctors testified to Speake's feeble-mindedness, one of them claim-
ing that Speake had a mental age of 9. Speake had in fact been
convicted of arson in November 1956, at which time the doctors
had said that he was not quite certifiable under the Mental Deficiency Act 1913. Speake was put on probation for three years; it was
while he was on probation that the killing occurred.

At his trial, Speake appeared to be more worried about a
subsidiary charge of bicycle theft than the murder charge; he did
not seem to appreciate what Crown counsel called "the monstrous
wickedness of his action".

The defence medical evidence was not rebutted by the prosecution and Speake was acquitted of non-capital murder but
convicted of manslaughter under section 2; he was *sentenced* by
Mr. Justice Diplock *to life imprisonment, Hereford Assizes,
12.6.1957.*

By leave of the single judge, Speake appealed against his sentence,
the grounds being that the trial judge should have made an order
under section 8 of the Mental Deficiency Act 1913, particularly
since imprisonment is used against persons under 21 in only rare
instances: see section 17(2) of the Criminal Justice Act 1948. The
Court of Criminal Appeal (Hilbery, Barry and Hinchcliffe JJ.)
held, however, that the trial judge was not bound to take some
other course than pass a sentence of imprisonment even where the
undisputed evidence was that the accused was a mental defective.
A sentence of imprisonment could properly be passed if the court

thought it right, having regard to the character and mental and physical condition of the accused: (1957) 41 Cr.App. R. 222.

[Authors' note: This case bears a remarkable resemblance to the situation that occurred in the case of Garlick (1958). Whenever a mentally sick person comes before the criminal courts, whatever the courts do by way of treatment, there is a need for some system of mental after-care to ensure that there is no repetition of the criminal behaviour.]

John Francis Spriggs   Harold Cunningham

Spriggs (29), tool maker, was alleged to have returned with a revolver to the public house from which he had earlier been ejected for trying to remove a beer tap label, knocked on the door and when the barman, Cunningham (43), answered it, to have shot him 4 times from very close range, twice in the back. Accused later found unconscious at home suffering from an overdose of drugs.

Defence submitted a plea of manslaughter under section 2, and offered evidence of Spriggs' mental state. Accused had long history of mental and neurotic trouble and treatment. Invalided from R.A.F. owing to mental illness. Evidence of psychopathic personality. "Suffered from an abnormality of mind which affected his emotions and made him liable to react much more strangely than a normal person to slight provocation" (such as his ejection from the bar.) However, Prison Medical Officer (for prosecution) stated that he found no evidence of insanity or mental abnormality.

Found guilty of capital murder and sentenced to death at Birmingham Assizes, 19.12.1957

Appeal to Court of Criminal Appeal on grounds that Mr. Justice Austin Jones had not given sufficient direction to the jury as to the meaning of the words "abnormality of mind" or "mental responsibility" in connection with his defence of diminished responsibility under section 2. The Lord Chief Justice (Lord Goddard) ruled that the judge had acted quite rightly in leaving to the jury the question of whether Spriggs' mental abnormality was sufficient to amount to diminished responsibility. Mr. Justice Austin Jones had confined himself to (1) handing to the jurors the terms of section 2, so that they could see it; and (2) going through the medical evidence meticulously to aid the jurors in coming to a decision.

"It was not for a judge, where Parliament had defined a particular state of things, as they had here, to redefine or attempt to define the definition." The matter here was entirely for the *jury* to decide (i.e. the interpretation of this section of the Act). *Appeal dismissed, 14.1.1958* ([1958] 1 Q.B.270). *Application for Attorney General's fiat to appeal to House of Lords refused, 20.11.1958.* The Attorney-General was questioned in the House of Commons by Birmingham M.P's, but refused to reconsider his decision. Petition of 500 signatures organised in Birmingham and sent to Home Secretary, appealing for reprieve. *Reprieve granted by the Home Secretary, 26.1.1958* (3 days before date of execution). *Life imprisonment.*

James Walter Storrs   Nellie Storrs

When his mother (69) went to hit him during a quarrel over his theft of £2 from her, Storrs (27), a labourer, hit her and she fell to the floor and screamed. As a result of his attempt to stop her screaming by putting his hands on her mouth, she became unconscious and then died. Afterwards he "panicked", dragged the body upstairs, pushed it under the bed, and then tidied the house. He did not report the crime at all.

Acquitted of non-capital murder but sentenced to 7 years' imprisonment on a conviction of manslaughter, Sheffield Assizes, 26.7.1957.

John Kenneth Swanston   Josephine Swanston

Swanston (25), a motor mechanic, who was very fond of his wife (21), impulsively stabbed her with a souvenir commando-knife, in the bedroom of their Exeter home. She had been living away from him but had just returned to the house; in the next room, with their daughter (16 months) was an N.S.P.C.C. Inspector who was trying to effect a reconciliation between the couple. But instead of discussing a reconciliation, his wife started to pack her clothes in her suitcase and told Swanston she was definitely leaving him. He picked up the knife and stabbed her once.

He was *convicted of manslaughter on grounds of provocation at Devon Assizes, 1.11.1957, and sentenced to 3 years' imprisonment,* "the least sentence I can impose" (the judge).

Arthur Taylor   Barbara Green

Taylor (52), colliery worker, had apparently formed an intense attachment for Mrs. Green (38) who was a librarian. She did not welcome the attentions which he pressed upon her. This preyed on his mind and he conceived her to be a "very loose woman". After drinking, he made up his mind to "finish it off, because I could stand it no longer". Went home to collect his rifle; then shot Mrs. Green in the library.

Evidence offered that accused had had frequent attacks of depression and was moody. Had been treated for nervous complaints.

Found unfit to plead at Leeds Assizes, 3.4.1957.

George Eric Taylor   David Gibson

Taylor (19), a farm labourer, was alleged to have stabbed Gibson (21) with a flick-knife (which he had bought a few days previously). He was attempting to run away from Gibson and his friends during a brawl after a dance. Evidence that (a) Taylor had been drinking earlier, and was jealous of Gibson for taking to the dance a girl with whom Taylor had been friendly; and (b) Taylor had prominently displayed his flick-knife to a number of people on the night of the incident.

Defence based upon "accidental" killing—victim must have "run on to his (Taylor's) knife".

Jury, after $3\frac{1}{2}$ hour retirement, returned verdict of *guilty of non-capital murder* with a rider expressing strong disapproval of the sale of flick-knives.

Sentenced to life imprisonment at York Assizes, 14.11.1957.

Lazarus Thomas   Thomas Aneurin Henry

Thomas (40), a sub-contractor, charged with the murder of his stepson (28). It was alleged that after a series of quarrels and fights instigated by Henry and his brother and sisters, Thomas left home. He returned a month later, but after a discussion about a business partnership, Henry, who had been drinking, became abusive and aggressive, and attacked Thomas with a chair. Accused fell on top of him and struck blows from which Henry died.

Prosecution admitted that it could not ask the jury to convict of murder on the evidence but invited a conviction of manslaughter. Defence plea of self-defence successful.

Found not guilty of non-capital murder or manslaughter at Glamorgan Assizes, 2.12.1957, and discharged.

[Authors' note: Thomas had been $5\frac{1}{2}$ months in prison awaiting trial.]

Michael Frederick Trout   John Clements

Trout (18), builder's labourer, stabbed Clements (20) in a street fight. Earlier in the evening at Bridgwater Fair, Trout and some friends had beaten up a youth in a fight, and at about 1 a.m. the following morning, when returning home alone he was accosted by Clements and several other youths who accused him of beating up one of their friends. Clements, a much bigger and stronger man, "invited" accused to "come round the corner" where he started beating Trout who took out a Woolworth's knife which he had been carrying in his pocket and defended himself with it, stabbing Clements as he came towards him. "Did not know Clements was dead until later."

Defence submitted pleas of provocation and self-defence, but accused *convicted of non-capital murder and sentenced to life imprisonment, Bristol Assizes, 15.11.1957. Application for leave to appeal refused by Court of Criminal Appeal, 14.1.1958.*

John Wilson Vickers   Jane Duckett

Vickers (22), a labourer, killed with blows and kicks Miss Jane Duckett (72) who interrupted his burglary of her small general store in Carlisle in April 1957. She flew at him, he got into a panic and knocked her down with his fist. Left her on the floor while he searched for money; escaped without finding any.

Defence was based upon a lack of *intention* to kill, and a pathologist said the blows were "moderately severe to slight". Nevertheless Vickers was *convicted of capital murder (in the course or furtherance of theft) and he was sentenced to death at Cumberland Assizes, 23.5.1957.*

Vickers appealed to the Court of Criminal Appeal, [1957] 2 Q.B. 664, on the grounds that the necessary implied malice, preserved by the 1957 Act, had not been proved. The Lord Chief Justice ruled that as there appeared to be a difference of opinion between the three appeal judges, the case must be heard before a full court of 5 judges. The *appeal was then dismissed* on the grounds that the appellant killed Miss Duckett because he realised that she would recognise him (Vickers had denied this at his trial) and that the intention to do grievous bodily harm sufficiently constituted "malice aforethought".

Fiat refused for appeal to House of Lords. Motion of censure upon the Attorney-General was signed by 68 Labour M.P's who described Vickers' case as involving a point of law of exceptional public importance.

Executed at Durham Gaol, 23.7.1957, the first hanging for two years and the first since the passing of the 1957 Act.

Vickers had only one previous conviction—for larceny at the age of 11.

[Authors' note: By a curious irony, the first man to suffer the death penalty under the changed law was almost certainly a bad case for demonstrating the utility of the categories of murder in the 1957 Act. Far from being an issue of the "open-and-shut" variety, the blows inflicted on the victim cast serious doubt on the "malice" implied by the law. The action of the victim, on the other hand, is an almost perfect paradigm of the situation described in our chapter on Victimology, p. 321]

Florence Wallace   Andrew Wallace

Wallace (49) was acquitted of murdering her husband (52) during a quarrel which developed into a fight at their home. The husband, who had been notoriously cruel to his wife, and had been associating with another woman, was particularly violent after drinking sessions. On night of incident Wallace knocked and hit his wife two or three times on the way home from the public house and later at home pushed her in the stomach over the end of the settee, then rushed at her. Accused said "I must have picked the knife up (bread knife), but I don't remember doing so". Stabbed husband in terror.

Defence plea of provocation and self-defence.

Not guilty, Leeds Assizes, 17.12.1957. (Also not guilty of manslaughter).

Discharged.

Herbert Leslie Watson   Joan Burton

Found *unfit to plead at Leeds Assizes, 4.12.1957*, charged with murder of girl (10) during course of an indecent assault. Watson (24), of no occupation, had a very long history of insanity and confinement to mental hospitals; was alleged to have battered the girl to death with a hammer which he was carrying in his pocket. Was reported to have said: "I have expected it to happen for years. I am frightened that it will occur again".

He had been removed from a mental hospital by his mother only 3 or 4 days before the killing. *H.M.P.*

Albert Victor White   Agnes Johnston

White (36), a scaffolder, a married man and father of 4, was *convicted at Durham Assizes 6.6.1957 of the non-capital murder* by strangulation of his mistress (and mother of his child) Agnes Johnston (24), with whom he had been living and associating on and off since 1953.

Apart from the somewhat questionable testimony of the chief prosecution witness, a teen-age girl, White was convicted on circumstantial evidence. He had admitted to having had, just previously, a quarrel with Johnston and that she had been constantly pressing him to obtain a divorce.

Sentenced to life imprisonment.

Gordon Henry Whitehead   John Whitehead
                                                 Peter Whitehead

After a quarrel with his wife, Whitehead (23), a steelworker, struck his twin sons (7 months) and beat them to death. It was stated that Whitehead was very fond of the babies and there was no apparent reason for the action.

His plea of *not guilty to the murder charge was accepted by the prosecution and he pleaded guilty to manslaughter.*

Sentenced to 21 months' imprisonment at Manchester Crown Court, 3.7.1957.

Mary Agnes Wignall   Leonard Wignall

Wignall (42) pleaded the defence of provocation to a charge of murdering her husband (38) at their home by stabbing him with a vegetable knife. It was alleged that the marriage had been a very unhappy one—husband gambled and drank heavily, constantly beating, insulting and threatening his wife, the accused. During one fight, while he was twisting her foot and throwing her from chair to chair, she grabbed a knife and cut her husband on the arm in order to make him stop. But he became more infuriated and lunged towards her, she stabbing him by accident.

Found not guilty at Leeds Assizes, 6.12.1957, and discharged.

Gunter Wiora   Shirley Marguerite Allen

Wiora (34), a Polish art student, used a 3 foot long *Samurai* sword to slash and stab his mistress (24) at their Kensington flat. He also stabbed his landlady when she tried to interfere, and afterwards attempted suicide by stabbing himself, cutting his wrists and turning on the gas. There was a strong suggestion of jealousy on Wiora's part, arising from an idea which he had that the girl was posing for pornographic photographs for another man and generally associating with other men. The stabbing occurred during a violent quarrel.

Defence successfully pleaded diminished responsibility at the Old Bailey, 25.7.1957, and Wiora was *convicted of manslaughter under section 2.*

Sentenced to 12 years' imprisonment.
Transferred to Broadmoor, 31.10.1958.

A 15-year-old Boy   Rosina Cotterell

In debt to a schoolfriend for £3, the accused lay in wait for 2 days on a footpath for a suitable person to rob, having already equipped himself with an iron bar and gloves to prevent fingerprints. Murdered Mrs. Cotterell (52) by beating her to death, and robbed her of an empty purse.

Defence offered evidence of diminished responsibility based upon the boy's development of schizophrenic illness, immaturity and maladjustment. Also a family history of mental illness. Prosecution produced doctors to rebut this evidence—"the history of the accused during the past few years was that commonly found in adolescents".

Convicted of capital murder (in the course or furtherance of theft) at the Old Bailey, 3.7.1957, and ordered to be detained during H.M.P.

1958

Accused   *Victim*

Kenneth John Alcock   Leonard George Philips

Philips (49), who had been drinking, saw Alcock (22), a coloured labourer, arguing with his (Alcock's) wife in the street at about midnight. He came up and said "You should not beat a white girl like that". Alcock knocked him to the ground and kicked him in the head. Philips died next day from injuries.

Alcock denied the kicking. Said he struck Philips because he thought he was going to draw a knife.

Convicted of manslaughter and sentenced to 21 months' imprisonment. Liverpool Crown Court, 20.11.1958.

Frank Vernon Armstrong   Mary Hancock

Armstrong (30), a clerk, was alleged to have battered his mistress (22) to death with an axe after she made insulting remarks about his wife and family. There had recently been numerous quarrels. Defence pleaded diminished responsibility and called medical evidence that Armstrong "showed a strong and intense tendency towards depressive attacks of a major nature". There were also several cases of inherent illness in Armstrong's family. Prosecution produced rebutting evidence and Armstrong was *found guilty of non-capital murder, Nottingham Assizes, 20.11.1958.*

Sentenced to life imprisonment.

Anthony Attard   Panglam Gopolam

Attard (39), a Maltese cook, *was acquitted at the Old Bailey* of murdering the man who, it was alleged, had just burst into a cafe and stabbed Attard's fiancée, who had previously been friendly with Gopolam.

Mr. Justice Gorman withdrew from the jury the possibility of finding a verdict of murder, and Attard was also acquitted of manslaughter, *8.12.1958.*

This case also raised an interesting point in the law of evidence. In the course of the trial the judge held that a detective-superintendent could not give evidence of a statement made by the accused to him via an interpreter. The evidence, which was said to incriminate the accused, was inadmissible since neither the police officer nor the accused (who spoke only Maltese) could understand what the interpreter was saying to the other person. As a result of this ruling, the Home Office at the suggestion of the Director of Public Prosecutions issued a circular to all Chief Officers of Police advising that in such cases the interpreter should be available to give evidence at the trial. It was also important that the interpreter either kept a full note of the interview or that he initialled the police officer's note from which he could subsequently refresh his memory: (1958) 43 Cr. App. R. 90.

Doreen Baird							June Croft

Baird (14), a schoolgirl, who was baby-sitting, tied a scarf around the neck of a child (16 months) to stop her crying. There were, in all, 5 children to be looked after and she "was fed up with one or the other crying". There seemed to be no intention to cause harm to the child, but the baby died of strangulation.

Defence evidence offered by consultant psychiatrist in plea of diminished responsibility. Baird of low intellect and emotionally immature; not a very happy home life.

Found guilty of manslaughter under section 2 and sent to Approved School. Sheffield Assizes, 27.11.1958.

Cebert Bastian						Stephen Bastian
										Francis Bastian

Bastian (31), an unemployed labourer, who was unable to work owing to tuberculosis, and therefore relied on his wife's earnings, was alleged to have become suspicious of his wife going about with another man. He confessed to killing his two sons (4 and 3) by beating them to death with a rolling-pin, perhaps in order to "spite" his wife who had gone to Birmingham. He had tried to commit suicide afterwards in a pond on Clapham Common. Described by prosecution as a "devoted father". He had, not very much earlier, been under observation as a mental patient.

Defence entered a plea of diminished responsibility. A Harley

Street specialist said Bastian was bordering on insanity—he might be suffering from melancholia or schizophrenia. Dr. Brisby, Principal Medical Officer at Brixton, claimed that accused was insane within the meaning of the law. Mr. Justice Donovan allowed the prosecution to set up insanity in rebuttal to the defence plea of diminished responsibility.

Not guilty of non-capital murder but guilty of manslaughter under section 2. Old Bailey, 28.2.1958. Sentenced to life imprisonment. [1958] 1 W.L.R. 413; cf. R. v. Price [1963] 2 Q.B.I.; R. v. Morris [1961] 2 Q.B. 237 at p. 240-1 and R. v. Russell [1963] 3 All E.R. 603.

Transferred to Broadmoor, 24.5.1958, under section 2 of the Criminal Lunatics Act 1884 (now replaced by section 72 of the Mental Health Act 1959).

John Thomas Batten   Elizabeth Batten

Batten (77), a retired civil servant, reported to be very devoted to his wife (63) who had been ill, battered her to death with a steel pipe during one of her hysterical attacks. He then tidied his affairs, wrote farewell notes, etc., and attempted suicide. Apparently a mercy-killing. In a farewell letter, Batten wrote, "As we get older we shall still less be able to attend to ourselves and to each other . . . so as not to depress me, my wife professes confidence that my operation will be successful but I know that she fears it will not be and she dreads the thought of being left alone after all these happy years and I cannot go on without her".

Found insane and unfit to plead at Old Bailey, 10.9.1958.

[Authors' note: The death of Mrs. Batten gave rise to subsequent proceedings over her estate. Mr. Justice Pennycuick in the Chancery Division held that a person who feloniously killed another while suffering from insanity was not disqualified from taking a benefit under his victim's will. Mr. Batten was therefore entitled to succeed to his wife's estate: (1961) 105 S.J. 529.]

Gilbert Francis Beaumont   Mabel Beaumont

Beaumont (43), a labourer, described by the judge as a "devoted husband", admitted to beating his wife (44) to death, probably with the butt of a gun, and then attempting suicide by shooting himself and taking an overdose of aspirins.

Defence offered evidence of severe melancholia brought on by the death of accused's mother. Beaumont had twice been a voluntary patient in a mental hospital and had attempted suicide in 1956. The Crown did not dispute this evidence and Beaumont was found *guilty but insane at Norfolk Assizes, 11.2.1958. Ordered to be kept in custody as a Broadmoor patient during H.M.P.*

David George Benfield   Derek Bacon

Benfield (18), a milk roundsman, was alleged to have stabbed his brother-in-law (27) 12 times with a knife during a fight. Bacon, who was a much bigger and stronger man—and who was at the time drunk—viciously attacked first his wife (Benfield's sister) who had taken refuge with her children at her parents' home, then Benfield's parents, and then Benfield himself. Accused picked up the knife to defend himself and his relations.

Acquitted of non-capital murder and discharged. Leicester Assizes, 22.10.1958.

Arthur John Bosworth (See: Francis Jacobs)

Alvin Lloyd Brown   Saled Abdo Saleh

After a series of incidents during which a group of young Arabs continued to follow and attack Brown (21), a Jamaican crane driver, in cafés and a public house, Brown armed himself with a penknife and stabbed Saleh (20) as they chased and attacked him outside the Town Hall in Sheffield.

Jury found that he had acted under provocation and *he was convicted of manslaughter at Sheffield Assizes, 4.3.1958; sentenced to 5 years' imprisonment.*

The accused had no previous convictions.

George Vernon Buckland   Marjorie Gladys Buckland

During a "sexual adventure", in which Buckland (31) bound and gagged his wife, Mrs. Buckland (22) died, presumably from asphyxiation. It was stated that the couple were "devoted to each other" and that the gagging and tying had undoubtedly been done with the wife's consent; she had evidently been drinking heavily during the evening.

Buckland's plea *of not guilty to non-capital murder was accepted by the prosecution. He pleaded guilty to manslaughter and was*

*sentenced to 3 years' imprisonment at Caernarvonshire Assizes,
9.5.1958.*

James Frederick Burden   Horace Potterton Papworth

Burden (38), a car-driver, was *found insane and unfit to plead* on
the charge of non-capital murder of his landlord, Papworth (50)
whom he hit on the head with a poker and then stabbed. *Old Bailey,
19.2.1958. H.M.P.*

Shortly after the killing he walked up to a policeman and said:
"I wish to report I've murdered my landlord, I did it this morning.
I've been to the pictures". When charged, he said "You want to
put him (Papworth) straight into the reactor . . . things will only get
worse until you put Jesus Christ into the reactor". In his statement
he also said: "I hit him several times. He's a 'multilith' which is a
functionary of the divine father chain which makes him a subtle
and powerful influence on the earth".

Tom Lionel Burns   Lavinia Murray
                                          Sheila Barnes

This was probably the most gruesome killing in recent years. It
was alleged that Burns (71), a retired motor-driver, sexually assaulted two girls (both aged 5) who wandered into his house while he was
playing the piano. There was evidence that he cut the throat of one
and tied and mutilated the other with a knife before she died of
multiple injuries and strangulation. Further mutilation and sexual
interference occurred after death, and it was alleged that both
bodies had been drained of blood, and that parts of both bodies
had been removed, cooked and eaten.

*Burns was found insane and unfit to plead at Lancaster Assizes,
21.10.1958; he was ordered to be detained during H.M.P.*

[Authors' note: Burns is still alive and completely mad. There is
evidence to suggest that he had suffered from acute organic brain
damage and had been hopelessly psychotic for many years before
the commission of the crime.]

David Andrew Campbell-Rose   Stella Joyce Smith

Campbell-Rose (23), a clerk, spent the day with his girl friend (28)
at his caravan home, and in the evening, when he learnt that she
had gone out with other boys, there arose a serious argument. He

took a wheel-brace, battered her unconscious and then strangled her.

Campbell-Rose *pleaded guilty to non-capital murder at Surrey Assizes, 25.6.1958, and was sentenced to life imprisonment.*

Brian Candish   Yvonne Hannaford

Candish (22), a builder's labourer, was alleged to have killed his former mistress (21) at her lodgings. She was pregnant by him and he was apparently concerned to know what would happen to the coming child. Medical evidence was that she died from vagal inhibition, as a result of punches, etc., probably after a short argument.

Candish was *acquitted on a charge of murder but convicted of manslaughter and sentenced to 7 years' imprisonment at Devon Assizes, 5.11.1958.*

This sentence was, however, reduced to 5 years by the trial judge, Mr. Justice Finnemore, some 12 days later; no approach for a reduction in the sentence had been made by the defence.

Brian George Candy   Lynne Diane Wilson

Candy (21), a motor mechanic, strangled his girl friend (16), whose naked body was found in a meadow near Basingstoke. Candy gave himself up to the police who found victim's ring, watch and locket on his person. Just previously, the girl's mother had refused her permission to get engaged to Candy.

Accused maintained a complete denial of the murder and said that as they walked past a stationary car he felt himself gripped and attacked, and became unconscious. When he came to, he found the girl's body and went straight to the police. Defence counsel, however, pleaded diminished responsibility and offered evidence of Candy's epileptic condition and his proneness to fits. "No one could make sense of this crime except on the basis that there was an abnormality of mind at the time of its commission."

Found not guilty of non-capital murder but guilty of manslaughter under section 2.

Sentenced to life imprisonment at Winchester Assizes, 26.3.1958.

Thomas Cassidy   Elizabeth McGill

Cassidy (37), a fitter's mate, was *found guilty at the Old Bailey*, of battering to death the mother (85) of the woman with whom he was living. All three lived in a flat in South London. When cautioned, Cassidy said: "I still cannot sort it out. I can't think of the reason why I killed her".

Cassidy was *sentenced to life imprisonment, 23.1.1958.*

Brian Chandler   Martha Dodd

Chandler (20), soldier in the R.A.M.C., went absent without leave and met two girls in Darlington who had run away from home; together they formed plans to steal some money in order to get to London. It was alleged that Chandler went to the home of Mrs. Dodd (83) who, he had been told by one of the girls, kept a lot of money with her; he asked for work and was given a task in the garden, but took a hammer and battered the old woman to death with 19 blows. Afterwards took about £4 from her handbag.

The defence submitted that one of the girls (Marion Munro) had gone along with Chandler, and that Chandler had come into the living room to find Mrs. Dodd already dying and the girl standing over her, holding her handbag. Accused claimed that the statement he had made to the police implicating himself (but intimating "self-defence") had been made to protect the girl, but she denied that she had gone to the house with Chandler.

He was *convicted of capital murder and sentenced to death at Durham Assizes, 29.11.1958. His appeal was dismissed; Chandler was hanged at Durham Prison, 17.12.1958*—the seventh man to be executed since the passing of the Homicide Act.

[Authors' note: He was reported as having come from a good home and had no previous record for violence of any kind, although he had one conviction for larceny and forgery a year earlier.]

Edith Chubb   Lilian Chubb

Mrs. Chubb (46) was alleged to have strangled her sister-in-law (52) at their home, to have taken the body in a push-chair and left it by the side of a road. She paid some outstanding bills with £12 taken from the dead woman's purse.

Defence offered evidence that accused was on the verge of a nervous breakdown due to mounting financial and family worries, which Miss Chubb had done nothing to alleviate. Accused stated that she strangled her sister-in-law in a period of "momentary mental blindness". Prosecution produced rebutting medical evidence.

Mrs. Chubb *acquitted of non-capital murder but found guilty of manslaughter* (*on grounds of lack of intent to kill or do grievous bodily harm*). *Old Bailey, 2.5.1958. Sentenced to 4 years' imprisonment.*

[Authors' note: A number of petitions were signed and sent to the Home Secretary after the daughter (17), who was left as "mother" to Mrs. Chubb's family, died in July. A Sunday newspaper ran a series of appeals for her release in February 1959, and Mrs. Chubb herself appealed for release to the Home Secretary in May 1959. All appeals were rejected. She had served her sentence by January 1961.]

Wesley Kenneth Churchman   Leonard Churchman

Churchman (23), a die-caster, inflicted 124 stab wounds on his brother—who was said to be "mentally peculiar"—after a family argument about the lighting of a fire. He then went to the police and said "I did it in self-defence". He claimed that his brother had previously made several attacks on him with a chopper, a chair and a knife. On the day of the incident, Leonard had a chopper and threatened he would kill accused. Wesley went upstairs and fetched a souvenir knife "to defend myself in case I was attacked". It was unsheathed in his trouser-pocket when Leonard attacked him.

He pleaded provocation and self-defence at his trial at Stafford Assizes, but was *convicted of non-capital murder and sentenced to life imprisonment, 4.7.1958.*

George William Collier   Edgar Adams

Collier (67), an unemployed old-age pensioner, was charged with the murder of Adams (60) 5 months after the victim's death. The murder was committed in the course or furtherance of theft of Adams' "horde" of money which he obtained by begging in the West End of London. (He was reputed to have earned and banked sums of £20 and £30, and the ragged clothes on his body contained nearly £80 in notes and a Post Office Savings Bank book showing a credit of £209).

Collier denied the charge but was found *guilty of capital murder and sentenced to death at the Old Bailey, 22.5.1958*, after the jury had been out for nearly 5 hours. *Appeal dismissed, 23.6.1958*, by the Court of Criminal Appeal: [1958] Crim.L.R.544.

The main ground of appeal was that an important witness, who could testify to having seen the deceased alive 16 days after the date of the alleged killing, had not been called by the prosecution. The court held that the only obligation on the prosecution in such cases is to so supply the defence with the names and addresses of witnesses whom they are not proposing to call; there is no further obligation to supply the defence with a copy of the statement which the Crown has taken; R. v. Bryant (1946) 31 Cr. App. R. 146.

Reprieve recommended by Home Secretary, 4.7.1958.

[Authors' note: Ground of reprieve might have been on account of either advanced age, or a "scintilla of doubt" about the verdict. The condemned man had written to his M.P., Mr. Victor Collins (now Lord Stonham), saying, inter alia: "I am writing to you on a matter of some importance to me. I am due to be hanged next Tuesday"]

Graham Colpoys-Johnson   Joan Winifred Colpoys-Johnson

Colpoys-Johnson (40), unemployed draughtsman, was found *guilty but insane at Hampshire Assizes, 6.7.1958*, of non-capital murder of his wife, Joan (46), at their home in Bournemouth. Accused had been unemployed for almost a year owing to illness and fits of depression, and, after a quarrel over money, took a spanner and beat his wife to death. It was alleged that the couple had been living in poverty-stricken surroundings—their flat being very bare and extremely dirty.

Some evidence was presented of accused suffering from paranoid delusions.

Ordered to be detained as a Broadmoor patient during H.M.P.

Leslie Gordon Colville   Edna Robinson

Colville (39), a labourer, battered to death with a hammer the woman with whom he had been living for six years (39). After an argument, she had told him to "pack his bags" and leave.

Defence presented medical evidence in a plea of diminished responsibility. It was stated that Colville was suffering from a depressive disorder and there was a history of insanity in his family. He had suffered from mental illness on 3 earlier occasions. Plea not successful.

Found guilty of non-capital murder at Nottingham Assizes and sentenced to life imprisonment, 19.11.1958.

Gerald James Cooke   Elizabeth Ann Stephenson

Cooke (32), a crane driver, was charged with the murder of Elizabeth Stephenson (16), whose body was found in a mud-filled ditch in a country lane. Death was due to suffocation caused by the inhalation of mud.

Prosecution said that accused drove past victim, who was walking along the lane, stopped his car, then walked back towards her, perhaps with the intention of committing a sexual offence. She died when the accused forcibly held her head down in the ditch in order not to be seen from a passing bus. Cooke, in defence, claimed that he had seen a person struggling in the ditch, had tried to pull "him" out (since girl was wearing short coat and jeans), but had "panicked" and been unsuccessful. After sitting dazed in his car for 20 minutes, he had reported the matter to the police. Accused was charged 7 days later.

Experiments were carried out with a life-size model by the police and it was alleged that Cooke's story, about being unable to remove the body, was in all probability (though not certainly) untrue.

Convicted of non-capital murder and sentenced to life imprisonment at Flintshire Assizes, 7.2.1958.

Valentine Cummins   Michael Softness

Cummins (61), a hotel chef, was acquitted at the *Old Bailey* of murdering his son-in-law (31) by stabbing him in the stomach with a bread-knife after he had heard his daughter sobbing and found Softness pulling her hair.

He was *convicted of manslaughter and sent to prison for 3 years, 26.11.1958.*

John William Davies   Newly-born child

Davies (37) *was sentenced to 9 months' imprisonment at Birmingham Assizes, 10.7.58, after pleading guilty to charges of concealment of birth and attempting to procure miscarriage* (of his wife). Prosecution withdrew a charge of murdering his newly-born child.
Judge:— "It seems to be quite clear that what you did was done

deliberately in order to rid yourself and your wife of an unwanted fourth child."

David Jordan Dennis   John Thomas Spriggs
                                        Florence Spriggs

Dennis (18), an apprentice motor mechanic, was accused of murdering his two grandparents, John (66) and Florence (68), who had helped to bring him up and with whom he was generally on extremely good terms, during the course or furtherance of theft. During his trial, Dennis defended himself on the capital charge and admitted that he had murdered his grandparents but not with the intention of stealing anything. He alleged that his girl friend threatened to leave him when he was placed on bail on a charge of shopbreaking and larceny; as a result of this his grandparents threatened to withdraw their surety for his bail, and after an argument at their home he beat them to death with 2 pokers and a hammer. He then took their car, drove to Brighton where he picked up his girl. They lived in various hotels for the next few weeks on money drawn by forged cheques from the grandfather's account, and also removed some furniture and other things from the grandparent's home. Dennis claimed that the only thing he took from home *at the time of the crime* was the car, which his grandfather had *already* lent him for a fortnight.

Acquitted of capital murder, but found guilty of non-capital murder at Lincolnshire Assizes, 5.6.1958. Sentenced to life imprisonment.

Jockine G. De Souza   Biscoe Walter Haynes

De Souza (39), an engineer, and Haynes (46), who were fellow lodgers, had been quarrelling in a public house over whose turn it was to put a shilling in the electric light meter at home, and this quarrel continued when they arrived home. It became violent and a fight broke out; Haynes picked up a steel rod in order to hit De Souza but the latter wrenched it from him and struck him 3 or 4 times with it.

De Souza was acquitted of non-capital murder at *the Old Bailey, 27.6.1958, but guilty of manslaughter and sentenced to 3 years' imprisonment.*

John Devine   James Hamilton Murray
Martin Russell

After drinking, Devine (19), a soldier, and Russell (21), a railway fireman, set upon Murray (18), a Cameron Highlander, in the street outside Folkestone Town Hall. They attacked him with a bottle and kicked him.

Devine claimed that his mate had been beaten up badly by 7 or 8 Cameron men and he was determined "that it was not going to happen to me". As they approached him, Murray apparently grabbed Devine by the lapels of his jacket and Devine then started to hit him.

Both accused were convicted of manslaughter and each sentenced to 4 years' imprisonment at Kent Assizes, 27.11.1958.

Herbert Ernest Dew   Clara Dew

Dew (35), who had returned home 10 days previously from the mental hospital where he had been a patient "for a long time", was alleged to have stabbed, in the breast, his mother (about 55) at their home. He admitted the killing saying, "I've been under a terrible strain. It's something that comes over me. I don't know why I did it".

Insane and unfit to plead on charge of non-capital murder. Old Bailey, 18.5.1958, H.M.P.

Dew had a long history of mental illness dating from 1943 when he was torpedoed while serving in the Navy. He was a chronic paranoid schizophrenic. He had previously attacked both his mother and sister. The last occasion, in 1955, when he was in a mental hospital he had discharged himself. He thought everyone was practising "psychology" on him.

Frederick Dewhurst   David Dewhurst

Dewhurst (27), a wireman, strangled with his tie his son (1 month) to whom he had shown "every kindness and care" in a fit of desperation when he was unable to quieten the baby after his wife had gone out.

Dr. Finkleman, medical superintendent of Rainhill Mental Hospital, for the defence, said that Dewhurst was suffering from an abnormality of the mind, an "incomplete development of the brain which could result in explosive outbursts". Plea of diminished responsibility accepted.

Acquitted of non-capital murder but guilty of manslaughter under section 2. Sentenced to 5 years' imprisonment at Liverpool Crown Court, 10.4.1958.

Mr. Justice Paull, in sentencing Dewhurst, said that the jury had taken the view that his mind was not normal and he (the judge) had that verdict in mind in assessing the proper sentence.

Charles Henry Dorrington   Arthur Charles Bisp

After an evening's drinking in a public house, there occurred a series of fist-fights between Dorrington (43) and Bisp (53) on their way home. Apparently each provoked the other to continue the brawl. After the third fight, Bisp received fairly severe facial injuries and went home. His doctor advised complete rest after he shortly returned from hospital; but, defence submitted, Bisp was soon out drinking again and leading an active life. He was taken ill 2 weeks after the fight, and died from a haemorrhage.

Dorrington acquitted of both non-capital murder and manslaughter at Bristol Assizes, 28.2.1958, and discharged.

Gerald Charles Elsmere   Duncan Whitelaw Brewster

The Judge upheld a defence submission at the Old Bailey that there was no case for Elsmere (18), a cinema projectionist, to answer on a charge of murdering his stepfather (42), with whom he lived together with his mother. The stepfather was quarrelsome and violent, especially when drunk. On the fatal evening, while drunk, he started beating up his wife and said to his stepson: "that's your mother—I'm going to kick her up and down the mews". Elsmere picked up a cricket bat and hit him four times on the head.

Discharged, 26.11.1958.

Ernest Fantle   Horace Lindsay

Lindsay, a wealthy fashion house owner (50), offered such provocation to Fantle (54), a travel courier, by his association with Fantle's wife and by his attitude towards the accused, that the charge of capital murder against Fantle for shooting him at his London flat was dismissed by the jury who returned a verdict of *manslaughter under section 3*. Fantle had suffered greatly from his

wife's association with Lindsay and was worried for the future of
his son (14), and on visiting Lindsay was greeted with such contempt that he shot him with a revolver he had brought with him.

*Sentenced at the Old Bailey by Mr. Justice Salmon to 3 years'
imprisonment, 25.9.1958.*

[Authors' note: Fantle's case seems to indicate a reception into
English Law of the concept of *crime passionel.*]

Maria Farrell   Joseph Farrell

Mrs. Farrell (47), the mother of 9 children, was acquitted of
murdering her husband (54) by stabbing him at their home. The
husband, described as "a drunken monster who stalked about the
house creating a temperature of fear", had consistently ill-treated
the accused ever since their marriage and had a list of 21 convictions, including some for assault, etc. During an assault with a
poker upon Mrs. Farrell, she grabbed a knife in self-defence and
stabbed him.

Defence plea of self-defence successful.

Acquitted and discharged, Liverpool Crown Court, 31.1.1958.

Barry Gordon Freeman (See: Roy Kenneth Nash)

Albert French   Rosemary French

Rosemary (2), of whom French, (43), unemployed labourer, was
said to be very fond, kept obstinately playing and kicking on her
bed. French lost his temper and "I put both hands on her neck and
pressed"; after strangling his daughter, he attempted suicide by
turning on the gas.

French was said to be suffering from a severe depression; he had
been off work since Christmas (2 months) with nervous trouble and
had been in mental hospital 3 years previously for treatment for
melancholia. He was found to be of diminished responsibility at
*Lancaster Assizes, 29.5.1958, and convicted of manslaughter under
Section 2.*

*He was put on probation with a condition that he underwent treat-
ment in a mental hospital*—under section 4 of the Criminal Justice
Act 1948.

3

Peter Fullelove   Patricia Fullelove

Fullelove (25), a clerk, strangled his wife (22), who was living apart from him, during a fight between them at her parent's home. He alleged that after calling her a slut for going out with another man, she attacked him and clawed at him, pulling his tie tightly; in order to stop her he grasped her throat.

Acquitted of non-capital murder but found guilty of manslaughter at Sheffield Assizes, 21.11.1958, and sentenced to 12 years' imprisonment.

Edward Donald Garlick   Wendy Garlick

Garlick (21) was a factory worker. Because they were in debt, Mrs. Garlick (19) went to Hyde Park as a prostitute in order to earn some money. When this failed to bring in any money, she and her husband agreed to commit suicide (by gas) together. She died but he recovered and was charged with her murder.

Found guilty of manslaughter under Section 4 (survivor of a suicide pact) at Kent Assizes, 29.11.1958, and placed by Mr. Justice Slade on probation for 3 years, with a condition of residence in a mental hospital for up to one year, under section 4 of the Criminal Justice Act 1948. He was discharged from St. Ebbas Mental Hospital, near Epsom, after five months. The doctors at his trial considered he was an inadequate personality and was suffering from mental abnormality as a result of the after-effects of coal-gas poisoning. When those effects had dissipated, it was felt safe to release him. He then remarried. On 1.2.1963 he was indicted and convicted of non-capital murder of a girl, aged 16, at the Old Bailey before Mr. Justice Paull. He unsuccessfully appealed to the Court of Criminal Appeal, 15.5.1963, on the ground that his confession after ten hours' examination at the police station was inadmissible in evidence. He alleged that the police had threatened that if he did not own up to the crime he would be put back in a mental institution.

[Authors' note: Garlick was undoubtedly an inadequate personality and probably psychopathic if not schizophrenic; the clinical diagnosis in 1958 was almost certainly wrong, the psychiatrists being misled by the effects on Garlick of the coal-gas poisoning. Even if it was right to have discharged Garlick from mental hospital in 1959, it was still necessary to have kept some medical check upon him. In this respect the law relating to mental health—the

Mental Health Act 1959 had not then come into force—was
defective, and still is. The same comment applies with equal force
to Speake (1957).

From evidence that one of us has since received, there are grave
doubts about the truth of Garlick's story of a suicide pact. It is
much more likely that he killed his wife immediately after or during
sexual intercourse, a pattern which was certainly evident in the
murder, in 1962, of Carol Ann White, a promiscuous adolescent
with whom he had intercourse in a field.]

Rosalia Garofalo   Tindaro Buzzanca

Garofalo (20), an Italian servant, became pregnant by the Italian
man (36) to whom she regarded herself "engaged". When she found
that he was already married, she packed her things to send back to
Italy and prepared to commit suicide. In a fit of desperation,
however, she stabbed her lover instead.

Defence plea of diminished responsibility on grounds of accused's
mental defectiveness coupled with emotional stress successful.
Found guilty of manslaughter under section 2.
Hertford Assizes, 7.10.1958.
Sentenced to 3 years' imprisonment.

John William Gaskin   Jean Holmgren

Gaskin (26), a clerk, stabbed to death, with a sheath knife, his
former fiancée (23). It was stated that he was subject to "violent
swings of mood" and was jealous of her friendship with another
man.

Defence of diminished responsibility successful. Prosecution
offered no rebutting evidence.
Acquitted of murder but guilty of manslaughter under section 2.
*Sentence of 5 years' imprisonment imposed at Bucks Assizes,
3.10.1958.*

Graham Geer   Kathleen Geer

Geer (17), a seaman on leave, beat and stabbed his stepmother
(35) to death at their home in Tunbridge Wells. He apparently used
five different weapons in the assault—2 knives, a pair of scissors, a
frying pan, and a set of kitchen scales—using each weapon one

after the other. After death, he sexually assaulted the body because "I wanted to show her how much I hated her".

Defence pleaded diminished responsibility, and the evidence of developing schizophrenia, offered by Dr. Brisby, Principal Medical Officer at Brixton, and Dr. T. C. N. Gibbens of Maudsley Hospital, was not refuted by the prosecution.

Acquitted of non-capital murder but guilty of manslaughter under section 2. Sentenced to life imprisonment at Kent Assizes, 11.3.1958.

Walter John Gilbert   Phyllis Kelleher

After Mrs. Kelleher (35) had left Gilbert (32), a lorry driver, with whom she had been living, in order to go out with another man, accused went to her house "to see if I could patch things up". When she refused to return to him, "I lost my temper and got jealous and mad"; picked up a knife from the shelf and stabbed her. Immediately called for an ambulance and tried to stop the bleeding.

Found not guilty of non-capital murder but guilty of manslaughter (on the basis that there was no intention to kill), Old Bailey, 28.2.1958. Sentenced to 5 years' imprisonment.

Lilian Giles   Derek Ronald Giles

Mrs. Giles (52), a housewife, was alleged to have drugged her son (16) (to whom she was devoted) by putting sleeping tablets in his cup of tea at lunch, and then "when he got sleepy over his meal, I got an axe and kept on hitting him with it", causing 54 head wounds. She admitted the killing and said that she did it because he had a girl friend whom she didn't like very much. "I have spoiled my son and neglected my husband. I have killed my son because I have let him down." She had had recurrent attacks of depression for over 10 years and had been treated in hospital for involutional melancholia twice. She had frequently contemplated suicide.

Unfit to plead. Old Bailey, 7.5.1958, H.M.P.

Robin Charles Grundy   Ada Arnold

Grundy (15), a tape recorder assembler, killed a widow (68) in her second-hand clothes shop in Chatham, while in the course or furtherance of theft. It was alleged that he battered her to death with a hammer, which he was carrying, when she started to scream.

Three medical witnesses for the defence stated that the boy was suffering from an abnormality of the mind, and this evidence was (apparently) not rebutted by the prosecution.

Grundy found guilty of manslaughter under section 2 and ordered to be detained for 5 years under section 53(2) of the Children and Young Persons Act 1933. Kent Assizes, 3.12.1958.

Alfred Gwynne   Leonard William Hall

Gwynne (36), a labourer, pleaded guilty to murdering a boy (9) whose half-clothed body was found on a stretch of waste land in Kidderminster. A post-mortem examination showed that the boy had been strangled and indecently assaulted. Gwynne was alleged to have said: "I want to say it was a sudden urge . . . I must have been mad".

Convicted of non-capital murder and sentenced to life imprisonment. Birmingham Assizes, 15.7.1958.

Douglas Richard Hamill   Joe Norris Birks

Hamill (27), a voluntary patient in a mental hospital, was *found guilty of the manslaughter on grounds of diminished responsibility at Leeds Assizes, 17.12.1958* of another patient (33). Birks' body was found in the grounds of the hospital after the two of them had been out walking.

Sentenced to life imprisonment.

[Authors' note: transferred to Broadmoor, 26.1.1959, under section 2 of the Criminal Lunatics Act 1884 (now replaced by section 72 of the Mental Health Act 1959).]

Richard Hannah   Thomas Hannah

Hannah (61), a fitter's labourer, the father of 19 children, *pleaded not guilty to murder but guilty to manslaughter (on grounds of provocation)* of his son (23). This plea was accepted by the prosecution at *Liverpool Crown Court, 13.2.1958*, and he was *sentenced to 6 years' imprisonment.*

Hannah's wife refused to let her son (who was very drunk) bring his girl friend in to sleep with him for the night—it was Christmas Day 1957. A quarrel then arose between the father (who was also drunk) and Thomas Hannah, which led to the son attacking his father. Hannah picked up a knife which he used in his work, and stabbed his son. No intention to kill, but used knife in trying to defend himself.

Thomas Hepburn   Mary Hepburn

Hepburn (41), a seaman, who had just been released from a mental hospital where he was a voluntary patient, met his wife (35) and they travelled to South Shields together to see if they could find a ship to take Hepburn back to sea. Being unsuccessful, they rented a room in a boarding-house for the night. Mrs. Hepburn's body was found the next morning. She had been strangled. Hepburn was found a few hours later when he attempted suicide (overdose of sleeping tablets) on a bus evidently going in the direction of his mental hospital.

Found unfit to plead at Leeds Assizes, 15.7.1958, on a charge of non-capital murder. H.M.P.

Harry Hill   Herbert Hill

Hill (38), a miner, *was acquitted of non-capital murder (at Manchester Crown Court, 1.7.1958) but convicted of the manslaughter* of his brother at the latter's home. Three fist-fights took place between the brothers after they had been drinking in a public house, during the third of which Herbert Hill (47) was strangled.

Sentenced to three years' imprisonment.

Albert Houghton   Dorothy Lilley

Houghton (21), an airman, on returning home for Christmas leave from National Service in Cyprus, learnt that his fiancée (20) wanted to end their engagement since she was going out with another boy. Houghton strangled her on sudden impulse and then attempted suicide by taking codeine and aspirin tablets.

Defence pleaded: (a) lack of intention; and (b) diminished responsibility. Senior Medical officer at Walton Prison testified that Houghton was suffering from a chronic anxiety state at the time of the incident.

Found not guilty of non-capital murder but guilty of manslaughter (under section 2) at Liverpool Crown Court, 17.2.1958. Sentenced to 8 years' imprisonment.

Francis Jacobs   John Edward Folkard
Arthur John Bosworth

While burgling a factory in Kentish Town, the two accused were discovered by the caretaker (55) who was beaten to death with a wooden mallet.

Charged with capital murder (during the course or furtherance of theft) *Jacobs* (17) pleaded that he had tried to restrain Bosworth (20), a labourer, from using violence, and was never violent himself.

Jacobs was acquitted of both capital murder and manslaughter but convicted, later, of breaking and entering, and of stealing a suitcase. Sent to Borstal.

Bosworth pleaded self-defence; said that he used the mallet after the watchman came for him with something in his hand and hit him in the face. *Convicted of capital murder, the jury (out for $4\frac{1}{4}$ hours) strongly recommended mercy.*

Sentenced to death. Old Bailey, 30.4.1958.

No appeal made to the Court of Criminal Appeal but to the Home Secretary for a reprieve. *Reprieve recommended, 16.5.1958,* 4 days before date of execution.

Life imprisonment.

Albert Jarrard   David John Jarrard

Jarrard (49), a labourer, was found *unfit to plead* to a charge of non-capital murder of his son (3). At the Magistrates' Court, Jarrard's wife said that she awoke and saw her husband pulling a rope around the child's neck as it lay in its cot. Jarrard was alleged to have told a police officer, "something went snap and it came over me to strangle somebody". David was stated to be the accused's "favourite son".

Dr. Brisby, Principal Medical Officer of Brixton Prison, testified that Jarrard was suffering from melancholia and was insane.

Essex Assizes, 16.6.1958. Ordered to be kept in custody during H.M.P.

John Jennion   Dorothy Jennion

Jennion (31), a process worker, was alleged to have strangled his wife (27) at their home after an argument about her association with another man. Jennion appeared to have been concerned for the well-being of his 4 children and said he had promised to forgive his wife (a second time) if she gave up the other man. Afterwards, he attempted suicide, first by cutting his throat and then by using the gas oven.

*Acquitted of non-capital murder but found guilty of manslaughter on grounds of diminished responsibility.**

Sentenced to 2 years' imprisonment at Liverpool Crown Court, 4.11.1958.

**N.B.* Owing to inadequate reports, it might just conceivably have been manslaughter under section 3, on the grounds that the wife's confession constituted provocation.

Yvonne Jennion   Ivy Vye

Jennion (23), an unemployed cook, killed her aunt (54) for whom, it was alleged, she had long held resentment, after a brief quarrel, by beating her with a heavy ash-tray and then strangling with a pyjama cord. Accused was a homosexual who had a long history of emotional instability and minor delinquency, and two doctors for the defence gave evidence of a schizophrenic disorder in a plea of diminished responsibility. This was rebutted by a medical witness for the prosecution. Counsel for the prosecution in summing up said: "You (the jury) may think that this case has shown you how dangerous is evidence of this sort, (i.e. medical evidence) that it is completely unreliable" and he suggested that the jurors use their "own commonsense" in reaching a verdict. Jennion's plea failed and she was *convicted of murder and sentenced to life imprisonment, Manchester Crown Court, 3.12.1958.*

A local petition urged the Home Secretary to review the sentence at an early date. Jennion applied 4 years later to the Court of Criminal Appeal for leave to appeal on the grounds that her mental state required reconsideration of the jury's verdict. But the court refused leave out of time, on the grounds that where there was a conflict of medical evidence—as in this case—the matter was one entirely for the jury: [1962] 1 All E.R. 689.

Lawrence Johnson   William Newton

Johnson (47), unemployed labourer, battered to death in a particularly brutal and frenzied manner, a fellow-lodger (55) at a Darlington Salvation Army Hostel. The victim interfered in a quarrel which developed into a fight between Johnson and another lodger, and Johnson picked up a chair and inflicted multiple injuries upon his head, from which he soon died.

Defence made a double plea of provocation and diminished responsibility, supported by evidence of Johnson's mental history and state of mind (low intelligence; schizophrenia) Latter plea successful.

Acquitted of non-capital murder but found guilty of manslaughter under section 2 and sentenced to life imprisonment. Leeds Assizes, 18.7.1958.

Ernest Raymond Jones   Richard Turner

During the course of burgling a co-op store, Jones (38), a moulder, heard the manager (38) returning, presumably to lock up the office safe which had been left open. As he came up the stairs, Jones hit him once and hurried away taking approximately £76 and 30,000 cigarettes. Turner died immediately from a fractured skull.

Charged with capital murder (during course or furtherance of theft), Jones' defence was based upon:

(1) There had been no intention to kill or do grievous bodily harm —he had hit the manager in his attempt only to push him aside and get down the stairs; and he had neither carried nor used any kind of weapon.

(2) At the time when he had hit Turner, the robbery had been "complete", so it could not be murder in the *course or furtherance of theft.*

Jones was convicted of capital murder and sentenced to death at Leeds Assizes, 10.12.1958.

Appeal to Court of Criminal Appeal, [1959] 1 Q.B. 291, was based on the definition of "course or furtherance of theft" but the Lord Chief Justice followed the ruling in H.M. Advocate v. Graham, 1958 S.L.T. 167—Lord Sorn:

"If a burglar is interrupted and if he murders in order to get away, it is still murder in the course of theft", *and dismissed the appeal, 26.1.1959.*

Jones was executed at Leeds Gaol, 10.2.1959.

Terrence George Jones   Mair Jones
Francis Joseph Schleising

After leaving a public house very drunk, the two accused, Jones (20), a labourer, and Schleising (25), a salesman, followed a girl (20) on her way home along a country lane after returning from a Salvation Army meeting, They both raped her and she died from suffocation when Schleising put his hand over her mouth to stop her cries.

Acquitted of non-capital murder but both found guilty of manslaughter by an all-male jury at Denbighshire Assizes, 15.10.1958. Both sentenced to 8 years' imprisonment.

Harbajan Kaur (See: Mehindar Kaur)

Mehindar Kaur (23), housewife   Banta Singh
Gurdev Singh (28), builder's labourer
Harbajan Kaur (23), housewife

The three Indians were accused of the murder of Mehindar Kaur's husband (56) by battering him to death with a chopper at their home in Leeds. The prosecution alleged that Banta Singh, who was much older than his wife (Mehindar Kaur), had started to have relations with an Englishwoman and kept his wife short of money. When she asked for money, he beat her; he had threatened to kill her and on one occasion had tried to throttle her. Crown claimed that Gurdev Singh and his wife, Harbajan Kaur, assisted her in murdering her husband.

At the end of the prosecution case at *Leeds Assizes, 12.12.1958*, there was found to be no case for *Harbajan Kaur* to answer: *she was acquitted and discharged.* Counsel for Gurdev Singh claimed that he had gone to Banta's house to act as peacemaker in the quarrel and had not been a party to the murder. Counsel for Mehindar Kaur made much of the emotional stress under which she must have been acting, but, as far as can be seen, made no attempt to plead manslaughter on grounds of provocation: instead said: "It was a reasonable possibility that at the time of the incident she had been deprived of her self-control and was not intending to kill her husband". *Both Gurdev Singh and Mehindar Kaur were found guilty of non-capital murder and sentenced to life imprisonment.*

Applications, on behalf of both, for leave to appeal, were refused by the Court of Criminal Appeal, 12.5.1959.

Matthew Kavanagh   Isaiah Dixon

Kavanagh (32), an Irish labourer, was found guilty of the capital murder of his fellow-lodger (60). It was alleged that he strangled hi with the man's own black tie after Dixon, a bachelor, had been drinking heavily, and stole from him about £5. (Kavanagh had been charged with murder once before, in 1957, when he was accused of strangling the married woman with whom he was associating. On that occasion, the charge had been reduced to manslaughter at the committal proceedings and, at Birmingham Assizes, 24.7.1957, Mr. Justice Lynskey had stopped the trial and instructed the jury to find Kavanagh not guilty after medical evidence of the victim's death had been presented).

This time, *Kavanagh was convicted of capital murder and sentenced to death at Warwick Assizes, 3.7.1958*, and the Home Secretary was "unable to find any sufficient ground to justify (him) in recommending the Queen to interfere with the due course of the law".

Kavanagh was executed at Birmingham Prison 12.8.1958—the fifth hanging under the Homicide Act.

Patrick Joseph Kehoe   Thomas Benedict Carolan

Kehoe (37), an Irish labourer, described as a "quiet, inoffensive, little man" was mending some shoes at his home, when he heard sounds from outside of Carolan molesting his (accused's) wife. He went out to protect her, but Carolan (34) who had been drinking heavily, started to attack him and, not realising he was still carrying his cobbler's knife, Kehoe stabbed him. Carolan died some hours later.

It was stated that the victim lived with Kehoe's wife before the accused met her, and she had had a child by Carolan.

Kehoe was acquitted of non-capital murder and discharged, Leeds Assizes, 15.7.1958.

Elijah Kendrick   Joseph Patrick Dunne

Kendrick (31), a labourer, and Dunne, fellow-lodgers, had been out drinking (fairly heavily). On the way home, Dunne knocked Kendrick to the ground and attacked him (as he had done on previous occasions). After a cup of tea upon returning home, Kendrick went to Dunne's room and strangled him with a tie.

Accused could not remember having the tea and was confused as to the circumstances of the killing, but said he remembered "being terribly afraid of Dunne and what might happen the next morning"

. . . "I have been shoved around by him and was more or less a lackey for him".

Kendrick was *found guilty of manslaughter on grounds of provocation at Warwick Assizes, 4.7.1958, and sentenced to 5 years' imprisonment.*

Gerald Theodore Lamarque   Eric Batty

Lamarque (37), a meat buyer, *pleaded guilty at the Old Bailey* to murdering the man (46) who had been associating with his ex-mistress. He stabbed him in the corridor of a hotel with a sheath knife which he had bought earlier the same day.

Sentenced to life imprisonment, 14.7.1958.

Alec Taylor Lawrence   Helena Emily Storey

Lawrence (19), a soldier home on leave, was alleged to have borrowed a .22 revolver from a neighbour and then shot his foster-mother (52) seven times in the head. It was stated that there was a great deal of love felt between the two, but accused had heard from his foster-father that Mrs. Storey might be going blind and he wanted to "put her out of her misery".

Two defence doctors gave evidence that Lawrence, who had had a kind home life and been given every opportunity, was suffering from hysteria, a disease of the mind. Plea of diminished responsibility successful. Lawrence *acquitted of capital murder but found guilty of manslaughter under section 2. Old Bailey, 8.5.1958. Sentenced to 3 years' imprisonment.*

Stanley Littlestone   Anne Littlestone

While on holiday in London, Littlestone (36), an accountant in the National Provincial Bank in Manchester, received a letter summarily dismissing him from his position because of "irregularities in the books". Instead of telling his wife, he said he had been promoted, and revealed the truth to her only when they got home. Evidently extremely worried about the future (he and his family lived in a flat owned by, and at the back of, the bank), he was overcome by a "profound and morbid depression and despair" and took a hatchet and attacked all the members of the family whom he "obviously loved". The next morning bank officials entered the flat and found the wife, mother-in-law, and one daughter, all suffering from severe head injuries; one daughter, Anne (6 months), dead in her pram; one other daughter, Sylvia (3), severely injured— she later died; and Littlestone with his wrists cut and two stab wounds in the chest.

When he recovered in hospital it was found that Littlestone was suffering from amnesia relating to all events up to his awakening in the ward.

Defence offered plea of diminished responsibility on the charge of non-capital murder of Anne Littlestone. Accused *found not guilty of non-capital murder but guilty of manslaughter under section 2. Sentenced to life imprisonment at Manchester Crown Court, 14.3.1958.*

Philip Alexander Maguire   Jessie Johnson

Maguire (47), a clerk, strangled Mrs. Johnson, who lived at the same house in Holloway, London, in early hours of New Year's Day, 1958. She was separated from her husband; she and Maguire had known each other for nine months and often drank together. Maguire began to suspect she was associating with someone else. One evening he got drunk and went home thinking how she was double-crossing him. He asked her to come to his rooms; when she refused he strangled her with his bare hands.

Defence entered a successful plea of diminished responsibility and Maguire was *convicted of manslaughter under section 2, at the Old Bailey, 19.2.1958.*

Sentenced to 10 years' imprisonment.

In 1937 Maguire had attempted suicide and had had two nervous breakdowns since. He was of an excessively jealous disposition.

John Stanley Marples   Mary Marples

Marples (42), a postman, took a shotgun and killed his mother (68) while she was sleeping, after he had been told by the doctor that she was suffering from cancer with little hope of recovery.

Defence plea of diminished responsibility, due to accused's acute mental depression, was accepted. *Marples acquitted of non-capital murder, and found guilty of manslaughter under section 2, at Derby- shire Assizes,* the jury adding a rider, asking the judge to give Marples "every consideration".

Sentenced to 18 months' imprisonment.

Mr. Justice Streatfeild said: "The sentence is not intended as a punishment; it is intended, as far as I am concerned, to provide you with the period in which I think and believe you will be given every consideration and such treatment as may be necessary to assist you to recover your balance", *11.6.1958.*

Albert Edward Matheson   Gordon Lockhart

This murder was described by Lord Goddard as "of the most horrible description, so revolting as to be almost beyond belief". Matheson (52), a casually employed labourer, met Lockhart (15) with whom he had a homosexual friendship, and took him to the St. James Boxing Hall, Newcastle. There Matheson killed the boy using a bottle and then a hammer in order to rob him of a registered envelope containing £35, "which I knew he had". He hid the body in a subway until the next day, then crudely bisected the body and put it into the sump underneath the boxing ring, after cutting open the body and removing parts of it. He then went to Edinburgh from where he sent anonymous letters to Lockhart's family about the boy's behaviour; he finally gave himself up to the police in Glasgow.

He was committed for trial on the charge of murder in the course or furtherance of theft (i.e. capital murder), but Mr. Justice Finnemore, putting the question on whether "furtherance of theft" meant that this had to be the motive or intention (or merely that in fact there was theft) said, "This is entirely new. I don't know whether you have considered that point—if the theft was the motive or the intention that led to the murder, or that the intention of the man was to murder (i.e. during the course perhaps of the sexual offence) and that the theft just followed". Defence was based on grounds of diminished responsibility and 3 doctors offered extensive evidence of Matheson's mental history. He had spent most of his life in a series of penal institutions and had been a voluntary patient in a mental hospital. He was obsessed by his sex perversion (sodomy) and had tried to get treatment for it, but this had been unsuccessful largely owing to his abnormally low intelligence (I.Q. of 73). Medical Officer of Durham Prison said that accused had a psychopathic personality and that his mental development was that of a 10 year-old boy.

All-male jury found him *guilty of capital murder and he was sentenced to death at Durham Assizes, 30.1.1958.*

Appeal to Court of Criminal Appeal heard before full court of 5 judges. Defence submitted: (1) three doctors had given evidence for the defence of diminished responsibility. There was no evidence the other way, and the jury's verdict was unreasonable and against the weight of the evidence; (2) was this capital murder—murder done in furtherance of theft? *Appeal successful, 24.3.1958.* The Lord Chief Justice said that the appeal was accepted on grounds of (1) for, while it was for the jury, and not the doctors, to decide the question of diminished responsibility (i.e. as in Spriggs (1957)), nevertheless the jury's verdict must be founded on the evidence offered. Though he could understand that the jury might think that such a "monster" ought not to live and therefore only a capital sentence was appropriate, they (their Lordships) had to bear in mind the present law. *Conviction reduced to manslaughter under section 2, and sentence altered to 20 years' imprisonment*: [*1958*] *1 W.L.R. 474.*

Michael Robert Mercer   Marion Beaver

Mercer (18), a packing machinist, stabbed his girl friend (20) outside her home when she told him she was going to leave him. "I took the knife out and stabbed her three times and stabbed myself once. The only reason I did it was because I loved her and thought I was going to lose her." He had afterwards attempted suicide.

Mercer was acquitted of murder, but found guilty of manslaughter and sent to prison for 7 years, Lancaster Assizes, 3.2.1958.

William Ernest Moodie   Patricia Moodie

Moodie (47), a prison officer, was described as "quite passionately devoted" to his daughter (12) who had been an imbecile since birth, could neither walk nor talk, and was subject to terrible epileptic seizures. Moodie was alleged to have killed her with an overdose of drugs at their home.

Defence pleaded diminished responsibility, and the senior Medical Officer of Durham Prison (where Moodie worked) said that accused was suffering from acute nervous depression. The prosecution offered no rebutting medical evidence and Moodie was *found guilty of manslaughter under section 2, the jury adding a strong recommendation for mercy, Durham Assizes, 27.10.1958. Moodie's sentence of 3 years' imprisonment was reduced on appeal to 12 months' imprisonment* on the grounds that the judge had not given full weight to the jury's recommendation.

[Authors' note: The first prison officer in this century to be indicted for murder. His colleagues in the prison service rallied round him and collected a large sum of money to insure his financial security after he came out of prison.]

Francis John Morris   Jessie Helen Morris

Morris (19), unemployed, was *found unfit to plead at the Old Bailey* on the charge of killing his mother (48) with a chopper. He was alleged to have conceived of a wildly fantastic plan to kill her and escape to Scotland. Accused was at the time a voluntary patient in a mental hospital. Morris had written out a plan headed "order for leading a full life" in which he planned to kill his mother. He said: "I didn't think it was a brave thing I did as I'm not in her class".

Ordered to be detained during H.M.P., 7.5.1958.

Roy Kenneth Nash   Alan Henry Compton
Barry Gordon Freeman

Nash (16), a shop assistant, and Freeman (16), an electrician's mate, were charged with murdering Compton (18) during a brawl at a dance-hall in Shoreditch. Although there was some evidence of provocative words and behaviour by Compton, who was drunk, it was alleged that the 2 accused returned to some nearby bushes where they had hidden a knife, collected it, and then went into the dance-hall where the fatal stabbing occurred.

Freeman was to some extent exonerated by the statement of Nash who had carried the knife and actually stabbed Compton. Nash claimed that he had not intended to do Compton any harm and that it had been an accident.

Freeman was acquitted of non-capital murder and discharged; Nash was found guilty of manslaughter and sentenced to 5 years' imprisonment. Old Bailey, 12.9.1958.

[Authors' note: Nash is the younger brother of James Lawrence Nash (1960)—see in relation to the "Pen Club" killing. They are members of a family notorious for their participation in violent professional crime.]

Lyndon Emrys Nott   Veronica Ryan

Nott (25), a butcher in a bacon factory, strangled and stabbed to death the girl (28) he had raped in a Hertfordshire lane. He fled

from his home and job the following day but gave himself up to the
police in Devon.

The defence offered strong evidence of Nott's mental state—
suffering from schizophrenia, long history of treatment in mental
hospitals, had attempted suicide, etc. Prosecution medical witnesses
disagreed with this evidence on his mental state but did not completely dispute it; Mr. Justice Elwes advised the jury to accept the
defence evidence that a schizophrenic attack had occurred, and
Nott was *found guilty but insane*, the prosecution having been given
leave to call evidence to show insanity, thereby rebutting defence
plea of diminished responsibility: (1958) 43 Cr.App.R. 8.

Bedfordshire Assizes, 8.10.1958, detained during H.M.P.

[Authors' note: In R. v. Price [1963] 2 Q.B.1 Mr. Justice
Lawton refused to allow the prosecution to call such rebutting
evidence. In this practice he was followed by Mr. Justice Elwes
himself: see Mitchell (1962), footnote to R. v. Price (1962) 47
Cr.App.R. 21 at p. 26. See also Bastian (1958) and, particularly,
Duke (1961) Mr. Justice Marshall in R. v. Russell [1963] 3 All
E.R. 603 did not adopt the practice but followed the decision in
R. v. Bastian [1958] *1* W.L.R. 413.]

Albert Edward Osborne   Sophia Barber

Osborne (26), a lorry driver, offered a lift to Mrs. Barber (61)
during the bus strike. He drove in a different direction and appa-
tently made an improper suggestion to her. When she started to
scream, he panicked, knocked her unconscious and strangled her
with a piece of string in the cab of the lorry, afterwards tipping the
body out by the side of the road.

*Pleaded guilty at the Old Bailey to non-capital murder and was
sent to prison for life, 21.7.1958.*

Barbara Page   Caroline Page

Mr. Justice Streatfeild instructed the jury to return a verdict of
"*Not guilty*" against Mrs. Page (23) on charge of non-capital
murder of her daughter (3 months) by purposely dropping her on
to the ground. He ruled that police evidence on the statement
alleged to have been made by Mrs. Page was inadmissible since
there was every indication that the statement, far from being voluntary, was the result of "the most bullying cross-examination of this
woman . . . she was reduced to such a state that she acceded to suggestion after suggestion that was made to her" (i.e. by the police).

Birmingham Assizes 22.7.1958. Discharged.

At the subsequent inquest it was stated that the baby had died from a rare type of illness.

Joseph Leonard Pantry   Sarah Newlett

Pantry (27), student male nurse, strangled his landlady (88) who lived at the same address. He was reported as saying, "I felt lonely for her and lonely for myself . . . since her husband died at Christmas 1956, she had always said she wanted to die to be with him and that is why I killed her".

Defence pleaded diminished responsibility and entered evidence of accused's bad home background. He had previously attempted suicide on a few occasions and was subject to fits of depression often induced by the worry resulting from his homosexual proclivities.

Found not guilty of non-capital murder but guilty of manslaughter under section 2 and sentenced to life imprisonment. Lewes Assizes, 24.3.1958.

Transferred to Broadmoor, under section 72 of the Mental Health Act 1959, on 12.1.1960.

Gour Krishna Paul   Mahboob Pulin Kumar Biswas

Paul (22), an Indian seaman, was alleged to have beaten to death two fellow seamen in the m.v. *Brockleymoor* in mid-Atlantic. There arose difficulties of language, etc., in the taking of police statements and Mr. Justice McNair later said: "I often wish that we observed in this country a practice, which I believe has been adopted in India . . . that no written statement by an accused man is accepted as evidence unless it has been taken down before a magistrate, then there is no dispute. Again and again one finds in these courts statements like this written in fair hand, stage by stage, in strict chronological order, and the jury is told that it was written down without any prompting".

Paul was acquitted of the double murder charge and discharged, Devon Assizes, 9.11.1958.

Geoffrey Pell   Lesley Kearney Pell

Pell (19), a railway cleaner, beat his recently-born child in a fit of temper/desperation when the child refused to take food. Lesley

Pell (13 weeks) died from shock and haemorrhage after being hit. Evidence that Pell was of good character and fond of the child.

Found guilty of manslaughter at Leeds Assizes and sent to prison for 7 years, 16.12.1958.

Gordon Pennington   Francis McVey

Pennington (27), unemployed cinema projectionist, was charged with the non-capital murder of the son (3) of his mistress. He claimed that there was never any intent either to kill or cause grievous bodily harm, but that he had chastised the child on two occasions for making a mess and that the child had fallen over. Defence offered medical evidence to show that death had resulted from a slow haemorrhage caused on the first occasion, not on the second, as claimed by the prosecution.

Convicted and sentenced to life imprisonment at Lancaster Assizes, 5.6.1958.

Appeal to the Court of Criminal Appeal on the ground that: (1) the direction upon the alternatives of murder and manslaughter, and a careful definition of each offence, had not been given by the Judge; (2) jury had disregarded the evidence in reaching that verdict.

Appeal successful. Conviction reduced to manslaughter and sentence reduced to 5 years' imprisonment. 28.7.1958. [1958] Crim.L.R. 690.

Donald John Perkins   Winifred Mullard

Perkins (20), electrician's mate, was alleged by the prosecution to have stabbed his aunt (40) with a poker at her home and to have stolen £15 to pay debts and take his fiancée (18) on holiday.

Perkins denied the capital murder charge, and after a long retirement the jury acquitted him of murder in course or furtherance of theft and found him *guilty of non-capital murder.* Perkins had stated that he went to his aunt's house in connection with his fiancée. The aunt had been described as Perkins' "second mother".

Life imprisonment at Nottingham Assizes, 17.11.1958.

John George Perkins   William Leyland

Perkins (44), a clerk, shot his neighbour (49) after a quarrel about Leyland's chickens who were constantly getting into the accused's garden.

Defence evidence of Perkins suffering from acute anxiety neurosis, for which he had obtained treatment in mental hospitals. Medical evidence not refuted by prosecution. Plea of diminished responsibility was successful. Perkins *found not guilty of capital murder but guilty of manslaughter under section 2.*

Sentenced to life imprisonment at Essex Assizes, 17.5.1958.

John Alfred Philips   Mabel Philips
                                                John Philips

Philips (55), a hospital porter, was so worried about the international situation and feared so much the idea of his family living "under the Russians" that he battered his wife (48) and son (8) to death with a hammer and then attempted suicide by an overdose of sleeping tablets and by gas.

Found guilty but insane at Sheffield Assizes, 25.11.1958. H.M.P. Broadmoor.

Clive Pickering   John Frederick Boucher

Pickering (26), unemployed, was alleged to have confessed in a statement to the police that he murdered a fellow-lodger (45) at his Salvation Army Hostel, by pushing him off the quayside into the water in Hull dock, after Boucher had refused to lend him 2/6d. Hull City Coroner had already recorded a verdict of accidental death.

At his trial defence offered extensive medical evidence of Pickering's mental state—long personal and family history of mental disorder, suffering from schizophrenia associated with delusions— and he was *found unfit to plead and sent to Broadmoor. York Assizes, 17.6.1958.*

He was examined and adjudged sane by 2 Broadmoor doctors in October 1958, and was sent for trial a second time. This time, he pleaded not guilty and claimed, as he had done originally, that Boucher had accidentally slipped to his death from the quay. He claimed he could not remember the statements of confession he had made, nor the first trial at all, owing to his mental incapacity at the time. The two main witnesses of the crime, 2 companions of Pickering and Boucher, now claimed also that death was accidental.

Pickering acquitted of non-capital murder at York Assizes, 10.11.1958, and discharged.

Pickering later made a most unusual statement, sworn before a Commissioner for Oaths, that he lived constantly under the impulse to murder a person—quite without motive—and claimed that he would undoubtedly murder "*again*". "For medical reasons I cannot have any sexual relations. Killing is my only means of gratification." He further stated that he had faked insanity before and at the first trial in order to get to Broadmoor from which he knew that he would soon be released, only to be acquitted in a second trial. He made a detailed confession of Boucher's killing. An investigation by the *Empire News* (albeit presented in a sensational fashion) brought to light other facts:

1. Pickering's long delinquent career and mental history (but he could not be *officially* recorded as a psychopath since there was no *legal* evidence of his having committed a crime of violence before the age of 18).

2. A third witness of the murder who had refused to come forward since he was himself in trouble with the police.

3. The two companions expressed doubts as to the correct nature of their testimony at the second trial.

On 22 January 1959 Pickering was arrested in Lincolnshire after local residents had complained of a "prowler". Magistrates committed him to Bracebridge Mental Hospital for observation, *where he was kept in the same ward as Boucher's brother, who had been admitted after a nervous breakdown following his brother's death*. The detention order for Pickering expired on March 6, and he released himself.

About the end of April, Pickering was imprisoned for 9 months at Lindsey (Lincs.) for stealing an axe. Alleged statement claimed: "I stole because I wanted to chop the head off a child".

Cyril Victor Pike   Margaret Ann Benbow

Pike (63), a farmer, after drinking a bottle of whisky, shot a farm girl (19) in the bathroom of the house where she lived with Pike and his wife. He then attempted to commit suicide by shooting himself twice. Allegedly, accused said (in a delirium) "why did I kill her when I needed her so much? She was not human. You did not know her. She led me a terrible life the last 2 years". Also said: "I know one thing: I would sooner hang for her than she break my son's home up. His wife told me about his staying out at nights". Benbow had given birth to an illegitimate child earlier in the year, but the father's identity was never disclosed at the trial. It was not known whether the child was Pike's or his son's.

Defence pleaded diminished responsibility (presumably on grounds of emotional stress). *Found guilty of manslaughter under section 2 and sentenced to 7 years' imprisonment at Hampshire Assizes, 11.12.1958.*

Abdool Rafik   Kenneth Pinnock

Rafik (28), an unemployed coloured man, was alleged to have stabbed Pinnock in a street fight after a series of arguments concerning custody of the child born to him (Rafik) and a woman who was now living with Pinnock.

Rafik was *convicted of non-capital murder at the Old Bailey, 2.12.1958, and sentenced to life imprisonment.*

His appeal to the Court of Criminal Appeal was on the grounds that the judge should have directed the jury on the defences of self-defence and provocation if, as Rafik claimed, it was Pinnock who attacked with the knife. *Appeal dismissed, 9.3.1959.* [*1959*] Crim. L.R. 336.

Roy Riddington   Keith Priestley

After Priestley (8) had "been cheeky" to Riddington (23), unemployed, his teacher at Sunday school, suddenly it occurred to the accused to "teach him a lesson" as they were walking home together along the bank of the Grand Union Canal near Leicester. Impulsively, he pushed the boy into the water and, after an unsuccessful attempt to get Priestley out, went home. The boy was drowned. No suggestion of sex involved.

Defence offered evidence by 2 prison doctors that Riddington was suffering from schizophrenia and was "apathetic, indifferent and wildly confused". While in custody, accused had shown no emotional response to the moral issues of the charge.

Found guilty but insane at Leicester Assizes, 3.2.1958. Judge stated that Riddington "would be taken to a place where he could be properly looked after". *H.M.P. Broadmoor.*

James Riley   Mary Riley

Riley (40), a woodwork machinist, was *found insane and unfit to plead at Manchester Crown Court, 2.12.1958,* on the charge of murdering his wife (40) by strangling her at their home.

In a statement to the police, Riley is alleged to have said:
"I didn't want her to suffer. I was making her suffer. I could see her suffering every night. I asked her to leave me but she wouldn't. I had been very depressed over the last 3 or 4 months and it had been making her ill with seeing me". *H.M.P.*

Ronald Roberts   Edna Roberts

Roberts (39), a driver, *pleaded guilty at Leicester Assizes* to murdering his wife (39) by stabbing and strangling her when he became suspicious that she was having an affair with their lodger. *Sentenced to life imprisonment, 21.10.1958.*

Joseph Nobel Rogerson   Ellen Rogerson

Rogerson (52), a metal worker, had been living apart from his wife (43) for some weeks, and shortly after they were re-united, Mrs. Rogerson told her husband she was going to leave him again. He put his arm round her neck to restrain her and she went limp. Death was due to asphyxia and cardiac inhibition. The Rogersons had been married for 24 years and there were 9 children.

Rogerson's plea of *not guilty to non-capital murder but guilty to manslaughter* was accepted by the Court and he *was sentenced to 7 days' imprisonment (meaning his immediate release) at Newcastle Assizes, 19.5.1958.*

Samuel Ronald   Elsie Lane

Ronald (22), a steel erector, throttled to death his landlady (64) after an argument about her switching off the electric current in her lodging house at night. He had previously been drinking quite heavily.

Defence plea of diminished responsibility was not accepted. A consultant psychiatrist, for the accused, had said that there was a history of epilepsy and that the killing might have taken place during an epileptic attack. This evidence was refuted by prosecution medical witness. Mr. Justice Ashworth said that section 2 of the Act was not to be regarded "as a charter for the passionate or quick-tempered, or those addicted to drink".

Ronald was *found guilty of non-capital murder and sent to prison for life at Durham Assizes, 25.10.1958.*

[Authors' note: Juries are notoriously sceptical of any defence involving epileptic fits when there is no history of epilepsy. The same cannot be said of amnesia (see Boshears 1961).]

Alan Edwin Rudd   Emma Lopez

Rudd (29), unemployed, returning home after drinking, had a quarrel with his mistress (31), when she suddenly decided she was going out "to get a man" and earn some money. He strangled her until she was unconscious and, uncertain whether he had killed her or not, stabbed her 20 times with a pair of scissors.

Rudd claimed he was emotionally upset and attacked her in revenge for her treatment of him. *Pleaded provocation successfully at Leeds Assizes, 28.4.1958. The Judge, sentencing him to 10 years' imprisonment, said:* "The jury have been very merciful—it was as near murder as it could be".

Martin Russell (see: John Devine)

Francis Joseph Schleising (See: Terrence George Jones)

Gurdev Singh (See: Mehindar Kaur)

Resham Singh   Ajit Singh

Resham Singh (36), an Indian labourer, was *acquitted of the non-capital murder* of Ajit Singh (28) during a street fight involving a number of Indians in Kettering.

The accused's defence of "self-defence" was accepted.
Northampton Assizes, 17.10.1958. Discharged.

Bernard Smith   Leah Gillman

Smith (68), an American furniture dealer, was alleged to have killed his sister (65) by hitting and kicking her during a quarrel and fight in his room at the Strand Palace Hotel in London.

On a charge of non-capital murder, defence entered a successful plea of diminished responsibility based on Smith's melancholia. *Acquitted on the murder charge, Smith was found guilty of manslaughter under section 2 and sentenced to life imprisonment. Old Bailey, 10.7.1958*

George Smith   Lilian May Cox

Smith (30), a dustman, was alleged to have taken Cox (30), described as "simple-minded and of immoral character", to the stockyard at the back of a factory where, after drinking, a quarrel arose between them, and accused strangled her.

Defence at *Stafford Assizes* presented evidence of Smith's low-grade feeble-mindedness in a plea of diminished responsibility. *Acquitted of non-capital murder but guilty of manslaughter under section 2. Sentenced to 15 years' imprisonment, 8.7.1958.*

Transferred to Broadmoor, 21.7.1961, under section 72 of the *Mental Health Act 1959.*

Eric Roy Stark   Elizabeth Flack

Stark (20), unemployed labourer, was charged with the capital murder of a part-time moneylender and club collector (66) at her home. Later, empty purses, normally used for collecting the subscriptions, were found abandoned, together with a hatchet, on an allotment.

The jury accepted Stark's unsworn statement read from the dock, and rejected prosecution evidence which was completely circumstantial; Stark was *acquitted of capital murder* (*in course or furtherance of theft*) *and was discharged, Lincolnshire Assizes, 30.10.1958.*

Helen Sterry   Christopher Vincent

Sterry (25), who was on leave from a mental hospital, took a baby (5 weeks) from its pram in a crowded shopping centre and threw it into the River Wye.

Faced with the charge of non-capital murder, defence pleaded diminished responsibility and offered very extensive evidence of accused's mental instability and abnormally low intelligence. Claimed that she was certifiable under the Mental Deficiency Act, and that there were no hopes that she could be improved by any treatment.

Found not guilty of non-capital murder but guilty of manslaughter under section 2. Sentenced to life imprisonment at Hereford Assizes, 19.2.1958.

Frank Stokes   Lynda Violet Ash

When he called in reply to an advertisement for a jobbing gardener, Stokes (44), an unemployed hotel porter, was offered

3/6d. per hour instead of the 4/0d. which he had asked the prospective employer. He was alleged to have picked up a hammer and beaten the victim (75) to death.

The prosecution alleged that a wallet found on Stokes when he gave himself up was identical with one which was missing from Mrs. Ash's home, and which normally contained an amount of money in bank notes. Stokes claimed, in his plea of not guilty to capital murder (in course or furtherance of theft) but guilty to non-capital murder, that he had gone there for an innocent purpose and had acquired the wallet elsewhere.

Nevertheless, he was *convicted of capital murder and sentenced to death at Leeds Assizes, 23.7.1958 [1958] Crim.L.R. 688.*

Appeal to the Court of Criminal Appeal was dismissed (no details available), *20.8.1958,* and the Home Secretary refused to recommend a reprieve.

Executed at Durham Prison, 3.9.1958.

Derek William Street   William Ernest Boddington

Street (23) was a forestry labourer. After his mother (48), Mrs. Love, had been living with Boddington for 25 years and had borne him 7 children, she decided to revert to her married name of Love and the children took her maiden name of Street. There were a series of domestic quarrels during which Boddington turned out the mother and children from his cottage without any money. There followed a number of fights on the same evening between the accused and his father; the latter died from injuries received from blows from a motor-car hand-pump.

Defence pleaded provocation, but Street *found guilty of non-capital murder and sentenced to life imprisonment, Leicester Assizes, 6.2.1958.*

Derek Sutcliffe   Anne Sutcliffe

Sutcliffe (23), a labourer, was found guilty of the murder of his daughter (4 months) at his home in Todmorden. The prosecution alleged that he had banged the child with considerable violence against a bedpost, apparently in a fit of temper or irritation when the baby kept crying.

The defence asked for a verdict of manslaughter on the grounds that there was no intention to kill, or alternatively, on grounds of diminished responsibility (it had been established that Sutcliffe had financial and hire-purchase worries and was constantly upset with sleepless nights through the baby's crying).

Sentenced to life imprisonment (probably on the grounds of diminished responsibility) at *Leeds Assizes, 18.12.1958.*

Vivian Frederick Teed   William Williams

Teed (24), an unemployed labourer, took a hammer with him when he went to rob the sub-post office in Fforestfach, Wales. He beat Williams (73), the postmaster, 27 times with the hammer when the latter grappled with him.

Charged with capital murder, Teed pleaded diminished responsibility and offered evidence of his psychopathic personality. The Medical Officer at Swansea Prison stated that Teed was a "dangerously jealous man who needs careful watching". Had many previous convictions for crimes of violence. The prosecution produced rebutting evidence.

Convicted of murder in the course or furtherance of theft and sentenced to death at Glamorgan Assizes 18.3.1958.

Appeal to Court of Criminal Appeal dismissed, 21.4.1958 (no details available). The Home Secretary refused a reprieve. *Executed at Swansea Prison, 6.5.1958.*

Eric Robert Norman Thorn   Phyllis Mary Thorn

Thorn (28), a gardener, was *found insane and unfit to plead at Lewes Assizes, 22.7.1958,* charged with murdering his wife. Dr. Brisby and Dr. Gibbens both said he was suffering from schizophrenia. *H.M.P.*

Thorn strangled his wife (34) and then phoned the police telling them: "I came over gassy . . . I have been having sexual trouble lately. I heard a cockerel when I put my hands round her throat". He had been suffering from mental illness shortly before the killing.

Robert Charles Tickell   Eva Gillings

Tickell (41), a railwayman, battered with a chopper his twice-married mother (68) after a quarrel over money. He lived with his mother with whom he frequently quarrelled, particularly after both had been drinking. The killing was committed after he had returned late following a drinking bout. After killing her he went to bed. At 8.30 the next morning he went and told the police.

Not guilty of non-capital murder but guilty of manslaughter (under section 2) and sentenced to life imprisonment at the Old Bailey, 23.1.1958.

He had three times—1933, 1934-37, and 1956—been a voluntary mental in-patient at a hospital.

Albert Arthur Watkins   Gladys Watkins

Watkins (44), painter and decorator, stabbed his wife (40) to death with a carving knife picked up during a fit of temper at their home. His wife had threatened to leave him following domestic quarrels. Medical evidence, at his *Kent Assizes trial, 28.11.1958*, that he was a "borderline case of insanity" was not rebutted by the prosecution. *Found guilty of manslaughter under section 2 and sentenced to 7 years' imprisonment.*

Harry Watson   Anne Watson

Watson (45), unemployed, was charged with beating to death his granddaughter (21 months) at his caravan home.

Defence admitted that he had slapped the child the previous day but that the child was often falling over and rarely attempted to save itself when it did so. Pleaded accidental death.

Mr. Justice Gorman stopped the trial at *Lewes Assizes* at the end of the prosecution's case, and directed the *jury to return a verdict of not guilty. Discharged, 27.3.1958.*

Roger Terence White   Douglas Leonard O'Brien

White (22), a shipwright, was alleged to have stabbed to death the man who was associating with his wife and by whom she was pregnant. It was stated that he used a spring-loaded flick-knife which he carried with him on the night he met O'Brien (27). White stated he never had any intention to kill.

The defence entered a successful plea of manslaughter by provocation, and White was *acquitted of non-capital murder at Bristol Assizes, 24.6.1958. Guilty of manslaughter under section 3 and sentenced to 7 years' imprisonment.*

Roy Frederick White   Gladys Philips

White (25), a farm worker, was alleged to have gone home and collected his gun, and then shot his employer and his employer's wife (54)—the victim—after a quarrel arising from White's improper association with Philips' 14 year-old daughter. They were distant relatives by marriage. Mrs. Philips died from her injuries.

Charged with capital murder, White pleaded insanity and entered evidence that he was suffering from a manic depressive disorder which rendered him incapable of knowing the nature and quality of his actions. The jury were unable to agree after 75 minutes, were discharged and a retrial was ordered. The second jury found White guilty but insane. *Winchester Assizes, 18.7.1958. Ordered to be detained during H.M.P.* The charge of attempted murder (of Mr. Philips) remained on the file.

Margaret Wiggins   Colin Michael Wiggins

Mrs. Wiggins (40), mother of 7 children, was charged with non-capital murder by pushing her son (7) into the River Foss at York, with the result that he drowned.

Evidence was offered by the defence that the accused had been mentally ill for a number of years and had gone into hospitals on six occasions for the treatment of two mental disorders. She had some form of epileptic attacks and was liable to outbreaks of depression. Had previously attempted suicide. Her father and two sisters had died at their own hands and another brother and sister were epileptics.

Found guilty but insane at York Assizes, 18.2.1958. Ordered to be detained at Broadmoor during H.M.P.

Roy Willington   Maureen Willington

Willington (24), labourer, after his brother had told him that he had slept once with Mrs. Willington (26), "brooded" over this confession of adultery, and the next day strangled her after a short quarrel, then held her head down in a bowl of water.

Defence asked for a verdict of manslaughter—"Willington grabbed his wife by the throat in a transport of passion".

Acquitted of non-capital murder but found guilty of manslaughter under section 3, and sentenced to 5 years' imprisonment. Manchester Crown Court, 7.7.1958.

Mary Wilson   Ernest George Wilson
                                          Oliver James Leonard

Mrs. Wilson (66), a widow, was charged with the double murder of her second and third husbands by poisoning. Each died within a few days of the wedding and in each were found traces of phosphorus. Motive in both cases seemed to be to obtain the husband's financial possessions. Suspicion was aroused when someone at the wedding reception commented that there were a lot of sandwiches and cakes left over and Mrs. Wilson replied: "Just keep them for the funeral, although I might give this one a week's extension".

Defence denied the charge but Mrs. Wilson *convicted of capital murder (murder on 2 separate occasions) at Leeds Assizes, 30.3.1958, and sentenced to death by Mr. Justice Hinchcliffe.* [*N.B.* Mrs. Wilson declined to enter the witness box.]

Appeal to the Court of Criminal Appeal on grounds that the judge had misdirected the jury. In referring to "contradictions in medical evidence, it was of the utmost importance that the judge should have pointed them out". *Appeal dismissed, 19.5.1958: (1958) 41 Cr.App.R. 226.*

Reprieve recommended by Home Secretary, 1.6.1958, presumably because she was an old woman. *Life imprisonment.*

Died in Holloway Prison, 10.1.1963, aged 71.

[Authors' note: Female murderers resort to poison to a much greater extent than men. Medea, in the myth of Jason and the quest of the Golden Fleece, is the prototype of female poisoners. Euripides portrayed Medea as the evil poisoner of her rival who punished her unfaithful husband by murdering the children she bore him. Some of the most heartless murders have been committed by female poisoners: Lucretia Borgia, Madame Voisin and Mrs. Merrifield.]

Herbert Alfred Wood   Anthony Wood

Wood (17), a locomotive fireman, was found guilty of murdering his son (8 months). In a statement he said the child always cried when he picked him up, and that on one or two occasions he had lost his temper and beaten the child with his shoe. On this latter occasion, he had again lost his temper, picked up a shovel and hit the child. Post-mortem revealed, in addition to fractured skull, from which death had resulted, a fractured thighbone (some months) and 10 broken ribs (4 weeks old).

Convicted at the Old Bailey, 20.6.1958, of non-capital murder, and ordered to be detained during H.M.P.

John Henry Wood   Eliza Roberts

After a quarrel with the woman with whom he had been living for some years, Woods (43), a van driver, left the room, returned with a shotgun and fired at Mrs. Roberts (49). He pleaded that the affair had been an accident, that he had only meant to frighten her, and that he thought the gun was unloaded.

Jury accepted defence and Wood, *acquitted of capital murder, was found guilty of manslaughter at Monmouth Assizes, 5.11.1958. Sent to prison for 7 years.*

1959

Accused   Victim

Annie Allman   Samuel Allman

Mrs. Allman (54) was *found guilty but insane at Birmingham Assizes, 16.12.1959,* of the murder of her husband (55).
H.M.P., Broadmoor.

The couple were found on the kitchen floor at their home with a chopper and a carving knife near them. Mr. Allman had head injuries and Mrs. Allman had wounds to the throat. She was stated to have had a history of delusion and depression.

Michael Francis Atherton   James Gibbons

Atherton (45), unemployed, who had been living apart from his wife for about a year, went to her home one morning; as he got to her door, he was set upon by his two stepsons, James (23) and Patrick, who attacked him. He claimed that he was so dazed from their blows that he did not remember pulling a knife from his pocket and stabbing them. James died a little while later in hospital. At his trial at *Liverpool Crown Court*, it would seem that defence pleaded diminished responsibility (no details except that Atherton was said to be always drunk), but he was *convicted of manslaughter on grounds of provocation and sentenced to 10 years' imprisonment, 11.11.1959.*

The charge of wounding the other stepson with intent to murder was not proceeded with.

Edmund William Barber   Carol Ann Soan

Barber (22), a bread packer, strangled his fiancée (18) in a park while seeing her home; she had just previously told him she wanted to break off their engagement in order to go out with another boy. (This latter boy committed suicide when he heard of her death.)

Evidence by a psychiatrist that severe emotional stress had caused a temporary abnormality of the mind supported a defence plea of diminished responsibility and Barber was found *guilty of man-slaughter under section 2. Sentenced to 3 years' imprisonment; Old Bailey, 16.4.1959.*

Ronald Herbert Benson   Elizabeth Ivatt
                                         Phyllis Squires

Benson (34), a clerk and church worker, battered to death in a frenzy two old ladies, Miss Ivatt (88) and Miss Squires (60), at their home in Wandsworth, London, when they told him they were not able to give him any money. He afterwards threw paraffin over them and set fire to their bodies.

Benson was *found insane and unfit to plead at the Old Bailey and was ordered to be detained during H.M.P., 27.10.1959.*

John David Berridge   Leonard Charles Berridge
                                    Irene Berridge

Berridge (19), an aircraftman, was apparently so impressed with the might of the Soviet Union that he felt the West could not win in the event of any conflict; and so he shot his father (42) and mother (38) as they lay in bed at their home. Later in the day, he showed their bodies to a friend and then went to the cinema.

Medical evidence was given at his trial on a charge of capital murder at *Pembrokeshire Assizes, 22.6.1959.* In the opinion of one doctor, Berridge was suffering from paranoid schizophrenia and was in need of hospital treatment. He was found *guilty but insane and ordered to be detained at Broadmoor during H.M.P.*

Dr. Ravindranath Shrinivas Bhonsle   Martha Giles

Dr. Bhonsle (31), an Indian specialist at a Wolverhampton hospital, was accused of murdering a nurse (45) at the hospital, by stabbing her and battering her to death in the grounds.

Prosecution could establish no motive of any sort and their evidence was all circumstantial. Blood found on Bhonsle's clothing was quite compatible with splashes during blood transfusions, etc., and the nature of the stabbing led suspicion *away* from someone with detailed knowledge of anatomy such as he would have. Bhonsle attempted suicide but this could have been due to worry over police investigations coming at a particularly inopportune

4

time in his family and personal life. *Acquitted on charge of non-capital murder at Stafford Assizes and discharged, 16.7.1959.*

William Douglas Biddick   Betty Moore
                                           Donna Moore

William Douglas Biddick (39), a fitter and a Special Constable, was alleged by the prosecution to have strangled in a frenzy of jealousy the woman with whom he had been living (60) and then to have strangled her daughter (14), perhaps because she had been a witness. The defence case was that he strangled Mrs. Moore quite by accident during an embrace and then strangled the girl while his mental responsibility was diminished as a result of finding the woman whom he loved very much, dead in his arms.

Biddick was *found guilty of non-capital murder on both counts at Cornwall Assizes, 6.6.1959, and sentenced to life imprisonment.*

Diana Bromley   Martin John Bromley

Mrs. Bromley (39) was *found insane and unfit to plead at Surrey Assizes, 25.2.1959,* on the charge of murdering her son (13). It was stated that she was suffering from melancholia and had been treated three times in mental hospitals. She had attempted suicide while awaiting trial.

At the hearing before the Magistrates' Court, it was alleged that after giving barbiturates to Martin and to her other son, Stephen (10), Mrs. Bromley carried the boys to a garage where she attempted to kill them with carbon monoxide. Afterwards she strangled Martin, whose body was found in the garage, and drowned Stephen in the bathroom. She also cut the boys' throats and, according to a statement, tried to drown herself in a pond. *H.M.P.*

Joseph Buckley   Ellen Buckley

Buckley (47), a boarding house keeper, was alleged to have unintentionally strangled his wife (46) at their home when she attacked him with a knife. She was constantly making false allegations that he "kept looking at other women" and it had become an obsession with her. It appeared that she had been suffering from paranoid schizophrenia. Buckley was described as a "devoted husband" by all his relations who gave evidence.

Acquitted of both non-capital murder and manslaughter, and discharged. Lewes Assizes, 23.3.1959.

Edward Bertie Butts   June Moorecroft

Butts (32), a garage hand, a native of British Guiana, was *convicted at Liverpool Crown Court, 22.6.1959,* of murdering a woman (20) with whom he was friendly, by stabbing her at home. Butts accounted for bloodstains on his clothing and a wound in his cheek by saying that he had received them during a fight with a man, who had attacked him some time before, while on his way to the woman's flat.

Butts was sentenced to life imprisonment.

Ernest Campbell   Paul Michael Lewis

Campbell (17), labourer, denied that it was for sex that he strangled a boy (6) whose body was found in a lavatory in the grounds of a mansion used as council offices in Twickenham. However, the boy's body was naked and his clothes were lying neatly folded at his feet. He had been strangled with one of his socks.

Evidence produced by the defence in a plea of diminished responsibility was apparently not rebutted by the prosecution and Campbell was found *guilty of manslaughter under section 2 at the Old Bailey, 18.6.1959. Sentenced to 10 years' imprisonment.*

Andrew Cassells   Ellen Harley (otherwise Hawkins)

Cassells (30) invited to his bed-sitter the victim (39), who was a prostitute, and during sexual intercourse put a towel over her face in order to prevent a person outside hearing a woman's voice and therefore knowing he had a woman in his room. Owing to the state of the woman's health and a hypersensitivity of the vagal nerve in her neck she died from asphyxia.

Cassells put the body under the bed and lived in the room for a week before he was arrested after having gone to Folkestone (from Manchester).

The offence bordered on an accident and Cassells was acquitted of non-capital murder, being *found guilty of manslaughter. Sent to prison for 12 months; Manchester Crown Court, 8.7.1959.*

Brian Cawley   Rupert Steed

In a quarrel, Cawley (30), unemployed, battered to death the
man (43) who had been a generous and friendly benefactor to him.
He had supplied Cawley and his family with rent-free accommodation, devoted a whole year's salary to assisting them financially,
bought presents, etc. Cawley, however, had been sacked from his
council job, took to drink, and his wife left him; seemed a very
unstable type.

*Pleaded guilty to non-capital murder at Winchester Assizes and
was sentenced to life imprisonment at a trial lasting 30 seconds,
14.12.1959.*

Eyyup Celal   Margaret Brindley

The Crown alleged that Celal (21), a Cypriot, beat to death the
woman (20) with whom he was living and who had become pregnant. It was stated that she was a prostitute and would therefore
be of no further use to Celal in bringing in money; he therefore
drove her in his new car—it was a flashy two-tone Vauxhall, and
as such was easily identifiable—out of London, ostensibly to take
her to her mother's home in Wolverhampton, but in fact murdered
her in a quiet country lane near Bicester and threw her body in a
river. Celal had in fact already "lined up" another prostitute to
take Brindley's place.

Celal denied the charge and produced an alibi; the case was,
however, described as a "classic example of the detection of crime
by forensic science" in the way that the prosecution was able to
break down the defence case. *Celal was convicted at the Old Bailey
of non-capital murder and sentenced to life imprisonment, 2.3.1959.*
His application to the Court of Criminal Appeal for leave to appeal
was refused after a hearing lasting only 15 minutes.

The woman's mother was also murdered, a year and a half later,
by a West Indian lodger. (See Nicholson (1960)).

Nellie Cheney   Maureen Cheney

Mrs. Cheney (43) was *found insane and unfit to plead at the Old
Bailey* on a charge or murdering her mentally defective daughter
(15). It seemed that the mother was overcome suddenly with pity
for the girl, who was quite ineducable and unable to fend for herself

at all; she evidently took a strap and strangled Maureen at their home in Clapham, London.

H.M.P., 27.1.1959.

Joseph Chrimes (see: Ronald Charles Pritchard)

Terence Cooney   Alan Johnson

During a gang fight in a dance hall Cooney (19), a labourer, stabbed Johnson (18) with a sheath knife which he had bought from a younger boy a few minutes earlier. He pleaded that he drew the knife in self-defence because he thought Johnson was going to draw one on him. (Johnson was not in fact armed). Cooney agreed that he had stabbed Johnson once, but denied that it was the fatal wound.

Cooney was *found guilty of non-capital murder and sentenced to life imprisonment at the Old Bailey, 8.6.1959.*

Edwin Cooper   Lilian Cooper

Cooper (70), a retired painter, misunderstood some initials on a prescription for ointment for his wife (75) to mean that she was going to be put in a mental hospital. Described as a "man who had focused all his attention on caring for his invalid wife", he had taken a mallet and beaten her to death, intending apparently a mercy-killing.

At his trial at Birmingham Assizes, 21.7.1959, a medical witness said that Cooper had been suffering from paranoid psychosis for weeks or months before the event and that he was insane at the time. *Found guilty but insane, and ordered to be detained H.M.P.*

John Hedley Cordon   Fred Foreman

Prosecution alleged that Cordon (32), a stoker, struck Foreman (54) four times with a shovel during a quarrel and fight in the boiler-house of a colliery where they were both on night work. Probably some degree of provocation involved on the part of Foreman, but he died as a result of one of the blows and Cordon was *convicted of non-capital murder, the jury adding a strong recommendation to mercy. Sentenced to life imprisonment at Birmingham Assizes, 9.12.1959.*

Demetrios Costas (see: Charalambous Panayi *et al.*)

Dennis Coster   Mary Coster

Coster (40), a lorry driver, claimed that he awoke one morning to find his wife (35) lying dead in the room, the body being covered with bruises. He immediately 'phoned the police.

Coster had, the previous evening, been drinking a good many bottles of lager at a neighbour's flat, and the defence called a doctor who stated his opinion that Mrs. Coster had been killed by her husband while he was suffering an epileptic attack. He concluded that Coster was an incipient epileptic and his attack had been induced by his large consumption of fluid. The fact that it was alcohol had aggravated the situation, but the doctor claimed that a similar amount of tea or even water would have had the same effect.

The Crown did not dispute this evidence and Coster was *found guilty but insane at the Old Bailey, 3.12.1959. H.M.P. Broadmoor.*

George Cotterill   Joan Mary McMahon

Cotterill (27), a lorry driver, *pleaded guilty at Stafford Assizes, 2.12.1959, to murdering* Mrs. McMahon (34) with whom he had been associating for some years. It was alleged that a struggle took place between them in the cab of his lorry after they had been to a dance (where they had been drinking); Cotterill stabbed her and beat her, then dragged the body on to some waste land.

An examination showed no signs of mental abnormality in Cotterill. *He was sentenced to life imprisonment.*

Arthur Cox   Eileen Cox

When his wife (25) left him and his son (3) to go and live with her parents, Cox (29), a gas fitter, armed himself with a jack-knife, wedged with wood and sticking tape so that it would remain open, and stabbed her at her parents' home. He then attempted to kill himself with the knife. It was stated that Mrs. Cox was associating with another man and the defence claimed that this amounted to sufficient provocation to reduce the murder charge to manslaughter.

Cox was, however, *found guilty of non-capital murder, the jury adding a strong recommendation for mercy. He was sentenced to life imprisonment at the Old Bailey, 1.6.1959.*

Ernest Bernard Crabb   Mary Jane Davies

Crabb (35), a builder's labourer, met Mary Davies (26) in a public house, bought her drink and afterwards took her home. After kissing in a lane near the hostel where she lived, she evidently ran away; as she did so, Crabb knocked her to the ground and then dropped a 45-lb. stone on her head two or three times. In a statement later, he said: "She laughed at me. I wanted to hurt her, but I never meant to kill her."

Crabb was *convicted at Glamorgan Assizes of manslaughter (probably under section 2), and sentenced to life imprisonment, 30.11.1959.*

Janice Diane Day   Unnamed Baby Girl

Janice Day (18), a factory worker, took a hotel room in Bath and lived there for a year with a married man who was separated from his wife. In November 1958, the girl gave birth to a female child, but gassed it a month afterwards in a fit of desperation. The man left the body in some bushes at a rubbish dump.

At *Winchester Assizes, 13.4.1959, Day's plea of not guilty to non-capital murder but guilty of infanticide* was accepted by the court and she was placed on *probation for 2 years* on condition that she did not associate with the man who had been the father of her child.

Fred Dennison   Rachel Dennison

Dennison (42), a weaver, was said to suffer from "periods of insanity" and was *found unfit to plead at Leeds Assizes, 1.12.1959,* on a charge of murdering his mother (72) at their home. *H.M.P.*

Dennison had been in a hospital for psychiatric treatment five times since 1956 and each time he had responded to treatment. His mother had been a patient in the same hospital four times. There was no evidence that Dennison had ever before been violent. The victim suffered from a heart disease without which her injuries might not have proved fatal. She was strangled and bruised. Dennison said: "I went for her . . . and put my hands round her neck, and she passed away then. I cannot explain why I did it. Something just came over me."

David Lancelot Di Duca   Herbert William Mullins

After drinking a great deal of rough cider called "scrumpy", Di Duca (21), a naval steward, broke into the flat of an antique dealer known locally as "Old Pandora" (66), who was reputed to keep large sums of money with him. He was evidently surprised in his burglary by Mullins, a tall and strong man, but beat him to death with a heavy wash basin in the bed sitting room. He escaped with about £44 and later gave some to one or two friends.

At his trial on a capital murder charge at *Winchester Assizes*, the defence was that Di Duca:

(1) killed Mullins in self-defence when attacked by the bigger man; and

(2) owing to the large quantity of alcohol he had drunk, was in "an unstable, irresponsible and impaired state of mind" (i.e. diminished responsibility).

Di Duca admitted to breaking in with intent to robbery but claimed that there was no intention to kill.

He was *found guilty, the jury adding a strong recommendation for mercy, 13.4.59, and sentenced to death.*

Appeal to the Court of Criminal Appeal. Defence submitted that the judge had given no direction to the jury on the question of malice and Di Duca's intention when he was involved in the struggle. Neither had he directed them on whether or not intoxication was capable of amounting to a defence of diminished responsibility. *Appeal dismissed, 26.5.1959,* (1959) 43 Cr.App.R. 167.

A petition was launched by Arthur Palmer, M.P. for Cleveland, and was based upon the jury's recommendation for mercy.

Reprieve granted, 8.6.1959. Life imprisonment.

Charles Frederick Dolby   Sylvia Natalie Lewis

Dolby (55), a turf accountant, was "extremely possessive" towards his mistress (31), and became convinced that she was cooling towards him and had started a friendship with another man. After a quarrel at her Chelsea flat, she told him to leave; he took a revolver from a cupboard and tried to shoot her but the bullet was inserted the wrong way and the gun did not go off. He then hit her with the butt of the gun and left. He returned an hour later to find her still unconscious, and not yet dead, so he strangled her with *seven* of her stockings. He then attempted suicide by gas-oven.

Defence at his Old Bailey trial pleaded diminished responsibility. Evidence was given that Dolby had been a highly strung, hypersensitive man all his life, and suffered from nervous fits. One doctor classified him as a psychopath with a mental abnormality due to "inherited causes". He also suffered from claustrophobia. Mr. Justice Edmund Davies instructed the jury to accept this defence and Dolby was *convicted of manslaughter under section 2; sentenced to 7 years' imprisonment, 8.10.1959.*

[Authors' note: If Dolby had been a little more skilled in weaponry he would have been indicted for capital murder and thus liable to the death penalty.]

Joszef Draboczi   Joszef Kukor

Draboczi (21), a Hungarian kitchen porter, lived with a girl in his basement flat in Westminster; a month before the incident he invited Kukor (also Hungarian) to live there also. Draboczi and the girl shared a double bed, and Kukor (28) had a single bed in the same room. One night, Kukor, who was drunk, tried to molest the girl when she was lying alone in bed, but she refused his advances and he told her to leave the flat. She told Draboczi when he returned from work. Kukor reached for a soldering iron as if to hit him, but Draboczi got hold of it and beat him to death with it.

At the Old Bailey, 7.12.1959, he was acquitted of non-capital murder but found guilty of manslaughter and sentenced to 6 years' imprisonment.

Hubert James Dughard   Miriam Ann Young

Dughard (21), a Eurasian plastics worker, was very fond of his friend (19) and she was very fond of him also, until a young French boy came to live with her family in Finchley, London. She wrote Dughard a letter indicating that she wanted to end their friendship. He met her to try to "win her back" but strangled her with a piece of cord which he had brought with him to their rendezvous in some public gardens near the North Circular Road.

He pleaded guilty at the Old Bailey and was sentenced to life imprisonment, 24.9.1959, by Mr. Justice Edmund Davies.

John Ellis   Grace Ellis

Ellis (25), a miner, and his wife (24) agreed to part for a month after quarrels. He returned home unexpectedly, however, to "patch things up", but found her with her lover in a darkened room; picked up the suspender belt her lover had bought her as a birthday present and strangled her with it; went straight to the police.

Ellis said in evidence: "I was very much in love with my wife and I loved my two children." He had become suspicious when his wife went out four or five times a week. When he learned who the man was, she taunted him about it and her lover's gift of the suspender belt.

Successfully pleaded provocation at Sheffield Assizes, 24.11.1959, and convicted of manslaughter under section 3. Sentenced to 5 years' imprisonment.

[Authors' note: This is slightly in excess of the normal sentence for a *crime passionel;* see Fantle (1958)].

George Fagerass   Iris Fagerass

After being out of work and faced with eviction from his house for failing to pay the rent, Fagerass (47), a painter and decorator, brooded, then exploded in a fit of temper when his wife (40) began to sell their furniture in order to get some money; he took a hammer and beat her to death at their home.

(Although full details are not available, it would appear that Fagerass pleaded diminished responsibility at his trial at *Chester Assizes.*) He was *found guilty of manslaughter under section 2 and sentenced to 8 years' imprisonment, 5.6.1959.*

Jordon Desmond Fenby   Florence Clements

Fenby (31), a labourer, was alleged to have taken an axe and beaten his mother (52) to death as she sat reading a newspaper at home. In a statement he claimed that she "hated the sight of my wife and children" and had interfered in his married life.

He was *found unfit to plead at Leeds Assizes,* having been under constant medical supervision since his arrest, and *ordered to be detained, H.M.P., 16.7.1959.*

Michael Peter Flegg   Lavinia Roberts

Flegg (23), a silk screen printer, stabbed his fiancée (20) with a souvenir sheath knife brought home from Germany. He stabbed her 26 times in a frenzied attack after a quarrel about their engagement at their home in Bromley. (Flegg lodged with the victim's parents).

He was *found guilty but insane at Kent Assizes, 9.7.1959, and ordered to be detained H.M.P.*

Alfred John Gasson   Mary Gasson

A few days after moving into their new bungalow, Gasson (65), a retired civil servant, battered his wife (63) to death with a hammer and then attempted to commit suicide by gas poisoning.

Gasson, *found insane and unfit to plead at Sussex Assizes, 13.3.1959,* was stated to have a history of mental instability and to be suffering from acute melancholia.
H.M.P.

Sarah Ann Gillies   William Henry Gillies

Mrs. Gillies (57) battered her husband (57) with an oven plate while he lay in bed some hours after a quarrel between them. She then "panicked", poured oil over the bed and set fire to it. She was found by the police four hours later wandering in the rain.

Defence entered plea of diminished responsibility and offered medical evidence that accused was highly neurotic and subject to fits of depression. This plea was not rebutted by the prosecution and Mrs. Gillies was *found guilty of manslaughter under section 2 at Liverpool Crown Court, 18.2.1959. Sentenced to 4 years' imprisonment.*

Thomas Anthony Gilsenan   Kathleen Annette Gilsenan

Gilsenan (24), an Irish labourer, had been having an affair with his sister-in-law (25) (he lived as a lodger with her and his brother) but when she became too attached to him and wanted him to take her away, he felt he wanted to break with her, especially since they were "carrying on " behind the back of his brother, who had been very generous and good to him. There was considerable dissension between them (Gilsenan and his mistress) for a few weeks until he finally shot her at their home after he had been drinking fairly heavily.

Defence presented medical evidence that he was little above a mental defective—mental age of about 11—when he faced trial on charge of capital murder at *Herts Assizes, 15.1.1959*. Plea of diminished responsibility was successful in spite of prosecution's rebutting evidence and he was *convicted of manslaughter under section 2; sentenced to 8 years' imprisonment*.

William John Goldsworthy   Brenchley Goldsworthy

Goldsworthy (31), an unemployed cripple, picked up a carving knife and stabbed his brother (38) during a fight at their home after a quarrel over switching on a radio.

Goldsworthy, who had three previous convictions for assaults on police officers, presented an alternative defence of provocation and self-defence (his brother—a bullying, domineering person—had attacked and assaulted him). The jury *acquitted him of murder but found him guilty of manslaughter under section 3, adding a rider that he had acted under extreme provocation. Sent to prison for 18 months, at Cornwall Assizes, 5.2.1959*.

Frank Goodchild   Grace Goodchild

Goodchild (53), a labourer, was found *guilty but insane, at the Old Bailey, 4.2.1959, of murdering* his wife (51) (to whom he had been married only a few weeks). It was stated that he had suddenly strangled her in a spasm of mental derangement.

H.M.P. Broadmoor.

Vernon Grant   Mary Walker

Grant (21), a quarry worker, went to the home of a spinster recluse (72) after a session of drinking, and there raped her before strangling her.

His defence at Derbyshire Assizes of diminished responsibility on grounds of inherent abnormality was not accepted; he was *found guilty of non-capital murder and sentenced to life imprisonment, 5.11.1959*.

John Harding   Henrietta Harding

Described as an "eminently respectable man" by prosecuting counsel, Harding (71), a retired schoolmaster, battered his wife (71) to death with an axe and a hammer and then attempted suicide by cutting his wrists. It was stated that the pair were exceptionally happy and devoted to each other, but after receiving a letter from the Inland Revenue, Harding wrongly got the idea that he was in taxation difficulties. His wife was also suffering from inoperable cancer.

Harding had been suffering from melancholia and was insane when the offence was committed. *Found guilty but insane at Newcastle Assizes, 14.5.1959. H.M.P.*

William Heathcote (see: William James Joyce)

Frank Heighway   Kevin Peter Heighway

In a fit of desperation to stop his son (5 months) crying during a favourite television programme, Heighway (25), a miner, punched him so hard that he died from the injuries.

Heighway's plea of not guilty to non-capital murder was accepted by the prosecution and he was *found guilty of manslaughter. Placed on probation for 3 years at Manchester Crown Court, 9.3.1959.*

Joseph Edward Hodgson   John Young

After drinking, Young (57) broke into the home of Hodgson (37), a labourer, (whom he knew, though not necessarily as a friend) as he and his wife were preparing to go to bed. Hodgson made a fruitless plea for him to leave, and in an attempt to frighten him away, brought a bayonet into the bedroom. He held it towards Young, intending to nick his arm, but Young moved forward and the blade pierced his stomach. He staggered out and collapsed in the street. Died a week later in hospital.

Hodgson found guilty of manslaughter at Durham Assizes, 27.10.1959, and sentenced to 5 years' imprisonment.

Richard Hodson   John O'Shea

Hodson (28), an unemployed Irishman, 'phoned a journalist and confessed to him that he had committed a hitherto unsolved murder in April 1956. He later made a statement to the police saying that he had seen O'Shea (43) "loaded with money" in a public house; some days later, armed with a hammer, he had gone to the man's home and beaten him to death; and robbed him. Asked why he wished to confess, Hodson said: "I have to. It is on my mind." He added that there was "another man" who knew he had done it.

Hodson, however, pleaded not guilty to capital murder at the Old Bailey and the only possible evidence against him were his curious confessions. The jury regarded them as the "imaginations of a drunken, drugged Irishman", and Hodson was *found not guilty, 2.12.1959*.

Stanley Walter Howard   Mary Howard

Howard (35), lorry driver, was alleged to have suddenly beaten his wife (33) with a branch from a tree while they were gathering firewood in a lonely lane. There was no motive save an impulsive mental disorder. Prosecution claimed that he then suffocated her by pressing his hands over her mouth, but her death by asphyxia might easily have been caused by the tongue blocking her air-channel as she lay unconscious after being attacked.

Howard's plea of diminished responsibility was successful and he was *convicted of manslaughter under section 2 at Leeds Assizes, 21.7.1959; sentenced to life imprisonment*.

Terence Howard   Lucy Howard

Howard (20), a sailor home on leave, battered his mother (45) to death with a poker during a quarrel over his relationship with a married woman who lived in the neighbourhood. In a statement to the police he was alleged to have said: "I did it. I have been thinking about doing it for some time . . . If I had two mothers like her I would have killed them both."

He was *found guilty of non-capital murder at Leeds and sentenced to life imprisonment, 21.7.1959*.

Michael John Hurley   Adrian Hurley

Hurley (24), a planning engineer, tied the shawl around the mouth of his baby son (6 months) and suffocated him in a fit of temper when he tried to stop the child crying as he and his wife were saying prayers.

Plea of *not guilty to murder but guilty to manslaughter* was accepted by the prosecution at *Warwick Assizes, 16.12.1959; sentenced to 15 months' imprisonment*.

George William Ingall   Elvina Ingall

Soon after they moved to a new home, Ingall (69) having

retired with 40 years' service on the railways, he attacked and battered to death his wife (65) with an axe. He then went to the police. Apparently motiveless; he said, "I don't know why I did it, because we had been good friends."

Defence pleaded insanity at his trial at *Birmingham Assizes, 14.12.1959, and he was found guilty but insane. H.M.P. Broadmoor.*

George Jackson   Ernest Crapper

During his burglary of Crapper's (81) barber shop, Jackson (28), a miner, spun the old man round in order to slip out of the house, and Crapper fell into the fireplace. He then put the man into a chair and bound his hands in case he again came after him as he continued to go through the drawers and sideboard. Left Crapper bound and injured when he escaped with £250. Was at large for over five months, during which an extensive police search was carried out involving mass fingerprinting, etc.

Finally charged with capital murder (in course or furtherance of theft), Jackson claimed that he had no intention to do grievous bodily harm to the old man. *Acquitted of capital murder, but convicted of manslaughter at Sheffield Assizes, 26.11.1959, after a three-day hearing. Sentenced to 12 years' imprisonment.*

Kenneth Jarman   Frances Susan Caddy

Jarman (25), a certified patient in Friern Barnet Mental Hospital, strangled another inmate (73) in the hospital grounds after she hit him with her handbag.

He was *found insane and unfit to plead at the Old Bailey, 11.3.1959, when charged with non-capital murder. H.M.P.*

Jerzy Jasiniak   John Hampton Morris

Jasiniak (29), a Pole, was found *guilty but insane at Glamorgan Assizes, 13.7.1959,* on a charge of capital murder of a night-watchman (60) found battered to death in the offices of a building site. Having been previously employed there, Jasiniak knew that money was kept there.

After arrest, accused acted very strangely, attempted suicide in prison, and attacked a witness at the Magistrates' Court hearing. Medical witnesses at his trial testified that he was suffering from acute schizophrenia; he had spent some years as a prisoner in a German slave camp.

H.M.P.

William Thomas Jenkin   Janice Ann Holmes

Jenkin (24), a tractor driver, raped and then strangled a girl (12) in a spinney near her home on a Lincolnshire farm. He was convicted largely upon the evidence of a man on remand in Lincoln Prison at the same time as himself, who claimed that Jenkin had admitted to him that he had "messed about" with the girl and knocked her unconscious in a panic. Jenkin was not able, either, to account for the presence of his empty tobacco tin found near the body of the girl.

The jurors at *Nottingham Assizes* were unable to agree after 100 minutes and a retrial was ordered. Jenkin was *convicted of non-capital murder at Birmingham Assizes, 16.7.1959, and sentenced to life imprisonment.*

William Johnson (see: Edwin Town)

Frederick Walter Jones   Edith Jones

Jones (23), a farm labourer, shot his mother (49) with a rifle kept on their farm in Shropshire. He had been a patient in a mental hospital a few months previously and was obviously suffering from paranoid delusions.

He was *found unfit to plead on a capital murder charge at Shropshire Assizes, 23.6.1959. H.M.P.*

George Jones (see: Henry Howard Mitchell)

William James Joyce   Graham John Osborn
William Heathcote

Heathcote (26), unemployed, stabbed in the stomach, and Joyce (27) punched, a guardsman (26) who was molesting a prostitute whom they knew, late at night (2.15 a.m.) in Piccadilly. Joyce denied that he was ever carrying or using a knife and claimed it was Heathcote who had produced and used it. The prostitute knew the two accused, and appealed to them for help. They both denied having been at the scene of the crime.

Both were found guilty of non-capital murder and sentenced to life imprisonment at the Old Bailey, 16.6.1959.

Further charges of wounding with intent were not proceeded with.

George Kell   James Boal

After both Kell (27), a miner, and Boal (50), had been drinking at a public house, they walked home together. Whether in the course of theft or as a result of a quarrel, Kell attacked and violently assaulted Boal, whose body was found by the roadside some hours later. His pockets had been turned out and he had no money on him.

At Kell's trial at *Durham Assizes*, two doctors testified that he had acted in a frenzied epileptic fury; he was subject to such fits and while in them "because unconscious for several minutes"—"he was insane within the legal sense". It was said that Kell was the kind of person who became aggressive or unmanageable after drinking.

Kell was *found guilty of capital murder but insane, 22.10.1959, and ordered to be detained, H.M.P.*

Lincoln Constantine Kelly   Michael O'Brien

Kelly (40), an unemployed West Indian, was involved in a fist fight, in a public house, with a white man. He was ejected, but came back with a screwdriver, bit and attacked the man. Again he was ejected, and the other man, bleeding badly from the face, went away. About twenty minutes later, Kelly again burst into the bar, with a flat iron in his hand; he made straight for a customer, O'Brien (45), who was standing with his back towards him and who had had no part in the fight, and struck him on the head with the iron four times. A case of mistaken identity!

Kelly's plea of diminished responsibility at his trial at the Old Bailey, 17.6.1959, was successful and he was *convicted of manslaughter under section 2. Sentenced to 6 years' imprisonment.*

James Whyte Kerr   Elsie Kerr

Kerr (55), a gatekeeper and retired police constable, whose health had been failing in recent months and who had been overcome by nervous worry, took a heavy metal file and battered his wife (47) to death at their home when, for some undisclosed reason, she told him he was mad. She died shortly after being taken to hospital.

Kerr was *found guilty but insane at the Old Bailey, 17.4.1959. H.M.P.*

Henry King   Sheila King
                              Detective-Inspector James O'Donnell

King (28), a labourer, was stated to have bought a shotgun and cartridges and to have spent the day drinking whisky. Later in the evening he went to the home of his wife's parents where she was living, separated from him, with the expressed intention of shooting her and their baby. He "terrorised" the household with the gun, and police officers were called to the scene. A police constable who entered the house to try and get the gun from King was shot in the groin, and then King turned and shot his wife (20) in the back. Inspector O'Donnell (age not reported) went into the room to try and pacify him but was shot in the chest and died later.

King faced a capital murder charge on 3 counts:—

(a) shooting,

(b) murder of police officer in the course of his duty,

(c) killing in avoidance of arrest.

He was also charged with the attempted murder of another police officer.

He put forward a plea of diminished responsibility and produced medical evidence of paranoid schizophrenia, low intelligence, history of mental certification and treatment, etc. Prosecution, in rebutting testimony, admitted that King was a psychopath, but claimed that this had not impaired his responsibility at the time of the shootings. The jury was out for $4\frac{1}{4}$ hours and returned when the jurors could not agree. They were sent out again and returned after 35 minutes. King was *acquitted of capital murder and found guilty of manslaughter under section 2. Sentenced to life imprisonment at Manchester Crown Court, 13.3.1959.*

George Levers   Patricia Ann Levers

Levers (30), a salesman who had eight jobs in nineteen months, raped his niece (12) at his home and then, in panic, strangled her with a stocking even though she promised to tell no one. He gave himself up to the police 24 hours later.

At *Nottingham Assizes* he pleaded diminished responsibility, and medical witnesses gave evidence that he had a schizoid personality bordering on schizophrenia, severe enough to amount to mental abnormality. The prosecution offered rebutting evidence and showed also that Levers had just previously been drinking heavily. Jury accepted prosecution evidence and Levers was *found guilty of non-capital murder; sentenced to life imprisonment, 25.2.1959.*

Alice L. B. Lyons   Alice Amelia Lyons

Lyons (39) was an epileptic and had recently assaulted her mother (71) a number of times in epileptic fits. As a result of a quarrel, the mother obtained a summons for assault which was served on her daughter. That evening the daughter assaulted her again in a fit of rage—hitting her and breaking her leg by jumping on it. The old lady was taken to hospital where she made a statement, but died twelve days after the incident from a blood clot following the fracture.

Alice Lyons was *convicted at the Old Bailey, 9.12.1959, of manslaughter* (probably a verdict of simple manslaughter, even though she was obviously mentally abnormal at the time). *Sentenced to 3 years' imprisonment.*

Elizabeth McCaffrey   Daughter (no name)

Immediately after discharge from hospital, McCaffrey (23), a cinema usherette, took her 10 days-old baby daughter to Blackpool beach, suffocated her and hid the body in the sand.

Her plea of *not guilty to murder but guilty to infanticide* was accepted by the prosecution and McCaffrey was *placed on probation for 3 years at Lancaster Assizes, 3.6.1959; an order for 12 months' residence in a mental hospital was made.*

John McNulty   Winifred Dunbar

Mrs. Dunbar (27) was attacked by McNulty (18), a swimming-bath attendant, as she walked alone along the beach at Tynemouth. He beat her about the head with a stone, raped her and then, probably in a panic, left her to die by drowning in the rising tide.

A defence plea of diminished responsibility owing to McNulty's extreme emotional immaturity and neuroticism was opposed by prosecution witnesses, and was rejected by the jury. McNulty was *convicted of non-capital murder at Northumberland Assizes, 14.10.1959, and sentenced to life imprisonment.*

Cavan Malone   Jan Momberg

Malone (22), an actor, was *acquitted at the Old Bailey, 11.3.1959, of murdering* Momberg (38), during a fight at Malone's home. He was also acquitted of manslaughter.

It was stated that, while Malone and his mother were entertaining Mrs. Momberg (an old family friend), her son, Jan Momberg, who was drunk, burst in and began behaving violently towards Malone's mother. Malone then pushed Momberg away and in the fight which followed he grabbed a kitchen knife, intending to scare his adversary into leaving, but accidentally stabbed him.

Defence successfully based upon self-defence: provocation pleaded alternatively.

Ronald Henry Marwood   P.C. Raymond Summers

Marwood (25), a scaffolder, was charged with the capital murder of a police constable who broke up a gang-fight outside a dance hall in Islington, in December 1958. It was alleged that, after drinking heavily, Marwood and two or three car-loads of young men went to the dance hall where a fight began. Someone aimed a chopper at Marwood and his hand was badly cut; but as he walked away, he saw one of his friends "being arrested" by P.C. Summers (25). He went after them, and Summers turned and told him to clear off, pushing Marwood on the shoulder. The prosecution alleged that Marwood then took a knife from his pocket and stabbed the policeman.

Marwood ran away and hid for 44 days, finally deciding to "face the facts"; he went to the police to whom he made a statement admitting to carrying a knife and stabbing the police constable inadvertently, i.e. "not knowing he was holding the knife". He claimed later that the police had "put down things" which he had not said. He never read what was in his statement and when he signed it he had been questioned for ten hours and was physically exhausted.

At the Old Bailey, Marwood denied the charge and said he had only hit the policeman. Defence claimed that he never had a knife in his possession that evening, and apart from what was said in the dubious statement, the prosecution never proved that he had. Nevertheless, the jury found Marwood *guilty of capital murder, and he was sentenced to death, 19.3.1959.*

He appealed on the grounds that Mr. Justice Gorman failed to remind the jury of certain points with regard to intent, (i.e. Marwood had apparently not used the knife during the gang-fight if he *had* had it on him). *His appeal was dismissed, 20.4.1959.* [1959] Crim.L.R. 784.

The Home Secretary refused to grant a reprieve. Two important petitions were presented—one signed by 150 M.P.'s called attention to 5 points: (1) apart from the disputed confession, there was little or no evidence; (2) it was never suggested that Marwood was of bad character, an habitual criminal, etc., although he was said to have been hidden by the Nash family—see *Sunday Pictorial*, March 5, 1961 (he had only one previous conviction—for larceny at the age of 14); (3) he was not trying to escape after, or in the course of, another offence; (4) he was not in fact concerned with the rival gangs in the fight; (5) there was no evidence of premeditated violence. There was much public outcry in newspapers, etc., and a motion was tabled in the House of Commons by Mr. Sydney Silverman, M.P. for Nelson and Colne.

A riot took place inside Pentonville Prison on the night before his execution, and only ten days after that of Joseph Chrimes [see Chrimes (1959)]; a demonstration of 1,000 people outside Pentonville Prison, when *Marwood was executed on 8.5.1959*, was dispersed by large numbers of mounted police. These were the first executions in Pentonville for five years.

Frank Matthews   Winifred Mary Matthews

The prosecution alleged that Matthews (49), an excavator driver, inflicted blows on the head of his wife (59) with whom he had shared a very unhappy and unsuccessful marriage, during a car journey on a lonely moorland road in Devon. He then ran the car over her head while she was lying in the road and did some damage to the car door, all with a view to giving the appearance of an accident. Defence was that it *was* an accident and that his wife received the injuries by falling out of the car when the door accidentally flew open (as it had done on occasions in the past).

Matthews was *found guilty at Devon Assizes, 19.6.1959, of non-capital murder and sentenced to life imprisonment.*

Theodore V. E. Matthews   Florence Matthews

Matthews (60), a retired clerk, attacked with a hammer and poker his aunt (82), who had come to live with him and his wife only 48 hours before. No apparent motive, but medical evidence given at *Bristol Assizes, 3.3.1959*, was that Matthews was labouring from a defect of reason due to melancholia at the time. He was *found guilty but insane, and ordered to be detained during H.M.P.*

James Alan Middleton   Cynthia Ruffy

Middleton (27), a photographer, was *sentenced to life imprisonment at York Assizes, 9.11.1959, after pleading guilty to the murder* of an ex-beauty queen and former girl friend (27), for whom he had a "passionate affection". It was stated that although he had spent hundreds of pounds on presents, etc., trying to impress her, she told him she wanted to end their friendship, and after drinking a good deal he stabbed her 16 times with a hunting knife on a footpath near her home in York.

Henry Howard Mitchell   Augustus Roberts
George Jones

Mitchell (25) and Jones (26) went to Roberts' (70) small newsagent's shop armed with an iron bar and intent on robbery. During the course of the crime Roberts was beaten to death with the bar; both men were charged with capital murder.

Each man accused the other of having delivered the blows and each claimed innocence with respect to causing bodily harm. However, since only the two men knew exactly what had happened in the shop, the prosecution was unable to prove which one in fact had beaten Roberts; *both were therefore acquitted of capital murder*. Mitchell's counsel said: "Far better that both men should be acquitted than that the wrong one should be convicted. Gus Roberts' death cannot be avenged by the hanging of an innocent man."

Both were found guilty of non-capital murder and sentenced to life imprisonment at Monmouthshire Assizes, 11.6.1959.

[Authors' note: This is a good example of the application of section 5(2) of the Homicide Act 1957 under which it is provided that only the person who by his own act caused the victim's death can be found guilty of capital murder; any other participant in the killing can be guilty of non-capital murder.]

Stanley William Moore   Rosina Moore

Moore (35), who was in a severe depression as a result of being out of work, gassed his mother (74), and then attempted to kill himself in the same way. He left a note to the coroner saying that he had fallen foul of an international political organisation of world power which apparently controlled the police as well. He could no longer fight against it. In a footnote he added: "My mother will be better off also, as no one cares for her."

Medical witnesses agreed that Moore was suffering from paranoid delusions and was insane. He was *found guilty but insane at Liverpool Crown Court, 18.6.1959, and ordered to be detained in Broadmoor during H.M.P.*

Albert Thomas Morgan   Arthur Pearson

Morgan (17), an unemployed labourer, was *found guilty at Flintshire Assizes, 15.10.1959, of non-capital murder* of Pearson (37), whose body was found on the bank of the River Dee with injuries to the face. Morgan was acquitted of murdering him in the course or furtherance of theft (capital murder) but convicted of non-capital murder and *ordered to be detained during H.M.P.* under section 53 (2) Children and Young Persons Act 1933.

Kenneth Francis Morris   Raymond Morris

Morris (47), a hairdresser, was living away from his wife, but with his son. He was stated to have battered to death his son (9); they were very fond of each other. The boy had happened to refer to the state of affairs at their home, with his mother living with another man. Morris afterwards hid the boy's body in the loft and told people that Raymond had gone away for a holiday.

Defence called two psychiatrists who told of Morris's unhappy married life, and said there was a long history of mental abnormality. Plea of diminished responsibility successful and Morris, *acquitted of murder, was convicted of manslaughter under section 2, York Assizes, 17.2.1959. Sentenced to life imprisonment.*

Joseph Anthony Neary   Vivian Aubrey Howard

Neary (27), an Irish labourer, told by an acquaintance that his wife was associating with Howard (48), a bookmaker, borrowed a leather knife and went to see Howard, intending to disfigure him in order to "stop him running round with married women". In fact, he stabbed and killed him.

Since he had admitted an intention to do grievous bodily harm (though not to kill), Neary was *found guilty of non-capital murder and sent to prison for life at Chester Assizes, 19.2.1959.*

Kevin Barry O'Connor   Irene Dorward

After taking Irene Dorward (31), who was a spastic cripple, on a tour of public houses, O'Connor (21), a boilermaker, bought her food and a pair of stockings. They then went to a derelict house, but when O'Connor tried to have intercourse with her, she resisted and he, in a temper, hit her two or three times so that she fell on to a pile of bricks. He left her there and she died some time later.

At his trial at Durham Assizes, O'Connor, who was described as "a decent young man and a regular churchgoer", pleaded not guilty to non-capital murder but *guilty to manslaughter*. This was accepted by the prosecution and O'Connor was *sentenced to life imprisonment, 26.10.1959.*

Ronald Douglas Orr   Joan Martin

Orr (32), a fruit salesman, strangled with his tie the woman (26) with whom he had been on very close terms and whom he is said to have loved. The girl's half-naked body was found at her home after Orr had gone next door to give himself up; it was found that a serious internal wound had been administered with a poker. The prosecution alleged that this was inflicted before death and that she was strangled while unconscious as a result of it. Orr, in talks with the prison doctor, said he had done it after strangling her. In either case it raises a curious question of motive—was it sex?—or jealousy? (one witness alleged that Orr thought Joan Martin was going out with another man)—or mental disorder?

Defence presented evidence of schizophrenia but this was rebutted by the prosecution and Orr was *found guilty of murder and sentenced to life imprisonment at Cumberland Assizes, 8.10.1959.*

Thomas Joseph O'Toole   Teresa Lyons

O'Toole (28), an Irish factory worker, and Miss Lyons (20), were orphans who had been brought up together in Ireland. They were supposedly very fond of each other and O'Toole wanted to marry her; but when she came home after going out with a man, with whom she had recently become friendly, O'Toole attacked her with a hammer and she died nine days later from her injuries.

O'Toole pleaded diminished responsibility (no details) at his trial at *Winchester Assizes, 4.4.1959, and was convicted of manslaughter under section 2.* After the Judge had consulted medical reports, O'Toole was, five days later, *sentenced to 5 years' imprisonment.*

Charalambous Panayi (20), labourer.   Andreas Panayi
Melis Pavlou (22), labourer.
Demetrios Costas (44), factory hand.

Three Cypriots were charged with the murder of the brother of one of them during a fight at a Cypriot Club in North London. It was Costas who battered Panayi with a chair, but at the Old Bailey it was said that Andreas Panayi was Costas' closest friend. When trouble broke out, Costas had tried to be a peacemaker; when fighting began, he picked up a chair to defend himself and by mistake hit his friend.

All three accused were acquitted of murder; Costas was found guilty of manslaughter, the jury adding a rider that the offence was committed under great provocation, He was conditionally discharged for 12 months. Old Bailey, 25.6.1959.

Charalambous Panayi was also found not guilty of wounding and of assaulting another man. *Discharged.*

Melis Pavlou found guilty of wounding two other men with intent to cause grievous bodily harm by stabbing them both with a penknife. Sentenced to 18 months' imprisonment.

Melis Pavlou (see: Charalambous Panayi et al.)

Günter Fritz Podola   Det.-Sgt. Raymond Purdy

This case presented one of the most interesting medico-legal issues in the history of English Criminal Law. Podola (30), German-born photographer, shot Det.-Sgt. Purdy in the foyer of a private apartment block in South Kensington while the latter and another police officer were attempting to take him into custody on suspicion of blackmail. He escaped, but was caught three days later when a number of policemen broke into his room in a Kensington hotel. He received injuries during the struggle and a doctor who examined him judged that he was not, at that time, in a fit state to be charged; Podola was removed to hospital.

At his trial at the Old Bailey in September 1959, the defence submitted that Podola was unfit to plead on the charge of capital murder owing to total amnesia resulting from the injuries received at the time of his arrest. This preliminary issue was then fought out for nine days, Mr. Justice Edmund Davies ruling that the onus of proof in establishing unfitness to plead lay upon the *defence*. Medical witnesses for the defence, led by F. H. Lawton Q.C. (now Mr. Justice Lawton), then gave evidence that in their opinion Podola was suffering from hysterical amnesia; this was refuted by doctors on behalf of the prosecution who claimed that the amnesia failed to show a number of significant clinical and other symptoms. After the conclusion of the medical evidence for both sides, Dr. Stafford Clark was allowed to give evidence to the effect that he had seen many cases of hysterical amnesia unaccompanied by clinical symptoms. *The jury found Podola's loss of memory to be not genuine and decided that he was sane and fit to plead.*

The next day, evidence pertaining to the case itself was heard. After counsel for the prosecution had finished, Podola offered no evidence; he read a statement saying that he understood the accusations but could not defend himself since he had no memory of the events surrounding the offence. He was *found guilty of capital murder, 24.10.1959, and sentenced to death.*

There were doubts whether there existed any established channel of appeal against a decision of fitness to plead, but the Home Secretary, under powers granted by section 19(a) of the Criminal Appeal Act 1907, referred to the Court of Criminal Appeal the issue whether the onus of proof of fitness to plead rested on the defence or on the prosecution. The Court ruled that there *was* a right of appeal by Podola to the Court, but *dismissed that appeal.*

The ruling was given that (1) no criticism could be made of the Judge's summing up on the preliminary issue of fitness to plead (nor of the ruling upon the onus of proof), and (2) even if the loss of memory had been genuine, that did not of itself render Podola insane so that he could not be tried on the indictment, and no other ground for alleging insanity was put forward. [1960] 1Q.B. 325.

The Attorney-General refused Podola his fiat for appeal to the House of Lords, and Podola was executed, 5.11.1959, at Wandsworth Prison.

[Authors' note: The best view of this case is that Podola did in fact suffer hysterical amnesia as a result of the incident on arrest, but that by the time he was put up for trial Podola had recovered his memory of the events. The Criminal Law Revision Committee, in its Third Report, Criminal Procedure (Insanity), did not think that any change should be made in the legal test of what constitutes unfitness to plead. By implication it endorsed the ruling of the Court of Criminal Appeal that amnesia, even if genuine, could not amount to unfitness to plead.]

Joseph Porter   Brenda McPartland

Porter (30), a labourer, was alleged to have stabbed McPartland (33), who lived at the same house, after the latter had provoked and punched him. There had just been a quarrel between the men's wives concerning the behaviour of the McPartland children. Defence claimed that there was no intention to kill.

Porter, who *pleaded not guilty to non-capital murder but guilty to manslaughter*, was *convicted on the latter count at Manchester Crown Court, 14.7.1959, and sent to prison for 2½ years.*

William Powney   Barbara Cashin

Powney (50), an Irish motor mechanic, had quarrelled with the married woman (43) with whom he was living over her bringing her daughters to stay with them. He tried to patch things up, but after refusing to speak to him for a few days, she suddenly attacked him one morning with a bread knife. In the struggle, he took the knife from her and stabbed her 15 times. He then attempted to gas himself.

Convicted at the Old Bailey, 26.11.1959, of manslaughter on grounds of provocation and sentenced to 5 years' imprisonment.

Ronald Charles Pritchard   Norah Summerfield
Joseph Chrimes

Chrimes (30), a stainer, and Pritchard (18), unemployed, broke into the bungalow of a widow (60), intending to burgle the house. When she came out and told them to go away, the prosecution alleged, Chrimes took out a tyre lever and battered her to death. The two accused then stole some small possessions—a clock, cigarette case, and some spoons.

At the Old Bailey, the prosecution offered no evidence against Pritchard on a charge of non-capital murder and he was acquitted. He then testified against Chrimes, charged with capital murder, and said he had tried to stop Chrimes using the lever and had never, himself, had any intention of hurting the woman, etc. Chrimes denied this and said that Pritchard had asked him for the tyre lever and when given it, had hit the woman with it on the head three or four times to stop her groaning. (Chrimes admitted to having pushed her violently to the ground).

The jury returned after an hour to ask why no evidence had been offered against Pritchard on the murder charge and why they had been instructed to find him not guilty. Mr. Justice Donovan replied: "The reason is, perhaps, a little technical . . . Pritchard could not be guilty consistent with the prosecution case unless, Chrimes having struck the blow, Pritchard was there urging Chrimes to do it, or that Pritchard knew that Chrimes was intending murder and so became a party to it." Largely upon Pritchard's evidence, then, *Chrimes was found guilty of capital murder, 4.3.1959, and sentenced to death. Pritchard pleaded guilty to breaking and entering and larceny; he was sent to Borstal.*

Chrimes appealed to the Court of Criminal Appeal, 11.4.1959, against conviction on the grounds that (1) Pritchard was an accomplice and therefore his evidence required to be corroborated; (2) there had been no proper direction about the necessity for corroboration of Pritchard's evidence and the meaning of corroboration. *His appeal was dismissed*, the Court ruling that there was corroboration in the evidence of other witnesses. (1959) 43 Cr. App.R. 149.

Chrimes was executed at Pentonville, 28.4.1959—the first execution there for five years. He had only one previous conviction—for three offences of larceny at the age of 15.

Michael Thomas Proctor (22)   Dennis Turnock
Robert Roberts (23)

After an extremely heavy drinking session, these two young builder's labourers accosted a man (32) who was standing at a bus stop with some friends, and demanded a cigarette. When he refused, they attacked this complete stranger and punched and kicked him to death. Later, after a violent struggle with four policemen they were arrested.

Found guilty of non-capital murder and both sentenced to life imprisonment at Stafford Assizes, 9.7.1959.

Maung Pu   David Essiet

Maung Pu (37), a Burmese seaman, and a Buddhist, was involved in a violent argument in the mess on board a cargo ship *Avisbrook* in the China Sea. It was Christmas Day and a Nigerian, Essiet (24), wanted to listen to Christmas music on the radio; Pu wanted to hear Burmese music. Afterwards, Pu went off and collected a hammer and before anyone could stop him, he struck Essiet two violent blows on the head from which he later died.

Pu was allowed complete freedom on board ship *and* ashore during the rest of the six month voyage; although he had many opportunities, he never tried to escape. He was finally flown from Venice to Southend and stood trial at *Essex Assizes, 19.6.1959.* Although full details are lacking, it would appear that he pleaded diminished responsibility and that this was successful. He was *convicted of manslaughter and sent to prison for 18 months.*

George Reynaud   Nancy Fillingham

During a quarrel with the woman with whom he had been living, Reynaud (47), a steel worker, strangled Nancy Fillingham (34), in a fit of temper when she attacked him with a poker.

He had been a voluntary patient in a mental hospital and the principal Medical Officer at Leeds Prison thought that he was certifiable as insane.

Reynaud was *found guilty of manslaughter under section 2 and sentenced to life imprisonment at Leeds Assizes, 9.7.1959.*

William Reynolds   Irene Elizabeth Kirby

Reynolds (31), an unemployed labourer, was *acquitted at York Assizes, 19.6.1959,* of murdering in his caravan home the woman

(38) who had been living with him. The jury found his mental responsibility diminished as a result of an epileptic fit at the time of the offence, and Reynolds was *convicted of manslaughter under section 2.*

Doctors called by the prosecution disagreed on the 'cause of death—was it a blow on the head with a lemonade bottle, or vagal inhibition as a result of pressure on the neck? For the defence, Reynolds admitted to hitting her with the bottle and said he then put his hands on her neck to pick her up—this may have accidentally caused vagal inhibition.

Reynolds was sentenced to life imprisonment.

Robert Roberts (see: Michael Thomas Procter)

Cecil George Robinson   Tasita Robinson

Robinson (36), a Jamaican plumber's mate, had been living apart from his wife (27), but met her and danced two or three times with her at a party given in Clapham. Just after midnight the two of them left the room and in a jealous quarrel outside, Robinson stabbed his wife in the throat. He was seen running away by the other guests.

He was *convicted of non-capital murder at the Old Bailey, 12.10.1959, and sentenced to life imprisonment.*

Levi Augustus Rowe   Vida Rowe

Rowe (35), a West Indian butcher, wrenched a kitchen knife from his wife when she attacked him in a fight after a quarrel; he then stabbed her in the struggle. It was alleged that Mrs. Rowe (27) had frequently insulted her husband, and had been associating with another man.

Defence based upon provocation. Rowe *acquitted of murder and found guilty of manslaughter. 4 years' imprisonment imposed at the Old Bailey, 14.1.1959.*

Judith Russo   Sarah Russo

Russo (29), it was alleged, put a plastic bag over the head of her daughter (13 months) and placed it in a bucket of water. She took the child's head out of the bucket and started artificial respiration, but when the baby showed signs of life, she discontinued her efforts and the baby died. She then attempted suicide by taking barbiturates and gin.

Mrs. Russo was *found insane and unfit to plead at the Old Bailey, 13.7.1959, and ordered to be detained, H.M.P.*

Hale Edgar Ryan   Kevin Hughes

Although Marylebone Magistrates decided that there was insufficient evidence upon which to commit Ryan (20), an American airman, for trial on a charge of murdering the son (14 months) of his girl friend, Ryan was committed for trail at the Old Bailey on a coroner's warrant.

No evidence was offered at the Old Bailey, where the coroner's inquest was described by the prosecution as "not an entirely satisfactory proceeding"; and Mr. Justice Cassels directed the jury to find Ryan *not guilty, 18.11.1959.*

Thomas Frederick Sanderson   Susan Sanderson

Sanderson (58), a colliery worker, during a quarrel with his stepson, collected a loaded gun and fired it (away from the boy) in order to frighten him. He shot his wife (60) in the head and she died in hospital three weeks later. Sanderson was stated to be extremely fond of his (second) wife and it was obvious that the offence was bordering upon an accident.

At Nottingham Assizes, 19.6.1959, he pleaded not guilty to capital murder but guilty to manslaughter. Sentence was deferred for five days, after which the Judge *sentenced* Sanderson to *5 days' imprisonment* (i.e. immediate release). Sanderson had been 3 months awaiting trial.

Herbert George Scott   Linda Brown

Scott (23), an unemployed labourer, was alleged to have gone off with a girl (6) into some woods where she was raped and battered to death with a milk bottle.

Scott denied the charge and claimed that a statement of confession had been made by him to the police only under threat of legal action against his mother and of physical violence against himself. He established an alibi for the time of the crime but his *conviction for non-capital murder* was based largely upon the evidence of identification given by Linda's 11-year old brother. Scott was *sentenced to life imprisonment at Lincolnshire Assizes, 5.6.1959.*

Application for leave to appeal against conviction was refused.

Anthony George Seller   Nancy Maud Higginson

Seller (22), an unemployed engineer, stabbed his former girl friend (19) and the mother of his illegitimate child, with a wood-chisel in an alley near her home. Prosecution charged him with capital murder on the basis of a statement he made to the police saying that he had killed her when she refused to give him some money. However, it appeared, later, that after a quarrel concerning their child, the girl left him and walked down the alley; he picked up the chisel intending to threaten her but did not produce it while their argument continued. When she asked a passer-by to see her home, Seller was overcome with emotional stress and frenziedly stabbed her. At the police station he made the statement about theft because he knew it would would involve the death penalty and he claimed that this was the only way he could "commit suicide" as he wished to do.

Defence pleaded diminished responsibility. Evidence was given of a history of violence, uncontrolled emotion, etc., and he was described as a "psychopath of immature development". Two prosecution doctors denied that his abnormality was sufficient to amount to diminished responsibility. He was acquitted on the capital charge, but *found guilty of non-capital murder, at Birmingham Assizes, and sentenced to life imprisonment, 23.7.1959.*

Winifred Shingler   Barry Shingler

Mrs. Shingler (28), said to be a "devoted wife and mother", gassed herself and her son (2) when in a severe depression. She imagined that she was suffering from a heart disease and had only a little while to live. In fact, she was found unconscious and the boy died.

Pleaded diminished responsibility for the above reasons, and was *convicted of manslaughter under section 2 at Sheffield Assizes, 26.11.1959. Placed on probation for 3 years.*

Derek Jeffrey Simpson   Teresa Simpson

After having broken into her home, Simpson (24), a painter and decorator, stabbed to death his recently estranged wife (24) when he became suspicious that she was associating closely with another man.

Defence pleaded provocation (of wife's behaviour) but there was a strong element of premeditation about the crime; *Simpson was found guilty of non-capital murder at Manchester Crown Court,*

1.12.1959, and sentenced to life imprisonment. The charge of
attempted suicide against him was not proceeded with.

Lal Singh (25)   Narang Singh (37)
Narain Singh (30)

Two Indians were *both found guilty at Warwick Assizes of non-
capital murder* of a fellow-countryman who was stabbed to death
during a fight outside a public house in Coventry. The victim was
stabbed 12 times. The fight may have been over a woman.

They were *both sentenced to life imprisonment, 9.7.1959,* after a
trial lasting 3½ days.

Manjit Singh   Gurmit Kaur

Manjit (30), an Indian labourer, was alleged to have dragged his
wife by the hair along a passage and strangled her in a locked room
at their home in Smethwick. No motive was ever suggested and
Manjit asserted that his wife had been taken ill, that she was prone
to epileptic fits and had such a fit at the time of her death. There
were witnesses in India, he claimed, who could speak of the
medical treatment which she had there.

*Found guilty of non-capital murder at Stafford Assizes, 19.3.1959,
and sentenced to life imprisonment* on the basis of medical evidence
on Gurmit Kaur presented by the prosecution. Although Singh
does not appear to have pleaded diminished responsibility, his
mental condition was found by the authorities to be such that the
Home Secretary ordered his transfer to Broadmoor where he is
now making a good recovery.

Narian Singh (see: Lal Singh)

Oscar Skyers   Sarah Anne Buxton

It was said that Buxton (25) had been a mental patient for the
last ten years, and had recently absconded from a hospital and
gone to live with Skyers (60), an unemployed Jamaican. During a
quarrel at their home in Cardiff she called him "a black bastard"
and hit him with a shoe. He flew into a rage, stabbed her and cut her
throat with a kitchen knife and battered her with the bent end of
a hatchet; he then wrapped her naked body in some rags and a
carpet and dumped it in the Cardiff sea-lock.

There was plenty of evidence that he was quite insane; a schizoid paranoiac of low intelligence, he had been certified in 1955, and had to be put in a strait-jacket twice while in prison awaiting trial. *Found unfit to plead at Glamorgan Assizes, 7.7.1959, and ordered to be detained during H.M.P.*

Robert Smith   Margaret Greig

Smith (46), a porter, suspected that his girl friend, Helen Gannon, had been taking his wages; he went to her house and climbed in through the window of the neighbouring flat. He strangled the woman (48) living there, though he apparently didn't know her, then burst into his girl friend's flat and attempted to strangle her while someone was going to call the police.

He pleaded diminished responsibility at his trial at the Old Bailey and Dr. Brisby of Brixton Prison gave evidence that Smith was a chronic alcoholic and bordering upon insanity. Smith was *found guilty of manslaughter under section 2. Sentenced to 7 years' imprisonment, 17.4.1959.* The charge of attempted murder was left on the file.

David Stanley Stewart   Margaret Widdison

During a quarrel in which Stewart (69), a retired electrician, objected to his married daughter's "immoral" way of life, she struck him, and in a period of mental unbalance he strangled her, at their home in Sheffield.

Stewart's defence of diminished responsibility was successful at *Sheffield Assizes and he was convicted of manslaughter under section 2. Sentenced to life imprisonment, 7.8.1959.*

William John Storie   James Joseph Tyrell

Not many hours after leaving his friend's home on friendly terms, Storie (52), a telephone supervisor, returned, on his way to night-work, and climbed through a window into the house. For no apparent reason, he attacked, with a hammer which he was carrying, both his friend and his friend's father (88), and the latter died some two weeks later from his injuries.

A defence plea of diminished responsibility was apparently not contested by the prosecution evidence and Storie was *found guilty of manslaughter under section 2. Sentenced to 4 years' imprisonment at the Old Bailey, 17.6.1959.*

Malcolm James Talbot   Marian Mary Bird

Talbot (20), a miner, had been courting Marian Bird (16) for some years, but recently their relationship had not been going smoothly because of objections by the girl's mother. Talbot strangled her in a field just off a lane, perhaps as a result of a quarrel or in a fit of despair. The girl was in an early stage of pregnancy.

He claimed at his trial at *Stafford Assizes, 2.12.1959*, that it had been an accident, but was *convicted of non-capital murder and sentenced to life imprisonment.*

Michael George Tatum   Capt. Charles Barrett

Tatum (24), an unemployed cinema projectionist, was probably interrupted by Barrett (85), a retired Army Officer, while burgling his home. He beat Barrett to death with a Zulu knobkerrie, which was displayed in the hall, and stole a wallet containing money.

Tatum, charged with capital murder, claimed that he was accompanied by another man who had struck the old man, but there was no evidence for this. He pleaded an alternative defence of diminished responsibility; a doctor said he was suffering from incipient schizophrenia. However, three doctors called for the prosecution agreed that though Tatum was abnormal, such an abnormality was not sufficient to impair his mental responsibility.

Tatum was found guilty and sentenced to death at Winchester Assizes, 23.3.1959.

In his appeal to the Court of Criminal Appeal, defence counsel complained of certain passages in the summing up. *Appeal dismissed, 27.4.1959*, and reprieve refused.

Executed at Winchester Prison, 14.5.1959.

Michael Brian Theakstone   Lyn Marie Theakstone
                                       Dorothy Tibbott
                                       Ellen Sutton

When Theakstone's wife left him and went to live with her baby, Lyn (9 months), at her mother's home, the accused bought a sheath knife and went to the house, his intention not being very clear. He stabbed his mother-in-law, Mrs. Tibbott (53) and then her aunt, Mrs. Sutton (68); he then stabbed the baby in its pram. He took the latter's dead body and wandered out along the road with it;

he is reported to have said, "If I can't have her, no one else will." When a policeman told him to put the knife down, he replied: "I have got to swing, so keep away from me." This interpretation was wrong since the three murders were committed on the same occasion.

Theakstone pleaded *guilty at Shropshire Assizes to non-capital murder* on all three counts and was *sentenced to life imprisonment, 19.11.1959.*

Harold Thirkettle   Iris Wilson

Thirkettle (36), a scrap metal dealer, with previous criminal convictions, killed the woman (27) with whom he had been living after a quarrel about her association with another man. He claimed that when he picked up the axe and battered her as she lay in bed at their home he was suffering from depression.

Found guilty of manslaughter at York Assizes, 18.6.1959, and sentenced to 12 years' imprisonment.

[Author's note: We were subsequently put in possession of the following information from a released prisoner (it has not been checked with official sources). In June 1961 Thirkettle was himself killed in Dartmoor prison. During a film show a coloured man had been stabbed in the back by an assailant who managed to make good his escape by crawling away in the darkness. The coloured man, severely wounded, pulled the knife from his own back and stabbed the two nearest men behind him—one of them Thirkettle —in an agonised frenzy; neither of the two men had in fact been responsible. Thirkettle died of his wounds.]

Margaret Thompson   William Thompson

Mrs. Thompson (20) was said to be 4-5 months pregnant and had been threatened with violence by her husband who was due home on leave from Borstal. Overcome by a severe mental depression— "No one wanted me or the baby"—she suffocated her son (14 months) in his cot and then attempted suicide by gas.

The jury at *Liverpool Crown Court* accepted the defence plea of diminished responsibility and Mrs. Thompson, *convicted of manslaughter under section 2, was sentenced to 21 months' imprisonment, 2.11.1959.*

Terrence Tippett   Michael John Smith

Tippett (20), a labourer, apparently picked a fight with Smith
(17) as the latter was waiting at a bus stop with a friend after attending a dance. Tippett came up in a group of youths and, after a few
words, punched Smith to the ground and then kicked him six or
seven times before running off. Smith died later on the operating
table.

Defence at *Stafford Assizes, 10.12.1959,* entered a plea of
diminished responsibility and presented evidence that Tippett was
a psychopathic personality. Nevertheless, Tippett was *found guilty
of non-capital murder and sentenced to life imprisonment.*

John Robert Toward   Mary Toward

Toward (26), a miner, strangled his wife (27), from whom he had
recently been separated, on a piece of waste ground and then went
back and cut her thoat with a razor blade to make sure she was
dead. He then drank a bottle of whisky and climbed on to the wall
of a dock in South Shields in the hope that he would fall asleep on
top then drop into the dock and kill himself. But he slipped and
hung upside down with his legs tangled in electric cables until he
was rescued. There had been trouble between Toward and his wife
during the previous two years over her drinking, associating with
other men, and neglect of their child.

Toward was *found guilty of manslaughter* and sentenced to 10
years' imprisonment at *Durham Assizes, 23.10.1959.* A few days
later, Mr. Justice Thesiger reduced the sentence, which he had
imposed, to *8 years' imprisonment.*

Edwin Town   Albert Gibbons
William Johnson

Town (20), a labourer, and Johnson (26), a miner, were two
members of a small gang of youths who, after drinking, molested
and then attacked, for no serious reason, Gibbons (31), who was
on his way home. It was alleged that Johnson punched Gibbons
to the ground but then left him there; Town then kicked Gibbons
viciously and it was from these latter injuries that the man died.

The jury at *Liverpool Crown Court acquitted Johnson* without
calling on the defence, but *convicted Town of manslaughter on
grounds of diminished responsibility* after his defence had presented

evidence of low mental age and feeble-mindedness. *Town was sentenced to life imprisonment, 19.2.1959.*

Howard Wainwright   Florence Wainwright
                                               James Wainwright

Wainwright (32), a poultry keeper, was found *unfit to plead* on the charge of murdering his parents (61) and (62) at their home. Their bodies were found badly battered with the barrel of an air-rifle.

Accused, who had been a voluntary patient in a mental hospital, was stated to be suffering from acute schizophrenia with religious delusions; his normal mental processes had greatly deteriorated since arrest. At the committal proceedings, his behaviour was bizarre—he insisted that "It wasn't murder, it was 'bloomferry' " and he ought therefore to be immediately released; the whole incident had been "an act of God" he said.

Flintshire Assizes, 3.2.1959. H.M.P.

Bernard Hugh Walden   Joyce Moran
                                                 Neil Saxton

Walden (33), a lecturer at Rotherham Technical College, had become infatuated with Moran (21), an administrative clerk at the College. They had spent a short holiday together and he had asked her to marry him, but she had laughed at the suggestion and was generally cool in her friendship towards him. In a fit of jealous temper, Walden took a loaded pistol from his locker and shot her and her 20 year-old student boy friend in an office at the College. Later, when found after he had run away, Walden was discovered to have three guns with ammunition upon him. He showed no remorse for the killings, although he claimed that he had meant only to "paralyse Saxton (the boy friend) from the waist down".

Defence submitted a plea of diminished responsibility. A consultant psychiatrist described Walden's condition as a "chronic paranoid development"; he was self-centred, yet felt insecure and thought of himself as a "victim singled out by fate". (While at University, his mother had died of cancer, he had developed polio —resulting in his being a permanent cripple—and he had eventually got only a poor degree.) He carried guns with him everywhere he went—"I am not as other men, I am a cripple and I must be armed to put me on fair terms with others . . . I have an absolute right to kill if I wish or find it necessary to do so." In 1949 when he was 24 Walden had been convicted of a homosexual offence against a 13 year-old boy. Medical witnesses for the prosecution (a Prison Medical Officer and a consultant psychiatrist), however, claimed that Walden showed good reasoning powers and showed no sign of mental abnormality. He was *convicted of capital murder and sentenced to death at Sheffield Assizes, 2.7.1959.*

His appeal was on the grounds that the Judge had misdirected the jury by attempting to define abnormality in section 2—i.e., contrary to the ruling of the Court of Criminal Appeal in R. v. Spriggs [1958] 1 Q.B. 270. However, the Court held that R. v. Spriggs decided only that there was no duty upon the trial judge to define or re-define "abnormality of mind" or "mental responsibility". The Judge was, however, entitled to assist the jurors by pointing out the sort of thing they could look for to see whether the case came within section 2. Here, the Judge had told the jurors that it was a matter for them and not for him, and he was right in that direction. *The appeal was dismissed, 27.7.1959.* [1959] 1 W.L.R. 1008.

The Attorney-General's fiat to appeal to the House of Lords was refused, and Walden was executed at Leeds Prison, 14.8.1959.

[Authors' note: The provisions of the Homicide Act seem curiously inapt to include Walden in the category of capital murderers.]

Robert Wardrope   Henry Ferguson

Wardrope (55), a stoker, Ferguson (80), and two women, returned all very intoxicated, to Ferguson's flat where a drunken quarrel broke out between the two men. The old man took a heavy belt, and swinging it at Wardrope, cut him on the face with the buckle. Wardrope went berserk; he hit and kicked Ferguson, then left for home, not thinking that anything was seriously wrong. When the women awoke in the morning, they found Ferguson dead; he had inhaled the blood from his facial injuries. Wardrope went immediately to the police when informed of this. The Judge directed the jury on the alternative defences of provocation, self-defence and drunkenness.

He was *found guilty of manslaughter at the Old Bailey, 16.10.1959, and sentenced to 5 years' imprisonment.* [1960] Crim.L.R. 770.

Michael Peter Waters   Margaret Dooley

After drinking heavily all afternoon, Waters (20), a labourer, met a little girl (9), and invited her to come home with him in order to run an errand. At home, he hit her with a piece of lead and raped her. He hid her body in the loft and spent the evening watching T.V. at his mother-in-law's home before giving himself up to the police.

His trial at *Chester Assizes, 8.6.1959*, at which he pleaded guilty to non-capital murder, lasted one minute. *Sentenced to life imprisonment.*

Leslie John Western   Ethel May Marshall

Western (39), labourer, beat his mistress (53), to death at her home with an iron bar when she told him that she wanted to go with another man.

Defence established diminished responsibility owing to accused's mental abnormality at the time; there was a long personal and family history of manic depression. This medical evidence was apparently not rebutted by the prosecution.

Found guilty of manslaughter under section 2 and sentenced to 7 years' imprisonment at Somerset Assizes, 23.10.1959.

William Alexander Wilkin   Dorothy Connor
                                       Michael Connor

Wilkin (32), a plater's helper, went in the afternoon to the home of a workmate, intending, the prosecution alleged, to break in and steal the hoard of savings which he knew was kept in the house. He carried a hammer with him, and had been drinking very heavily during the lunch hour. At home, however, were his friend's wife (25) and son (2); in a frenzied attack, he beat them to death with the hammer and then ransacked the house in his search for the money, but he was unsuccessful and got away with only a little small change from the woman's purse.

Afterwards he suffered from amnesia relating to the actual period of the two killings and apparently could not even remember the presence of children in the house at the time.

Defence at *Durham Assizes, 26.10.1959*, entered a plea of insanity on the charge of capital murder. A doctor claimed that Wilkin had been suffering from a form of mental instability known as "hypobulic crisis"—a "sudden abrupt discharge of primitive, intuitive, uncontrolled behaviour, a sort of violent explosion of mental abnormality, and alcohol was a common contributor to this condition". Doctors giving evidence for the prosecution stated that Wilkin had a very high I.Q.—122; his loss of memory was probably genuine, but had been induced by the previous large consumption of alcohol. One doctor called Wilkin's mental state an "hysterical crisis" and his diagnosis came very near that of the defence doctor, but he denied that it amounted here to insanity.

After 100 minutes' retirement, the jury *acquitted Wilkin of capital murder, and found him guilty of non-capital murder, but insane. Wilkin was ordered to be detained during H.M.P.*

Eric Francis Wilson   Evelyn Daniels

Wilson (22), a shop assistant, strangled his mistress (27) whom he was said to have loved very much, at the flat which he rented for her in Leytonstone, London. He had found another man with Mrs. Daniels (both accused and victim were already separately married).

Defence pleaded diminished responsibility on grounds that Wilson was "lovesick" at the time. He was *found guilty of manslaughter under section 2 at the Old Bailey, 20.11.1959, and sentenced to 7 years' imprisonment.*

Thomas Henry Wilson   Maxwell Barfield Harrison

After a very heavy drinking session, Wilson (25), a steward, and Harrison (46), 2nd engineer, started fighting for no apparent reason, on board the private yacht *Aronia*, berthed in Weymouth harbour. Harrison was later found dead on the deck.

Wilson was alleged to have beaten and kicked Harrison, but death resulted not so much from the injuries themselves as from asphyxia as a result of blood from the nose blocking the man's air channel while he was unconscious. Nor was there apparently any intention to kill.

Wilson *found guilty of manslaughter at Hampshire Assizes, 9.12.1959, and sentenced to 3 years' imprisonment.*

Bronislaw Zakowski   Damita Zakowski

Two days after being allowed home on leave from a mental hospital, Zakowski (34), an unemployed Pole, turned on the gas fire at his home in an effort to kill himself and his daughter (3) while his wife was out. It was said that he believed his state of ill-health was incurable, that he had not long to live, that his little girl had the same thing, and that the best thing to do was to kill her so that she would not suffer as he did.

He was *found guilty but insane at Warwick Assizes, 9.7.1959, and ordered to be detained, H.M.P.*

[Authors' note: This case raises doubts about the efficacy of mental health administration. Either the authorities were unaware of Zakowski's violent propensities or else they should never have granted home leave.]

1960

Hilde Maria Adames   Phyllis Shields

Mrs. Adames (40), German born, was *found unfit to plead at Bedfordshire Assizes, 12.10.1960*, on the capital murder charge of shooting Miss Shields (43), at the house of Adames' husband.

It would seem that Shields was living there with the husband and that the accused had, in fact, meant to kill him and not the woman.

Adames was certified insane in prison, on remand, and transferred to a mental hospital. She was stated to have a long history of mental disorder and was suffering from paranoid schizophrenia.

Ordered to be kept in strict custody, H.M.P.

Henry Atkinson (see: Leonard Thomas et al.)

Margaret Atkinson   Rosemary Atkinson

Mrs. Atkinson's husband left her (39) and her two children and went off with another woman; his wife gradually sank into a depressive state and eventually decided to kill her daughters and commit suicide. After having a good deal of difficulty in strangling one daughter (12), because she put up such a struggle, Mrs. Atkinson decided not to kill her other daughter, but went downstairs and turned on the gas. The girl ran for help and Mrs. Atkinson was prevented from even becoming unconscious.

At *Leeds Assizes, 27.4.1960*, unrebutted medical evidence of her nervous depression supported a successful plea for a verdict of *manslaughter under section 2; she was sentenced to 3 years' imprisonment.*

Douglas Aves   Cecil William Pietersen

On the day in question, Aves (17), a sheet metal worker, was late for work and was sacked. He took a walk in the park and Pietersen (52), spoke to him, told him he could get him a job and invited him home for a cup of tea. Aves claimed that, once there, Pietersen showed him some obscene photos and started to make indecent advances towards him. A fight broke out, during which Aves struck Pietersen with a milk bottle; he claimed it was self-defence. He "never intended to do serious injury". The room was reduced to considerable disorder; Pietersen died soon after being taken to hospital.

After a 3 hour retirement, the jury at the *Old Bailey, 6.12.1960,* found Aves *guilty of manslaughter.* Mr. Justice Slade, passing *sentence of 12 months' imprisonment,* said it was "quite clear the jury and the court had not heard the whole truth of what had happened".

Jhulam Sarwar Azad   Mohammed Aslam

Azad (27), a Pakistani railway worker, was alleged to have practically beheaded, with a butcher's knife, his brother-in-law, and then left letters by the body from a mysterious "Albert" and "John" in order to throw suspicion upon another person or persons. It was said that Azad believed that his wife's relations were trying to kill him in a family feud and it was certain that bad feeling had been present between the accused and his victim, whom he was said to have treated like a servant.

Azad was *convicted of non-capital murder at Nottingham Assizes, 21.11.1960, and sentenced to life imprisonment.*

Elaine Baker   Ronald Leonard Cross

Elaine Baker (23), striptease dancer in a London club, raised her hand in self-defence when attacked by the man with whom she was living; not realising she was holding a potato knife she stabbed him. Defence counsel described her as the "Oriental chattel" of her "work-shy boy friend".

She pleaded that the act had been done accidentally while defending herself, and she was *acquitted of both non-capital murder and manslaughter at the Old Bailey, 23.5.1960.*

George Frank Baker (see: Ernest William Bell Snr. et al.)

Henry Baker   Charles William Martin

Baker (39), metal polisher, saw his wife apparently struggling with a man (Martin) (28), in the street outside their home and stabbed him with a carving knife because he thought he was trying to rape her. Mrs. Baker had earlier been drinking heavily with Martin and another man who had both seen her home. All three were very drunk.

Baker pleaded provocation; he was, however, *acquitted of both non-capital murder and manslaughter at the Old Bailey, 15.9.1960.*

James Robert Barclay   Nancy Brians

Barclay (31), labourer, took a prostitute (45), to a hotel room in Newcastle. Her naked body was found later; she had been battered to death and then violently assaulted. Barclay, in escaping, apparently stole a nightdress and club-card from the bedroom of the hotel-owner.

The defence at *Newcastle Assizes, 21.1.1960*, entered a plea of diminished responsibility; Barclay was stated by medical witnesses to be a psychopathic personality, and had a long history of mental abnormality, sadism and sexual perversion, coupled with violent attacks on women. The Judge, Mr. Justice Edmund Davies, directed the jury: "It is your duty, your positive duty, to hold that the defence had been made out."

Barclay was *found guilty of manslaughter under section 2 and sentenced to life imprisonment.*

[Authors' note: Murder is the occupational hazard of prostitutes, particularly of those who work alone and go to hotels or other rooms rather than to premises used by the prostitute, where a maid is often in ready attendance.

Detection of the murder is made more difficult by the clandestine nature of the victim's association with her killer; and the clients who seek the services of a prostitute very frequently have perverted sexual desires that are often inseparable from guilt complexes and sadistic proclivities which are formed by the inadequacies of normal sexual activities. See Dowdall (1960). For the pimp-prostitute relationship, see Greenwood (1960).]

Lester Vincent Barrett   Indiana Barrett

After a violent quarrel with his wife (35), at their Walsall home, Barrett (41), a Jamaican labourer, packed a case and left the house.

He returned a little while afterwards, and when he attempted to "make it up", she took a vegetable knife from under her pillow and attacked him. He grabbed it and stabbed her to death. There was evidence of provocative behaviour by the wife, apart from her attempt to stab him.

At Stafford Assizes, 7.12.1960, Barrett was said to be suffering from a reactive depression. *He was convicted of manslaughter under section 2, and was sentenced to 7 years' imprisonment.* Barrett was later transferred to Broadmoor and subsequently repatriated to Jamaica.

John George Bates   Jordon Rayner

The prosecution alleged that Bates (29), a labourer, battered to death his friend (24), in whose house he was temporarily lodging, and then, leaving the body where it was for a week, disposed of the dead man's property, pawning some of it.

Faced with a charge of capital murder (in the course or furtherance of theft), Bates admitted that he had stolen Rayner's property after his death but denied that he had killed him. He said that a man named Fred had also stopped at the house on the night of the murder; he had been unable to trace Fred since. He had discovered the body after Fred had left the house, but did not go to the police because of his record of previous convictions for dishonesty. "I just got panicky."

Bates was *acquitted of capital murder but convicted of non-capital murder at Durham Assizes, 29.1.1960. Sentenced to life imprisonment.*

Keith Baynham   Patrick Landy

In a scuffle with his brother-in-law at his home, Baynham (25), a newsagent, with an underarm upward blow, struck Landy (31), with a carving knife, stabbing him in the heart. Baynham claimed no intention of killing or causing injury, and said that it was done in self-defence in a moment of panic during a fight with a stronger man. Baynham's daughter (2) witnessed the killing.

He was acquitted of murder, but *found guilty of manslaughter at Leeds Assizes, 16.12.1960, and sentenced to 7 years' imprisonment.* In Mrs. Baynham's subsequent divorce proceedings, Baynham was denied any prison visits by his daughter, *The Times* Law Report, 24.10.1963.

Ernest William Bell Snr. (46), lorry driver.
Peter Edward Bell (23), labourer.   James David Hannington (23)
Sydney Bell (18), car breaker.   (known as Billy Smith)
Ernest William Bell Jnr. (26), lorry driver.
George Frank Baker (24), painter.

E. W. Bell, Snr., three of his sons, and Baker, were charged with
capital murder after Smith was shot during a gang fight involving
them and others in Notting Hill. The fight—an attack by the five
accused, armed with various weapons, upon Smith and some
companions—was in the nature of a reprisal after a series of
quarrels and fights going back over previous weeks between the
two gangs.

E. W. Bell junior had carried and used the gun, a .22 rifle, but
successfully pleaded that he had had no intention of killing or
causing grievous bodily harm to Smith—he had carried it "to
scare him". *Found guilty of manslaughter and sentenced to 7 years'
imprisonment.*

Baker did not cause Smith's death by his own hand but, the
Judge said: "Nevertheless, you took a prominent part." *Convicted
of manslaughter and sentenced to 5 years' imprisonment.*

*E. W. Bell senior, P. E. Bell and S. Bell, all acquitted of capital
murder* but charged with causing grievous bodily harm to one of
Smith's companions and being in unlawful possession of a rifle.
They were all acquitted. *Old Bailey, 15.7.1960.*

William Bowman   Jane Bowman

Bowman (38) was *found unfit to plead at Durham Assizes,
29.1.1960,* on the charge of strangling his wife (40), at their home.
The prosecution alleged that he apparently suspected her of
squandering his savings and of committing adultery with his father
and another man.

Medical Officer at Durham Prison said Bowman was suffering
from paranoid schizophrenia, with delusions and hallucinations;
he still refused to accept the idea that his wife was dead.

Ordered to be kept in strict custody during H.M.P.

John Brookes   George Samuel Tate

Brookes (32), labourer, beat, kicked and finally battered to death
with a brick the man (29) whom he had met for the first time only

an hour before in a public house. He went through his pockets and his wallet, but there was no money; or at least, he was not able to get at 19/6d. in Tate's trousers pocket because his hands were too big. He then went straight to the police where he became violent during questioning, and threatened to kill the first police constable he saw when he got out.

Brookes was charged with capital murder (during course or furtherance of theft), but *found unfit to plead at Sheffield Assizes, 16.11.1960, and ordered to be detained, H.M.P.* Said to be suffering from delusions of persecution.

Ernest Vincent Brown (see: Thomas Patrick McNamara)

George Morris Brown   Joseph Alderson

Prosecution alleged that Brown (22), labourer, was convicted of stealing chickens and he believed that his friend, Alderson (43), had "split" on him to the police. The two men left a public house arguing together and went for a walk to "have it out". Brown knocked Alderson down in a field and kicked him unconscious. The next day, he returned, tried to revive him but went away later when he failed. Alderson was badly battered and died 2 weeks later from his injuries. Brown was on the run when the police caught him.

Defence pleaded diminished responsibility based upon Brown's backwardness and illiteracy; he was "of subnormal intelligence and feeble-minded". *Convicted of manslaughter under section 2 at Durham Assizes, 20.10.1960, and sentenced to life imprisonment.*

Reginald James Bruce   Rose Plain

Bruce (39), bricklayer, widower-father of six children, saw in Mrs. Plain (47), a woman who could provide once more a happy home life and be a "mother" to his disunited family. He thought she was divorced and discussed their coming marriage at her home; but she suddenly told him that she was still married and did not want him. He then strangled her with her scarf and gave himself up.

Medical evidence that Bruce was suffering from a sudden acute depression when he killed his mistress was refuted by the prosecution witnesses, but Bruce was *found guilty of manslaughter under section 2 and sentenced to 8 years' imprisonment at Northants Assizes, 26.1.1960.*

Winifred Budden   Michael Budden

Mrs. Budden (34), was alleged to have drowned her son (8), by floating him out to sea on an air mattress at Swanage. She then intended to drown herself but ran away and was found three days later in thick woods, exhausted.

It was stated that she felt herself a "hindrance" to her husband, who spent little time at home, and she was in the throes of a mental depression associated with an inferiority feeling and mounting emotional stress at the time, sufficient to amount to diminished responsibility. She was *found guilty of manslaughter under section 2 at Dorset Assizes, 13.10.1960, and placed on probation for 2 years. A residence order for treatment in a mental hospital was made for the first 12 months of this period.*

Ali Bin Nagi Bin Buraiki   Alim Salim Bugail

Buraiki (24), an Arab from the Aden Protectorate, was said to have stabbed his cousin (36), after an argument over Buraiki's wife. Two other lodgers found the accused with a knife in his hand on top of Bugail; but he said that Bugail had pushed him down and jumped on top of him. "I was frightened of him because I thought he was going to kill me. I pulled a knife from my pocket and hit him with it."

Convicted of non-capital murder at Birmingham Assizes, 14.7.1960, and sentenced to life imprisonment.

David John Burton   Patricia Weeden

It was alleged that Burton (31), farmer, broke into the home of a neighbouring farmer (and friend), Mr. Weeden, and his wife (68) at six o'clock in the morning with a loaded shotgun. He burst into their bedroom where they were asleep and fired at them, injuring both of them. Mr. Weeden struggled with him and pushed him out; he was later found wandering the streets in a dazed condition.

He was brought for trial at Herts. Assizes on five charges, including shooting with intent to kill, wounding with intent to cause grievous bodily harm, etc., etc. He was said to have been foaming at the mouth and his eyes were "flaming"; he said he saw a lot of doves flying about the room and opened fire at them. Medical evidence that he was certifiably insane—acute schizophrenia. *Found unfit to plead, 17.5.1960, and ordered to be detained H.M.P.*

Mrs. Weeden died in hospital on 26.5.1960 without regaining consciousness after the incident. Burton was *charged with capital murder*, but *found unfit to plead on this charge at Sussex Assizes, 19.7.1960.*

Patrick Joseph Byrne   Stephanie Baird

Byrne (27), an Irish labourer, confessed in a detailed statement to the horrible murder of Stephanie Baird (29), in a Birmingham Y.W.C.A. hostel just before Christmas 1959. Byrne prowled about the hostel in the character of a "Peeping Tom" and burst into the girl's room when she discovered him at her window; he strangled her and indulged in a bout of perverted sexual behaviour with her body. He cut off a breast and the head of the girl with a table knife and inflicted other mutilations. In spite of a long and extensive police investigation, Byrne was not caught until he confessed to the police six or seven weeks later.

At his trial at *Birmingham Assizes*, Byrne entered a plea of diminished responsibility and medical witnesses gave unrebutted evidence that Byrne was an aggressive psychopath with a long history of gross sexual abnormality; his sexual emotions took complete control of him so that he could not stop himself from these perverted actions. In spite of this, he was *convicted of non-capital murder, 24.3.1960, and sentenced to life imprisonment.*

Appeal was made against this conviction on the grounds of the Judge's misdirection of the jury. Defence counsel alleged that Mr. Justice Stable, in his interpretation of section 2, had in fact removed from the jury the possibility of finding a verdict under this section. The Court ruled in favour of Byrne and said that "properly directed, (the Court) did not think the jury could have come to any other conclusion than that the defence (of diminished responsibility) was made out". The Court's interpretation of "abnormality of mind" and "mental responsibility" in section 2 was approved by the Judicial Committee of the Privy Council in Rose v. The Queen [1961] A.C.496. *A verdict of manslaughter under section 2 was substituted. The sentence of life imprisonment was not altered.* [1960] 2 Q.B. 396.

[Authors' note: It is commonly thought that the sex offender does not graduate from minor to major crimes involving sexual practices. Voyeurs (Peeping Toms—offences which are not classified in law as sexual), exhibitionists (indecent exposure cases) and

fetishists (those worshipping material objects as a female love
symbol, such as women's underwear) do not often indulge in
violent crime. Occasionally, as in the case of Byrne, there is an
unhappy and violent sequel to these minor sexual quirks. In these
cases the sexual perversion occurs in the context of severe socio-
pathic personality disorder: see also Dowdall (1960).]

Evan George Carter   Ruby Carter

The prosection alleged that Carter (29), an asbestos worker,
took an iron bar from his place of work and battered his wife (33)
to death as she lay in bed; it was also asserted that he beat, at the
same time, his son Alun (6), who did not die but sustained permanent serious injury to the brain. Afterwards, Carter staged a fake
robbery in the living room to mislead the police, and threw the bar
away in a field half a mile from the house. It was stated that Mrs.
Carter was five months pregnant with an unwanted child.

Carter denied the charge but was *found guilty of non-capital
murder at Glamorgan Assizes, 28.3.1960, and sentenced to life
imprisonment.*

Colin Chapman   Carol Chapman

Chapman (21), a joiner, went to attend his daughter (6 weeks)
at 2.45 a.m. She was grunting, as though something had stuck in her
throat. He got in a panic and, in a fit of exasperation, tapped the
baby's head on the sink in order to loosen the obstruction. She
died from a fractured skull.

6 years' imprisonment at Leeds Assizes, 21.3.60, for manslaughter.

Kathleen Nora Clark   David Michael Clark

In a statement to the police, Mrs. Clark (22) admitted that she
hated her son (2), partly because she "had a bad time" when he
was born, and had suffered from "all sorts of pains and headaches"
since. She admitted that she went out of her way to beat the child
(sometimes with a metal-studded belt) and deny him things which
she gave to her other son, Paul. She said: "He sent me crazy and
I pushed him over and he probably knocked his head on the settee",
when the child refused to go to bed.

However, at *Leeds Assizes, 30.4.1960, a formal verdict of not
guilty* was returned upon the Judge's direction, after the end of

the prosecution case, that there was "no evidence upon which she could be found guilty".

Veronica Collins (see: Eamonn Hamilton.)

Johannah Connolly   Patrick Connolly

Suffering from a long mental depression, Mrs. Connolly (45) decided to gas herself and her son (4) at the same time. Only the child died.

She was stated to have had a long history of mental disorders and was *found guilty but insane at the Old Bailey, 11.5.1960. Ordered to be detained as a Broadmoor patient during H.M.P.*

John Louis Constantine   Lily Parry

Constantine (22), a boxmaker, was alleged to have broken into the shop kept by a woman (75) in Nottingham, but, when she interrupted his burglary, he battered her with his crowbar and she died from her injuries some days later. He stole some money and various items of personal property.

Faced with a charge of capital murder, Constantine claimed that he had been accompanied on the burglary by another man who had gone upstairs with the crowbar, and must have killed the woman. This man, however, had a complete alibi for the time of the offence, and the other evidence against Constantine was fairly substantial. Constantine who was, all-round, a delinquent and irresponsible type with a number of previous convictions, was *found guilty of capital murder at Birmingham Assizes, 22.7.1960, and sentenced to death.*

His appeal on the grounds that words in the Judge's summing-up and the summing-up as a whole were unfavourable to the defence, *was dismissed 15.8.1960*, and the Home Secretary refused a reprieve.

Constantine was hanged at Lincoln Prison, 1.9.1960.

Thomas Coyne   Ronald Lee

Coyne (21), a labourer, was evidently attacked by a number of men in the street whilst returning home after drinking very heavily. He said that he felt a bang on the head and remembered nothing more until he woke up next morning in a police cell. However, it appeared that Coyne had kicked Lee (25), while he lay unconscious on the ground in the fight.

A consultant neurologist gave an opinion that the loss of memory was genuine and could have been due to the bang on the head. He thought it was sufficient to amount to an abnormality of the mind, but Coyne was *convicted of non-capital murder at Leeds Assizes, 17.3.1960, and sentenced to life imprisonment.*

Ann Craggs   Janice Davison

Mrs. Craggs (49) was alleged to have battered her grand-daughter (16 months) to death with a stone in order to stop her crying when she fell from a window and "bumped her head". She had been an in-patient in a mental institution six times since 1955 and had a long history of mental disorder.

Found unfit to plead at Durham Assizes, 20.10.1960, and ordered to be kept in strict custody during H.M.P.

Martin Graham Crump   James Martin Crump

Crump (40), a labourer, stabbed his son (10) in the chest at their home. When charged, he said, "I did not know what I was doing to the little chap. I did not mean to harm him."

It was said that Crump had suffered from his prisoner-of-war experiences so much that his mind became affected and he was re-patriated by the Germans. Since 1944 he had been in and out of mental hospitals both as a certified and a voluntary patient. He suffered badly from delusions, and thought at times that he was a German. *Found unfit to plead at Gloucestershire Assizes, 25.5.1960, and ordered to be detained H.M.P.*

Christopher Darby (see: Norman James Harris et al.)

John Day   Edna Day

Mrs. Day (58) had been nursed devotedly by her husband (61) who was also an invalid. They had one daughter, a blind invalid, who had died seven years previously, to whom Day had also been devoted. Her death left him in a very depressed state of mind. It would appear that Day turned on the gas-tap at their home, killing his wife, but being found unconscious himself. His memory was afterwards affected by the gas poisoning but the defence submitted that it was possible that the tap had been turned on accidentally in a moment of absent-mindedness in his depression. No evidence of intent to kill wife or self, though Day was reported as saying: "I sometimes felt as if I could stand it no longer."

Jury accepted defence case, and Day was *found not guilty of murder at Stafford Assizes, 13.12.1960, and discharged.*

William Henry Dixon   Jean Dixon

Dixon (37) was an electrical fitter. When his wife (29) came in at 3 o'clock in the morning and told him she had just been with a man, and had had intercourse with him in his caravan, and that she was taking their baby away with her to live with him, Dixon picked up a hammer and frenziedly beat her to death at their home.

He was *found guilty but insane at Glamorgan Assizes, 5.12.1960, and ordered to be detained during H.M.P. at Broadmoor.* [1961] 1 W.L.R. 337.

Michael Douglas Dowdall   Veronica Murray

Dowdall (19), a Welsh Guardsman, went with a prostitute (31), to her home in Kilburn. After intercourse, a quarrel arose and during the fight which followed Dowdall battered her to death with an ornamental dumb-bell which lay on the mantelpiece. After death he forced two coathangers into her body and mutilated her. He was eventually arrested when, after a similar attack on another woman eleven months later (which she survived), his description was circulated and the fingerprints found at the latter woman's home tallied both with those found at Murray's home and with those discovered at a series of homes in the London area which had been broken into and from which property had been stolen.

Defence offered extensive evidence of Dowdall's mental abnormality and therefore diminished responsibility for the crime. The Principal Medical Officer of Brixton described him as a psychopathic personality, liable to aggressive and violent behaviour "without sufficient cause". He had been said to be a "difficult and precocious type" and his Commanding Officer said Dowdall seemed to have delusions of grandeur occasioned by the fact that he was "small, weak and insignificant". He was well on the way to becoming an alcoholic—he thought nothing of drinking two bottles of spirits at one time, and in his statement to the police he said: "It is when I get drinking I do these things, I'm all right when I'm sober."

He seemed to be suffering from amnesia with respect to his infliction of curious circular mutilations which were found on the bodies
of both women and was unable to throw any light upon solving
this problem. He had attempted to hang himself two years
previously.

The prosecution offered no rebutting medical evidence and Dowdall was *convicted of manslaughter under section 2 and sentenced by
Mr. Justice Donovan to life imprisonment at the Old Bailey,
21.1.1960.*

[Authors' note: see Barclay (1960) and Byrne (1960).]

Robert Earl   John Little

Earl (42), a farmer, was accused of the capital murder by
shooting, of a neighbouring farmer (45). It was alleged by the
prosecution that the two men were not on friendly terms by any
means and that Earl had deliberately shot Little in the back with
a .22 rifle. Earl claimed that it had been an accident, that the gun
(which had a very faulty safety catch) had gone off while Earl was
climbing a fence.

Earl, to whom there attached a strong underlying suggestion of
mental abnormality, was *acquitted of capital murder at Cumberland
Assizes, 10.10.1960,* and he was discharged.

Arthur Eastwood   Margaret Alice Bean

Eastwood (19), a married bus conductor, "formed an association" with a girl passenger (15) and took her out once or twice.
He did not tell her he was married until after he had invited her to
his home for the first time. When she realised, she told him she
would wait until his wife returned and then tell her. In a frenzied fit
of desperation, Eastwood battered her to death with a hammer and
cut her throat. He then attempted suicide.

He pleaded diminished responsibility at his *Leeds Assizes,*
trial *12.7.1960,* and a doctor testified that an injury to his brain
which he had received previously while playing rugby, had led to a
mental abnormality sufficient to impair his responsibility. He was,
however, *convicted of non-capital murder and sentenced to life
imprisonment.*

Frederick Ellison   Annie Ellison

Ellison (72), a retired textile worker, and his wife (70), had been
married for 50 years. But when Annie became ill from a heart

complaint, accused gave up his work to look after her. He did all the domestic duties but eventually became physically and mentally exhausted. He had had little or no sleep and had not taken his clothes off for three months when he killed her in a "mercy killing" at their home.

Defence plea of diminished responsibility based upon emotional stress and mental exhaustion, was successful and Ellison was found *guilty at Leeds Assizes of manslaughter under section 2; sentenced to 3 years' imprisonment, 12.7.1960.* In November he appealed against sentence to the Court of Criminal Appeal. *Appeal successful, sentence reduced to 141 days, i.e. immediate release.*

Ellison had been in custody for 141 days, his condition had improved and his son and daughter-in-law were anxious to look after him. This was not, the Court said, a case for a probation order. [1961] Crim.L.R. 269.

Lily England   Susan England (7)
                          Dorothy Jane England (6)

Separated from her husband since early in 1959, Mrs. England (52), felt that "things were getting too much for her" and decided to commit suicide and take her two young daughters with her. Turned on the gas, the children died, but she was found unconscious. Said to be a devoted mother and cared for the children well.

Found guilty of manslaughter on grounds of diminished responsibility at Lancaster Assizes, 26.10.1960. Placed on probation for 2 years on condition that she take treatment in a mental hospital.

John Ferguson   Margaret Ferguson

On Christmas morning, 1959, Ferguson (22), a railway signalman, and his wife (18) left their home to seek an apology from a man who had apparently insulted Mrs. Ferguson, perhaps at a party the night before. Ferguson was very drunk; and as they walked along a road by a river, whether as a result of an argument or during "larking about", he pushed his wife; she staggered through a fence into the river. He said he was unable to get her out, so "floated" her across to the other side. After unsuccessfully trying to make her take a cigarette, he put her back in the water, floated her across again, then carried her home, hiding her from the sight of a milk van on the way. He laid her on a settee, covered her with blankets and left her. She was later found to be dead.

There appeared to be no possible reason for the act except drink and little intention even to harm his wife. Ferguson was, however, *found guilty of non-capital murder at York Assizes, and sentenced to life imprisonment, 3.5.1960.*

Albert Flint   Caroline Beatrice Ellis

Flint (54), a nightwatchman, met Mrs. Ellis (49), whom he had known for about a year, and took her to his room and gave her a meal. She was very drunk on either methylated spirits or surgical spirits. After the meal an argument developed and Mrs. Ellis began to scream. As she was extremely deaf, she would not have heard Flint telling her to stop, and he grasped her throat in an effort to stop her. She died from asphyxia. He hid her body under the bed and went to the police two days later.

At Manchester Crown Court, 18.7.1960, he denied an intention to cause bodily harm and was *found guilty of manslaughter. Sentenced to 12 months' imprisonment.*

Flint was later tried and convicted of manslaughter of a woman (59) in almost identical circumstances. He was sentenced at Manchester Crown Court on 11.12.1962 to life imprisonment. (See Flint (1962).)

Francis Forsyth (see: Norman James Harris et al.)

Wasyl Gnypiuk   Louise Surgey

The prosecution alleged that Gnypiuk (34), Polish Ukrainian refugee, unemployed, was in serious financial difficulties; knowing that Mrs. Surgey (63) kept large sums of cash about her (since he had lodged with her for some time previously), he broke into her house and strangled her when she interrupted him. He chopped the head off her body and hid the latter on an allotment. He then hid the head over a mile away in a paper-bag. He stole two handbags, one containing £250, the other £350. The second bag was found underneath the paper-bag containing the woman's head.

Gnypiuk disputed a statement of confession which he had made to the police and claimed at the trial that what had happened was very different. He said he got fed up with living in a wooden hut on the allotment and after drinking a quarter bottle of brandy, went to Mrs. Surgey's house to see if she would let him sleep there for the night. He broke in, shouted to Mrs. Surgey, but she was upstairs in bed; so he drank some spirits which he found in a bottle and went to sleep on a couch. During the night he had a violent nightmare in which he dreamt he was defending himself. The next morning he found Mrs. Surgey lying strangled on the floor. In a panic he chopped the head off and put it in a carrier-bag, not noticing that the bag already contained the other bag with £350 in it. He then hid the body and the head.

Defence produced evidence of Gnypiuk's violent war experiences in a German camp, after which he had constantly suffered from these terrible nightmares, and submitted that the killing had therefore been committed in the nightmare without conscious intent. Two persons who knew him said Gnypiuk was of a particularly gentle nature. Neither could the killing have been in course or furtherance of theft, since the stealing of the money and the idea of taking it were not formed till much later. Nevertheless, Gnypiuk was *found guilty of capital murder at Nottingham Assizes and sentenced to death, 18.11.1960.*

Appeal to the Court of Criminal Appeal was on the grounds that the Judge's summing up had omitted certain important matters of fact and had contained misdirections. *Appeal dismissed, 19.12.1960.*

Gnypiuk then applied for leave to *appeal to the House of Lords* under the new procedure laid down in the Administration of Justice Act 1960 (which abolished applications for the Attorney General's fiat). *The Court of Criminal Appeal* refused to give leave to appeal to the House of Lords, since the case "did not involve a point of law of general public importance".

Reprieve refused. *Executed at Lincoln Prison, 27.1.1961.*

Charles Goodby   Pauline Blaney

Goodby (47), a factory foreman, was alleged by the prosecution to have battered his mistress (18) with a cider bottle and to have then strangled her. He hid her body in a cupboard and fled to London the next day.

Goodby claimed that after they had made love, the girl began talking about other men she had been with and the shame she felt as a result. She had handed him a cider bottle and said: "Why don't you kill me now and get it over?" He had intended to fake a blow, but had accidentally hit her and tried, he said, to stop the blood stemming from a cut by putting pressure on the neck.

Goodby was *convicted of non-capital murder at Birmingham Assizes and sentenced to life imprisonment, 1.4.1960.*

George Grant   Edward Thomas Grant

While his wife and her mother went out for the evening, Grant (22), labourer, remained at home to look after his son (16 months), whom he was said to idolise. But some time during the evening he drowned the baby in a bowl of water and left the house. Some hours later he went to the police.

Defence at *Liverpool Crown Court* offered alternative pleas of "manslaughter on grounds of diminished responsibility" or "guilty but insane". Grant was said to suffer from epilepsy. In July 1959, just after the second child was born, he disappeared and was found naked on the shore at Southport. He was at that time taken to a mental hospital and kept for a week.

Mr. Justice Paull allowed the Crown in this case to contend that the correct verdict was guilty but insane, although the burden of proving it was to establish it beyond reasonable doubt. [1960] Crim.L.R. 424; cf. R. v. Price [1963] 2 Q.B. 1. where Mr. Justice Lawton refused to allow the prosecution to raise the plea of insanity although in that case there was no alternative defence plea of insanity.

Found guilty but insane, 12.2.1960, and ordered to be detained as a Broadmoor patient, H.M.P. Grant was refused leave to appeal, 18.4.1962, on the grounds that the trial verdict was an acquittal, against which there was no right of appeal, *The Times* Law Report, 19.4.1962: see Duke (1961).

Vivienne Greenwood   Ernest Patrick Lynch

Greenwood (31), a prostitute, and Lynch, a pimp, had been living together for ten years; for some time previously he had been living upon her earnings as a prostitute and upon money obtained through her constant petty larceny.

After a Boxing-night party at which Lynch became drunk, an argument broke out between them when they returned home. Lynch was upset because Greenwood had been dancing with other men; he grabbed a knife in order to attack her and in the struggle which followed they both fell to the ground, the knife going into Lynch's stomach.

Greenwood pleaded not guilty to murder, but on the second day of her trial at the *Old Bailey, 9.2.1960,* she pleaded *guilty to manslaughter on grounds of provocation.* The prosecution accepted this plea and she was *sentenced to 5 years' imprisonment.*

[Authors' note: A prostitute is frequently the victim of her procurer, the maquereau (or pimp). The theory is that, once the prostitute becomes dependent on the pimp, the only escape is death. A pimp is often brutally cruel to the prostitute who fails to earn enough money for them both. Occasionally the tables are turned and the prostitute kills either in self-defence or owing to terrible jealousy because often she loves her protector as well as procurer.]

Robert Derek Griffiths   Christine Griffiths

Griffiths (36), sales representative, was alleged to have strangled his daughter (10) whom he loved, after his mistress had broken with him and returned to her husband and son. Griffiths had told her that he would have to kill himself or his daughter, or both of them, because there was no one to look after the girl.

Defence did not dispute the factual evidence, but claimed that Griffiths was mentally abnormal at the time with a "reactive depression". *Found guilty of manslaughter under section 2 at Birmingham Assizes, 27.7.1960, and sentenced to 5 years' imprisonment.*

Lucien Gruszka   Josephine Brennan

Gruszka (34), a naturalised Frenchman born in Poland, attacked a housekeeper (51) in a Roman Catholic presbytery, and raped her on the lawn by the Church. She died from suffocation as he held his hand over her mouth. He had previously been drinking heavily.

Gruszka was *convicted of manslaughter at Stafford Assizes, 14.12.1960, and sentenced to 12 years' imprisonment.*

Eamonn Hamilton   Alexander Walton
Veronica Collins

The prosecution alleged that Hamilton (23) stabbed Walton (20), with a flick knife during a street fight between a group of youths outside a café in Birmingham. It was claimed that the knife was carried by Hamilton's girl friend, who handed it to him just before he entered the fight.

Hamilton *was convicted of non-capital murder at Birmingham Assizes, 13.12.1960, and sentenced to life imprisonment.* Collins *was acquitted and discharged.*

Edward Hanlon   Doris Hanlon

Hanlon (41) battered his wife (35) to death with a hatchet at their home, as a result, apparently of domestic difficulties caused by Hanlon's unfounded belief that his wife had been unfaithful to him. She had borne him ten children.

Medical evidence was given of his delusional symptoms and general history of mental disorder at *Birmingham Assizes, 19.12.1960,* where he was *sentenced to life imprisonment, upon a conviction of manslaughter under section 2,* by Mr. Justice Winn. Transferred to Broadmoor, 2.2.1961.

Norman James Harris (unemployed).   Allan Jee
Francis Forsyth (road labourer).
Terence Lutt (unemployed).
Christopher Darby (coalman).

The prosecution alleged that the four accused, aged respectively 23, 18, 17 and 20 years, decided to rob someone. They waited in a lonely alley in Hounslow and when Jee (23), who had become engaged on the day before, came along he was punched in the face by Lutt. His pockets were then rifled by Harris while he was held down by the others. Forsyth, who was standing above, kicked Jee unconscious with his pointed Italian-type shoes in order "to keep him quiet", and Jee died in hospital some 26 hours later as a result of the injuries sustained. The ten shillings he had been carrying had not been found by the accused.

At their trial at the *Old Bailey,* there was some evidence to suggest that Darby had not played such an active part in the killing as the other three and at the end of the prosecution's case, the charge against him was reduced from capital to non-capital murder. Although it was admitted that none of the boys had any intention to *kill,* it was sufficiently proved that there had been intent to commit grievous bodily harm and *all four were found guilty,* (Darby of non-capital murder and the others of capital murder). *Lutt being under 18 was ordered to be detained during H.M.P., but Harris and Forsyth were sentenced to death; Darby was sentenced to life imprisonment, 26.9.1960.* Although only Lutt and Forsyth caused injury to Jee (though, by his own confession, Harris also laid hands on him), it was established that there was "a common purpose or design" in which all four were involved.

Appeals by all four accused against their convictions were dismissed by the Court of Criminal Appeal, 27.10.1960.

Various public appeals and petitions were made to obtain a reprieve for Forsyth and Harris, but this was not granted and they were both *executed, Forsyth at Wandsworth and Harris at Pentonville, 10.11.1960.*

Both Forsyth and Harris had a number of previous convictions, mostly for larceny.

Herbert Samuel Harrison   Beryl Harrison

It was alleged that Harrison (31), sales representative, stabbed his wife (20), at their home in order to leave himself free to marry another woman. Evidence suggested that his wife had frequently refused him a divorce and letters between him and his girl friend mentioned in indirect terms the possibility of him "doing" something to his wife.

Defence claimed that death had been accidental during a struggle after his wife had attacked him with a kitchen knife. Harrison was *found guilty at Kent Assizes, 11.7.1960, of non-capital murder and sentenced to life imprisonment.*

Phyllis Harrison   John Philip Harrison

Mrs. Harrison (29) was alleged by the prosecution to have beaten and kicked her son (3), one of her five children, so that death resulted from peritonitis set up by a rupture of the intestines.

It was reported that the child had not developed naturally, was deformed and could not help himself at all—needing constant attention. In defence, Mrs. Harrison claimed that, instead of *kicking* the boy, she gave him a push with her foot because he was getting nearer and nearer the fire while she was dressing another child, while another was crying out for food.

She was *acquitted of both non-capital murder and manslaughter at York Assizes, 26.4.1960.*

Sarah Jane Harvey   Frances Knight

Mrs. Harvey (65), a widow, was alleged by the prosecution to have strangled Mrs. Knight (50), who lived with her, some time in

1940 after the latter had given Mrs. Harvey permission to draw £2 a week for her on a maintenance order. It was said that accused had continued to draw this money every week for 20 years until the mummified body of Mrs. Knight was found in a cupboard at her home. Mrs. Harvey claimed that the woman had died from natural causes but that after death she had hidden the body in order still to be able to draw the payments.

Much evidence of a scientific nature was called on behalf of the prosecution, at the *Denbighshire Assizes* trial, concerning the ligature (there for 20 years) found around the dead woman's neck and possible injuries to the neck; but before completing his case, the Solicitor-General announced that on the evidence as it stood, it would not be right for the Crown to ask the jury to find a verdict of murder; the charge was withdrawn and Mrs. Harvey was *formally found not guilty, 18.10.1960.*

She then pleaded *guilty to 2 charges of obtaining money by false pretences and was sentenced to 15 months' imprisonment.*

Brian George Hatcher   Ann Hatcher

Hatcher (21), a National Serviceman, was sent money every week by his wife (19), so that he could come home at the weekend. One week she failed to send him any and he became suspicious that she was being unfaithful. While on his next leave he strangled her with a stocking at their home but did not carry out his intention to commit suicide.

Hatcher was said to be "overwhelmingly jealous and extremely possessive", and was suffering from melancholia at the time.

He was *found guilty but insane at Bristol Assizes, 23.11.1960, and ordered to be detained at Broadmoor during H.M.P.*

Robert Boston Hay   Martin Adair

Hay (17), a labourer, was found not guilty of murdering Adair (48), whose body with stab wounds was found in a public lavatory. He was *convicted of manslaughter at Kent Assizes, 12.7.1960, and sentenced to 3 years' imprisonment.*

The killing in some way had homosexual overtones, for in a statement Hay said: "I did it for what he did to me. I pulled out my knife and stabbed him."

Robert Haynes   Brenda Haynes

A few weeks after his wife (31) left him and went with her five children to live with her mother, Haynes (37), a mechanical excavator driver, armed himself with a dagger, went to her home and stabbed his wife and her mother. He was detained a few days later after a motor accident, and his wife died in hospital 11 days after the attack. Her mother recovered.

Haynes *pleaded guilty to non-capital murder at Stafford Assizes, 2.3.1960, and was sentenced to life imprisonment.* He was also charged with the attempted murder of his mother-in-law.

Mildred Heffernan   Thomas Heffernan

Mrs. Heffernan (45) divorced her first husband on grounds of cruelty and married Heffernan (38). Eight weeks after their marriage, he brought home a young girl (17), and in a quarrel told his wife he was going to bed with her. In a sudden fit, the wife picked up a bread knife and stabbed him. He was a heavy drinker and had previously treated her brutally, using foul language, kicking and beating her.

Defence of provocation succeeded and Mrs. Heffernan was *convicted of manslaughter, 22.11.1960. Sentenced to 2 years' imprisonment at Sheffield Assizes.*

Alfred Rubython Hickman   Winifred Hickman
                                             Jean Hickman

Hickman (55), an instrument maker, was *found insane and unfit to plead at the Old Bailey, 29.3.1960,* to a charge of murdering his wife (about 50), and daughter (19), at their home, both of whom he stabbed and beat to death. Hickman admitted the killing to the police. Mr. Justice Donovan *ordered him to be detained during H.M.P.*

The family was reasonably happy, the parents having been married for over 30 years. He had twice been treated for mental disorders; on the day before the killing he had told his doctor he contemplated suicide, whereupon he had been sent to Maudsley Hospital where he was given sleeping tablets. Early next morning he woke up and "that feeling came over me . . . I hit my wife with a hammer on the head. I possibly knifed her . . . I did the same thing to the girl". He then cut his own wrists and neck. A ligature had been put round the daughter's neck after her death.

Miriam Hill   Dennis Hill

Mrs. Hill (49) pleaded self-defence at her trial at *Stafford Assizes* on a capital murder charge of shooting her husband (19). They had been married only ten weeks, but for the past six weeks the young husband had been abusive to her and had frequently assaulted her. He had left their home, taking her daughter with him, and he had been bound over by the Justices to keep the peace. A few days later he returned, went to attack her, and Mrs. Hill picked up a shotgun and shot him in "self-defence". (There was every indication that Hill had married Mrs. Hill, a wealthy widow with four children, for her money.)

She was *acquitted of both capital murder and manslaughter, 27.7.1960.*

Albert Edward Hinds   Lilian Kate Crane
                                       Robert Newby Garrett

Hinds (59), painter, battered to death the elderly woman, with whom he had lodged for several years, and her brother, at their home in Sheerness. He used an axe; then phoned the police.

Found guilty but insane, of murdering Mrs. Crane, at Kent Assizes, 28.11.1960, and ordered to be detained at Broadmoor during H.M.P. The other charge of murder was not proceeded with.

George Cuthbert Hinkson   Lorenzo Lovelock

Hinkson (51), a West Indian book-shop manager, was *acquitted* of non-capital murder of another West Indian, Lorenzo Lovelock (24), whose body with stab wounds was found in an alley in Manchester. He was also cleared of manslaughter at *Manchester Crown Court, 2.12.1960.*

William Horrocks   Brenda Hardman

Horrocks (18), gardener, was infatuated with his girl friend (18), and, when she told him she could not see him the next day, in a fit of jealous temper he stabbed her with a putty knife which he carried.

He pleaded the defence of provocation, but was *convicted at Manchester Crown Court of non-capital murder and sentenced to life imprisonment, 24.11.1960.*

6

Mohamed Ismail   Michael McFarlane (21)
                                                        Thomas Owen (29)
                                               George Frederick Morris (32)

Ismail (30), unemployed labourer, a native of British Somaliland, was *found insane and unfit to plead at Sheffield Assizes, 25.2.1960*, on the capital charge of shooting three men in a public house. At an earlier hearing it was alleged that Ismail had said he wanted to commit suicide, but this was against his religion and he would go to Hell. It would be all right, however, if he killed someone else and was then killed himself. He therefore suddenly produced a revolver in a public house and fired five shots—killing three men and wounding two others.

Medical witnesses said he was suffering from paranoid schizophrenia and was quite insane. *Ordered to be detained in strict custody during H.M.P.*

George Ernest Johnson   David Johnson

Johnson (40), an Army Major, grew obsessionally depressed and worried as it gradually became clear that his baby son (3 months) was a mongol child. Eventually, this man, whom witnesses described as "very fond of children", gassed the boy in his sleep and immediately informed the police.

He presented a defence of diminished responsibility at his trial at *Surrey Assizes*, and was *found guilty of manslaughter under section 2. Sentenced to 12 months' imprisonment, 28.6.1960*, by Mr. Justice Slade.

Albert Michael Kelly   Thomas Henry Russell

Apparently after Russell (49), a tramp, had started to commit an indecent act with him in a tent in a field, Kelly (21), a railway foreman, picked up two stones and threw them at him in a fit of temper.

His defence at *Manchester Crown Court* was on grounds of provocation provided by the tramp's behaviour; but, although there had been no intention to kill, the jury found that there had been intent to do grievous bodily harm and Kelly was *convicted of non-capital murder and sentenced to life imprisonment, 29.11.1960*.

Kelly claimed that he did not previously know that Russell was homosexual, and if this had been established he would probably have got off with manslaughter; however, he had mentioned the fact to two boys earlier in the evening and it would seem that he *was* aware of it.

Hubert Roy Lane   Beatrice Wiles

Lane (47), a railway dining-car attendant, and Mrs. Wiles (40), had been living together and had had a child. The woman had, however, recently obtained from the Justices a non-molestation order keeping Lane away from the house and she had a Turkish Cypriot living with her. Lane went to the house and after a quarrel over their child, he stabbed her two or three times in the neck and chest.

He was *convicted at the Old Bailey, 19.10.1960, of manslaughter on grounds of diminished responsibility and sentenced to life imprisonment.*

David Calude Lazell   Lily Agnes Coote

Lazell (23), a spot-welder, was *sentenced to life imprisonment at the Old Bailey, 8.4.1960,* for the murder of his landlady (64), at their home. He had hit her on the head with a hammer. She died from suffocation with a pillow while unconscious. She had been ill with lung trouble. Lazell had lodged there for three months during which time the landlady nagged him about his drinking habits and about a paternity order against him. He killed her at 8 a.m., went out for the day, played billiards, went to the cinema, came home at 1.30 a.m. and then reported her dead. He finally told the police: "If I knew why I did it I probably would not have done it." He was a paranoid psychopath; his plea of diminished responsibility failed, and his appeal to the Court of Criminal Appeal, 11.7.1960, was dismissed.

Conrad Lecointe   Jagtar Singh
                                                       Sadhu Singh

Lecointe (35), a Jamaican bricklayer, was alleged to have stabbed his landlord, Jagtar Singh (55) and the landlord's son (19), in a street fight after a quarrel over the cooking and heating arrangements in his room. There was some evidence that Lecointe was attacked first—i.e. provocation and self-defence. But his counsel also entered a plea of diminished responsibility and medical witnesses claimed that Lecointe was suffering from schizophrenia associated with a persecution complex.

He was *found guilty at Birmingham Assizes, 13.12.1960, of man-slaughter (under section 2) and sentenced* by Mr. Justice Winn *to 10 years' imprisonment* on each charge (to run concurrently). He was transferred to Broadmoor on 26.4.1961.

Gladys Lavinia Linger   Alick William Linger

Mrs. Linger (48) battered her husband (50) to death with an iron bar as he lay sleeping at their home in Bromley, Kent. She said she did not want to leave him behind. She was deeply attached to him and did not wish to give him pain.

Defence plea of diminished responsibility was successful at her trial at the *Old Bailey* and she was *found guilty of manslaughter under section 2. Sentenced to life imprisonment, 9.2.1960.* Transferred to Broadmoor, 26.2.1960. She had a history of bouts of mental depression over 20 years and at the time was suffering from involutional melancholia. She was morbidly depressed and had illusions she was going insane. She felt she was two persons.

Alfred Albert Little   Sandra Toms

Little (32), an Army sergeant and father of five, invited a girl (13) into his home on a pretext of running an errand for him, "because he was fed up and wanted someone to talk to". He put his hand on her knee—a habit of his when talking to people—and she screamed. In his panicky attempt to stop her, he strangled her. He hid the body in his garage and then later put it down a manhole.

He claimed that there had been no intention to kill. Evidence was presented of his wife being in hospital and the housework "seemed to get on top of me". He seemed to be under a great mental strain, but apparently defence was not based upon mental abnormality; he was *convicted of simple manslaughter, 27.7.1960, at Hampshire Assizes. Sentenced to 2 years' imprisonment.*

Terence Lutt (see: Norman James Harris et al.)

George McLachlan   Frances McLachlan

McLachlan (27), a driver, attacked his wife (19), in the street with a hammer on the day the local Justices had found him guilty of desertion and of wilful neglect to maintain. The Magistrates had made maintenance orders against him for the wife and her two children. It was alleged that, after the hearing, McLachlan had told his wife: "You will never get money off me. I would rather kill you."

McLachlan was *convicted of non-capital murder at Lancaster Assizes, 2.6.1960, and sentenced to life imprisonment.*

He was *refused leave to appeal against the conviction and sentence* on the grounds of the Judge's misdirection of the jury.

Thomas Patrick McNamara   Rose de Maria
Ernest Vincent Brown

Brown (32), a driver, and McNamara (23), a fishmonger, attacked Mr. and Mrs. de Maria in the fog while they were walking home. The two accused had been drinking, and after attacking these two middle-aged people, they attacked some young boys and girls a few minutes later—all apparently without reason. Mrs. de Maria (56), it was said, was pushed to the ground and kicked; she died 24 hours later.

McNamara was acquitted at the Old Bailey, 19.1.1960, but held on a second charge of assaulting Mr. de Maria. *Brown was found guilty of manslaughter and sentenced to 7 years' imprisonment, 20.1.1960.*

Harold Hampsden Marsden   Andrew Robertson

Prosecution alleged that Marsden (61), a salesman, battered his stepfather (76) to death at their home with a metal bar in order to prevent him changing his will in favour of someone else. Robertson was soon to go and live in lodgings with a woman who had offered to look after him. Marsden claimed that a quarrel between them had broken out on the stairs and that Robertson had struck at him first with the metal bar. The bar fell and Marsden picked it up and struck Robertson who had grabbed him by the throat. Robertson eventually fell downstairs, "I remember kicking him, but I do not know for how long. I jumped on him."

Marsden was *convicted of non-capital murder at Lancaster Assizes, 26.10.1960, and sentenced to life imprisonment.* The killing gave rise to litigation over Robertson's will under which Marsden was the chief beneficiary, but because of his felony he could not take the benefit from the will. See, *Re Robertson, dec'd, The Guardian* Law Report, 11 April 1963.

Herbert James Marsh (see: Frank Alexander Williams)

Joseph Martin   Pamela Masterson

Martin (27), unemployed, visited the house where his mistress (22) lived, but, finding her to be not at home, went to bed with her friend who lived in the same house. In the morning, while showing her the working of a Luger pistol which he was carrying with him (because "there was someone looking for him with a gun"), the gun went off and Mrs. Masterson was killed instantly.

Martin was *acquitted at the Old Bailey, 24.5.1960, of capital murder but convicted of manslaughter (i.e. accident with gross negligence). He was sentenced to 6 years' imprisonment.*

Lilian Medd   Denise Kay Medd (4)
                                                 Michael Medd (1)

Mrs. Medd (28), a widow, who was in part-time employment, became very depressed and worried about her financial prospects and about the prospects for the children, so she turned on the gas tap in the room in which they were all sleeping. Mrs. Medd was found unconscious but survived.

Defence pleaded diminished responsibility on account of acute melancholia and Mrs. Medd was *convicted of manslaughter under Section 2 at York Assizes, 12.2.1960. Sentencing her to 2 years' imprisonment,* Mr. Justice Salmon said: "This is one of the most terribly sad cases which I have ever had to deal with."

Philip Morris   Matilda Morris

Morris (59), an unemployed sheet metal worker, was *found guilty, on grounds of diminished responsibility, of the manslaughter* of his invalid wife (72)—a "mercy killing"; he was *sentenced to life imprisonment by Mr. Justice Austin Jones at Glamorgan Assizes, 6.12.1960.* During the trial two doctors gave evidence that Morris was suffering from depression superimposed on a chronic anxiety state. Mr. Justice Austin Jones refused to allow the prosecution to raise the issue of insanity although the prosecution's medical evidence showed an even greater degree of mental abnormality than the defence doctors (cf. Price 1962). The Court of Criminal Appeal, [1961] 2 Q.B. 237 at pp. 240-1, had this point argued but declined to rule on the question as not being directly in issue. It upheld the life sentence because the provisions of the Mental Health Act gave a wide discretion to the judge. But it laid down that, normally where punishment is not intended, it was better to make a hospital order and not leave it to the Secretary of State to transfer the person from prison to a mental institution (see Duke (1961)).

James Lawrence Nash, steeplejack.   Selwyn Keith Cooney
James Alexander Read, unemployed.
Joseph Henry Pyle, street trader.

Nash (28), Read (28) and Pyle (25) were accused of murdering Soho club-owner Selwyn Cooney (31) in the Pen Club in Stepney. Cooney was shot as an act of revenge during a gang feud, and all three faced charges of capital murder, though it was alleged that it was Nash who had carried and used the revolver.

At their trial at the Old Bailey, there was evidence that witnesses were being intimidated and others were remaining in hiding, and that jurors were being tampered with. Mr. Justice Gorman stopped the trial and dismissed the jury.

At the re-trial before Mr. Justice Diplock, objections were made by counsel to 9 of the 12 people called for the jury before the prosecution announced that it was offering no evidence against *Read and Pyle* on the capital murder charge; *they were formally found not guilty*. During Nash's trial, there were further intimations of false evidence and witnesses disappearing before Nash was *acquitted of capital murder, 4.5.1960*, owing to lack of sufficient evidence, the principal prosecution witness having deliberately failed to attend the trial. All three were then tried on charges of causing actual bodily harm to Cooney. *Nash was sentenced to 5 years' imprisonment*, and *Read and Pyle to lesser terms*.

[Authors' note: The events surrounding this trial suggest there may be times when the power of the criminal underworld defeats the ends of justice. It might be argued that where Crown witnesses, themselves embroiled in associated criminal activities, are likely to be intimidated, there is a case for key witnesses also being placed under automatic police protection or house arrest pending the trial.]

Eric Thomas Nicholson   Margaret Brindley

Mrs. Brindley (48), the mistress of a Jamaican who owned a house in Wolverhampton, was battered to death by one of their

West Indian lodgers and left lying on her bed. Nicholson (45), claimed that he had lost his job and, wanting to send some money to his wife and 6 children in Jamaica, asked Mrs. Brindley for £5 which she owed him. When she said to him: "I don't have time now to talk to any black bastard", he lost his temper and hit her with the shoe he was cleaning.

At Staffordshire Assizes, 2.12.1960, Nicholson was *found guilty of non-capital murder, the jury adding a recommendation for mercy;* he had pleaded provocation. *Sentenced to life imprisonment.*

(*N.B.* Mrs. Brindley's daughter, Margaret, was also murdered, in December 1958 by a Cypriot, Eyyup Celal (1959). She was a prostitute. Mrs. Brindley's cousin, an R.A.F. Sergeant, was killed in a fight outside a dance hall. A man was jailed for his manslaughter.)

James Anthony O'Shaughnessy   Maud Miller

O'Shaughnessy (19), Irish labourer, who was out of work and short of money, had already raided Mrs. Miller's tobacconist's shop twice within the previous few weeks when, on February 17th, he visited it for a third time. He pulled out an iron bar from under his coat, the prosecution alleged, battered the old lady (75), as she tried to stop him opening the till, and got away with about 15/-. She was found with a fractured thigh, caused when she fell over, and a large lump on the back of her head. She died in hospital five weeks later from a blood clot following the fracture.

O'Shaughnessy admitted to going to the shop, but claimed that when he produced the iron bar, Mrs. Miller remained behind the counter and he had not touched her.

At his trial on a charge of capital murder (in course or furtherance of theft) at the *Old Bailey,* defence counsel submitted successfully that there was a break in the link of causation between the events of February 17th and Mrs. Miller's death on March 22nd. The Judge directed the jury to return a formal verdict of *not guilty of capital murder. O'Shaughnessy then pleaded guilty to armed robbery and was sentenced to 4 years' imprisonment, 29.4.1960.*

Florence Margaret Owen   George Martin Semple

Owen (45) took the son (3) of a family who had been friendly towards her for a walk along the cliff-top near Brighton. When "he would not behave", she pushed him over the edge and he was killed on the rocks below.

She was found *guilty but insane at Sussex Assizes, 12.12.1960, and ordered to be detained as a Broadmoor patient during H.M.P.*

Costas Panayi   Arthur Griffin
                                                 David Michael Lacey

Panayi (43) kept a coffee bar in Birmingham. The two victims were the "hard core" of a gang of young men who had been refused admission to Panayi's coffee bar because they had made trouble there before. They returned a while later and refused to leave; they insulted Panayi's wife and threatened to attack her. On an impulse of panic, Panayi picked up a carving knife from the counter and struck Lacey (22); Griffin (24) was stabbed in the ensuing fight. Accused said: "I only tried to protect my wife."

At *Birmingham Assizes, 14.12.1960, prosecution accepted his plea of not guilty to murder but guilty to manslaughter on grounds of provocation, and he was sentenced to 4 years' imprisonment.*

Jessie Isobella Parkinson   Henry Parkinson

Found *unfit to plead at Liverpool Crown Court, 9.2.1960,* on a charge of murdering her son (17 months), Mrs. Parkinson (34), who was divorced, was said to have drowned the child in the bath, then put it to bed. "I didn't want it to suffer any more; it had to die." Her father said at the Magistrates' Court that she had always been more or less mentally unbalanced.

H.M.P.

Frank Payne   Bertha Payne

Payne (63), retired caretaker, was said to have strangled his wife (67) in her sleep because he thought she was suffering; he then tried to commit suicide by cutting his throat and wrists and taking barbiturates. It had been a happy marriage (since 1920), but since the beginning of the year both had suffered from bad health —but not so bad as Payne imagined. Became very depressed.

Found *insane and unfit to plead at Sussex Assizes, 20.7.1960. H.M.P.*

Terry Leonard Penny   Ellen McMillan
James Thake

A fight broke out in a seamen's club in Limehouse during which Thake (36), a haulage contractor, picked up a lighted oil heater and chased people out of the club, saying: "I will kill you." The fight continued in the street and police arrived. Then Penny (20), a driver, picked up the heater and threw it towards the club doorway where a number of people were standing. It hit a wall and burning oil was splashed over several persons including Ellen McMillan (31), a friend of the two accused, who had been with them earlier. She died some weeks later in hospital.

Prosecution offered no evidence against *Thake and he was formally acquitted at the Old Bailey, 20.5.1960. Penny was also acquitted of non-capital murder but found guilty of manslaughter and sentenced to 4 years' imprisonment.*

Mihaly Pocze   Frederick Gallagher

Pocze (25), a Hungarian labourer, battered Gallagher (55) to death with an iron bar in his pawnshop in Blackburn. Between £180 and £200 were missing from the safe, and Pocze was arrested in London.

At his trial at Lancaster Assizes, Pocze pleaded diminished responsibility to a capital murder charge, and evidence was given that he was a high-grade mental defective with an abnormality of mind due to arrested or retarded development.

He was *convicted of murder in course or furtherance of theft, 1.6.1960, and sentenced to death. His appeal to the Court of Criminal Appeal was dismissed,* but he was *reprieved* by the Home Secretary, 4.8.1960, presumably on mental health grounds. *Life imprisonment.*

Josef Popis   Antonio Sebastian Lobo

Popis (52), a Pole, was *found unfit to plead at Chester Assizes, 12.2.1960,* on the capital murder charge of shooting his lodger (37). He had earlier claimed that it had been an accident.

Evidence was given that Popis was suffering from paranoid schizophrenia. He was *ordered to be detained during H.M.P.*

David Francis Posse   Esther Posse
                                                 Walter Posse

Posse (32), a process-artist, protested loudly that he was sane and able to stand trial when he was *found insane and unfit* to plead at the Old Bailey, *2.3.1960,* on the charge of murdering his parents with a bayonet. He said, "I can follow the court procedure. This is an attempt to stop my trial being heard. Can I have an independent medical opinion?"

Principal Medical Officer at Brixton had testified that Posse was suffering from paranoid schizophrenia. He was mentally very ill and his powers of concentration were impaired. *H.M.P.*

Elfinsond Ferdinand Powell   Julia Powell

Powell (50), a Jamaican, twice found his wife (38) in bed with his nephew, and there were continual quarrels between them. She left him and practically "stripped the house". About fourteen days before her death, he received a Magistrates' Court summons from his wife alleging cruelty and desertion. Prosecution said he armed himself with a "switch"-knife and stabbed her in the street in a premeditated plan to kill her. Also battered her with an iron bar.

Powell claimed that as he approached his wife and put his arm around her, she pulled a knife from her bag and cut his hand. In the ensuing struggle, he fell on top of her and she was accidentally stabbed.

Found guilty of manslaughter on grounds of provocation at Bristol Assizes, 1.7.1960, and sentenced to 7 years' imprisonment.

Rita Powell   Albert Powell

Despairing at her husband's unloving attitude towards their children and disgusted by his sexual behaviour with her, Mrs. Powell (30) gave her husband (33) some sleeping tablets, telling him they were to prevent mumps; as he lay in bed she took a hammer and beat him to death. She also tied stockings around his neck and thrust a tea towel in his mouth.

At her trial at *Wiltshire Assizes, 13.5.1960, she was acquitted of non-capital murder but found guilty of manslaughter* (probably under section 3), and *sentenced to 7 years' imprisonment.*

Sidney Aubrey Price   Marian Price

After quarrels over the way she was neglecting their 8 children, Price's wife left to live at a neighbour's house. Price (38), an unemployed miner, went to see her, begged her to come back, but when she refused he went back to their home, picked up an axe and battered two of their children, killing Marian (4 weeks) and injuring a son. He then gave himself up to the police. He was charged with non-capital murder of Marian, and of causing grievous bodily harm with intent to murder his son.

Price was *found guilty but insane at Glamorgan Assizes, 11.7.1960, and ordered to be detained H.M.P.*

Joseph Henry Pyle (see: James Lawrence Nash et al.)

Adolfas Rastenis   Ida Mary Spradbury

The woman who had been living with Rastenis (46), a Lithuanian celluloid dipper, went away on holiday with Miss Spradbury (70), and while on holiday met a man whom she later married. When she returned, she broke with Rastenis and there was a violent quarrel. Rastenis went drinking and was kept in a police cell over-night, charged with being drunk and incapable. While there, he tried to hang himself. An hour or two after being bailed out the next morning, he went to Miss Spradbury's house, broke the glass in the front door with a hammer and when the old lady appeared, holding a knife, he stabbed her with it 11 times. He said he had done it in a fit of temper because the woman had called him a "bloody foreigner" and had "taken Annie from me".

Described as "mentally a very sick man" by the prosecution, Rastenis was *found guilty of manslaughter under section 2 at Leicester Assizes, 26.10.1960. Sentenced to life imprisonment.* Transferred to Broadmoor, 16.12.1960.

James Alexander Read (see: James Lawrence Nash et al.)

Cleveland Reid   Frances Tucker

Reid (32), Jamaican painter and decorator, and Tucker (38), both coloured, lived together in Stepney, but after a quarrel over Reid's possessions at their flat, Reid appeared before Old Street Magistrates' Court (probably on an offence causing a breach of the peace). He was released and the same day returned to the house. Frances Tucker ran out the back way but was seen to go in with Reid. There another quarrel evidently started and Reid grabbed hold of her by her scarf and strangled her. He panicked, threw paraffin all over the place and set fire to it.

In a statement to the police, Reid also referred to improper photographs which he claimed Tucker had taken of him when he was doped, and which she threatened to show to his family. She was known to be in the drug traffic in the East End.

Reid was *convicted of non-capital murder at the Old Bailey, 17.3.1960, and sentenced to life imprisonment.*

George Riley   Adeline Smith

Riley (21), butcher's assistant, was *convicted at Stafford Assizes, 12.12.1960, of the capital murder* (during course or furtherance of theft) of an elderly neighbour (62) whom he had known well. She was found battered to death at her home—but there was no sign of any disturbance and no fingerprints, etc. Riley made a statement to the police in which he "confessed" that he had intended to rob the widow and had brutally murdered her in a panic.

He disputed this statement at his trial and claimed that he had written it down "at the suggestion" of the Detective Inspector in charge. It was noticeable for its conciseness; neatly written, it was not cluttered up with the irrelevant details usually found in such confessions. Also, it was written after Riley had been questioned for several hours. Once they had it in their hands the police looked no further into the case and made no more investigations which might have suggested an alternative culprit. Riley said that he had been out drinking, heavily, and arriving home late, he decided not to disturb his family but slept on a sofa in the garage. He had had a fight earlier in the evening and he suggested that this accounted for some minute specks of blood found on his coat (too small to analyse).

There were other disturbing features:

(1) the whole attitude of the police towards his questioning and investigation;

(2) their failure to produce at the trial two pieces of wallpaper smeared with blood, alleged to have come from the murderer's coat as he left the house;

(3) the woman had been brutally murdered, but no weapon was found and there was no confirmatory evidence of beating from the medical examination of Riley's hands and fingers; and

(4) no evidence of there having been any theft at all.

Riley had a criminal record, including minor offences and, just recently, grievous bodily harm. He was convicted on his confession alone, and *sentenced to death.*

His appeal to the Court of Criminal Appeal was dismissed in 10 minutes, 23.1.1961.

Following an *Observer* article, 6.2.1961, the matter was taken up by several M.P's in the Commons but the Home Secretary refused a reprieve.

Riley was executed at Shrewsbury Prison, 9.2.1961.

See also Blom-Cooper, Louis, "The Trial of George Riley", [1961] Crim.L.R. 292, where the legal points of the case, not touched on during the appeal, are discussed.

Aldrick Rockhead   Brian Cross

Rockhead (26), West Indian labourer, and a voluntary patient in a mental hospital, suddenly escaped, picked up a piece of scaffolding and battered a boy (7) to death in the street. He was alleged to have said: "I did it because I thought they would put me in prison and take me away from the hospital."

Rockhead was undergoing treatment for paranoid schizophrenia. *Found unfit to plead at Birmingham Assizes, 14.7.1960. Ordered to be kept in strict custody, H.M.P.*

Adolphus Augustus Rodney   Beatrice Elgiva Douglas

Rodney (29), a Jamaican metal shearer, became very jealous and depressed when the woman (31) with whom he was living became friendly with another man and told him she was not going to marry him. He battered her to death with an axe which he had borrowed from a neighbour.

At *Stafford Assizes, 12.12.1960, found guilty of manslaughter on grounds of diminished responsibility and sentenced to 5 years' imprisonment.*

John Rogers   William Tripp

Rogers (20), a brewery clerk, armed himself with a sawn-off shotgun and hired a taxi in Bristol intending to rob the driver when they got to a lonely stretch of road in order to get money to pay for his trip to a jazz festival in Hampshire. Whether by design or by accident in a panic (as Rogers claimed), he shot the driver, robbed him and spent the week-end at the festival and in London.

Rogers was *convicted at Somerset Assizes, 20.10.1960, of capital murder (in course or furtherance of theft) and sentenced to death.*

His appeal to the Court of Criminal Appeal was on grounds that the Judge had not put before the jury the submissions made on behalf of the accused; neither had he invited the attention of the jury to the evidence of witnesses for the prosecution which tended to support Rogers' case that it was an accident. *Appeal was dismissed 21.11.1960, The Times Law Report, 22.11.1960.*

A petition for reprieve was signed and presented to the Home Secretary by W. A. Wilkins, M.P. for Bristol.

Rogers was reprieved, 7.12.1960, on the grounds, it is thought, that there was a scintilla of doubt. *Life imprisonment.*

[Authors' note: It is an inviolable practice for the Home Secretary not to disclose the reasons for his decision whether or not to grant a reprieve in any particular case. It was widely assumed that Rogers' reprieve was due to his mental condition, but it appears, from what we have been able to discover, that ballistics experts informed the Home Office that it was possible the shotgun went off accidentally. The reprieve would in those circumstances have been granted on the grounds that there was a "scintilla of doubt" about the correctness of the jury's verdict.]

William Lawrence Ross   Eva Booth

Mrs. Booth (71), a widow, was found dead at her Plymouth home. Her body, showing signs of severe beating, was found in a cupboard, but she had died as a result of pressure on the mouth. In spite of extensive police investigations, the culprit was not found for five months until Ross (18), a shipwright apprentice on remand in Exeter Prison on another charge, started boasting to fellow-prisoners that he had committed the crime. Interviewed by the police, Ross confessed, but certain details of his story did not fit in with the facts as established, and he changed his account two or three times, maintaining all the while that he had killed Mrs. Booth.

He said that he was burgling her home when he saw someone behind him; he turned and hit the woman with a bunch of keys which he was carrying, took her upstairs and put her in a cupboard after she had started to struggle again and he had hit her. He searched for money, but found none, and left. Threw his gloves and the bunch of keys away.

The woman's injuries were not consistent with being hit with the keys, neither did the keys fit the door of the house, as Ross said they did. Nevertheless some of the important details in Ross's story fitted in, and it would seem that he was on the scene of the crime. At *Devon Assizes, 10.11.1960*, the jury, on the direction of the Judge, *acquitted him of capital murder but found him guilty of manslaughter. He was sentenced to 4 years' imprisonment.*

There was some evidence that Ross had had an unhappy and broken home life. He had a number of convictions for minor delinquency and was described as suffering from some sort of inferiority feeling which led him to brag and boast a lot.

Amelia Caroline Rowley   Stephen Rowley

Mrs. Rowley (39) strangled one of her three children, Stephen (5), with a silk stocking at her home, and then tried to revive him by massage. In a statement to the police, Mrs. Rowley, who lived at home with her husband and children and was described by the prosecution as "of perfectly good character and fond of her children", was alleged to have said: "It all began when I had Keith. No one seemed to want to get near to me. They said I was rotten."

Mrs. Rowley was said to be suffering from a schizophrenic illness with a severe depression; she had delusions both of persecution and about her health. First signs of mental abnormality had appeared after the birth of her third child.

Defence plea of diminished responsibility successful and she was found guilty of manslaughter under section 2. Sentenced to life imprisonment at the Old Bailey, 18.7.1960. Transferred to Broadmoor, 2.8.1960.

Mohammed Sajawal   Mohammed Sultan

Sajawal (25), a Pakistani, pleaded not guilty to non-capital murder but *guilty to manslaughter* of his nephew (27) at *Birmingham Assizes, 23.3.1960.* Plea accepted. *Sentenced to 2 years' imprisonment.*

Sultan was stabbed with a flick-knife in a street fight which was evidently the culmination of a continuous feud between groups of Pakistanis living in Birmingham. Sajawal's action was probably impulsive under provocation. A second charge, of maliciously wounding another man with intent to cause grievous bodily harm, was not proceeded with.

Basil Scarlett (see: Leonard Thomas et al.)

Gurdev Singh (see: Jugtar Singh et al.)

Joginder Singh (see: Jugtar Singh et al.)

Jugtar Singh (27), labourer.   Sarwan Singh
Joginder Singh (29), labourer.
Gurdev Singh (33), labourer.
Swarn Singh (37), labourer.
Sadhu Singh (40), moulder.

The five accused, all Indians, were alleged to have beaten another fellow-countryman (33) to death during a street fight outside a public house in Coventry. Others were also involved in what was probably a kin feud.

At *Birmingham Assizes, 27.7.1960, the first four, Jugtar S., Joginder S., Gurdev S., and Swarn S., were all convicted of non-capital murder and sentenced to life imprisonment. Sadhu S., was found not guilty of either murder or manslaughter.*

All were charged with maliciously wounding three other men; charges not proceeded with except in the case of Sadhu Singh. No details of this prosecution are available.

Sadhu Singh (see: Jugtar Singh et al.)

Swarn Singh (see: Jugtar Singh et al.)

Barry Charles Smallman   Jean Harrison

Smallman (19), labourer and local rock-n'-roll singer, strangled his girl friend (17) during sexual intercourse in a wood. He claimed that she had dared him to do so and he had done it in a fit of temper. There was plenty of evidence that intercourse was with the girl's consent and had been performed on several occasions before. Smallman had been drinking heavily.

He *pleaded guilty to non-capital murder at Shropshire Assizes, 25.11.1960, and was sentenced to life imprisonment.*

Ernest Smedley   Jesse Maskery

Smedley (72), the landlord of a lodging house, was apparently under delusions that lodgers at his home were teaming up with his wife against him; after returning from a drinking session, he battered one of his lodgers (40) to death by beating his head against the wall.

Smedley had been certified, had mental and physical disease which affected his mind and suffered from chronic delusional insanity. He had been a patient in a mental hospital five times.

He was *found guilty but insane at Nottinghamshire Assizes, 29.6.1960, and ordered to be detained during H.M.P.*

Arthur John Smith   Phyllis Pearce

Smith (20), a shipwright, who had been drinking, bumped into Mrs. Pearce (48) in the road; when she told him to get out of the way, he pulled out a sheath knife and stabbed her. His father later threw his knife into Portsmouth Harbour.

Smith *pleaded guilty at Hampshire Assizes to non-capital murder and was sentenced to life imprisonment, 11.7.1960.*

Jim Smith   (P.-C.) Leslie Meehan

Smith (26), a gypsy dealer, and another man were in a car containing stolen metal when they were approached by Police Constable Meehan (34). The car was seen to accelerate, but Meehan hung on to it and was hit by two or three cars coming in the opposite direction before being thrown on to the road where he was run over by a bubble-car and killed.

Smith's defence at the *Old Bailey* was that, although he was trying to avoid arrest, he never had any intention of killing or doing grievous bodily harm to P.-C. Meehan, and his counsel asked for a verdict of manslaughter. *Smith was convicted of capital murder and sentenced to death, 7.4.1960.*

Smith appealed to the Court of Criminal Appeal on grounds that Mr. Justice Donovan's summing up and direction might have led the jury to consider they were entitled to infer guilty intent. The Judge had introduced the test of the "reasonable man" rather than Smith's actual intent at the time of the killing. *Appeal was successful and the conviction was reduced to manslaughter and sentence to 10 years' imprisonment substituted.*

The Director of Public Prosecutions then obtained leave to appeal against this judgment and take the case to the *House of Lords.* There it was ruled that the Court of Criminal Appeal's "subjective" approach to the problem of intent (i.e. what was in *Smith's* mind rather than what would be the attitude of "the reasonable man") was contrary to the normal approach of the English courts and that the original (Old Bailey) approach had been the correct one. The *verdict of capital murder and the sentence of death were restored, 28.7.1960:* [1961] A.C. 290. The Home Secretary had already announced that in the event of this reversal, a *reprieve* would be granted, so that *Smith's final sentence was life imprisonment.*

[Author's note: This case raised issues of quite exceptional importance in the field of English Criminal Law. It is usual in the House of Lords for each Law Lord to deliver a judgment. Unusually one judgment is given. In this case, the Lord Chancellor, Lord Kilmuir delivered the one judgment. But, on good authority it is believed that the judgment was written by the Lord Chief Justice, Lord Parker, who was a member of the Court. The other members of the Court were Lord Goddard, a former Lord Chief Justice, Lord Tucker, and Lord Denning, who subsequently (and particularly on a lecture tour the following summer in Israel) sought to explain away the unfortunate effect of the decision. Since the case, there has been a movement away from the rigid application of the objective test of intent. The legal profession generally regards the decision as wrong, and to be confined in the future only to its particular facts. See, for example, R. v. Grimwood [1962] 2 Q.B. 621. The High Court of Australia recently said that while hitherto it had adopted the policy of loyally accepting the decisions of the House of Lords it would no longer adhere to that policy. The Chief Justice of Australia, Sir Owen Dixon, speaking for all the members of Australia's highest Court, said that the decision in Smith's case was palpably "misconceived and wrong"; the case would not be used as a judicial authority in Australia at all: see Parker v. The Queen, *The Times* Law Report, 12 June 1963.]

Wesley Smith (see: Leonard Thomas et al.)

Dominik Soltysiak   Rose Haywood

Soltysiak (46), a Pole, was *sentenced to life imprisonment at Stafford Assizes, 3.3.1960, for the murder* of the woman with whom he was living. The prosecution alleged that he cut Mrs. Haywood's (40) throat in the street after leaving a working men's club where they had been drinking.

Michael Roland Stimson   Doreen Elsie Stimson

After going to see a couple of horror films, Stimson (20), a confectioner, came home and, in a brainstorm, stabbed his aunt (33) four times with a Boy Scout knife when she started nagging him. At the *Old Bailey, 9.9.1960, prosecution accepted his plea of guilty to wounding her with intent to cause grievous bodily harm.* (The woman had died from a pulmonary embolism in a lung *not* affected by the stab wounds. She died ten days after the incident, and the stabbing was not a contributory factor to the death).

Stimson, who was backward and had a defect of speech, was constantly teased by his workmates and nagged by his aunt, with whom he lived. She was always throwing in his face the fact that he was illegitimate.

Stimson was placed on probation for 3 years, with the condition that he receive hospital treatment for 12 months.

Michael James Stockton   Unnamed newly-born male child

Stockton (26), electrical fitter, put a towel over the child's head as soon as his wife gave birth to it, since neither of them wanted another baby. The body was found at Stockton's home in a cardboard box by a police-constable who had gone there on a different matter.

At *Bedford Assizes, 11.5.1960,* the prosecution offered no evidence on the charge of non-capital murder and *Stockton was formally acquitted.* He *pleaded guilty to endeavouring to conceal the birth of the child* by secretly disposing of the child's body—was *sentenced to 10 months' imprisonment.*

William Studley   Margaret Studley

Studley (42), farmer, was *found guilty but insane at Chester Assizes, 7.6.1960,* of the murder of his wife (39). It was alleged that he had attacked her with a hammer while she was in bed.

Studley had had a nervous breakdown and evidence was given that he was suffering from schizophrenia. He had been asked to go into hospital but was unwilling to do so.

Ordered to be detained at Broadmoor during H.M.P.

Istvan Szabo   William Davies

Prosecution alleged that Szabo (21), a Hungarian, went to Davies' (55) flat, stabbed him in the chest and stole a cigarette case and wallet. He then put the knife in the man's hand to make it appear that Davies had stabbed himself; the pathologist said that, as it was found in the hand, the knife could not have caused the injury.

Szabo claimed that Davies, a complete stranger, stopped him in the street and invited him to his flat for a drink. There, Davies made homosexual suggestions to him and discovered a dagger-type knife in Szabo's trousers. A struggle followed in which the knife, held by Davies, went into his chest.

Szabo was *acquitted of capital murder but found guilty of non-capital murder and sentenced to life imprisonment at the Old Bailey, 16.12.1960.* The Judge said: "Should you be released, I recommend that you be deported to the country from which you came."

John Barry Tapper   Maureen Tapper

Tapper (25), lorry driver, who was separated from his wife (24), visited her at her lodgings to ask her if he could take out their child, over whom she had custody. She refused and a violent quarrel arose during which Tapper picked up a knife and stabbed her 52 times.

Tapper pleaded guilty, at York Assizes, to non-capital murder and was sentenced to life imprisonment, 7.11.1960.

James Thake (see: Terry Leonard Penny)

Leonard Thomas (34)   Maurice Britton (30)
Basil Scarlett (23)
Henry Atkinson (28)
Wesley Smith (27)

Four West Indians were charged with non-capital murder of Britton after he had been stabbed during a brawl in a public house in Ipswich where he worked as a barman.

At the *Old Bailey, 28.11.1960* and *6.12.1960, Thomas and Scarlett were acquitted of murder and manslaughter, and discharged. Atkinson and Smith were both convicted of manslaughter* (Atkinson had apparently carried and used the knife), and were *sentenced to 5 years' and 18 months' imprisonment respectively.* Smith alone appealed to the Court of Criminal Appeal (consisting of five judges) on 6 and 7 November 1961; his appeal against conviction was dismissed.

George Todd　　　　　　　　　　　　　　Frederick Blenkey

Todd (35), an unemployed engine fitter, killed his landlord (50) by strangling him during an argument at their home after returning from drinking. He hid the body in the coal cellar but did not go to the police for some weeks.

Defence at *York Assizes, 4.11.1960,* did not call Todd to give evidence and brought no other evidence. Todd "had gone downhill with heavy drinking, and beer had become the ruling force of his life". On the night in question, it was said, Blenkey had been drinking more than usual, and the argumentative side of his nature came out. There was never any intention by Todd to do harm or injury to Blenkey whose death was accidental.

Found guilty of non-capital murder, the jury adding a recommendation for mercy; sentenced to life imprisonment.

Norman Tomlinson　　　　　　　　　　　Carol Tomlinson

Tomlinson (37), an unemployed textile worker, who was in the throes of a severe depression and was going to enter a mental hospital for treatment on the day in question, conceived the idea that if he killed someone he would be charged and put to death for the offence; he wanted to die. After his wife had got up in the morning, he strangled his daughter (4), then went to the police soon afterwards.

Medical evidence that he was suffering from melancholia at the time; had attempted suicide three times before; had recurrent depressions. *Found guilty of manslaughter under section 2 and sentenced to life imprisonment at Leeds Assizes, 22.7.1960.*

James Edward Towell　　　　　　　　　　Michael Hanley

Towell (21), a painter, joined his landlord, with his friends, and some fellow lodgers in the kitchen of the restaurant above which they lived. Over the meal, an argument arose during which Hanley, a fellow lodger, punched Towell who was holding a carving knife by his side, and almost at once Towell pushed it into Hanley's body. Towell claimed that although he had been slightly drunk, he knew what was happening. "When he punched me, I did not realise I was still holding the knife in my hand . . . it all happened as an accident."

Found not guilty of both non-capital murder and manslaughter at the Old Bailey, 8.12.1960. Discharged.

Robert James Townsend   Louis Cassell

Townsend (38), a collector, who had been dismissed from his previous employment for stealing money, was alleged by the prosecution to have taken a tyre-lever with him when he visited the office of an old moneylender (87) and to have beaten him to death with it. It was claimed that he then took a number of white £5 notes, two of which were passed in the next few days by the accused. Townsend's thumb print was found on a receipt book in the office.

Accused admitted that he had been in financial difficulties but claimed he had posed as a manager in order to borrow £20 from Cassell (i.e. in white £5 notes). He admitted visiting the office on the day of the crime and having picked up the receipt book from the floor when Cassell knocked it off his desk, but denied any part in the crime.

He was *acquitted of capital murder at Worcestershire Assizes, 1.2.1960, and discharged after jury was out for 4 hours.*

Michael Twells   Angela Greaves

Twells (23), coalman, forced a girl (12) off her bicycle in a lonely lane, pursued her down a footpath, then strangled her and cut her thoat with his sheath knife. No attempt at sexual interference.

Three doctors for the defence at Nottingham Assizes gave evidence that Twells' mind was substantially impaired at the time and he was *convicted of manslaughter under section 2. Sentenced to life imprisonment, 21.11.1960.*

Sophie Walsh   Mark Walsh

Mrs. Walsh (28), described by her husband as "a good and loving wife and mother devoted to her children", had apparently strangled her son (18 months) and attempted to kill her other two sons by stabbing and strangulation. She was reported as saying: "It just happened. I just felt the urge. Someone was telling me to kill for God ... I weren't intent to murder the child. I thought they had the devil. It was the devil I was trying to kill."

Found insane and unfit to plead at Lancaster Assizes, 30.5.1960, and ordered to be detained during H.M.P.

Herbert Oswald Ward   Ada Roberts

Ward (61), an unemployed miner, stabbed his neighbour, a

spinster (68), in the backyard which their two houses shared, after a quarrel over a "trivial matter". He used a carving knife with which he was chopping wood at the time.

Defence pleaded diminished responsibility at the trial at Nottingham Assizes and evidence was given that Ward suffered from periodic coughing fits caused by his bronchial condition, and one of these could have affected his mind temporarily because of reduction of oxygen supply to the blood cells. "This could cause confusion, excitement, loss of memory."

Ward, *convicted of manslaughter under section 2, was sentenced to 10 years' imprisonment, 23.11.1960.*

Samuel Johnston Wiggins   Helen de Georgio

Wiggins (27), an Irish labourer, picked up Mrs. Georgio (55), a prostitute, and went with her to her room. There, perhaps after a quarrel, he stabbed her to death with a penknife. He was traced through the numbers on four new £1 notes found in the woman's bag, given to her as payment, and which he had received in change for a fiver in a chemist's shop.

At his trial at *Manchester Crown Court, 29.11.1960,* he was described as "a pitiful figure" and *convicted of manslaughter* (under section 2); *sentenced to 4 years' imprisonment.* He had a mental age of 9 years and was unable to make friends of either sex.

Alfred Williams   Marion Williams

Williams (39), a Jamaican labourer, was *convicted at Birmingham Assizes, 18.3.1960, of murdering his wife* (33). It was alleged that Williams was bitter and jealous because his wife had left him and suspicious that she was associating with another man. He traced her to her lodgings and stabbed her 17 times with a knife which he carried.

Williams denied that he had any intention of killing his wife, and said that he lost his temper and stabbed her after she threw a bottle at him.

Sentenced to life imprisonment.

Azariah Williams   Raymond Hall

Hall (22) behaved very provocatively towards Williams (37), a Jamaican factory hand, and another man over a period at the factory where they worked, interfered with their work and threw coal dust in Williams' face. Williams never retaliated until Hall jumped on him one day and the two men fought; Williams sustained a fractured nose and the pair were separated by the foreman. As he walked away, however, Williams picked up an iron bar and struck Hall with it, since he was afraid Hall was going to hit him with a shovel.

At *Gloucestershire Assizes, convicted of manslaughter and sentenced to 3 years' imprisonment, 27.5.1960.*

Frank Alexander Williams (21), an unemployed
   builder's labourer.   William Southon (50)
Herbert James Marsh (32), a builder's labourer

It was alleged that Southon, who lived alone and was reputed to keep a lot of money near him, was killed by having a gag thrust forcibly into his mouth, after Marsh and Williams had followed him to his home that night. The place had been ransacked and the two men were caught red-handed on the spot after a neighbour had become suspicious and called the police.

A specialist, called for the defence of Williams, said that Southon had an extremely rare case of adenoids. He had seen only three similar cases out of 10,000, where a mass of adenoids obstructed breathing to any degree in middle age. The indications were that Southon did not necessarily die from having a gag thrust into his mouth forcing the tongue back. *Both accused were acquitted of capital murder but found guilty of manslaughter at Kent Assizes, 15.7.1960. Marsh was sentenced to 10 years' imprisonment and Williams to 4 years'.*

William Clifford Workman   Janice Workman

Workman (52), a labourer, was *found insane and unfit to plead at the Old Bailey, 18.5.1960,* on a charge of stabbing his daughter (6) at their home. He was also charged with the attempted murder of his wife who had been found, at the same time, with serious throat wounds. *H.M.P.*

He was apparently devoted to his family. A neighbour heard a bump and a scream, and went next door to find the daughter dead (an hour earlier) with stab wounds in the neck and the wife also with knife wounds in the throat. Workman himself had superficial lacerations on his arm. In hospital afterwards he said, "My darlings, you are out of it all now". He said he had chest pains and had been severely depressed.

An 11 year-old boy   Iris Dawkins

An 11 year-old boy was alleged by the prosecution to have frenziedly stabbed a 9 year-old playmate 39 times in a park near their home. During questioning, the boy made three very conflicting and confused statements to the police concerning the incident which occurred during games in the park, but his "confession" was not substantiated by further investigations. The murder weapon was never in fact discovered. No evidence of sexual interference.

He was found not guilty upon the direction of the Judge after he had agreed with the defence that there was insufficient evidence. *Discharged. Winchester Assizes, 13.7.1960.*

A 15 year-old boy   James Michael Ullah

The accused, who was in a children's home, strangled, with his belt, an Anglo-Pakistani child (8) who also lived in the home. The boy's body was found in the orphanage grounds after a search.

At *Northampton Assizes, 19.10.1960*, the defence submitted, in a plea of diminished responsibility, that the accused was suffering from a mental abnormality springing from a retarded or arrested development, emotional in character. In a statement to police, the accused had said: "I wanted to get away from here. That's why I did it."

He was *found guilty of manslaughter under section 2 and ordered to be detained for 10 years, 19.10.1960, under section 53(2) of the Children and Young Persons Act 1933 (as amended by section 9 of the Homicide Act 1957).*

1961

William Henry Abernethy   Arthur Charles Henwood

Abernethy (34), a labourer, had been friendly with a girl, previously engaged to Henwood (34). They continued to see each other. Abernethy found the girl and Henwood in a car in the street (they had been looking for Abernethy), whereupon Abernethy stabbed Henwood 19 times. He told the police: "I was mad with jealousy—hatred if you like."

At *Durham Assizes, 30.5.1961, Abernethy was found not guilty of murder but guilty of manslaughter under section 2.* Defence doctor said he was abnormal, but not insane, and the ferocity of the attack was in keeping with a possible epileptic seizure. He was *sentenced by Mr. Justice Austin Jones to life imprisonment.*

Harry Stanley Adams   Rosemary Adams

Adams (25) was a crane driver, whose wife (34) had been committing adultery with another man. On 21 June she asked Adams to take her back, but went on seeing the other man. On 26 June, Adams was upset and stayed at home; his wife went out and returned in the evening saying nothing. Adams could not sleep and in the night strangled her. They had two children.

At *Birmingham Assizes, 21.7.1961,* Adams was *found guilty of murder and sentenced to life imprisonment.* Leave to appeal to the Court of Criminal Appeal refused, 11.12.1961. The Court held that provocation was available as a defence to murder only so long as the action of the person provoked bore some reasonable relationship to the type of provocation received (see *The Guardian* Law Report, 12.12.1961). This conduct, even the breaking of promises to return and taunting Adams with the other man's sexual prowess, did not in these circumstances amount to provocation in law because the taunting did not operate at the time of killing. Jury strongly recommended mercy.

Hassan Mahamad Adan   Noel Morgan

Adan (59), a Somali, was employed as a cook in a Stepney café. Morgan (28) and some other seamen had a meal there and then were involved in a fight over the bill in which Adan was alleged to have stabbed Morgan with a dagger. Adan denied the dagger was his or that he worked or was involved in the room where the fight occurred.

At the *Old Bailey, 21.11.1961*, Adan was *found not guilty of murder and discharged.* Only one witness claimed to have seen him strike the blow. The jury stopped the case.

John Airey   Patricia Airey

Airey (32), a builder's labourer, stabbed his wife (25) and later admitted doing it. They had been living apart. He said, "I thought if she was going to live away on her own, life would not be worth living, so I thought I would kill her and I would get hung and we would both go together."

At *Cumberland Assizes, 5.10.1961*, Airey was *found not guilty of murder but guilty of manslaughter under section 2.* Doctors said he had physical damage to his brain and he was abnormal within section 2. He was *sentenced to life imprisonment* by Mr. Justice Fenton Atkinson.

Khan Asfar   Mohammed Younis Khan

Asfar (30), a Pakistani, stabbed his cousin (25) several times with a sheath knife in a fight in the street. He told the police: "This man has been giving me a lot of trouble. He has been drugging me." He admitted the crime.

At *Birmingham Assizes, 13.12.1961*, Asfar was *found guilty but insane, and detained during H.M.P.* He had been an outpatient in a mental hospital.

Samuel Leo Thomas Ashworth   Lisbeth Ashworth

Ashworth (38), a Warrant Officer in the Army, was quarrelling with this third wife who wanted his six children by a previous marriage to be adopted when they went to Germany on duty. During the row she said . . . "choose between me and the children", whereupon Ashworth hit her on the head with a bottle, and strangled her.

At *Berkshire Assizes, 21.1.1961, Ashworth was found not guilty of murder but guilty of manslaughter. Sentence—4 years' imprisonment.*

Leonard Edward Askham   Helen Patricia Johnston

Askham (22), a Royal Navy engineer mechanic, had been living with Mrs. Johnston (25) for 12 months before she decided to leave him and return to her husband. Askham said: "She kept on and on until I could stand it no longer. I saw red." He then strangled her. Since she was not robust, only a little pressure was required. Askham said he had no intention of killing her.

At *Hampshire Assizes, 8.12.1961, Askham was found not guilty of non-capital murder but guilty of manslaughter. He was sentenced to 3 years' imprisonment.*

Daniel Attard (see: Xanthos Zacharia et al.)

Rodney William Bailey   Sandra Pickering

Bailey (17), a farm labourer, battered his victim (16) on the head with a blunt instrument, causing injuries from which she died. The crime occurred at night in a country lane.

Bailey suffered for several years from epilepsy and apparently had a blackout just before meeting the girl. He told the police he had a number of blackouts and then got an "urge to do something to clear my mind".

At *Leicester Assizes, 25.5.1961*, three experienced doctors said that Bailey came within section 2 in that he was abnormal owing to epilepsy. The prosecution did not dispute this and Mr. Justice Hinchcliffe told the jury the evidence was "all one way". Despite this, the jury brought in a verdict of murder and *Bailey was sentenced to be detained during H.M.P.* under section 53(2) of the Children and Young Persons Act 1933.

On 23.10.1961, the Court of Criminal Appeal allowed Bailey's appeal. The Court held that, while the jury was not bound by what medical witnesses said, it must act on the evidence and if there were nothing to throw doubts on the medical evidence, the jury was bound to accept the uncontroverted medical evidence. Nothing that the Court had said in Byrne (1960) threw any doubt on the decision in Matheson (1958). In these circumstances the Court of Criminal Appeal would conclude that the verdict of the jury was unreasonable.

A verdict of manslaughter under section 2 was substituted for that of murder; and the sentence varied to one of life imprisonment: [1961] Crim.L.R. 828.

[Authors' note: Compare this case with the case where there *is* evidence other than of a strictly medical character which the jury can take into account in deciding whether diminished responsibility is established. See Ahmed Din (1961).]

Rose Vera Baker   Martha McGee

Baker (34), a patient in a mental hospital, strangled a fellow patient with a sheet because she annoyed her by singing.

At *Essex Assizes, 1.11.1961, she was found unfit to plead. She was detained during H.M.P.* She had been suffering from mental illness, and had been a patient for seven years.

Shirley Barker   Lee Jeffrey Barker

Barker (25) was pregnant at the time of killing her son (3). She already had four children and was very distressed with her pregnancy. "I could not face starting again nappy-washing and bottle feeding." Lee was dirty and played her up. Barker apparently broke his spine. He was also bruised. She could not remember how it was done at all.

At *Leeds Assizes, 2.5.1961, Barker was found not guilty of murder but guilty of manslaughter* on the ground that she had no intention to do any serious injury. The jury recommended mercy. *She was put on probation for 3 years.*

Horace George Barrett   Julie Barrett

Barrett (21), a baker's assistant, had a row with his wife over the choice of television programmes. After he struck her, she left the baby and him alone in the house for thirty minutes. During this time the baby started to cry and Barrett attacked it, breaking four ribs and rupturing the liver.

At *Nottingham Assizes, 27.2.1961, Barrett was found guilty of non-capital murder and sentenced to life imprisonment.* The Court of Criminal Appeal dismissed an appeal, 3.11.1961, based on a defence submission of no intention to kill. The severity of the injuries negatived such a submission. (See *The Guardian* Law Report, 4.11.1961).

Lemuel Bartley   Eulalie Henry

Bartley (30), a Jamaican, spent all his money on his mistress (20). One day when the girl said she was leaving him for another man, Bartley visited her and in an argument, stabbed her 37 times. He then went and told the police: "I am vexed and annoyed . . .I keep hitting her." "I would like to hang."

At *Birmingham Assizes, 12.12.1961*, Bartley was *found not guilty of murder, but guilty of manslaughter under provocation*, as she said she was leaving. *He was jailed for 7 years.*

Douglas Bates   John William Phillips

Bates (44) and his wife had cared for her father, Phillips (74), for 12 years. Phillips was partly paralysed and suffered from silicosis. Bates was alleged to have strangled him with his scarf, but said he simply put it round his neck at his request as he was cold. The Home Office pathologist said death was due to strangulation, while the defence said it was due to heart failure caused by pneumonia.

At *Warwick Assizes, 9.3.1961, Bates was found not guilty of murder or manslaughter and was discharged.*

Kenneth Black   Christakis Phitides

Black (22), a Jamaican, was involved in a fight in a coffee bar with Phitides (20), a Cypriot, and another man. According to witnesses, Phitides was pushed into Black, who drew a knife and stabbed him three times. Black went berserk and was wild and screaming.

At *Birmingham Assizes, 20.7.1961, Black was found guilty of noncapital murder and sentenced to life imprisonment.* In the defence submission, Black used the knife, which he carried on him, only when he was attacked, i.e. in self-defence. Black said he used it only on Phitides' friend and not on Phitides himself. Black was of previous good character.

Robert Bernard Black   William Walker

Black (27) killed Walker (30) in a fight. Walker had been associating with Black's wife and had fathered her child. The wife had left Black some time previously, but at the time of the offence was no longer living with Walker. Walker had also smashed the furniture at Mrs. Black's home after Black had told him that she was a loose woman. Black said that Walker had started the fight.

At *Manchester Crown Court, 22.3.1961, Black pleaded guilty to manslaughter and was sentenced to 3 years' imprisonment:* he had told the police the killing was unintentional.

Aston Bolt   Ellen Chapman

Bolt (35), a Jamaican labourer, broke into Mrs. Chapman's (37) bedroom and slashed her 18 times with a razor. He also injured two of her children who came to her aid. He later admitted the crime to the police. He said they had been friendly for 2 years and he was the father of her baby. That day she had told him to leave and not return. He said he did not know what he was doing when he slashed her.

At *Maidstone Assizes, 27.11.1961, Bolt was found guilty of murder and sentenced to life imprisonment.*

Willis Eugene Boshears   Jean Sylvia Constable

Boshears (29), a U.S.A.F. Staff-Sergeant, married with three children, met Jean Constable (20) and another man in a pub on New Year's Eve. After drinks they all went to Boshears' flat where the other man had intercourse with the girl. Later she went to sleep on a mattress on the floor. The other man left and Boshears lay down beside her and passed out. "The next thing I remember was something scratching . . . at my throat. Jean was lying there under me and I had my hands round her throat: she was dead then." He panicked, dressed the girl, cut her hair to prevent recognition and two days later dumped the body in a ditch.

At *Essex Assizes, 21.2.1961,* Mr. Justice Glyn-Jones told the jury: "This woman died of asphyxia, suffocation, and Dr. Camps has told you of the stages through which she must have passed before she died. Firstly, a struggling or resisting by her even if involuntary; secondly, she must have sunk into unconsciousness, next there must have been a convulsion, and finally her death. Dr. Camps said how long all that took would be a matter of conjecture. He said it might be half a minute, but it would be an appreciable length of time." Mr. Justice Glyn-Jones urged the jurors to use their commonsense.

"Have you ever heard of a man strangling a woman while he was sound asleep? We have no medical evidence that there exists any record, in all the records of the medical profession, that such a thing has ever happened." The Judge continued: "Is it, do you think, reasonably within the bounds of possibility that this man could have moved from his position beside the girl, removing any covering that might have been upon him, removed the blanket which was covering her, and so arranged himself that she was lying on her back, that he was sprawled across her facing downward, that he could then have extended his hand and applied the pressure, and continued to apply it, while she passed through all the stages of resistance, unconsciousness, convulsion and death without his being awakened either by his own exertions or by her struggles? Do you really think such a thing could happen?" The jury thought it could. There was a doubt, which had to be resolved in the accused's favour.

Boshears was found not guilty and discharged.

Dora Bradley   James Bradley

Bradley (31) was the mother of seven children. Her husband (31) punched and maltreated her until she could stand it no longer. After a row, he tipped over the washing machine and threw a bowl at her, whereupon she stabbed him once, with a small kitchen knife. She told the police: "I did it. I'd had enough. I couldn't stand it any longer. He was drunk." She had frequently been beaten up.

At *Stafford Assizes, 27.11.1961, Bradley was acquitted of non-capital murder, and discharged.*

Terence Brennan   Thomas McKeown
Frank James Murrow
George Raymond Monaghan
James Anthony Shiels

Brennan (19), an R.A.F. Serviceman, Murrow (21), labourer, Monaghan (21), labourer, and Shiels (23), dumper driver, set out to beat up McKeown (19), who had attacked one of their friends. McKeown suffered a scalp wound, but died nine days later of tetanus. His wound was probably caused by injuries inflicted by "winklepicker" shoes.

At *Liverpool Crown Court, 20.4.1961, all were found not guilty of murder, but guilty of manslaughter.* Brennan was *sent to prison for 18 months, as were Murrow and Monaghan. Shiels got 2 years.*

Daniel Brocks   Tom Bouling Simpson

Brocks (37) was a patient in a mental institution. He was charged with the murder of a fellow patient (56), who was killed in a scuffle.

At *Leeds Assizes, 10.3.1961, he was found unfit to plead and detained during H.M.P.* He had been in hospitals since 1950 as an advanced schizophrenic. It was impossible to contact him; he could not tell right from wrong and would not understand a plea. He had a long history of mental illness.

Richard William Bryant   Mary Bryant

Bryant (79), a Naval pensioner, strangled his wife with a dressing gown cord at home. They were devoted to each other.

At *Hampshire Assizes, 23.3.1961, Bryant was found not guilty of murder but guilty of manslaughter under section 2.* Doctors said he suffered from arterio-sclerosis. Mr. Justice Elwes made a hospital order with restriction for 12 months under sections 60 and 65 of the Mental Health Act.

Edwin Albert Arthur Bush   Elsie May Batten

Bush (21), a labourer, was the son of a Pakistani father and English mother. He made enquiries at a curio shop just off Charing Cross Road about a ceremonial sword. The body of Mrs. Batten, who worked in the curio shop, was found some time later with three daggers in it and the skull fractured by a stone jar. Bush said that she had called him a "nigger" and "I lost my head and hit her with the stone. I cannot remember much after that".

At the *Old Bailey, 12.5.1961, Bush was found guilty of capital murder (in the course or furtherance of theft) and sentenced to death.* His appeal to the Court of Criminal Appeal was dismissed. A petition was refused by the Home Secretary: its grounds were:

(1) Bush had had an appalling life as a product of a broken mixed marriage and had been in an orphanage. The L.C.C. Children's Department said he was emotionally immature.

(2) The killing was unconnected with the theft. He went berserk when called "nigger".

Bush was executed at Pentonville, 6.7.1961.

Albert Edward Cannon   Doris Mabel Cannon

Cannon (55), a painter and decorator, killed his wife (57) by hitting her head with a piece of wood. They were married in 1937 but had not been happy. She would not grant him a divorce. He made a full confession to the police.

At *Leeds Assizes, 19.7.1961, Cannon pleaded guilty to non-capital murder and was sentenced to life imprisonment.*

Richard Clark   Florence Clark

Clark (38), a builder's labourer, walked into the police station and said he had strangled his wife (33), who was found lying on the scullery floor. They had been fighting.

At *Hants Assizes, 16.3.1961, Clark was found guilty but insane and detained during H.M.P.* A psychiatrist, whose evidence was uncontested, said Clark was a paranoid schizophrenic and did not know he was doing wrong. He "believed his wife was, in some way, destroying him by exercising a malign influence over him". He had spent three periods as a voluntary mental patient; in 1959 left hospital against medical advice.

Jack Clarkson   John Francis Walsh

Clarkson (18), a zoo attendant, was walking with his girl friend in the street after they had been drinking together. Walsh (40), a rag gatherer, was also drunk and was offensive about the girl and Clarkson's mother, whereupon Clarkson drew a sheath-knife and stabbed Walsh seven times. Walsh had shown no violence. The accused had no record of violence.

At *Chester Assizes, 29.10.1961, he pleaded guilty to non-capital murder and was sentenced to life imprisonment.*

Anthony Joseph Collop   Anthony James Tomlin

The body of Tomlin (13) was found naked in the undergrowth near Maldon. He had been strangled with a cord. Collop (21), a cinema projectionist, had been seen with the boy and at first pretended to help the police look for him, but finally admitted strangling him.

At *Essex Assizes, 2.11.1961, Collop was found not guilty of non-capital murder, but guilty of manslaughter under section 2.* Two defence doctors (unchallenged), said he had a schizoid personality and was retarded. Collop had admitted to having had homosexual tendencies since he was 13. When Tomlin repulsed his advances, he knew he could not see him again and so he killed him. *Mr. Justice Havers sentenced him to life imprisonment.*

Anthony Brian Cooper   Sidney Gazzard

Cooper (24), a ship's porter, was *found unfit to plead to a charge of capital murder* of Gazzard (64). Two doctors said he was a paranoid schizophrenic. At *Stafford Assizes, 30.6.1961, he was sentenced to be detained during H.M.P.*

He told the police: "I was feeling in a bad temper at being unemployed and I am afraid I deliberately shot at the back of the man walking along the pavement in front of me." He was carrying his shotgun because he had been out shooting squirrels.

Gordon Dunhill Davy   Kathleen Conway

Davy (34), an electrician, had been living with Mrs. Conway (30) and was planning to marry her, as they were both separated from their own spouses. "Mrs. Conway came in one evening and said I, Davy, had to go. It was all through. We talked and disagreed and then we went to bed . . . I suddenly woke up at 4.30 a.m. I don't know whether I was asleep or mad, or what I was. I fetched the knife and stabbed her"; he then told the police. He said he never intended to harm her, as he had changed his life for her. Mrs. Conway was intending to return to her husband.

At *Sheffield Assizes, 27.2.1961, he was found guilty of non-capital murder*. The jury recommended mercy. He was sentenced by Mr. Justice Thesiger to *life imprisonment*. No medical evidence was tendered.

Jack Day   Keith Godfrey Arthur

Day (30), a car salesman, shot Arthur (25) at Day's home when he found Arthur talking to his wife. Day was very keen on firearms (his home contained no fewer than 177 weapons), and always carried a loaded gun. Arthur's body was found later buried in a field.

At *Bedford Assizes, 20.1.1961, Day was found guilty of capital murder and sentenced to death.* He refused to allow his counsel to plead diminished responsibility at the trial, even though one medical witness, Dr. Rowland Hill, was convinced he was a psychopath. His defence was of accident and he panicked when Arthur died on the way to see a doctor. *Appeal to the Court of Criminal Appeal dismissed, 6.3.1961. Reprieve refused, 27.3.1961.* He showed no emotion at his trial.

Day was executed at Bedford Prison, 29.3.1961.

[Authors' note: Day's case was interesting in that, had he allowed his counsel to put forward the defence of diminished responsibility, his plea might well have succeeded, either at the trial or on appeal.

Day's solicitor issued a writ from the death cell against the *Spectator* which, in an article, had stated that Day had already been executed. The move failed to forestall his execution.]

Lillie Dean   Jeffrey Dean

Dean (35) was a "wonderful mother" to Jeffrey, aged 1½, who was very destructive and badly behaved. She, however, became very depressed after his birth. He was accepted by her husband though he was the child of another man. She had been previously treated for anxiety and nervous tension. On this occasion the child was screaming, "so I put the scarf around his neck and pulled it". Then she smothered him with a pillow.

At *Manchester Crown Court, 27.4.1961, she was found not guilty of murder but guilty of manslaughter under section 2.* Mr. Justice Veale put her on *probation for 3 years.* "Doctors regard you as being cured now, and I agree."

Ahmed Din   Abdul Ansara

Din (46), a Pakistani sheet-metal worker, lived with his wife and some of his ten children. Ansara had been friendly with them for years and frequently stayed with them, sleeping with the accused while the wife and children slept together. Din believed that Ansara was cuckolding him and asked his wife to make Ansara leave. She refused. One night he stabbed Ansara in a frenzy.

At *Birmingham Assizes, 11.12.1961, Din was found guilty of non-capital murder and sentenced to life imprisonment.* Two defence doctors said he came within section 2 and was a paranoiac, having delusions about his wife's faithfulness. Mr. Justice Stable, however, told the jury to decide whether the accused's beliefs were delusions or reasonable beliefs.

The Court of Criminal Appeal dismissed the appeal, saying doctors should stick to medical evidence and not concern themselves with facts (i.e. whether or not the wife was unfaithful). [1962] 1 W.L.R. 680. The jury was entitled to look at surrounding circumstances— such as the custom among Pakistanis with regard to the position of a wife vis-à-vis a third party—to test whether the husband's delusions were substantive. [Compare with Bailey (1961).]

Maxwell Douglas   Audrey Douglas

Douglas (31), a miner, stabbed his wife seventeen times on a seat in the park, after she had left home with another man.

At *Durham Assizes, 19.10.1961, he was found not guilty of murder, but guilty of manslaughter. He was sentenced to 8 years' imprisonment.* Douglas claimed that he was provoked, and when he came home from hospital, he found the children, previously well cared for, were dirty and ill-fed.

Ruby Dovaston   John Dovaston

Dovaston (39) was the mother of John (2), who was a somewhat difficult child. She strangled him with a stocking and fractured his skull with a hammer. She told the police: "He would not dress. I tried to strangle him first with my hands. He was slow dying, then I used a hammer and I covered him over." She was very distressed. She was normally a devoted mother.

At *Carmarthen Assizes, 28.6.1961, she was found not guilty of murder but guilty of manslaughter under section 2.* She suffered from a severe depression precipitated by her sister's death, anaemia and pains in the face, and the stress of having to cope with the child. She was *ordered by Mr. Justice Finnemore to be detained in a mental hospital under section 60 of the Mental Health Act 1959.*

Renson Solomon Drummond   Frigyes Borsos

Drummond (20), a Jamaican welder, was mercilessly tormented by two Hungarian workmates, including Borsos (26). Drummond was deeply religious and turned the other cheek constantly until one day he was told to hand over 50/- within ten minutes. He had been hit earlier that day and on this occasion he lost control, picked up a 7 lb. hammer and killed Borsos.

At the *Old Bailey, 9.6.1961, Drummond pleaded not guilty to murder, but guilty of manslaughter. He was gaoled for 10 months.* Provocation did not arise. Drummond said he intended to hit Borsos on the shoulder, but Borsos moved and Drummond hit his head.

Christopher John Duffy   Frederick Sydney Skinner

Duffy (16), was on holiday from an approved school and on Christmas Eve he had been drinking and visited the cinema. On his walk home, he met Skinner (78), who was very drunk, lying in the gutter. Duffy helped to pick him up but he clung to Duffy. Duffy said, "I hit him over the head with a dustbin lid" and left him. Later he admitted strangling Skinner with a tie or belt and taking his wallet with £3 or £4 in it.

At the *Old Bailey, 20.3.1961, Duffy was found guilty of capital murder and sentenced to be detained during H.M.P.* Duffy gave no evidence, but one doctor said he was suffering from an abnormality of mind and schizoid instability. This was refuted by the Prison Medical Officer at Brixton, who thought Duffy was quite normal.

Irene Mary Duke   William John Duke

Duke (28) shot her husband (31) four or five times at their home. She told the police: "I don't know what made me do it. The gun was in the . . . cupboard . . . I kept hearing noises in my head. I feel like two people . . . I am a wicked woman but he said he was going to leave me and I'd be better off."

At the *Old Bailey, 5.7.1961, she was indicted for capital murder.* The jury found: *Guilty of manslaughter but insane: not guilty of capital murder.*

The Court of Criminal Appeal dismissed the appeal on 8.10.1961. The Court, however, certified that a point of general public importance was raised but, in view of a binding decision of the House of Lords, refused leave to appeal to that Court. Duke's petition to the Appeal Committee of the House of Lords for leave to appeal was dismissed on 20.10.1961 without any reasons being stated: [1961] 1 W.L.R. 1434. On 11 September 1962 the Home Secretary referred the problem raised in the case, and other related issues on the question of pleas of insanity in criminal trials, to the Criminal Law Revision Committee under the chairmanship of Lord Justice Sellers.

[Authors' note: The Court recorded the verdict as "guilty of the act charged, but insane at the time of commission". Section 3 of the Criminal Appeal Act 1907 gives a right of appeal to persons "convicted on indictment". In Felstead v. The King [1914] A.C. 534, the House of Lords held that a special verdict was an acquittal; therefore the Court had no jurisdiction to entertain an appeal. Before 1800 if a jury found an accused person to have been insane when he committed the act, he was simply acquitted and went entirely free. By the Criminal Lunatics Act of that year, however, a special verdict empowered the Court to order the person's detention during His Majesty's Pleasure. The present form of verdict—guilty but insane, which is essentially illogical—was introduced by the Trial of Lunatics Act, 1883. This piece of legislation resulted from the personal insistence of Queen Victoria, following an attempt on her life by Maclean in 1883, that, insane or not, the man was "guilty". And so the law has remained. The Royal Commission on Capital Punishment (1949-53) endorsed the view of the Atkin Committee of 1922-1923 that the form of verdict was unsatisfactory, but no legislation has been forthcoming. Hopes for legislation have been brightened with the recent publication—on 24 September 1963—of the Third Report of the Criminal Law Revision Committee on Criminal Procedure (Insanity). The Committee recommended, and drafted a Bill, to the effect that the special verdict would be, "not guilty by reason of insanity". While the Atkin Committee declined to recommend a right of appeal because the accused himself might put forward the plea that he was insane and because the issue of insanity was never raised where there was any real question whether the accused committed the act, the recent Committee supported the view of the Lord Chief Justice, Lord Parker, in R. v. Duke [1963] 1 Q.B. 120, that the absence of an appeal "may work injustice". This sentiment was prompted largely by the fact that an accused might have claimed, in addition to insanity, that the killing was accidental, against which finding there would be no appeal although the jury had been misdirected by the judge. The Committee was in favour of allowing an appeal against either the special verdict or the finding that the act was committed, or both.

The criticism of the decision in *Felstead* and, of course, *Duke*, related not merely to form but to substance. Suppose there is no evidence of a crime having been committed by the accused, but evidence of his insanity, and the jury find the accused guilty but insane? The difficulty has been aggravated by the Homicide Act 1957, for, according to R. v. Bastian [1958] 1 W.L.R. 413, where the accused sets up the defence of diminished responsibility the prosecution would appear to be entitled to cross-examine the medical witnesses for the defence and call its own evidence to prove that the accused was insane. If the prosecution's case was accepted by the jury there could be no right of appeal. The Committee thought that the point of not allowing the prosecution to counter a plea of diminished responsibility by adducing evidence of insanity would be less valid once there was a right of appeal. It recommended, however, that the issue should be resolved by the legislature providing that the prosecution could give evidence of insanity to rebut a plea of diminished responsibility, and vice-versa. In R. v. Russell [1963] 3 All E.R. 603, Mr. Justice Marshall, in following the practice in Bastian but declining to adopt the attitude of the court in R. v. Price [1963] 2 Q.B. 1, hoped that the Committee's recommendations would be speedily implemented.]

Brian J. Edgington   Belinda Mary Edgington

Edgington (26), a labourer, failed to make a success of his marriage. His wife left him more than once, and finally he got fed up with hearing her and their daughter's voices. While his wife watched, he gagged the daughter (2), tried to strangle her and then drowned her in the canal. The wife failed to take any action to save the child. Edgington had made several unsuccessful efforts to persuade relatives to foster the child and at least one child welfare agency to take her into care.

At *Oxford Assizes, 11.10.1961, Edgington was found not guilty of murder but guilty of manslaughter under section 2.* Doctors said he was "barely semi-literate, simple and childish". He was a psychopath. *Mr. Justice Sachs sentenced him to 15 years' imprisonment.*

Jean Elsegood   Paul Jeremy Elsegood
                                                Serena Ruth Elsegood

Elsegood (30) and her husband adopted the two children, both aged 2. One day in his absence she gassed them and attempted to gas herself. She was weak and ill at the time.

At *Hampshire Assizes, 30.11.1961, she pleaded not guilty to murder, but was found guilty but insane and detained during H.M.P.* Mr. Justice Hinchcliffe said it was "completely out of character".

She was a good mother and a devoted Christian. Her father had died in a mental home and she was pregnant (after attempting to procreate for seven years). Doctors said she had an acute depressive illness and would not have known she was doing wrong.

David James Emery   Jacqueline Birri

Emery (22), a process worker, visited a prostitute's flat to see a girl called "Ruby". Instead Birri (25) was there and attempted to take £2 from him. He pushed her away and she picked up a poker and hit him, whereupon he lost his head, seized the poker and struck her. He then returned home to Stevenage. He confessed to the police.

At the *Old Bailey, 19.12.1961, he was found not guilty of murder but guilty of manslaughter. He was sentenced to 6 years' imprisonment.*

Norma Rose Everson   Winifred Lord

Everson (33), a van driver, found Mrs. Lord in her flat with a Miss Power, with whom she (Everson) shared. She was furious and ordered her to go. Mrs. Lord pushed her and she panicked and stabbed her with a knife. Everson's relationship with Miss Power was admittedly lesbian. At the time of the offence, Everson had not eaten for some time and had taken both drinks and barbiturate.

At the *Old Bailey, 25.7.1961, she was found guilty of murder and imprisoned for life. The Court of Criminal Appeal, 20.10.1961, refused leave to appeal.*

Walter Frederick Faulkner   Violet Faulkner

Faulkner (24), a private in the Gloucestershire Regiment, strangled his wife (17) at home. She was six weeks pregnant. Faulkner said, "She called me a bastard and I strangled her with my hand." He had previously attacked her.

At *Kent Assizes, 8.3.1961, before Mr. Justice Stable, Faulkner was found not guilty of murder, but guilty of manslaughter under section 2.* Defence doctors said he was depressed and apathetic with no social sense or responsibility. He had "the emotional control of a child". This was not contested. *Sentence: life imprisonment.*

Alice Fletcher
Roy Fletcher
Boleslaw Zimnowodzki   Melvin Stephen Smith

Alice (51) and Roy Fletcher (26), a painter and decorator, and
Zimnowodzki (28), a salesman, got together to revenge themselves
on a man who had beaten them up. They used petrol to set fire to
the house where he lodged with a prostitute and her child (2). The
child was burnt to death.

At *Birmingham Assizes, 27.7.1961, all three were found guilty of
non-capital murder and sentenced to life imprisonment.* They had
more or less admitted the crime. Mr. Justice Edmund Davies said
he regarded Roy as less to blame than the others, and Zimnowodzki
as the "dominant one". *Appeal to the Court of Criminal Appeal,
18.4.1962, dismissed.* Two witnesses retracted their evidence about
supplying Zimnowodzki with the petrol. Lord Parker, the Lord
Chief Justice, said he couldn't accept anything they said: [1962]
Crim.L.R. 551.

Roy Fletcher (see: Alice Fletcher et al.)

Albert Edward Michael Foy   Shirley Foy

Foy (24), a Lance-Corporal in the Army, shot his wife (23) in
their caravan late one night with a shotgun. Foy maintained that
he tripped over the carpet and shot her by accident.

At *Hampshire Assizes, 5.12.1961, Foy was charged with capital
murder and found not guilty. The jury said it was an accident. Mr.
Justice Streatfeild agreed.*

John Alex. Fulton   Margaret Florence Fulton

Fulton (34), an unemployed crane driver, was unhappily married
to Margaret (34), who was instituting separation proceedings. He
arranged to meet her and their three children in the park, but bought
a shotgun and a sheath knife. At the meeting he shot and stabbed
his wife and then stabbed himself. Fulton made a full admission to
the police. He shot her accidentally when she grabbed the gun.

At *Birmingham Assizes, 11.12.1961, Fulton was found unfit to
plead and detained during H.M.P.*

Joseph Gamroth   Kathleen Gamroth

Gamroth (37), a former German P.O.W., strangled his wife (37)

during an argument when she said: "You are nothing but a low-down German." He had suspected her, and when he accused her of sleeping with another man she said: "What if I did?" He did not mean to kill her and had always loved her.

At *Bristol Assizes, 30.6.1961, Gamroth was found not guilty of murder but guilty of manslaughter. He was sentenced to 12 months' imprisonment.*

Brian Gardner   Lorna Gardner

Gardner (18) had been married only six months to Lorna (17), but they frequently quarrelled. Lorna was found in their caravan with six stab wounds from a sheath knife. Gardner said there was a quarrel and she came at him with the knife. In the struggle she was stabbed. He "went mad". Her mother had caused most of the rows and Gardner intended to leave to frighten Lorna, who had threatened to go back to her mother.

At *Lancaster Assizes, 1.2.1961, Gardner was found not guilty of murder but guilty of manslaughter on the grounds of provocation. He was sentenced to 7 years' imprisonment.* In addition to her family's interference, Mrs. Gardner had thrown things at her husband and stabbed him with a fork.

Paul Geis   Maud Elsie Holderness

Geis (27), a factory worker, who lodged with his victim (69), strangled her after a row, when she asked him for 10/- towards the purchase of a new mattress on account of his bed-wetting. "I put my hands above her shoulders and she dropped down dead." He later gave himself up to the police. Mrs. Holderness's body was found naked on the bed.

At *Buckingham Assizes, 13.1.1961, Geis was found not guilty of murder but guilty of manslaughter under section 2.* Four defence doctors gave evidence of abnormality. Geis was partly blind and his family had a long history of mental illness and he had been seen by a consultant psychiatrist at an out-patient's clinic; he was diagnosed as being mentally disturbed but not sufficiently so as to be detained under the Mental Health legislation. He was a compulsive handwasher. He did not know right from wrong. *Mr. Justice Streatfeild sentenced him to 15 years' imprisonment.* Geis was later transferred to Broadmoor.

[Authors' note: This is another case of bad sentencing by the courts: see Sims (1961).]

Richard Allen Gillmore   Ellen Irene Gillmore

A grammar school boy "of above average intelligence" but with a violent temper, killed his mother (53), with a carving knife after a quarrel over a sandwich.

At the *Old Bailey, 25.9.1961, the boy was charged with non-capital murder, alternatively with manslaughter. He pleaded guilty to manslaughter and the first indictment was dropped. Mr. Justice Lawton committed him to the care of the Middlesex County Council as a "fit person" under section 57 of the Children and Young Persons Act 1933. His education would thus continue undisturbed.*

Geoffrey Ernest Gooch   Florence Elizabeth Gooch

Gooch (30), a joiner, was happily married to his wife (30), but made an inexplicable attack on her and hit her with a cold chisel before strangling her.

At *Bedford Assizes, 12.10.1961, he was found not guilty of murder but guilty of manslaughter under section 2.* Doctors said he suffered from a rea-ctive depression as a result of his circumstances. *He was ordered by Mr. Justice Thesiger to be detained under section 60 of the Mental Health Act 1959.*

Robert Harold Gorman   Leslie Bailey

Gorman (18), a window cleaner, stabbed Bailey (17) in a fight at a fun fair. Gorman said, "There was a fight. I had a knife in my hand. He ran towards me and the knife stuck in him."

At *Leeds Assizes, 19.7.1961, Gorman was found not guilty of manslaughter.* He maintained that Bailey had started the fight. *He was sentenced to 3 years' imprisonment.* Mr. Justice Nield said: "It is . . . my duty to . . . deter the use of knives."

Wallace Anthony Goulding   William New

Goulding (31), a labourer, and his wife lived with his parents-in-law, William New and his wife. New (53) was a powerful and domineering man who constantly abused and argued with Goulding. One night, when the two wives were out, Goulding hit his father-in-law over the head with a coal hammer picked up from the coal house, and killed him. He at once telephoned the police. At the time he was under a doctor for nervous trouble as he could not concentrate at work.

At *Lancaster Assizes, 29.5.1961, Goulding was found guilty of murder and was sentenced to life imprisonment. The jury recommended mercy.* Mr. Justice Veale ruled there was no evidence of provocation.

Roger Grist   Susan Whitlock

Grist (21), a labourer, was a shy, immature man who was desperately in love with Susan (17). When she finally terminated their association, he, after unsuccessful pleading, met her at her bus stop, stabbed her with a kitchen knife and threw himself under two cars (unsuccessfully). He told the police: "There is nothing to live for. I loved her . . . I am unable to face life."

At *Hampshire Assizes, 15.3.1961, Grist was found not guilty of murder but guilty of manslaughter under section 2. Mr. Justice Howard ordered him to be detained in Broadmoor under section 60 of the Mental Health Act 1959, and made a restriction order for five years under section 65 of the same Act.* Two defence doctors said he was abnormal, an epileptic type, grossly immature and a suicide risk.

Albert Stuart Hall   Mabel Hall

Hall (66), a barman, was apparently devoted to his wife (66). However, he strangled her and then put his head in a gas oven.

At the *Old Bailey, 28.3.1961, Hall was charged with non-capital murder, but was found insane and unfit to plead. He was detained during H.M.P.* A prison doctor said he was suffering from a mental disease due to coal-gas poisoning, superimposed on a depressive illness.

Edward James Hall   Walter Charles Wood

Hall (50), a butcher, became suspicious of his wife, followed her from work to a rendezvous with Wood (53) in a car park. He had picked up a carving knife at home. When Wood approached, "he had his hands up as if to grapple ... My immediate reaction was to use the knife. I lunged and thrust and the man went backwards." Next day Hall went and told the police. He said: "My natural reaction was to have a suspicious mind", as his wife had confessed to going out with Wood. His wife had on another two occasions associated with other men.

At *Sussex Assizes, 21.3.1961, Hall was found not guilty of murder but guilty of manslaughter*. Mr. Justice Glyn-Jones said there was no evidence of provocation. *Sentence: 5 years' imprisonment*. Appeal to the Court of Criminal Appeal, on grounds of a misdirection with regard to the intention of the accused, dismissed, 31.7.1961; (1961) 45 Cr.App.R. 366. If Hall went to the car park with unlawful intent and a fatal accident ensued, this was manslaughter.

John Harrison   Harold Cook

Harrison (34), a miner, had been drinking with Cook (19) and his brother. Cook had asked Harrison about a remark Harrison made earlier concerning Cook and his girl friend. A fight ensued and Cook was stabbed in the neck.

At *Carlisle Assizes, 5.10.1961, Harrison was found not guilty of murder and of manslaughter; he was discharged*. No evidence was offered on wounding with intent.

George Edward Henshall   Frank Botto Hammond

Henshall (50), a factory worker, strangled Hammond (68) in a lavatory behind a pub. He went straight to the police and said: "He called my mother a prostitute and I . . . strangled him." "I definitely did it."

At the *Old Bailey, 19.10.1961, Henshall was found guilty of murder and gaoled for life*. Prison doctor said he was below average in intelligence (I.Q. 86), but otherwise was normal. Not an epileptic.

Derek Alan Hill   Edith Connell

Hill (25), a machinist, believed himself to be in love with Miss Connell (25), although he never took her out. He used to pester her with letters and was told to desist. One night, when she was in a car with her boy friend, Hill walked up with a shotgun bought specially and shot her through the car window. He then slashed his own arm. He admitted it to the police.

At *Lancaster Assizes, before Mr. Justice Fenton Atkinson, 19.10.1961, Hill was found not guilty of capital murder but guilty of manslaughter under section 2.* Two doctors gave unchallenged evidence that he was a schizophrenic. He was emotionally shallow and depressed. *Life imprisonment.*

Anthony Reginald Hitchcock   John Clarence Neale

Hitchock (29) battered to death Neale (35), his partner in a jobbing gardening firm, and then dialled 999. His defence was that Neale swung at him with a rake and he struck Neale with a stone. He pleaded provocation.

At *Hampshire Assizes, 25.7.1961, Hitchcock was found guilty of murder and sentenced to life imprisonment.*

Melvyn Charles Hodges   Ann Hodges

Hodges (21), an unemployed labourer, strangled his wife (19) with his tie. He then tried to gas himself but the meter ran out. His wife was found on the bed with their son (15 months) beside her. His wife had told Hodges that the child was not his. He had been drinking.

At *Sheffield Assizes, 22.11.1961, Hodges was found guilty of non-capital murder and sentenced to life imprisonment. The jury strongly recommended mercy.* The defence said that Hodges had a stormy marriage and that he acted on an impulse. Provocation was pleaded. Appeal to Court of Criminal Appeal, on grounds that the Judge's summing up was inadequate, dismissed 20.3.1962. See *The Times* Law Report and *The Guardian* Law Report, 21.3.1962.

William Thomas Holding   Eleanor Holding

Holding (73), a caretaker, walked into Marylebone Police Station and said: "I have just killed my wife." She (81) was found in the bedroom strangled with a stocking. Holding was very distressed. He told the police that they had rows over the dog and she unjustly accused him of breaking her dentures. Holding put his hands round her throat: "I would not have done that in my right senses."

At the *Old Bailey, 13.9.1961, Holding was found unfit to plead and detained during H.M.P.*

William Holland   Mary Holland

Holland (34), a labourer, was mowing the lawn when his wife (52) precipitated a quarrel. Later there was an explosion and a fire in their caravan, and the wife was found dead and Holland with self-inflicted wounds. She had been strangled.

At *Oxford Assizes, 11.10.1961, Holland's plea of not guilty to murder but guilty of manslaughter, was accepted. He was gaoled for 3 years.* The prosecution said they would have, in any event, invited the jury to bring in a verdict of manslaughter due to provocation.

Alan Alfred Hosier (see: Victor John Terry et al.)

Bernard David Howard   Rosemary Ann Cook

Howard (26), a timber porter, was a married man who wanted a divorce in order that he might marry Miss Cook (21); at first Miss Cook agreed but she wrote later saying she could not go through with it. Six days later he visited her home and she went outside with him. Next day she was found strangled with a nylon sock from the clothes line. Howard denied strangling her but told the police: "We had a row: she slapped my face and I hit her back."

At *Norfolk Assizes, 26.11.1961, he was found guilty of murder and sentenced by Mr. Justice Havers to life imprisonment.* The defence pleaded diminished responsibility and the doctor said Howard was an aggressive psychopath. Dr. Brisby, the Brixton Prison Medical Officer, and another doctor called for the prosecution, said Howard was normal. Howard had had several previous convictions for wilful damage to property.

George Ernest Howard   Beatrice Howard

Howard (69), a part-time gardener, strangled his wife (61), to whom he had been married for one year. He attempted to gas himself after the crime.

At *Glamorgan Assizes, 30.11.1961, he was found not guilty of murder but guilty of manslaughter on the grounds of provocation. He was sentenced to 12 months' imprisonment.* His wife had tormented and provoked him. Mr. Justice Hinchcliffe said: "What you did was quite out of character and due to sudden and temporary loss of self-control."

Betty Hurdle   Roy Hurdle

Hurdle (30) was married to Roy (29), who was a bully, constantly beating her up and terrorising her. One night, after she had returned from having, to her husband's knowledge, drinks with a man friend, he threatened her with a knife and came at her. She picked up another knife and he ran into it.

At *Hampshire Assizes, 11.12.1961, Hurdle was acquitted of murder.* Mr. Justice Streatfeild described her as a woman of "great character and courage". She had stuck to her husband partly for the child's sake.

Fazal Hussain (see: Mohammed Sabar et al.)

Atkiar Hussain (see: Mohammed Sabar et al.)

Constance Ann James   Paul Andrew James

James (32) was the mother of Paul (6). During a state of anxiety she obtained sleeping tablets from the doctor, ostensibly for her mother, but used them to kill the child.

At *York Assizes, 12.6.1961, James was found not guilty of non-capital murder but guilty of manslaughter under section 2.* Evidence was given that she suffered from extreme melancholia leading to acute depression for which she had been treated. During her second pregnancy she became more anxious and gave the pills to the child. *Mr. Justice Austin Jones sentenced her to 3 years' imprisonment.* The Home Secretary had had her transferred to hospital under section 72 of the Mental Health Act 1959. The Court of Criminal Appeal thought that James did not merit punishment. It was right to substitute a hospital order under section 60 of the Mental Health Act 1959 with a restriction order under Section 65 of the Act without limit: [1961] Crim.L.R. 842.

Robert John James   Annie James

James (62) had had an exemplary career in the police rising to Chief Superintendent. For the four previous years he had been caring for his wife (66), who was dying of cancer. In twelve months he had lost 9 stone in weight and was very depressed. "In a fit of frenzy", he strangled her. He had been a devoted husband.

At *Devon Assizes, 10.3.1961, he was found not guilty of murder, but guilty of manslaughter under section 2. Mr. Justice Elwes followed the jury's recommendation of mercy and made a hospital order under section 60 of the Mental Health Act 1959, with a restriction under section 65 of the Act limited to 2 years.* A psychiatrist had said that James had been mentally ill for at least a year.

Arthur Albert Jones   Brenda Nash

Jones (44), a fitter-welder, was alleged to have strangled Brenda (12), a Girl Guide, whose body was found on a common six weeks after the crime. She had been raped.

At the *Old Bailey, 19.6.1961, Jones was found guilty of murder and sentenced to life imprisonment.* His defence was an alibi that he was with a prostitute at the time. Jones was already serving a sentence of 14 years' imprisonment for the rape of a young girl (11), also a Girl Guide. At that trial he had offered the same alibi which the jury rejected.

Appeal to the Court of Criminal Appeal on 25.7.1961 was dismissed. The point of law involved was finally determined by the House of Lords, [1962] A.C. 635. All the Law Lords were agreed in dismissing the appeal but for different reasons. Viscount Simonds, Lord Reid and Lord Morris of Borth-y-Gest held that the evidence of the rape in the earlier case would not have been admissible as tending to incriminate the accused of the charge of murder but the cross-examination tending to show that he had committed another offence did not reveal to the jury anything they did not already know, and was therefore admissible. Lord Denning thought that direct evidence of the rape would have been admissible and Lord Devlin thought that the questions were admissible as being relevant to the issue of the alibi. Anything relevant could not be excluded by rules forbidding questions about offences tending to reveal other offences.

The sentence of life imprisonment consecutive upon the existing sentence of 14 years' imprisonment, passed on Jones by Mr. Justice Sachs, was upheld.

[Authors' note: Mrs. Jones was subsequently granted a divorce on the grounds of her husband's adultery admitted by him as part of his alibis which were not accepted by the two juries. Mr. Edgar Lustgarten in an article in the *Evening Standard* of 12 June 1963 was contemptuously scathing about these two alibis but overlooked the fact that only a few weeks earlier a divorce court, on a higher burden of proof, had been prepared to accept these as material evidence in support of Mrs. Jones's petition.]

Clifford Jones   Elvira Davies

Jones (28), a labourer, killed his mother when he struck her with his fists during a quarrel.

At *Staffordshire Assizes, 12.12.1961, he was found not guilty of murder but guilty of manslaughter under section 2.* He was *gaoled for 12 months.* Mr. Justice Sachs said there was no question of mental treatment, as "there is no danger of a recurrence". The judge said that the case was a tragedy. Jones, after 22 years in institutions, sought affection, and his mother was incapable of giving it. Two doctors said Jones was abnormal and his development was retarded.

Jack Jowett   Stephanie Jowett

Jowett (39), a former male nurse, stabbed his Austrian born wife (33) in October 1960 in the street. They had married in June but lived together for only two weeks. Accused wanted a reconciliation. When his wife refused, he bought a knife and stabbed her four times.

At *Sheffield Assizes, 21.11.1961, he was found guilty of non-capital murder and sentenced by Mr. Justice Nield to life imprisonment. The jury recommended mercy.* A defence psychiatrist produced a 27,000 word statement—it took the court ninety minutes to read—made by the accused telling how he had run away and was picked up in Glasgow living under an assumed name. The statement was "highly dramatised, colourful and with inconsistencies". He was a psychopath and pleaded section 2. The prison doctor at Wakefield denied that he was suffering from such abnormality of mind as to reduce substantially his mental responsibility.

Neil Kane   Keith Gordon Muncey

Kane (16) and his brother went to a cinema and sat in front of Muncey (17) and a friend. After they all left, Kane said, "Next time . . . stop staring at us (in the cinema)." Knives were drawn by the friend and Kane who carried a fish knife (he was a fishmonger's assistant). Muncey was stabbed and died. It seems that Kane was the one who picked the quarrel.

At the *Old Bailey, 10.1.1961, Kane was found not guilty of murder but guilty of manslaughter. He was sentenced to 4 years' imprisonment.* He had several previous convictions, and had twice absconded from an approved school.

Hilson Philmore Kennedy   Stanley George Wright

Kennedy (28), a labourer and a coloured man, lived in the same house as the girl-friend of his victim (20). One night as Wright and the girl were saying goodnight, Kennedy stabbed him five times. He told the police: "Something came over me; I went to my room and got a knife . . . stabbed him several times . . . I am not just a chap who would normally stick a knife into someone."

At the *Old Bailey, 2.3.1961, Kennedy was found insane and unfit to plead; he was ordered to be detained during H.M.P.*

Stanley Kennedy   Adrian Linward

Kennedy (26), a labourer, was accused of murdering Linward (29). Kennedy said he was being followed by Linward, whom he thought was a homosexual. He complained to a police officer about this, but later was approached by Linward and thought Linward would hit him, so he hit Linward, who fell and died from blood blocking his windpipe. Kennedy dialled 999 but there was a delay in the arrival of an ambulance. With prompt treatment, Linward would not have died.

At *Leeds Assizes, 12.12.1961, Kennedy was found not guilty of murder but guilty of manslaughter. Mr. Justice Nield sentenced him to 3 years' imprisonment. He had no intention to kill.*

Charles Edward Kinley   Ruby Turnbull

Kinley (29), a farm labourer, strangled and partly stripped a teacher (58) whose body was found at her home.

At *Durham Assizes, 12.10.1961, Kinley was found not guilty of murder but guilty of manslaughter under section 2.* Defence doctors said he had "a serious form of psychopathic disorder substantially impairing his mental responsibility". He had at least seven previous assaults recorded against him, including one of attempting to strangle his wife. He had once attempted suicide. He said he had been drinking. *He was sentenced by Mr. Justice Winn to life imprisonment.*

Thomas Ralph Kirk   Miriam Kirk

Kirk (39), a ship's steward, murdered his second wife (40) at home in bed by hitting her with a small bricklayer's hammer. Kirk said they had had financial differences and they went to bed in a state of tension. Next day he got up, went into the kitchen and remembered nothing more till he put the hammer away.

At *Hampshire Assizes, 12.12.1961, Kirk was found guilty of murder and sentenced to life imprisonment.* A defence doctor said Kirk believed in ghostly visitations from his first wife, but was not insane. He "could not exclude" the possibility that Kirk did the crime in a state of automatism. A doctor called for the prosecution disagreed.

Walter Frederick Kneller   Nancy Ann Kneller

Kneller (36), a pipe-fitter, and his wife were found in bed in a gas-filled room. She was dead but he survived. Kneller admitted that he had switched the gas on, but said she knew what he was doing. He had been depressed and out of work. He intended to commit suicide. She would not do as she was told, but was a good wife.

At the *Old Bailey, 14.2.1961, before Mr. Justice Hinchcliffe, Kneller was found not guilty of murder but guilty of manslaughter under section 2. A hospital order was made with a 12 months' restriction under sections 60 and 65 of the Mental Health Act 1959.*

Jack Colin Knight   Veronica Eleanor Foy

Knight (21), a butcher's assistant, met Foy (15) at a dance at the end of an evening where he had drunk 15 or 16 pints of beer. Next morning her body was found in the ice on a pond in the park. She had been raped and strangled both manually and with a stocking. Knight had been seen taking her home. When charged, he remembered nothing at all from the time when she had pushed him away and he hit his head on a wall until he found himself in the park running home. At first he lied to the police.

At *Lancaster Assizes, 28.1.1961, Knight was found guilty of murder and sentenced to life imprisonment.* The defence had suggested "a blackout" and questioned his intent. There was a suggestion, without any medical evidence being adduced, that he was a section 2 case because Knight's conduct was abnormal in that he had been seen with the girl at the spot and would obviously be arrested at once.

Brian Lee   Nellie Macreadie

Lee (28), a plasterer, was a married man who had been carrying on an affair with Mrs. Macreadie (36) for several months. They were in the habit of making love in hotels and on building sites. One

night she admitted associating with another man. Lee then pushed
her head against the wall; he then strangled her, first with his hands
and then with his tie. He concealed the body in a partially built
block of flats. Four days later he surrendered to the police and
confessed in full. He also admitted taking her rings.

At *Sheffield Assizes, 26.6.1961, Lee pleaded not guilty to capital
murder, but guilty to non-capital murder.* No evidence was called,
and he was sentenced to *life imprisonment*.

Francis Christopher Leonard   John James McHugh

Leonard (22), a labourer, apparently accompanied McHugh to
his home where at 4 a.m. a quarrel was heard. It seems that
Leonard was the victim of a homosexual attack and took a knife
from the wall and stabbed McHugh five times. Leonard had been
drinking. He gave himself up to the police and made a statement.

At the *Old Bailey, 3.5.1961, he was found not guilty of murder
but guilty of manslaughter. Sentence: Bound over for 2 years on
condition he returned to Dublin during that time.* A probation officer
said he was a good worker but drifted during leisure hours.

Alan Don Ralph McCalmont   Cecil Hardy

McCalmont (35), a Ghanaian warehouseman, shared a room
with another coloured man, Hardy (38). Hardy was known to be
violent. On this occasion, McCalmont saw him stealing from the
gas meter and remonstrated, whereupon Hardy attacked him with
a cosh. McCalmont lost his temper and butted Hardy, seized the
cosh and battered him to death.

At the *Old Bailey, 29.11.1961, he was found not guilty of non-
capital murder but guilty of manslaughter* (almost certainly *provocation*). He was sentenced to *3 years' imprisonment*.

Brendan Joseph McCann   Pentti Avlis Halonen

McCann (20) was a linesman. He was alleged to have killed
Halonen (31) with a piece of timber in a fight on a jetty in the dark.
Several men were involved and all were drunk. McCann stood by
at first, but finally panicked and struck the blows.

At *Essex Assizes, 2.11.1961, McCann pleaded not guilty of
murder but guilty of manslaughter. This was accepted. He was
sentenced to 3 years' imprisonment*.

Peter Mark McFarquhar   Newly-born child

McFarquhar (17) was alleged to have murdered a newly born child by drowning it in the bath. There was medical doubt whether the death was due to drowning or to another cause.

After consultation with the Judge, both counsel agreed that McFarquhar should be *allowed to plead guilty to attempted murder. He was sentenced to 9 months' imprisonment at Kent Assizes, 3.7.1961.*

John Christopher McMenemy   Valerie Sellers

McMenemy (24), a labourer, was engaged to be married to Valerie Sellers (19), who was found to be eight weeks pregnant. One evening, they had an argument over some money he had demanded from her to "get some rum and go away". She refused and he stabbed her 13 times. Then he took her purse and other items. He shortly afterwards told the police and confessed fully.

At *Liverpool Crown Court, 1.11.1961, McMenemy was found guilty of capital murder and sentenced to death.* He gave no evidence himself and he refused to allow his counsel to plead diminished responsibility despite entreaties from his family and his legal advisers. He changed his mind after being sentenced to death but, since the evidence establishing a case of diminished responsibility was available at the trial, the Court of Criminal Appeal, on 17.11.1961, declined to allow fresh evidence to be called: [1962] Crim.L.R. 44. In this case the medical evidence available had been collated by the doctors called in by the Crown to examine McMenemy. *The Home Secretary*, not unnaturally in these circumstances, *recommended a reprieve*, 24.11.1961.

Robert Ward Mitchell   Florence Mitchell

Mitchell (45), a sailmaker, was charged with the murder of his wife (38) who had recently divorced him. She was stabbed with a penknife in the heart during a quarrel over (possibly) access to their child. Mitchell said he went to her house to seek a reconciliation. She became hysterical and punched him. He lost his temper and hit her with his fist. As he left, she came at him. There was a struggle in which she was stabbed—he never intended to do it. The knife was sharpened and carried by Mitchell.

At *Essex Assizes, 8.8.1961, Mitchell was found guilty of non-*

capital murder and sentenced to life imprisonment. The jury recommended mercy.

George Raymond Monaghan (see: Terence Brennan et al.)

Donald Alex. Mooney (see: Geo. Wood et al.)

Lester Philip Morgan   John Stark

Morgan (21), a Jamaican, stabbed Stark (21) in a fight in a club. The weapon was a metal file which Morgan carried with him. He was seen to hit Stark who crumpled up. He told the police: "I hit him but I didn't stab him."

At the *Old Bailey, 23.3.1961, Morgan was found guilty of non-capital murder and sentenced to life imprisonment.*

Rupert Morrison   Hazel May Dacres

Morrison (31), a labourer, had been the lover of Dacres (31) for some months. In a quarrel in the kitchen, Morrison stabbed Dacres no less than 16 times. He made a statement: "I did not mean to do anything to her ... I love her very much. But she said she did not want me." He said she first picked up the knife, but he took it from her.

At *Birmingham Assizes, 28.3.1961*, Morrison said it was an accident. Dacres had said she was leaving him. *Mr. Justice Pilcher said that intention to injure seriously was enough to establish murder in law. Guilty of non-capital murder. Sentenced to life imprisonment.*

Frank James Murrow (see: Terence Brennan et al.)

Arthur Sidney Nash   Patricia Ann Nash

Nash (45), a clerk, was the father of Patricia (16), who was an epileptic. Nash felt she had no future in the world; she was hopelessly wayward and could not keep a job and "she seemed to have a liking for coloured men". One morning, after she had a fit, he gave her 50 pheno-barbitone tablets and strangled her with his tie and her stocking. He then took 100 tablets himself.

At the *Old Bailey, 29.6.1961, Nash was found not guilty of murder but guilty of manslaughter under section 2.* Two doctors gave unchallenged evidence that Nash was suffering from "acute depression known as melancholia"; he was a perfectionist who felt he had failed. Mr. Justice Lawton made a hospital order under section 60 of the Mental Health Act 1959.

[Authors' note: The physician superintendent of Long Grove Mental Hospital, near Epsom, discharged Nash within a matter of a few weeks of his admission to the hospital. Nash's return to his home environs caused some disquiet among his neighbours and excited adverse public comment in and out of Parliament. Nash's discharge from hospital, medically quite justified, lacked that sense of public relations required by the mental hospital authorities; the effect on the judiciary has been for the courts since then invariably to attach restrictions on discharge when making hospital orders: see Rose (1962). Some consultant psychiatrists are loth, or even refuse, to admit patients where the court has attached a restriction order to the hospital order, since they strongly disapprove of judicial or administrative restraints upon their rights to declare a mental patient fit and ready to return to the community. Thus a number of persons who successfully pleaded diminished responsibility will find it more difficult to ask for a hospital order.]

Clifford Newsam   Patrick Mulligan

Mulligan (22) was stabbed to death in a fight in a Worcester public lavatory. Newsam (39), a marine engineer, then living rough, was identified by two witnesses as the assailant. However, at the trial, a policeman of the British Transport Commission said he had seen Newsam in London on the night of the crime.

At *Stafford Assizes, 12.7.1961, Newsam was charged with murder. In view of the evidence, Mr. Justice Stable withdrew the case from the jury before final speeches. Newsam was found not guilty and discharged.*

Albert Henry Nickells   Ann Sarah Nickells

Nickells (44), a charge hand at Fords, Dagenham, was devoted to his wife (40), who left him for another man (27). Despite his entreaties, she refused to return to him. One day he visited her and stabbed her with a knife 12 times. He then stabbed himself.

At *Essex Assizes, 20.2.1961, Nickells was found not guilty of non-capital murder but guilty of manslaughter under section 2.* Doctors said he suffered from an acute depression, and mental dissociation resulted from this. He had a genuine amnesia from the time of the offence. He had previously been in a mental hospital. *He was sentenced by Mr. Justice Glyn-Jones to 3 years' imprisonment.*

Hendryk Niemasz   Hubert Roderick Buxton
                                   Alice Bateman (Buxton)

The bodies of the two victims, aged 35 and 32, who were living as man and wife, were found at their Kent cottage. Buxton had been shot with a shotgun and Bateman battered to death with its butt. It was alleged that Niemasz (49), a married man, who had committed adultery with Bateman, had shot Buxton, and clubbed Bateman on being discovered.

At *Lewes Assizes, 20.7.1961, Neimasz was found guilty of capital murder of Buxton and guilty of non-capital murder of Bateman. He was sentenced to death and to life imprisonment for each respectively.* As a defence, Niemasz alleged that a man named George (who could not be traced) had left him at the gate and gone in and done the killings. He further alleged that Bateman was urging him to leave his own wife and family for her and said she would kill them if he didn't. He therefore paid "George" to kill her.

The appeal to the Court of Criminal Appeal was dismissed, 15.8.1961. (See *The Times* Law Report and *The Guardian* Law Report, 16.8.1961). Although there was some evidence that Niemasz had suffered mental and physical deprivation as a prisoner during the war, no reprieve was recommended, 6.9.1961. *He was executed at Wandsworth, 8.9.1961.*

Leslie Nixon   Catherine Mary Nixon

Nixon (36), a security patrolman, throttled and stabbed his wife (36), and then attempted to kill himself by cutting his wrist and throat and trying to strangle himself.

At *Birmingham Assizes, 14.3.1961, he was found not guilty of murder but guilty of manslaughter and sentenced by Mr. Justice Streatfeild to 10 years' imprisonment.* He was said to have been haunted by a fear that he had a disease and was passing it on to his wife. This fear was groundless. It is not certain whether section 2 was pleaded and, if pleaded, successful.

John Anthony O'Neill   Eileen Harris
O'Neill (26), unemployed, had been courting Miss Harris (18) for

three months, but their friendship was breaking up. He took her out for the last time and strangled her with his tie. He was a lonely young man. He told the police "(She defied me) . . . She said: 'Go on, kill me then' . . . I have no regrets at having killed her." She had been hard towards him.

At *Stafford Assizes, 28.6.1961, he pleaded guilty to non-capital murder and was sentenced to life imprisonment.*

Violetta Osuagwu   Joseph Osuagwu

Osuagwu (38) was the Nigerian mother of four children, including Joseph (6½). She married someone other than the child's father. She was alleged to have beaten the child with a coal shovel and generally starved and maltreated the child till he died.

At the *Old Bailey, 20.10.1961, she was found not guilty of murder and discharged.*

Marie Pachy   Pandelis Phillippidis

Pachy (24), a Greek woman, lived with a Greek married man and cared for his son (2) "like a mother". The Greek promised to get a divorce and marry her, but took no active steps. There were quarrels and he made her sleep alone one night, though he knew this frightened her. Next day she strangled the son with a dressing-gown cord and then told the police straight away.

At *Leeds Assizes, 26.7.1961, she was found not guilty of non-capital murder but guilty of manslaughter under section 2.* The defence gave unchallenged evidence that she was not responsible owing to morbid depression. She was preoccupied with suicide and depressed, partly due to childhood difficulties and partly to the Greek not marrying her. She had nearly had a nervous breakdown, but the Greek did not let her see a doctor. *Mr. Justice Howard sentenced her to 3 years' imprisonment. Appeal to the Court of Criminal Appeal against sentence was dismissed, 13.11.1961:* see *The Guardian* Law Report, *14.11.1961.*

[Authors' note: This appears to us to be penologically a regressive sentence.]

Zsiga Pankotai   Eli Myers

Pankotai, a Hungarian miner (31), learnt that Myers (50) had money in his house and had won £1,275 on the football pools. He broke into the house and was surprised by Myers who chased him. In the struggle Myers suffered injury, which would normally not have been fatal, but was in his case, due to the presence of a heart disease. Pankotai escaped with a large quantity of clothing. A medical witness said that there was a remote possibility that the victim might have died from heart disease independently of his wounds.

At *Leeds Assizes, 26.4.1961, Pankotai was charged with capital murder and was found guilty.* He maintained he used a knife only to scare Myers.

His *appeal to the Court of Criminal Appeal, 5.6.1961, was dismissed:* [1961] Crim.L.R. 546. Leave to appeal to the House of Lords was refused on 14.6.1961 by the Appeal Committee of the House of Lords. The Home Secretary declined to recommend a reprieve and Pankotai was *executed at Leeds Prison, 29.6.1961.*

Doreen Grace Pateman   Michael Pateman

Doreen (14) had an argument with her brother (16) over his terrier dog and later shot him with his shotgun.

At *Sussex Assizes, 13.12.1961, she was found not guilty of capital murder but guilty of manslaughter under section 2.* The defence said that she suffered from epileptic fits and was an informal patient in a hospital for sub-normal people. *Mr. Justice Finnemore ordered her to be detained in a similar hospital under section 60 of the Mental Health Act 1959.*

Malcolm John William Peck   George Taylor Warwick

Peck (16) was an inmate in a mental hospital where he had been sent from an approved school. He was alleged to have taken George (4) away from a game and murdered him by hitting him on the head, probably with a brick. It appeared that there had been some indecency. George's father worked at the hospital.

At *Cumberland Assizes, 19.5.1961, before Mr. Justice Veale, Peck was found not guilty of murder but guilty of manslaughter under section 2. Sentence: life imprisonment.* Peck had had a very unhappy childhood and had lived in homes since he was eighteen months old.

William Ewart Perkins   Sarah Jane Teal

Perkins (69), a retired storekeeper, had been caring for his mother Mrs. Teal (94), for 14 years. She was cantankerous and violent and gave him no reward. One morning, after a night of quarrels, there was a fight and she was strangled and asphyxiated. Perkins gave himself up at once.

At *Birmingham Assizes, 20.3.1961, Perkins was found not guilty of murder, but guilty of manslaughter. Mr. Justice Pilcher made a 12 months restriction order under section 65 of the Mental Health Act 1959.* This was clearly a section 2 case although the available reports do not specifically mention the section. Two doctors said his mental responsibility was impaired owing to early senile dementia.

George Ernest Picter   Bernadette Morris

Picter (19), a naval rating, was accused of murdering Morris (36), a prostitute, known as "Irish Moll", whose body was found strangled at her home. It had been mutilated with a kitchen knife and a garden trowel. The police said it was the work of a "sex-maniac". The murder occurred on 19.1.1961.

At *Devon Assizes, 15.6.1961, Picter was found not guilty and discharged by Mr. Justice Melford Stevenson.* The prosecution evidence was largely based on "confessions" obtained after nearly thirty hours of questioning. Picter was of good character.

Jan Piechowicz   Jan Biernat
                                                 Rozalia Jandy

Piechowicz (42), a Pole, thought that Biernat (39) had been associating with his wife. His wife died on 15 March. Two days later, Piechowicz shot Biernat at his home and also Mrs. Jandy (34), who tried to reason with him. He also wounded a police-constable.

At *Gloucester Assizes, 25.5.1961, he was found unfit to plead and ordered to be detained during H.M.P.* Doctors said he could not understand the proceedings and was violent. He had twice attempted suicide. He was a manic depressive.

Muriel Lilian Pillinger   Stephen Edward Pillinger

Pillinger (25) threw her son (2) into the Thames off Lambeth Bridge and then told a policeman.

At the *Old Bailey, 9.1.1961, she was found not guilty of murder but guilty of manslaughter under section 2. She was ordered by Mr. Justice Fenton Atkinson to be detained in a mental hospital.* She was suffering from a depressive disorder from which she could recover if given treatment.

George Anthony Porritt   Albert Leonard Porritt

Porritt (27), a car dealer, and his stepfather (48), were involved in gang warfare with the Copley family. After an evening of quarrels and fighting, Porritt and his victim were attacked by the Copleys at their home. Porritt saw his stepfather held by two men with a knife at his throat and fired at them. In error he killed his stepfather. He later shot, but not fatally, two of the rival gang.

At the *Old Bailey, 4.7.1961, Porritt was found guilty of capital murder and sentenced to death. The jury strongly recommended mercy.*

On appeal, 26.7.1961, the verdict was set aside on the grounds that, whenever the facts raise the possibility of a finding of provocation, the Judge must direct the jury that the alternative verdict of manslaughter is open, and must leave the question of provocation to the jury even though the defence did not seek to raise the defence at the trial: [1961] 1 W.L.R. 1372. Since the Judge had failed to deal with provocation the conviction was quashed and manslaughter substituted. *Sentence: 10 years' imprisonment.*

Samuel Poynton   Annie Miller

Poynton (62), a widower, had been living in squalid circumstances with Miller (67), a widow. She was found dead with a tie round her neck.

At *Leeds Assizes, 15.3.1961, Poynton was found not guilty of murder but guilty of manslaughter under section 2.* He was a "quiet" man, while his victim was coarse and foul-mouthed. She suffered from a heart condition. Poynton gave himself up to the police. In 1946 Poynton had served six months for the attempted murder of his daughter (7) and was unhinged. He had attempted suicide in 1945. Doctors said he had an "inherent defect in moments of great stress". *He was given life imprisonment* by Mr. Justice Thesiger.

The *Court of Criminal Appeal, 21.9.1961, refused Poynton leave* to appeal against his sentence. The Court held that in view of Poynton's mental condition and the brutality of the crime he needed care and attention; and he would receive this only if he were sentenced to a long term of imprisonment. Life imprisonment was an appropriate sentence and not unduly severe. See *The Guardian* Law Report, 22.9.1961.

[Authors' note: It is all too typical for the courts to think that psychiatric treatment is readily available in prison. Now that the first psychiatric prison, at Grendon, has been opened, cases like Poynton's may be handled in such an institution which will be, one hopes, geared primarily to medical and not purely to custodial treatment.]

Edward Laurence Prescott   Beryl Prescott

Prescott (50), a fettler, was a Roman Catholic who had married his Protestant wife (52) in 1939. In 1952 they were divorced, but since 1958 they had been seeing each other again. On December 27 there had been a quarrel in which the wife had hit Prescott with a poker, and on December 29 there was a further row, when she refused to be reconciled and Prescott stabbed her over 50 times with a kitchen knife. He then told the police, saying, "I just panicked."

At *Manchester Crown Court, 17.3.1961, Prescott was found guilty of manslaughter under Section 2 but not guilty of murder.* Medical evidence was given that he was "mentally deranged" and suffering from delusions about his ex-wife. *Mr. Justice Nield sentenced him to life imprisonment.* In 1939 he had been bound over for unlawfully wounding his wife, and in 1950 jailed for 12 years for wounding her with intent to murder. Prescott also tried to kill himself at the time of the killing.

Patricia Grace Rainbow   Stephen Rainbow

Rainbow (24) was the mother of Stephen (3). She was alleged to have punched and shaken him when he whined. He died three days later when he was found to have severe bruising all over.

At *Bristol Assizes, 27.2.1961, she was found not guilty of murder but guilty of manslaughter under section 2.* She had a mental age of 11 and was an epileptic. She had lived in institutions as a child. *Mr. Justice Elwes ordered her to be detained in a mental hospital under section 60 of the Mental Health Act 1959.*

Karri Vee Reddy   Sartaben Patel

Reddy (35), a cotton-spinner, apparently visited Mrs. Patel (22) and her husband and stabbed her to death, stabbed the husband and tried to kill himself. He was piqued because they refused to dine with him.

At *Liverpool Crown Court, 14.2.1962, he was found guilty of non-*

capital murder and sentenced to life imprisonment. He claimed that Mr. Patel had first attacked him and in the fight he had gone giddy and could remember nothing until he came to in hospital.

Edward Henry Robins (see: Geo. Wood et al.)

William George Rodgers   Emanuel King

Rodgers (24), a Tyneside labourer, had gone with King and a prostitute to King's rooms after drinking together; they took eight bottles of beer with them. Later King ordered Rodgers and the woman out and then tried to drag Rodgers out of bed, whereupon Rodgers picked up a bottle from the floor and hit him. King, who was West African, was left badly injured all night.

At *Durham Assizes, 29.5.1961, Rodgers pleaded guilty to manslaughter, which was accepted. He was sentenced to 3 years' imprisonment.*

Barry Anthony Roe   Roland Ned Victor Bushnell

Roe (15), a baker's apprentice, studied bakery at the same college as Bushnell (15). Bushnell and another boy were in the habit of taunting and hitting Roe. Finally, one evening they broke his bicycle and let the tyres down. Roe became very angry and plunged his baker's knife, used at the classes, into Bushnell's back.

At the *Old Bailey, 18.7.1961, Roe pleaded not guilty to noncapital murder but guilty to manslaughter.* This was accepted because of the provocation. In view of this and Roe's excellent character, Mr. Justice Megaw put him on *probation for 3 years.*

William Horace Rogers   Mabel Rogers

Rogers (67), a pensioner, had been married for 42 years to his wife (62). They had been legally separated and had frequent troubles on account of his drinking. On this occasion his wife asked him to leave again, and his daughter changed her mind and refused to have him at home. When his wife grinned about this, "I lost my temper." He got a hammer from the cupboard and attacked her. He later told the police.

At *Birmingham Assizes, 13.12.1961, Rogers was found guilty of murder but insane; he was detained during H.M.P.* Evidence was given that he had a hole in his skull as a result of First World War injuries.

8

William Roughley   Olive Roughley

Roughley (23), labourer, was deeply fond of his wife (22) and baby. For some years she had been associating with another man, and she finally said she wanted a separation. Later that day she told him she was pregnant, whereupon he hit her and stabbed her with a knife he had picked up.

At *Liverpool Crown Court, 2.11.1961, Roughley was found not guilty of non-capital murder but guilty of manslaughter. Lord Parker, the Lord Chief Justice, sentenced him to 5 years' imprisonment.*

Patrick Lionel Ruler   Albert Duncan

Ruler (19) struck Duncan (35) in the street and left him dead with severe facial injuries. Ruler told the police that he had been drinking and found himself followed by Duncan, whom he thought to be a homosexual. He chased him and struck several blows, but had no intention of causing him serious injury.

At *Manchester Crown Court, 6.9.1961, Ruler was found not guilty of non-capital murder but guilty of manslaughter. Mr. Justice Megaw sentenced him to 5 years' imprisonment.*

Henrikus Wilhelmus Rumping   Margaret Gregory Hughes

Rumping (29) was the mate of a Dutch ship docked at Menai Bridge. During the stay there Rumping was alleged to have entered a doctor's house and there raped and strangled his victim, a house-maid (21). Rumping left fingerprints, and fragments of paint, etc. were found on him.

At *Chester Assizes, 26.10.1961, Rumping was found guilty of non-capital murder and sentenced to life imprisonment.* He did not give evidence. A lynchpin in the prosecution's evidence was a letter written by Rumping to his wife in which he virtually confessed to the killing. The letter in a sealed envelope had been handed by Rumping to a fellow shipmate, asking him to post it to his wife in Rotterdam. The mate had, however, handed it over to the captain of the ship who in turn gave it to the police. Mr. Justice Hinchcliffe at the trial ruled that the letter was admissible as evidence. The defence argued that there was a principle of the Common Law that communications between husband and wife, which are not intended to be disclosed to others, were protected from disclosure in court.

The Court of Criminal Appeal upheld the ruling of the trial Judge, 26.10.1961, and the House of Lords (Lord Radcliffe dissenting) dismissed the appeal, 18.7.1962. [1962] 2 W.L.R. 763.

Mohammed Sabar	Patrick Coyle
Atkiar Hussain	
Fazal Hussain	

Mohammed Sabar (30), Atkiar Hussain (26) and Fazal Hussain (35), all three Pakistani labourers, were alleged to have murdered Coyle (29), an Irish labourer, in a fight at a hotel between Pakistanis and Irishmen. The trial lasted six days and the evidence was mostly very confused. Jealousy over a girl was a suggested motive.

At *Liverpool Assizes, 24.2.1961, Fazal Hussain was found guilty of non-capital murder and sentenced to life imprisonment.* He carried the knife which stabbed Coyle. *Sabar and Atkiar Hussain were found not guilty and were remanded for trial on wounding charges.* At that trial no evidence was offered against Atkiar Hussain. Sabar was convicted and sentenced to 2 years' imprisonment.

Hassan Said	John Hunt

Said (25), a labourer from Aden, was charged with the murder of Hunt (18), in the street in Middlesbrough, just before or during the race riots there. Hunt and some friends were looking for coloured men to fight, after one of their friends had been beaten up. Hunt had drunk seven pints of beer. He was stabbed in the stomach by a coloured man who threw the knife away. This was alleged to be Said.

At *York Assizes, 6.11.1961, Mr. Justice Winn directed the jury to acquit Said of murder* since there was insufficient evidence to support a conviction. *Discharged.*

Keith Samuel (alias Douthwaite)	
	Maud Eleanor Braithwaite-Smith

Samuel (24), a salesman, lived in the same block of flats in Baron's Court, London, as his victim (62), who had invited him to her flat for a drink. Later on in the evening, after he had been drinking, Samuel went up to her flat at 11 p.m. and came down at 2.30 a.m. and told his flat-mate he had murdered her; he then left for the North of England. He later rang the police and told them of the murder. Mrs. Braithwaite-Smith was found with head wounds from a mallet; her throat had been slashed, and she had eighteen chest wounds inflicted by a bread knife. Some of her property was found in hotels which Samuel had later visited.

At the *Old Bailey, 17.5.1961, Samuel was found not guilty of capital murder but guilty of non-capital murder. He was sentenced to life imprisonment.* A defence doctor had said that section 2 should apply, as Samuel's family tended to epilepsy and Samuel possibly suffered from this complaint. The possibility would be increased by alcohol.

Terence Michael Sansom   James Hawney

Sansom (24), a car dealer, was accused of the capital murder, in the course or furtherance of theft, of Hawney (60), a pay roll guard, who was coshed during a wages snatch. Sansom was identified by two Crown witnesses, but had an alibi.

At the *Old Bailey, 20.4.1961, Mr. Justice Paull withdrew the charge of capital murder and the jury found him not guilty of non-capital murder. Discharged.*

Alex Leopold Saundry   William Ernest Saundry

Saundry (61) attacked his son (30) with an axe at their home. The son subsequently died. There was no motive and they had always got on well. Saundry told the police: "I don't know what came over me." The son was asleep.

At *Cornwall Assizes, 1.6.1961, Saundry was found guilty but insane and ordered to be detained during H.M.P.* Saundry had been attending a psychiatrist as an outpatient and suffered from depression and nervous trouble.

John Joseph Sheenan   Charles Sheenan

Sheenan (37), a labourer, lived with his brother Charles in one room. Charles was argumentative, and one evening, when John had been drinking, he said something, whereupon John picked up a kitchen knife and stabbed him in the neck. He made a full confession to the police. He said: "I did not intend to . . . I lost my temper."

At the *Old Bailey, 31.5.1961, Sheenan was found not guilty of murder but guilty of manslaughter. He was jailed for 4 years.*

James Anthony Shiels (see: Terence Brennan et al.)

Edwin David Sims   Lilian Edmeades
                                                 Malcolm Johnson

Sims (28), a carpenter's mate, walked into the offices of the *Daily Mirror* and confessed in detail to the double murder of a young couple as they were walking on the marshes near Gravesend. He held them up with a sawn-off shotgun, tied them and gagged them. Then he strangled the boy and threw him in a dyke. Next the girl was strangled and then mutilated before she too was thrown into the dyke. Certain items (watches, etc.) were taken by Sims. He also took certain human parts in a plastic bag, which he displayed at the offices of the *Daily Mirror*.

At *Maidstone Assizes, 29.11.1961, Sims was found not guilty of capital murder but guilty of manslaughter under section 2.* Doctors said he was, and had been for some time, an aggressive psychopath, with grossly perverted sexual inclinations. He had inherent defects. His crime "was almost an end product of the insidious degeneration of his pervert instincts". "His abnormality developed . . . from morbid fantasy into pathological obsession." Mr. Justice Finnemore sentenced him to *21 years' imprisonment*. Sims has been transferred to Broadmoor under section 72 of the Mental Health Act 1959.

[Authors' note: The transfer of Sims to Broadmoor demonstrates most forcibly the futility of the judiciary's manifesting the public opprobrium for the more sordid killings by passing long sentences of imprisonment on persons who have successfully pleaded diminished responsibility. It would be much simpler to recognise the gross mental disturbances of these people and commit them forthwith to a mental hospital. The judiciary has every right to ensure that the public shall be protected and can do so by attaching a restriction order, unlimited in time, to the hospital order: see Sowle (1961).]

Sidney Singleton   Samuel Rowney

Singleton (17) was an office boy in the block of offices where Rowney (63) was the night watchman. Rowney was hit several times with an iron bar from behind and then pushed down a lift-shaft from the 5th floor. In a statement, Singleton said he had lost money on the dogs and planned to steal from one of the offices. Singleton alleged that he had two accomplices. A briefcase and £18 were stolen.

At *Manchester Crown Court, 1.5.1961, Singleton was found guilty of capital murder and sentenced to be detained during H.M.P. under section 53(2) of the Children and Young Persons Act 1933.*

Kathleen Smith   Vivienne Smith

Smith (51) killed her daughter (8) while the father was out, by giving her drugs, then attacking her with scissors and a hammer and finally strangling her with a scarf. She then put the child in a bath of water. She took sleeping pills. She told the police: "The little girl was going to be taken up the mountain and stoned."

At *Lincoln Assizes, 5.6.1961, she was found not guilty of murder, but guilty of manslaughter under section 2. She was ordered to be detained under section 60 of the Mental Health Act 1959 and her discharge was restricted under section 65 with no time limit specified.* Doctors said she was abnormal within the meaning of section 2. She had delusions and felt her enemies were closing in on her. She was a devoted mother.

Ronald Derek Sowle   Diana Locke

Sowle (29), a former mental hospital patient, strangled Diana Locke (17) with her own scarf as she walked by the river Trym, near Bristol. She was not sexually assaulted. Sowle had the mental powers of a child of 8 and had been subject to orders under the Mental Deficiency Acts most of his life. In 1958 he was re-classified and just before the murder had released himself from Berwick Lodge Mental Hospital. He made a rambling confession to the police, later retracted. Dr. Fenton, Bristol police surgeon, and Dr. Gibson of Bath said that Sowle was suffering from severe subnormality warranting his detention. They did not think there was any prospect of a change or improvement in his condition in the foreseeable future.

At *Bristol Assizes, 29.6.1961, Sowle was found not guilty of murder but guilty of manslaughter under section 2. Sentence: Detention at Rampton under section 60 of the Mental Health Act 1959, with a restriction, under section 65, for 40 years* ordered by Mr. Justice Melford Stevenson.

The Court of Criminal Appeal, 19.10.1961, held that, in view of the medical evidence that Sowle would not recover, the restriction order—though long—was justified (*The Times* Law Report, 20.10.1961). The case aroused considerable public disquiet and the Minister of Health called for a report, which revealed that Sowle had discharged himself and that there had therefore been no negligence by the authorities of the mental hospital.

[Author's note: It seems quite unnecessary for judges to place restrictions on the operation of a mental health order for such long periods, since the Home Secretary is highly unlikely to allow release for a very long period. A restriction order of unlimited duration is adequate to protect the public.]

Freda Squires   Frank Squires

Squires (39) had had a very unhappy married life and her husband (40) had been cruel, physically and mentally; he had boasted of his other women to her. One night, when the husband had been out with another woman, she met him on the doorstep and stabbed him.

At *Lancaster Assizes, 20.10.1961, she was found not guilty of murder, but guilty of manslaughter under section 2. She was imprisoned by Mr. Justice Fenton Atkinson for 3 years.* She suffered from a morbid depression, due to her husband's treatment of her.

Joyce Alice Stock   Thomas Goodwin

Stock (31) was living with Goodwin's step-son next door to Goodwin (84). One morning, for no apparent reason, she went next door while the son-in-law was waiting for breakfast, and attacked Goodwin with bottles. He later died. She was originally sentenced to 12 months' treatment in a mental hospital for wounding with intent to kill, but when he died she was recharged. She told the police: "I have no idea at all what happened."

At *Cambridge Assizes, 17.5.1961, Stock was found not guilty of murder but guilty of manslaughter under section 2.* A doctor said she was acutely depressed. She had had various in- and out-patient mental treatments. *Mr. Justice Barry made a hospital order under section 60 of the Mental Health Act 1959, with a restriction order under section 65 not limited in duration.*

Wladyslaw Stojalowski   Kazemierz Gielniewski

Stojalowski (53) was alleged to have battered to death Gielniewski (63), a former Polish judge, who was his landlord. Stojalowski claimed it was another lodger who had done it.

At the *Old Bailey, 13.9.1961, Stojalowski was found insane and ordered to be detained during H.M.P.* Doctors said he suffered from delusions and chronic paranoid schizophrenia with considerable deterioration. He thought the police were communists and perjured themselves.

Hilda Maria Stokes   Thomas Frederick Stokes

Stokes (44), a housewife, was alleged to have stabbed her husband (45) with a carving knife which she picked up from the kitchen. Both had been drinking. The husband was a bully and very violent towards her. His girl-friend had been to the house that night.

At the *Old Bailey, 19.1.1961, she was found not guilty of murder but guilty of manslaughter. She was sentenced to 2½ years imprisonment. Provocation* was successfully pleaded on the ground that the husband had hit her and made a very offensive remark.

Budhi Chan Sud   Kehar Singh

Singh's body was found in his house with multiple head and chest injuries caused by a knife. There were signs of a struggle. Three weeks later, Sud (28), apparently unemployed, gave himself up.

At *Birmingham Assizes, 18.7.1961, Sud was charged with capital murder (in the course or furtherance of theft). He was found not guilty of capital or non-capital murder, but guilty of manslaughter. Sentence: 10 years' imprisonment.* The prosecution alleged an intent to steal, but nothing was taken. Sud's defence was that he went to collect a pedlar's licence but Singh made an indecent suggestion and threatened him with a knife. In the struggle Sud stabbed Singh in self-defence. He then searched Singh's clothing for the licence.

George Henry David Sutton   Jean Mellors

Sutton (31), a crane driver, took Mellors, a prostitute, into a churchyard which she frequented. Next day, her body was found naked and she had been strangled and stabbed at least seven times. Sutton told the police: "She started arguing and I gave her a back-hander . . . I have had intercourse . . . twice before and we had gone there for intercourse." He lost his temper and used the knife he was carrying. Other witnesses said Sutton was angry before the event, because Mellors had apparently told the N.S.P.C.C. that Sutton was maltreating his child.

At *Sheffield Assizes, 27.2.1961, the defence doctor said Sutton was below average intelligence but not subnormal within the Mental Health Act.* There was some degree of psychopathic personality. The prosecution doctor agreed with the latter statement, but said it would not impair Sutton's mental responsibility. Sutton had spent one year in a mental home as a psychopath. Mr. Justice Thesiger described the murder as being like Jack the Ripper's. *Guilty of non-capital murder. Life imprisonment.*

Ronald Sweary   Sylvia Simpson (Coleman)

Sweary (32), a bricklayer's labourer, had been the lover of Simpson (29) for over eighteen months. She was a barmaid and drank heavily, and was apparently very promiscuous. Sweary wished to marry her and became very jealous when she refused to stop associating with other men. One night, after seeing her kiss two men, he took her home. When he remonstrated with her over these men she said she was "her own boss" and started laughing, where-upon Sweary strangled her with his own scarf behind a bungalow. He then dialled 999 and later made a full confession to the police, saying: "I had no intention of killing her . . . (she) made me jealous."

At *Nottingham Assizes, 1.3.1961, the defence pleaded diminished responsibility and produced evidence that Sweary was of subnormal intelligence* (age 10) and also suffered from reactive depression, due to his affair with Simpson. Two prosecution doctors disagreed and said jealousy was the cause. His mental age was $12\frac{1}{2}$; there was no mental disorder, merely features of it. Mr. Justice Streatfeild ruled that there was no evidence of provocation. *Guilty of non-capital murder. Sentenced to life imprisonment.*

Harry Swift   Ellen Sproson

Swift (50), a railway cleaner, was alleged to have murdered his sister, Mrs. Sproson (62), a widow.

At *Manchester Crown Court, 13.3.1961, he was found insane and unfit to plead. He was ordered to be detained during H.M.P.* Doctors said he had a long history of mental illness and suffered from illusions. Swift had acted "in response to the voice of God, as he believed it".

Victor John Terry   John Henry Pull
Phillip Tucker
Alan Alfred Hosier

Terry (20), a labourer, Tucker (16) and Hosier (20) all took part in a well-planned and concerted robbery at a Worthing bank, where they stole £1,372. Terry was the leader and he had bought a shot-gun, which he used at point-blank range on Pull (61), a bank guard, who attempted to seize the gun. Tucker entered the bank with Terry and took the money away, while Hosier waited in the car. Both knew Terry had the gun. The killing took place on the morning of 10 November, 1960, within an hour of the execution of Forsyth and Harris (see Harris, 1960) whom Terry was acquainted with in gang activity in the Hounslow area of London.

At *Sussex Assizes, 28.3.1961, Terry was convicted of capital murder and Tucker and Hosier of non-capital murder. Terry was sentenced to death, Hosier to life imprisonment and Tucker to detention during H.M.P. under section 53(2) of the Children and Young Persons Act 1933.* Two defence doctors said Terry was living in a dream world and believed he was possessed by the spirit of a New York hoodlum of the 1920s, "Legs Diamond". He was a schizophrenic, who also took drugs, enhancing his dreams. His responsibility was therefore diminished. A prosecution doctor denied this. Terry alone appealed to the Court of Criminal Appeal, 8.5.1961, which dismissed his appeal. The appellant claimed that the trial judge (Mr. Justice Stable) had merely referred the jury to the terms of section 2 and, instead of reviewing the medical evidence, had handed to the jury a single copy of the transcript containing the passages of the medical evidence, heavily marked by the Judge in red pencil with certain edges of the pages turned down to mark significant passages.

The *Court of Criminal Appeal held that such a practice was objectionable* and would not ordinarily constitute an adequate direction to the jury. But in this case the issue was not an evaluation of the medical evidence—on which the jury would hear careful direction and guidance from the Judge—but on the sole question whether Terry was fooling the psychiatrists or whether his story about "Legs Diamond" was genuine. In the circumstances there was little else the Judge could do but tell the jury to answer that sole question, depending as it did on Terry's evidence rather than on the psychiatrist's. [1961] 2 Q.B. 314.

The Home Secretary declined to recommend a reprieve. Executed at Wandsworth, 26.5.1961.

[Authors' note: Terry's girl friend, Valerie Salter, who was simultaneously tried and convicted of a charge of receiving, was placed on probation. She and Terry, immediately after the crime, travelled from Worthing to Portsmouth where Terry was able to purchase, with no apparent difficulty, yet another shotgun. The lesson of the case, which has never been taken up, is the laxity of the present law with regard to the purchase of smooth-bore guns.]

James Tibbs (see: Geo. Wood et al.)

Philip Tucker (see: Victor John Terry et al.)

Margaret Mary Wade   Stephen Wade

Wade (39), a housewife, strangled her son (8) at home. She told the police and stated: "I thought it was the only thing to do to deliver myself from Satan."

At the *Old Bailey, 3.5.1961, she was found unfit to plead and was ordered to be detained during H.M.P.* She was suffering from depression (involutional melancholia) with gross impairment of her reason. She did it "to further God's plan". Her younger son was especially dear to her.

Kathleen Mary Warnock   Pauline Mary Warnock

Warnock (33), a housewife, battered her only child (2) with the butt of a shotgun. The child died in hospital five days later. Warnock took fifty aspirins afterwards.

At *Wiltshire Assizes, 15.1.1961, she was found not guilty of murder but guilty of manslaughter under section 2. Mr. Justice Slade gave her an absolute discharge.*

Warnock suffered from a slipped disc and became depressed at the prospect of leaving the child during hospital treatment. In 1954 she had had a still birth. She was anaemic. She was a devoted mother and had no idea why she did the killing. In 1952 she had been an in-patient for mental treatment. Two doctors agreed that she was suffering from such mental abnormality as to justify a verdict of diminished responsibility. She was willing to undergo voluntary mental treatment.

Ernest Alfred Webb   Alice Gray

Webb (52), a labourer, had been living with Mrs. Gray (63) for six months. They had many quarrels; she drank heavily and was very abusive. One morning she hit him and he lost his temper and strangled her. Another man was frequently mentioned in the quarrels. Webb later gave himself up to the police and made a full confession.

At the *Old Bailey, 2.3.1961, Webb was found not guilty of murder but guilty of manslaughter. He was jailed for 12 months.* Provocation was the ground. A defence doctor said he suffered from diminished responsibility. The prison doctor denied this, but agreed that his intelligence was low.

Thomas Welsh   New-born baby
Winifred Wray

Welsh (41) lodged with Wray (37), a widow. Wray gave birth to a girl and then told Welsh to drown her in the bath. The body was later found with a fractured skull in a culvert on some mud-flats.

At *Leeds Assizes, 13.12.1961, Welsh was found guilty of murder and was sentenced to life imprisonment. Wray was found guilty of infanticide and placed on 3 years' probation.* The defence said that Wray's mind was disturbed. She was depressed but very fond of children. Welsh was in a state of "mental panic" and didn't know what he was doing.

Arthur Albert Weston   Ellen Weston

Weston (36), a boot repairer, battered his wife (26) to death with a roller out of the washing machine. She was a nervous type and had woken him early after hearing a noise in the flat. He investigated with the roller and then "something came over him"; he struck her several times and strangled her. He gave himself up next day and said: "I must have blacked out. Goodness knows what came over me." They were a devoted couple.

At the *Old Bailey, 18.7.1961, Weston was found guilty of murder and imprisoned for life.* Defences of sleepwalking and automatism were raised. The prison doctor said Weston did not come within section 2. He had no mental history and no earlier blackouts. He had amnesia of the event which was not consistent. He was not an epileptic. He was inadequate and emotionally shallow. Jury did not accept these defences.

William Wibberley   Paul Friend

Wibberley (15), the son of an N.C.O. in B.A.O.R., battered and strangled Paul (6), probably with his tie. The crime occurred in Brunswick, West Germany. Wibberley told the police, "Paul chased me . . . and I swung round and knocked him over . . . He started crying and would not stop, so I put my hand over his mouth to stop him and he bit my hand. Then I put my hands round his throat and choked him. I didn't mean to." Wibberley had earlier been in a psychiatric treatment centre. The body was buried in a cellar.

At the *Old Bailey, 26.6.1961, before Mr. Justice Glyn-Jones, Wibberley was found not guilty of murder but guilty of manslaughter under section 2. A hospital order was made with unlimited restriction under sections 60 and 65 of the Mental Health Act 1959.*

N.B. This case is not recorded on the Homicide Returns because the crime was committed in Western Germany.

Agnes Wilkinson   Hazel Vera Wilkinson
                                             Kenneth Harry Wilkinson

Wilkinson (36) was divorced and lived with her two children, aged 13 and 12. She was a devoted mother. She had been suffering from depression and having electrical shock treatment for this. The cause was that she had been associating with a man 14 years younger than herself, who promised to marry her but then broke it off. She turned on the gas, and she and the two children went to sleep. She was rescued in time. She left a note saying: "Don, I have ended everything for Harry and Hazel. The world is too cruel to let them live. Only God knows why you did this to us." In a statement she said the children were upset that Don had left them and she turned on the gas, as "I only wanted to be with the children".

At *Stafford Assizes, 6.3.1961, she was found not guilty of murder but guilty of manslaughter under section 2. Mr. Justice Finnemore said she was not ill enough to be irresponsible for her actions. Sentence: 3 years' imprisonment.*

Malcolm Keith Williams   Andrew Edward Bonnick

Williams (21), a fitter's mate, took his victim (14) into a pillbox and there made homosexual advances. When the boy repulsed them, Williams hit him on the head with a piece of wood and then told the police, pretending he had found the boy.

At *Glamorgan Assizes, 28.3.1961, he was found guilty of non-capital murder and sentenced to life imprisonment.*

Alan Victor Wills   Amanda Graham

The body of Amanda (6) was found under the bed in the room of Wills (33), a hotel porter. She had been raped, criminally assaulted and strangled. Wills told the police: "I don't remember anything that happened . . . I woke up in the morning and seen her there." He had been seen with the girl on the previous evening.

At *Liverpool Assizes, 10.11.1961, Wills was found guilty of murder and sentenced to life imprisonment.* A defence doctor said Wills was on the borderline between sub-normal and low average. His mental age was 11; he was not mentally responsible. Two doctors for the prosecution denied this, saying his intelligence was low but that he was responsible and knew right from wrong.

George Wood (38)   Ronald Thos. Coomber (28)
Edward Henry Robins (37)
Donald Alex. Mooney (47)
James Tibbs (33)

Wood and Robins, both fruiterers, Mooney and Tibbs, a general foreman, were charged with the murder of Coomber in a brawl outside the Ranch House Club at Ilford. Evidence was given of offensive behaviour by Coomber and others. No witness could say that any of the accused hit Coomber, who died of head and face injuries.

At the *Old Bailey, 8.3.1961, Mr. Justice Edmund Davies ordered the jury to find all four men not guilty of murder or manslaughter.* The evidence was highly unsatisfactory. The accused were *discharged* and awarded costs.

Winifred Wray (see: Thomas Welsh)

Andreas Xanthou (see: Xanthou Zacharia et al.)

Frederick York   Louise Charlotte York

York (83) was charged with the murder of his wife (old, but age not known) in their bedroom with an axe. York admitted hitting her and said to the police: "I had a feeling come over me in the night . . . that I wanted to . . . kill my wife and myself if possible."

At the *Old Bailey, 24.11.1961, York was charged with non-capital murder but was found unfit to plead. He was ordered to be detained during H.M.P.* He suffered from acute mental depression.

Xanthou Zacharia   Stanley Roach
Andreas Xanthou
Daniel Attard

Zacharia (28), a waiter, Xanthou (20), a chef, and Attard (22), a seaman, were charged with murder, having stabbed and battered to death Roach (21), a U.S. airman. Roach and another airman, both drunk, had kicked a girl whom Xanthou and Attard knew. Xanthou was the one who used the knife.

At the *Old Bailey, 9.10.1961, Xanthou and Attard were found guilty of murder and jailed for life. Zacharia was found not guilty and discharged.*

An application by the two prisoners was made for leave to appeal to the Court of Criminal Appeal, 5.3.1962, when the Court granted legal aid so that counsel could settle the grounds for appeal and argue the application. [1962] 1 W.L.R. 608. Since there are no further reports of the case, it is presumed that on advice the applications were withdrawn.

Boleslaw Zimnowodzki (see: Alice Fletcher et al.)

1962

Brian Abbott   Albert Edward Crabb

Abbott (16), a tea boy, attacked Crabb (46), the storekeeper, where he had previously worked. Crabb was hit with a hammer, robbed of £15 and burned alive. Abbott then locked him in a burning store. Abbott later claimed Crabb had made improper advances towards him, but the defence declined to rely on this allegation.

At *Essex Assizes, 28.6.1962, Abbott was found not guilty of capital murder but guilty of manslaughter under section 2. Mr. Justice Hinchcliffe ordered Abbott to be detained during H.M.P.*

The prison doctor said Abbott had a history of epilepsy and was immature. The Home Secretary referred the case, under section 19(a) of the Criminal Appeal Act 1907, to the Court of Criminal Appeal for that court to consider the propriety of the sentence. The court, on 19.2.1963, held that, in the case of an infant found guilty of manslaughter under section 2, the Court could deal with the case only under section 53(2) of the Children and Young Persons Act 1933, as amended by section 9 of the Homicide Act 1957. The question was whether detention for life qualified as detention "for such period as may be specified in the sentence". On the whole the Court, not without difficulty, came to the conclusion that a period might be specified under section 53(2) as life. In any event the trial judge's sentence of H.M.P. was wrong. That sentence was the obligatory one under section 53(1) only for a young offender convicted of capital murder, who because of his age was not liable to the death penalty. See R. v. Abbott [1963] 2 W.L.R. 1011.

Thomas Henry Adams   Catherine Adams

Adams (35), an engineering mechanical inspector, had just been discharged from three years in a mental hospital, when he lost his temper with his mother and strangled her. He also killed their budgerigar. He told the police: "I have killed the only two things I loved." "She kept on at me about going away again—she called me a coward . . . something just snapped. I must have had a black-out. I loved her you know." After the killing, he slashed his wrists and tried to gas himself.

At the *Old Bailey, 2.7.1962, he was found unfit to plead and detained during H.M.P.*

While in hospital he had had hysterical pains.

Sami Ahmed   John Breen

Ahmed (25), a Turkish Cypriot, railway porter, attacked Breen (34) and his brother in the street as they got out of their car. Breen died of a stab wound. No knife was seen or found during or after the fight. The accused and the victim had had a row earlier. Ahmed claimed that the two brothers attacked him.

At the *Old Bailey, 24.9.1962, he was found guilty of non-capital murder and sentenced to life imprisonment. The Court of Criminal Appeal refused him leave to appeal.*

Faiz Alam   Zaib Alam

Alam (30), a Pakistani bus-conductor, attacked his wife (32) with a knife while she slept. Because she wanted to divorce him, he had threatened to kill her on several occasions. The couple lived apart. Mrs. Alam had seven wounds on her throat. The eyes and nose and ears were mutilated. Alam claimed she had picked up the knife first; but, when he had seized it, he had got "out of control". "I don't know what I did." Defence pleaded provocation.

At *Newcastle Assizes, 9.5.1962, he was found guilty of non-capital murder. Sentence: Life imprisonment.*

Victor Armstrong   George McKenna

Armstrong (16) killed McKenna (45) by repeated kicks to his head. The body was found in the long grass in a Sunderland park. Armstrong admitted the killing.

At *Durham Assizes, 18.10.1962, he was found not guilty of murder, but guilty of manslaughter under section 2. He was sentenced to life imprisonment.*

Defence doctors had said that he suffered from abnormality of mind. He may have attempted suicide while in prison awaiting trial.

Samuel Edwin Arno   Julius Arno

Arno (25), a cinema projectionist, lived at the same address as his father. One day he killed his father (69), a property manager, by hitting him on the head with a hammer. He went and told the police "I killed my father this morning. He has been cruel to me for years." He said he had thought a lot about killing him. He had bought the hammer a year before. Before giving himself up he went to the West End "to have a last look at Piccadilly".

At the *Old Bailey, 22.5.1962, he was found not guilty of murder but guilty of manslaughter under section 2. Mr. Justice Paull made a hospital order with restriction unlimited in time.*

Marilyn Anne Bain   Jeannette Doreen McVitie
                                          (known as Blake)

Bain (25), a nurse, shared a flat with McVitie. At first their relationship was lesbian, but when Bain became fond of a man McVitie became jealous. McVitie also prostituted herself to men. One evening, they had both been drinking and had a quarrel, in which McVitie was stabbed. Bain told the police.

At the *Old Bailey, 23.10.1962, she pleaded guilty to manslaughter. This was accepted. A charge of murder was not proceeded with. She was sentenced to 3 years' imprisonment.*

Alastair Hind Ball (see: John McCarthy)

Joseph Barker   Daisy Barker

Barker (68), a retired railway-worker, worshipped his wife (69), but she was deaf, difficult and unpopular with the neighbours, who said she smelt. Barker woke up early on Sunday morning and while she slept, he strangled her with a stocking. He went straight to the police and said: "I did not want her to be humiliated—we loved each other so very much."

At *Nottingham Assizes, 6.3.1962, before Mr. Justice Melford Stevenson, he was found not guilty of murder, but guilty of manslaughter under section 2. He was ordered to be detained in a mental hospital under section 60 of the Mental Health Act 1959, with a restriction for one year under section 65 of the Act.* Two doctors said he was depressed and unbalanced.

Selian Leslie Bernard   Sidney Lansord Constantine Miles

Bernard (37) struck Miles (42) in the face with a stone from a garden rockery. (The reports of this case are scanty.)

At *Manchester Crown Court, 20.3.1962, he was found not guilty of murder, but guilty of manslaughter. He was sentenced to 3 years' imprisonment.*

John Robert Prior Billings   Tessa Billings

Billings (26), a fisherman, had been married for six years to his wife (23). Their marriage was not always happy. One day Billings, after he had been drinking, was told his wife had been seen with another man. He immediately bought a filleting knife and visited his wife. She refused to return to him and so he stabbed her 10 to 12 times. He still protested that he genuinely loved her.

At *Lincoln Assizes, 12.2.1962, Billings was found not guilty of murder but guilty of manslaughter under section 2. He was sentenced to 12 years' imprisonment by Mr. Justice Howard.*

Two doctors said he had a mental history. He was a heavy drinker, emotionally unstable and a psychopath. He had suffered from a reactive depression since the crime.

Albert Edward Bilton   Gladys Bilton

Bilton (46), an electrician, married his second wife (49) in 1957. There was trouble from the beginning and they were living apart at the time of the killing. In January 1962 they met in a club. Bilton twice offered her a drink and on the second occasion stabbed her in the neck. She was quickly released from hospital, but died 12 hours later through loss of blood. The friction between the killer and victim was because she wished to put Bilton's spastic son (24) in a home. He pleaded that he had no intention to stab her, but admitted he lost his temper. When he asked why she wore no wedding ring, she told him to mind his own business.

At *York Assizes Bilton was found guilty of murder and sentenced to life imprisonment.*

Appeal to the Court of Criminal Appeal was dismissed on 23.7.1962: [1962] Crim.L.R. 710.

Edith Agnes Birch   Joyce Birch

Mrs. Birch (64) had been under a considerable strain for years.

Her husband had died of cancer and she cared for her spastic daughter (29). The crisis came when she had to leave her cottage and the daughter did not want to. In her depression, she "had a sudden impulse and put the stocking round her neck".

At *Nottingham Assizes, 11.7.1962, she was found not guilty of murder but guilty of manslaughter under section 2. The judge made an order of unlimited duration under the Mental Health Act 1959.*

Percy Alfred Blanks   Reginald Bartholomew Blackshaw

Blanks (46), an agricultural contractor, was alleged to have shot Blackshaw (43), a cowman. He said: "I shot him. He said I was lazy." Blanks was a frequent visitor to the Blackshaws who treated him as one of the family.

The Detective Inspector who arrested Blanks said that, when making a statement, Blanks seemed indifferent. He did not grasp the position he was in. He asked if he was going to be locked up and said, "I suppose I will go to prison for this." His main worry seemed to be that he had to sort out his income tax papers because he had been late in sending in his return. Medical evidence was given by Dr. Brisby, principal Medical Officer at Brixton Prison, and by Dr. Gibbens of the Bethlem hospital. Dr. Brisby testified that from reports of neighbours Blanks was regarded as peculiar. He had been able to earn his living as an agricultural contractor but it was clear that although he worked hard he had no grasp of the business side of his job. He could not cost his work and merely guessed what he could charge. He was described as always being in a muddle. His I.Q. was 75. Dr. Brisby assessed him as being little above the highest level of mental deficiency envisaged by the Mental Deficiency Act 1913 (now replaced by the Mental Health Act). Dr. Brisby's diagnosis was that Blanks suffered from a retarded development of the mind, having a mental age of 10 or 12, and that he had substantial defects of judgment and perception. Dr. Gibbens agreed with this view.

At *Essex Assizes, 1.3.1962, he was found not guilty of capital murder but guilty of manslaughter under section 2. Mr. Justice Lawton postponed sentence to consider whether to deal with him under the Mental Health Act.*

At *Surrey Assizes* a week later Blanks was order to be detained in a mental hospital. A restriction order, unlimited in duration, was made under section 65 of the Mental Health Act 1959.

Eric Green Bowler   Janice Yvonne Bowler

Bowler (27), an unemployed driver, had three children, including Janice (6 weeks). One evening he was looking after her and she would not stop crying. He shook her and "at that instant, I lost control and smacked her on the face". He smacked her again "to make both her cheeks red". Dr. Francis Camps said he exaggerated the force of the blows and trivial ones could kill a baby.

At *Glamorgan Assizes, 9.4.1962, he pleaded not guilty to murder but guilty to manslaughter. Both pleas were accepted. Mr. Justice Veale sentenced him to 19 days' imprisonment, permitting his immediate release.*

Charles Brown   Phoebe Brown

Brown (49), a labourer, was very depressed and feared he had to go into hospital. He was worried what would happen to his wife in his absence so he hit her and, when she struggled, he strangled her.

At *the Old Bailey, 19.9.1962, he was found guilty but insane. He was detained during H.M.P.*

In 1958 he had had a mental breakdown and later suffered from a depressive psychosis with paranoid delusions. He was happily married, but heard a voice saying, "She must die before dawn."

Kenneth Robert Leon Burrell   George Henry Howard

Burrell (32), a seaman, came home unexpectedly one night to find his wife in bed with Howard (48), whom the accused knew and had once worked with, lying on the bed partially clothed. The accused had been drinking but was not drunk. At the sight of the man he thereupon set upon him, kicking and punching him to death. The victim was Mrs. Burrell's driving instructor with whom she had been out at night leaving three young children in the care of a neighbour.

*Before Mr. Justice Thesiger at Essex Assizes, 19.2.1962, he pleaded not guilty to non-capital murder but guilty to manslaughter—*clearly a case of provocation—which was accepted by the prosecution. *He was sentenced to 4 years' imprisonment.* The judge said: "The accused undoubtedly had very, very severe provocation, but on the other hand the large number of divorces do indicate that this sort of situation, though not quite in such a dramatic form, is apt to arise and it would be a terrible thing if all people who commit misconduct while their husbands are away, were subjected to a violent attack like this."

Michael Butler   Joseph McEwan
James Martin Meaney
Thomas William Price

Butler (20), Meaney (19) and Price (18), all labourers, took part in a battle between soldiers and civilians in the street, in which McEwan (23), a R.E.M.E. private died. He was kicked to death.

At *Hampshire Assizes, 11.12.1962, no evidence was offered on the charge of murder:* the three accused and 8 others admitted to, and were bound over to keep the peace on a charge of affray.

Mr. Justice Glyn-Jones said it was impossible to pick out any one as being more blameworthy than the rest.

George Chappell   Mavis Chappell

Chappell (24), a wire-drawer, killed his wife (21) with a pickaxe at their home. They had two children and the wife was pregnant. On arrest Chappell said: "I did not kill her on purpose, she dared me." His diary showed he contemplated suicide. He was bankrupt and worried about money. His wife did not know he had not been working.

At *Sheffield Assizes, 5.6.1962, Chappell pleaded guilty to murder and was sentenced to life imprisonment.*

Colin Chisam   Hugh Tait

Chisam (55), a garage proprietor in Berwick-on-Tweed, killed Tait (21) in odd circumstances. Tait was one of a number of youths who had irritated Chisam by playing a transistor radio outside his house late at night. Chisam had taken out a gun and shot in the air —it was at first thought that Tait had died as a result of the gun shot wound. The youths immediately forced their way into Chisam's house. There ensued a fight during which Chisam was assaulted; he then brought out a swordstick in order, so he claimed, to defend himself, and his family. Two youths were injured and Tait died.

At *Durham Assizes, 19.10.1962, the jury accepted that death resulted from the swordstick and not from the shotgun, and therefore would have convicted Chisam of non-capital murder, but for the fact that a further plea of diminished responsibility was accepted. Chisam was sentenced to life imprisonment.*

Chisam appealed to the Court of Criminal Appeal, 12.3.1963, on the grounds that the trial judge, Mr. Justice Lyell, had misdirected the jury on self-defence. The Court of Criminal Appeal, in an important judgment on the question of self-defence, found that while the judge had omitted a part of the direction, such omission was wholly favourable to the defence. *The appeal was dismissed.* See *The Guardian* Law Report, 13.3.1963 (Manchester edition only) and [1963] Crim.L.R. 353.

The Court held that the judge ought to have put two questions to the jury: (1) Did Chisam honestly believe himself or his family to be in danger of death or serious injury?; and (2) if so, were there reasonable grounds for that belief? The judge had left only the first question for the jury's consideration. The court accepted that the judge had failed to direct the jury on the second issue; but the failure to direct the jury that the belief must be based on reasonable grounds was, if anything, highly favourable to Chisam, since it meant that, if the jury had been satisfied of his genuine belief, he would have been acquitted even if there had been no reasonable grounds for that belief.

Victor Clark   Gladys Florence Creek

Clark (36), a labourer, shot his neighbour Mrs. Creek (40) with a double-barrelled shotgun as she went to her dustbin. He admitted buying the gun for this purpose and told the police: "She had it coming to her . . . she had been talking about me and stopped me getting a job."

At *Chester Assizes, 6.6.1962, Clark was found guilty of capital murder but insane. He was ordered to be detained during H.M.P.*

Arrangements had earlier been made for him to enter a mental hospital voluntarily. Two doctors—their evidence was unchallenged—said he suffered from paranoid schizophrenia and he did not know what he was doing.

Michael William Clarke   Joseph Golding
Wyndham John King

Clarke (25) and King (22), both merchant seamen, served in the s.s. *Camito* with Golding (65), with whom they shared a cabin.

One evening they broke into the bosun's cabin and stole rum. They were both drunk, and, when Golding remonstrated, they threw him overboard into shark-infested waters 70 miles from land. King said he was drunk and remembered only putting Golding over the side. Clarke said he took no active part in the escapade; he also pleaded diminished responsibility.

At *Hampshire Assizes, 30.7.1962, both men were found not guilty of capital murder (in the course or furtherance of theft) but guilty of murder. Both were sentenced to life imprisonment.*

Clarke had a psychiatric history and was a schizoid psychopath of a violent disposition—the more so after drink. Three doctors said he came under section 2. The Crown doctors agreed he was a psychopath, but said he did not come under section 2. The Court of Criminal Appeal dismissed King's appeal, holding that his defence of drunkenness was fairly put to the jury who rejected it. The Court, however, allowed Clarke's appeal on a misdirection relating to the medical evidence. The case involved the difficult question of the diminution of an accused's mental responsibility by the taking of drink. [1962] Crim.L.R. 836.

Enid Connelly   Guilym Connelly

Connelly (46) was of good character. She had been married for 16 years to her husband (46), to whom she was devoted, and by whom she had two children. While she was cutting sandwiches with a sharp knife and gesticulating at the same time, the knife went into the husband's back. The defence consequently was that death was accidental.

At *Carmarthen Assizes, 13.12.1962*, it was held that there was no case to answer.

She was found not guilty of murder and discharged.

Joan Mary Coupland   Gillian Kerry Coupland

Joan Coupland (37) was the mother of 3 children, Sean (5), Gillian (1½) and Andrew (3 weeks). She was found unconscious in a gas-filled room with the 2 younger children, Gillian and Andrew beside her dead. She took 2 days to regain consciousness.

At the *Old Bailey, 20.2.1962, she was found not guilty of murder, but guilty of manslaughter under section 2. She was put on probation for 2 years by Mr. Justice Havers.* The charge of infanticide of Andrew was not proceeded with.

She said: "I intended to commit suicide." She suffered from depression after the pregnancy.

Maurice John Cox   Mary Jones

Cox (22), a photographic printer, was engaged to Miss Jones (27). One evening he strangled her at her lodgings with his hands and a dressing gown cord. They had been kissing and she was naked. He told the police: "They will hang me for it won't they? I gave her a good kiss then I got astride of her and put my hands round her throat . . . I felt like it, so I did it."

At the *Old Bailey, 31.1.1962, he was found unfit to plead and detained during H.M.P.*

William Aston Cragg   David Marshall

Cragg (24), a machinist, was alleged to have knocked down Marshall (40) and kicked him to death outside the Public Hall in Preston. It appeared that Marshall had been drinking, was very aggressive and had started the fight, despite Cragg's efforts to pacify him. Cragg gave himself up to the police when he heard of the death. There was no evidence that Cragg's blow caused the death.

At *Lancaster Assizes, 12.2.1962, Cragg was found not guilty of both murder and manslaughter; he was discharged.*

Charles Henry Curtis   Harry Gordon Bartlett

Curtis (39), a merchant seaman, was at a family party at his home when everyone drank too much. The prosecution alleged he used a shotgun to shoot Bartlett (24), another seaman, who lived at the same address. Curtis said "I had no intention of doing him any harm. I just wanted him . . . out of the house. He grabbed for the end of the gun. I heard a shot and he fell down."

At *Leeds Assizes, 20.12.1962, he was found not guilty of capital murder, but guilty of manslaughter. The jury recommended mercy. He was jailed for 12 months.*

Bryan George Edward Davis   Ann Pervaiz

Davis (27), unemployed, was the landlord of Mrs. Pervaiz (28), who was separated from her husband. He was on intimate terms with her. He was alleged to have strangled her and prepared to bury her under the floorboards. She was discovered in bed having been dead for 8 days, after her child (2½) had been left on the steps of Westminster Hospital. Davis maintained he knew nothing of her death and was merely trying to mend an electricity fault under the floorboards. He had, however, been seen with the child between Mrs. Pervaiz's death and the discovery. He gave no evidence at his trial.

At the *Old Bailey, 12.7.1962, he was found guilty of murder and sentenced to life imprisonment. The Court of Criminal Appeal, 12.11.1961, dismissed his appeal.* [1963] Crim.L.R. 40.

Anthony Charles Dawkins   Brian Dawkins

Anthony Dawkins (16) had a quarrel with his brother, Brian (14), over whether the door should be open or shut while the T.V. was on. In the quarrel Anthony struck Brian in the chest with a pen-knife. Anthony later ran away to the local vicar.

At the *Old Bailey, 8.1.1962, Anthony's plea of not guilty of murder but guilty of manslaughter was accepted. He was put on probation for 3 years.*

Donald Dawson (see: George William Fox)

June Norah Dolby   Robert John Dolby

Mrs. Dolby (32), a housewife, was found with her son (2) in a gas-filled kitchen at home. The son died. As a result of oxygen starvation at the time, she suffered organic brain damage.

At *Northamptonshire Assizes, 23.1.1962, she was found unfit to plead as a result of the damage to her brain, and was ordered to be detained during H.M.P.*

William Henry Dudding   Ethel May Walker

Dudding (32), a carpet-weaver, broke into his wife's home, armed with a knife, an air-pistol, a torch and other items. He entered her bedroom and found her in bed with Mrs. Walker (65), the mother of friends of the wife, who was keeping her company. He may have thought she was a man, as she was stabbed in the throat and received multiple injuries.

At *Sheffield Assizes, 23.7.1962, he was found guilty of murder and sentenced to life imprisonment.*

The Leeds Prison Medical Officer said he had retrograde amnesia from a car crash subsequent to the murder.

Charles Anthony Dunn   Roy Blakey

Dunn (19), a miner, visited several pubs one evening and then got into a "pointless quarrel" with Blakey (18), who apparently had looked at him unduly. Blakey was found unconscious behind a pub. Dunn was 6 ft. 2 in. while Blakey was only 5 ft. 9 in. Dunn told the police: "I hit him . . . he fell and his head hit the floor."

At *Leeds Assizes, 10.4.1962, he pleaded not guilty to murder but guilty to manslaughter*. Both pleas were accepted. *He was sentenced to 4 years' imprisonment.*

Dunn was said to be deeply shocked and to have learned his lesson.

Ronald Eastwood   Adrian Eastwood

Eastwood (26), a reeler, beat his son Adrian (6 weeks) to death.

At *Leeds Assizes, 10.5.1962, he was found not guilty of murder, but guilty of manslaughter under section 2. He was sentenced to life imprisonment by Mr. Justice Phillimore.*

He suffered from epilepsy, was of low intelligence and was erratic, uncontrollable and unstable. He was very violent.

Charles Carmel Falzon   Benjamin Mason

Falzon (46), unemployed, was a Maltese, whose family was engaged in a vendetta with the Masons, another Maltese family. He had been involved in a fight with Mason (43) as a result of which he spent 5 days in hospital. On the occasion of the killing, it was alleged that Falzon was seen with a knife in his belt before a fight in the street occurred between them, in which Mason died. Falzon said that Mason was drunk and challenged him to come outside. As he was in the kitchen, he picked up a knife and Mason walked on to it.

At the *Old Bailey, 25.7.1962, he was found not guilty of murder but guilty of manslaughter, probably on the grounds of provocation. He was sentenced to 6 years' imprisonment.* He had previous convictions.

Albert Flint   Patricia Trevor

Flint (56), a night-watchman, strangled Trevor (59) in his room in a lodging house and hid her naked body under the bed. He later told the police.

At *Manchester Crown Court, 11.12.1962, he was found not guilty of murder, but guilty of manslaughter.* Mr. Justice Brabin said, "he was so drunk as to be incapable of forming an intent sufficient for murder." *He was sentenced to life imprisonment.* Couple met at a bus stop and went to his room.

[Authors' note: At Manchester Crown Court in July 1960, Flint had been sentenced to 12 months' imprisonment for manslaughter of a widow (49) in almost identical circumstances. She was strangled and hidden under the bed; he then told the police. He had also been drinking (see Flint (1960)).]

Thomas Walter Flynn   Jean Flynn

Flynn (33), a window-cleaner, strangled his wife (28) at their home. The wife had been carrying on with, and was pregnant by, a Jamaican schoolboy (18). The husband had forgiven her many infidelities but this time he had had enough. He told the police: "These coloured men think they can do what they like. I want to die. I want to join Jean."

At *Leeds Assizes, 9.5.1962, he was found not guilty of murder but guilty of manslaughter.* Defence submitted both provocation and diminished responsibility. Flynn was of low intelligence and emotionally unbalanced. *He was sentenced to imprisonment for life by Mr. Justice Phillimore.*

George William Fox   Francis William Townson
Donald Dawson

Fox (29), a labourer, and Dawson (25), a driver, were charged with the capital murder (in the course or furtherance of a theft) of Townson (65), a coal merchant, who was found strangled with a red tie (not his own) outside his office. An attaché case containing £60 was missing. When arrested, Fox and Dawson told the police where the case was to be found, but denied any intention to kill Townson. Townson died from inhaling blood from facial injuries. Dawson said, "I tried to gag him with my tie . . . I only meant to shut him up. I only wanted money for my kids for Christmas."

At *Leeds Assizes, 6.4.1962, both were found not guilty of capital murder but guilty of manslaughter. Both were sent to prison for 10 years.* Dawson also received another 4 years, to run consecutively, for another robbery with violence.

Brian Gardiner   Marjorie Amelia Grace Pattison

Gardiner (22), a milkman, was stealing money from his employers and, to make up the deficiency, he went to the flat of a widow, Mrs. Pattison (71), to steal. She found him and went to telephone the police and, since she recognised him as her milkman, he grabbed her scarf and pulled it tight; in this way she was strangled.

At *Essex Assizes, 19.10.1962, he was found not guilty of capital murder, but guilty of manslaughter.* He had no intention to kill her. *He was sentenced to 12 years' imprisonment.*

Derrick Garnett   Michele Garnett

Garnett (21) was the father of Michele (3 months). He lost his temper and struck the baby with his fist several times when she would not go to sleep.

At *Leeds Assizes, 12.3.1962, he was found guilty of murder. He was sentenced to life imprisonment.* Defence pleaded manslaughter, as he had lost control and did not intend to cause grievous bodily harm.

Martha Patterson Gibson   Evelyn Margaret Gibson
                                                 Keith Gibson

Mrs. Gibson (29) strangled her daughter (6) and son (3) at their home. She had suffered from mental trouble since the birth of her first child. She told the doctor: "My babies being parted from me is my punishment. My worries died with my children." She was worried that they would inherit her mental condition.

At *Newcastle Assizes, 19.11.1962, before Mr. Justice Veale, she was found not guilty of murder but guilty of manslaughter under section 2. She was ordered to be detained in Broadmoor.*

She had twice been in a mental hospital during 1962 and after the murder she had tried to gas herself.

Hilda Golder   Ernest Cyril Golder

Mrs. Golder (55), the wife of an employee of a radio firm, had a long quarrel with her husband (58) about another woman, during which he struck her many times. Next day when he was eating breakfast, she shot him with his shotgun at point-blank range. She then called for help. She told the police, "He beat me up badly last night and tried to kick me in the tummy . . . I had to defend myself. I did not realise what I was doing."

At *Hertford Assizes, 6.12.1962, she was found not guilty of capital murder, but guilty of manslaughter under section 2. Mr. Justice Hinchcliffe ordered her to be detained in hospital under section 60 of the Mental Health Act 1959.* A doctor said she was very depressed following a major operation in 1961.

Frank Goodman   William Nelson

Goodman (22), unemployed fitter, battered Nelson (48) to death at the latter's flat in April 1962. In August he sent messages in code to the police and finally was picked up by the police, while ringing 999 to give them another message.

In a 2-minute hearing at *Manchester Crown Court, 3.12.1962, his plea of not guilty to capital murder* (presumably in the course or furtherance of theft) *and guilty to non-capital murder was accepted. He was sentenced to life imprisonment.* A further charge of attempted murder of another man was not proceeded with.

Stephen Michael Green   Stephanie Green

Green (20), a post-office linesman, killed his daughter Stephanie (9 months) by hitting her to stop her screaming. His wife was out at the time and she returned to find him asleep and the baby dead. He said: "I lost my head and kept on hitting her." He had been drinking.

At *Birmingham Assizes, 19.7.1962, he pleaded not guilty to murder, but guilty to manslaughter. Both pleas were accepted. Mr. Justice Stable sent him to prison for 5 years.*

His wife was said to be remaining loyal to him.

Panayiotis Gregoriou   Costas Vassiliou

Gregoriou (28) got into an argument with Vassiliou (27), another Greek Cypriot, outside a café in the Seven Sisters Road. Apparently he had been leaning on Vassiliou's car. He said he picked up a gun from the ground and shot Vassiliou, who weighed 15 stone. At any rate he told the police: "I am a small man, he hit me and I shot him." Another man was wounded by the shots.

At the *Old Bailey, 19.9.1962, he was found not guilty of capital murder but guilty of manslaughter under section 2.*

Dr. Brisby, the Brixton Medical Officer, said he came within section 2. He was a depressive neurotic and hysterical. He had been in hospital with a hysterical abdominal complaint. *He was sentenced to life imprisonment by Mr. Justice Roskill. The Court of Criminal Appeal, 9.11.1962, refused him leave to appeal.*

Oswald Augustus Grey   Thomas Arthur Bates

Grey (20), a Jamaican baker, shot Bates (46) in the latter's newspaper shop one evening. Grey was desperate for money, having been on National Assistance for 12 months. There was, however, no evidence that anything was stolen. Grey had stolen a pistol and admittedly had it in his possession at 3.30 p.m. and again at 10 p.m. The killing occurred at 6.30 p.m. Grey gave 5 different versions of what happened to him or the gun at that time of the killing.

At *Birmingham Assizes, 12.10.1962, Grey was found guilty of capital murder and sentenced to death.*

The Court of Criminal Appeal, on 29.10.1962, dismissed Grey's Appeal: [1963] Crim.L.R. 440.

The Home Secretary declined to recommend a reprieve, 17.11.1962.

Grey was hanged at Winson Green Prison, Birmingham, 20.11.1962.

Eric Anthony Morton Hadfield   Mary Felicia Hannah Hadfield

Hadfield (54), a retired mining engineer, strangled his wife (61) at their home the day after an order had been made committing her to prison for contempt of court following a legal action over a will. He said, "I am not allowing my Molly to go to Holloway. We had a couple of drinks and she died with her lips on mine. Her last words were 'Don't make a mistake'."

At *Devon Assizes, 13.2.1962, he was found unfit to plead, and Mr. Justice Widgery ordered him to be detained during H.M.P.*

James Hanratty   Michael John Gregsten

Hanratty (25), unemployed, shot Michael John Gregsten (34), a physicist. Gregsten was with Miss Valerie Storie (23) in his car in a cornfield, when the killer approached with a gun and forced Gregsten to drive them away. Some hours later they stopped in a lay-by, where Hanratty shot Gregsten twice in the head. He then was alleged to have raped Miss Storie when she was in the back of the car; he afterwards shot her 5 times leaving her for dead.

At *Bedford Assizes, 17.2.1962, after a trial lasting 21 days*—the longest in English legal history for a murder trial—Hanratty *was found guilty of capital murder and sentenced to death.*

[Author's note: Hanratty's defence was that he was in Rhyl at the time of the murder. He had earlier told the police he was in Liverpool, but admitted he was lying to cover up the fact he could not remember where he stayed in Rhyl. The jury was out for nearly 10 hours before returning its verdict. The appeal to the C.C.A. was hopeless—the judge's summing up, being meticulous in detail but omitting some important matters, was entirely favourable to the accused. The C.C.A. said it was "clear, it was impartial, it was not only fair but favourable to the prisoner . . ." The appeal was dismissed on 14.3.1962. A petition for a reprieve was launched amid a welter of publicity; there were grounds for suggesting that Hanratty was an inadequate psychopath—he had once been diagnosed, perhaps not very convincingly, as a mental defective. The reprieve was not forthcoming and he was *executed at Bedford Prison on 4.4.1962.* On 2 August 1963 Mr. Fenner Brockway M.P. initiated an adjournment debate in the House of Commons calling on the Home Secretary to order a public inquiry into the case. He presented a long memorandum to the Home Office in which a police-discarded suspect in the investigations into the crime gave a rambling, largely incoherent and confused confession. The Home Secretary, replying to the motion, called the confession "bogus" and "spurious", adding that the memorandum contained virtually nothing that was not already known to the authorities. (See Hansard, H.C., Vol. 682, Col. 795).

See Blom-Cooper, *The A.6. murder, R. v. Hanratty; The Semblance of Truth* (Penguin Special). 1963.]

Francis Joseph Hardy   **James Kenyon**

Hardy (25), a painter and decorator, was alleged to have murdered Kenyon (38) who died after falling in a fight with Hardy in the street outside a dance hall which both men had been frequenting.

At *Liverpool Crown Court, 12.10.1962,* the defence was not called upon and *Hardy was found not guilty of murder and was discharged.*

Mr. Justice Stable said: "You leave this court without a stain on your character. A charge of murder ought never to have been brought against you. If anyone ever says you were charged with murder, you can say that I think you ought not to have been."

Rene Hargreaves   Ernest Massey

Hargreaves (54), a spinster, lived in an isolated cottage in Cornwall with another woman and Massey (78), the husband of Hargreaves' late nurse. Hargreaves put weed-killer, sodium chlorate, in Massey's tea and so poisoned him. She said: "I gave him (it) to make him ill so that he would go into hospital." Massey was dirty, unwashed and unkempt. He was very nosey and spent much time tasting odd things like turpentine and methylated spirits, etc.

At *Hampshire Assizes, 5.4.1962, Hargreaves was found not guilty of murder but guilty of manslaughter.*

She was sentenced to 18 months' imprisonment.

Mr. Justice Finnemore said: "You intended to do him some harm."

Willoughby Harland   Joyce Harland

Harland (46), a tile-maker, was of good reputation and devoted to his wife. There was, therefore, no apparent reason for his strangling her one night and then trying to gas himself.

At *Kent Assizes, 27.11.1962, he was found not guilty of murder, but guilty of manslaughter under section 2. Mr. Justice Melford Stevenson sentenced him to 2 years' imprisonment,* saying there were no grounds for making a hospital order under the Mental Health Act 1959.

Two doctors (unchallenged) said at the time of the killing Harland had been suffering from transient depressive melancholia.

Frederick Roy Harvey   Anne Harvey
                                                 Gillian Harvey

Harvey (40), a gardener, strangled his two daughters, aged 10 and 8, and battered his wife unconscious with an axe. He had apparently realised for some time that he was in danger of having to go to a mental institution, so he decided to kill himself after

9

killing his family, to avoid leaving them as a public charge. After the killing he tried to drown himself, but went to the police and said: "I've done my family in." He was soaking wet.

At *Hampshire Assizes, 11.12.1962, before Mr. Justice Glyn-Jones, he was found not guilty of murder, but guilty of manslaughter under section 2. He was sent to Broadmoor.*

Thomas Hatton   Maureen Hatton

Hatton (28) was, at the time of the killing, living apart from his wife (23); he went to the radio shop where she was manageress to discuss a divorce. When she started screaming, he lost his head and strangled her.

At the *Old Bailey, 13.4.1962, Hatton was found not guilty of murder, but guilty of manslaughter. He was sentenced to 7 years' imprisonment.*

Ronald Frederick Hawkes   Gladys Hawkes

Hawkes (38), a footwear-worker, axed his wife to death at their home. He met the police and showed them the room and the weapon and told them: "I don't know why I did it."

At *Birmingham Assizes, 20.7.1962, he was found unfit to plead and detained during H.M.P.*

Doctors said he showed no concern for his fate and could not understand the proceedings.

Margaret Hebden   George Hebden

Hebden (71) became so depressed nursing her invalid husband (70) that she finally strangled him to end his misery. He had been suffering grievously and was paralysed.

At *Leeds Assizes, 29.11.1962, before the Lord Chief Justice (Lord Parker), she was found not guilty of murder but guilty of manslaughter under section 2. At the time of the offence she was deeply depressed. A hospital order, under section 60 of the Mental Health Act 1959, was made.*

David Michael Helbing   Pauline Mary Crane

Helbing (29), a finance company's representative, was told by his girl-friend (21) that they must stop seeing each other. She may have lost her temper with him. She was strangled with a dressing gown cord at his flat, and he then attempted suicide beside her.

At *Birmingham Assizes, 12.10.1962, he pleaded guilty to murder and was sentenced to life imprisonment.*

John Henshaw (see: Albert Henry Quigley)

James M. W. J. Heron   D. Field

Heron (19), a warehouse boy, walked into the newspaper shop kept by Field (68), picked up a bottle of Tizer, hit Field over the head and stole £12 10s. 0d. Field later died in hospital. Heron confessed to his family and then ran away. When arrested a week later, he told the police: "(I hit him) I had no intention of doing it, but I suddenly picked up the bottle and hit him . . . I did not intend to kill him."

At the *Old Bailey, 17.9.1962, he was found not guilty of capital murder but guilty of manslaughter under section 2. He was sentenced by Mr. Justice Roskill to life imprisonment.*

Two doctors said he was below average intelligence, and was withdrawn and isolated.

Veral Hey   Enez Hey

Hey (31), a West Indian, stabbed 5 people with a knife, including his wife (35) who died from the wounds. He apparently ran amok.

At *Manchester Crown Court, 24.7.1962, he was found unfit to plead and detained during H.M.P.*

A prison doctor said he suffered from schizophrenia.

Peter Hinds   Stephen Hanrahan

Hinds (23), a fish buyer, used a knife and stabbed Hanrahan (24) in a scuffle in the street in a small Welsh village. It seems that Hanrahan was the aggressor and Hinds acted in self-defence. The row was over Hinds' ex-fiancée. He said: "This man got out of the van and hit me . . . I let him have it."

At *Flintshire Assizes, 9.10.1962, Hinds pleaded not guilty to murder but guilty to manslaughter. Both pleas were accepted. Mr. Justice Howard said it was an exceptional case and put him on probation for 3 years.*

Terence Hughes   June Roberts

Hughes (18), a soldier in the Royal Fusiliers, punched and jumped

on the body of Roberts (23) and left her dead behind a bakery.
She had been raped. Hughes had picked her up one evening when
he had been drinking; apparently she was quite willing to be picked
up. He told the police: "We started kissing and then I went sort of
mad and started hitting her."

At *Denbighshire Assizes, 15.10.1962, Hughes pleaded guilty to
murder and was sentenced to life imprisonment.*

Ishmael Beresford Jones   Florence Eugenie Brown

Jones (24), a Jamaican labourer, had lived on intimate terms
with Miss Brown (29) both in Jamaica and in England. When she
refused to continue the association despite his entreaties he stabbed
her seven times outside her flat. He told the police that he had killed
her and said, "She said she no want me. I not good enough." He
could not remember killing her, but knew he had done wrong with
the knife.

At the *Old Bailey, 19.7.1962, he was found guilty of murder and
gaoled for life. A recommendation for deportation was made under
the Commonwealth Immigrants Act 1962.*

Mr. Justice Lawton overruled a defence submission of provocation, saying there was not enough evidence of this. Dr. Brisby said
Jones fell within the low category of normality.

[Authors' note: There was some doubt whether the courts have
the power to recommend deportation of a Commonwealth citizen
in addition to passing a mandatory sentence of life imprisonment,
since the sentence in those circumstances is literally a sentence for
life and that, although the convicted person might be let out of
prison within approximately ten years, the release is only on
licence and subject to recall. Section 7(1) of the Commonwealth
Immigrants Act 1962 does, however, provide for a recommendation for deportation of a person convicted of an "offence punishable with imprisonment" without any qualification. Any actual
deportation after release would make the Home Secretary's power
of recall ineffective.]

Alfred Kemp   Shirley Kemp

Kemp (26), a machine operator at Ford's (Dagenham),
quarrelled with his wife (25) about him working night-shifts. She
complained; he shook her and she went limp. "It was an accident. I
didn't mean to do it."

At *Essex Assizes, 22.10.1962, he was found not guilty of murder and was discharged.*

His defence was that he was trying to comfort her, with his arm about her neck, when they both fell to the floor. It was then that she went limp.

William Kent   Lilian Kent

Kent (58), a market gardener, shot his sister in the head with a sports gun while she was sitting at the breakfast table. He thought she was poisoning him.

At *Hampshire Assizes, 10.12.1962, he was found guilty of capital murder but insane.* He was ordered to be *detained during H.M.P.*

Doctors said he was a paranoid schizophrenic.

Afyal Khan   Zilda Ruth Mitchell

Khan (21), a Pakistani, stabbed his English mother-in-law during a quarrel. He also stabbed his wife.

At *Nottingham Assizes, 17.7.1962, he was found not guilty of murder, but guilty of manslaughter. He was sentenced to 7 years' imprisonment.*

Khan claimed he carried the knife only to frighten them.

Albert Harold King   Edith King

King (69), a retired insurance agent and former Councillor in the Borough of Woodstock, married his second wife in 1959. She was then 69. They had frequent quarrels. He said, "Every day she would start up a row by throwing things." On the occasion of the crime, on Good Friday morning, it was the first time he struck her. He went to the police and said, "Good morning, I am afraid I have hit my wife over the head with an axe"—the skull was shattered in at least eight places with a minimum of two blows. She died in hospital. He later said: "I didn't do it to murder her. I think I was temporarily deranged at the time." He said that his life had been a misery.

At *Oxford Assizes, 7.6.1962, he was found not guilty of murder, but guilty of manslaughter under section 2. A hospital order was made with a restriction order of unlimited duration.* Mr. Justice Veale said that, as these were "very, very exceptional circumstances", in his case he did not propose to send King to prison.

Doctors said he was prematurely old and had an impaired

memory. He could not remember his own date of birth. Dr.
Mandelbrote said that King was not, however, M'Naghten mad,
as suggested by the prosecution (cf. Price (1962).)

Wyndham John King (see: Michael William Clarke)

Ena Jeannett Lambert   **Richard Lambert**

Mrs. Lambert (29), the wife of a farm-worker, was alleged to
have strangled her son (4). She also had a daughter (2).

At *Sussex Assizes, 8.6.1962, she was found insane and unfit to
plead and was ordered to be detained during H.M.P.*

The Holloway senior medical officer said that Mrs. Lambert
was in a very depressed melancholic condition and sat gazing out
of the window for hours. Two other doctors agreed she was unfit
to plead. One doctor said she was mentally ill, but was fit to plead.

Doret Cynthia Legore   **Cecil Taylor**

Legore (20), a West Indian, had been living with Taylor, a
coloured man, for 2 or 3 months. She was 8½ months pregnant by
another man. One day they had a quarrel in which she picked up a
glass water jug and hit him twice on the neck. He was stabbed by a
fragment. She told the police: "my husband and I have just had a
row and I hit him with the jug . . . he hit me first." She was mentally
normal, though somewhat backward. This, combined with her
pregnancy and Taylor's earlier violence towards her, could have
impaired her self-control.

At the *Old Bailey, 20.11.1962, she was found not guilty of murder
and discharged.*

Glenford Linton   **Harbhajan Singh Basi**

Linton (39), a Jamaican carpenter, stabbed Basi (21), an Indian,
in a back entry in the coloured quarter of Derby. They were
quarrelling over a broken lodging-house window.

At *Derbyshire Assizes, 6.6.1962, he was found guilty of murder
and sentenced to life imprisonment.*

Stanley Lister   **Edith Woodhams**

Lister (41), unemployed, lived with his common-law wife who
collected rents for Miss Woodhams (79). One day Lister went up

to her rooms and strangled her with a woollen hood and her hearing aid. He told police: "I honestly don't know why I did it . . . she has always been nice to me." He remembered the killing only vaguely. He took a little money from a tin box.

At the *Old Bailey, 6.4.1962, he was found not guilty of capital murder (in the course or furtherance of theft) but guilty of manslaughter, presumably under section 2. Mr. Justice Salmon ordered him to be detained under section 60 of the Mental Health Act 1959.*

Since a fall, Lister had been prone to have black-outs. He had frequently been in hospital. He said, "I've been upside down for a couple of years."

James Robert Lowe   Evelyn Lowe

Lowe (43), a cotton operative, father of five children, strangled his wife in a quarrel over another man at their home. She worked in a mill and had formed an affection for a man who worked there. She wrote letters to him signed: "Your dearest lover", which Lowe discovered. He gave her "a good hiding" and forgave her. However, there were more rows and finally: "She took off her wedding ring and threw it at me. I went mad. I looked at her. I thought there might be a chance, so I walked to the police station."

At *Leeds Assizes, 19.10.1962, the jury retired for 8 minutes and brought in a verdict of not guilty of murder, but guilty of manslaughter on the ground of provocation. The jury also recommended mercy. Mr. Justice Stable gave Lowe an absolute discharge.*

John McCarthey   Eric Haley
Alastair Hind Ball

McCarthey (21), a labourer, and Ball (23), a fish-filleter, entered the home of Haley (39), whose body was found both battered with a poker and cut with a knife. It was alleged that both accused intended to steal. The defence was that all three men were homosexuals, that Haley had a letter written by Ball and was blackmailing Ball. McCarthey and Ball went to get the letter. Haley just laughed and a fight ensued. A briefcase was taken from the house.

At *Leeds Assizes, 24.5.1962, both were found not guilty of capital murder but guilty of non-capital murder. Both were sentenced to life imprisonment.*

Michael Henry McCowliff   Mona Errington

McCowliff (22), a miner, had been engaged to Miss Errington (19) for one year, when they began to quarrel over their holidays and money matters. He said: "I lost my temper. I got hold of her by the throat and strangled her. I had no intention of strangling her. I still loved her." The death was caused by only slight pressure.

At *Durham Assizes, 15.10.1962, he was found not guilty of murder, but guilty of manslaughter. He was sentenced to 5 years' imprisonment.*

Bernard Joseph McCrorey   Mary Elsie Salter

McCrorey (29), a labourer, was a frequent visitor to a public house kept by Mrs. Salter (57) and her husband. One day she refused to lend him money, so he hid after closing time and brutally attacked and killed her with a hammer belonging to workmen on the premises. He took £18 from the till.

At *Manchester Crown Court, 20.7.1962, he was found guilty of murder (capital) and sentenced to death.*

Defence doctors said that McCrorey came within the defence of diminished responsibility; but the prosecution doctors, while recognising McCrorey's mental illness, thought that the impairment of his mental responsibility was not substantial. McCrorey had a long mental history and was classified as a psychopath. He had repeatedly attempted suicide and had been deported from Canada for this very offence. He had been a voluntary mental patient. McCrorey's appeal, 31.7.1962, was allowed on the grounds that Mr. Justice Lyell had inaccurately heard and relayed to the jury a part of the evidence of one of the medical witnesses. The doctors were generally of the opinion that, if the killing had been premeditated, this would destroy the theory of substantial impairment of responsibility; if the killing were in a crisis caused by surprise, then the theory applied. Mr. Justice Lyell, in his summing up, had included a "not", so that he directed the jury whether or not there was premeditation the doctors could not say impairment was substantial. The report of the case, R. v. McCrorey [1962] Crim. L.R. 703, is not very satisfactory on this point.

The Court of Criminal Appeal substituted a verdict of manslaughter under section 2, and a sentence of life imprisonment.

Ada Patricia McCusker   Joseph John McCusker
Alfred Edwin Musgrave

The victim (56) was killed as a result of three blows with an axe at his home at Whitfields, Lancashire. The only two other people in the house were his wife, Ada Patricia McCusker (38) and Alfred Edwin Musgrave (32), whom the McCuskers had befriended and provided with a home since his release from prison a few weeks before the killing on 26 July 1962.

Mrs. McCusker had married her husband in March 1962 while Musgrave, whom she had known prior to her marriage, was serving a sentence for an offence of fraud. She herself had spent 17 years in a mental hospital since the age of 19 where she had been sent from an approved school to which she had been committed at the age of 15 for stealing. She had been certified as feeble-minded and on her discharge in 1960 she had been declared as having a mental age of 11. On her discharge she had first been a maid but had then taken to prostitution in Manchester. Musgrave was an unstable character, having several times attempted to commit suicide.

On the evening of the killing, the husband, who was financially well off and had lent money to Musgrave, came home late after a bout of heavy drinking. It was not at all clear which of the two accused had wielded the fatal blows—they both made conflicting statements and at the trial attempted to throw the blame on the other.

It was clear that both accused were in a highly emotional state, resentful of the deceased, that they were both mentally unstable, and that they too had been drinking. There was some evidence that Musgrave had asked Mrs. McCusker to get hold of her husband's money and to run away with him. The deceased had been suspicious of their relationship and had been jealous of Musgrave, who in turn found the deceased getting on his nerves.

The two were indicted jointly for *non-capital murder at Manchester Crown Court* before *Mr. Justice Brabin* and a jury. At the end of a long trial, ending on *3.12.1962*, the jurors were warned by the judge on several occasions that they must be absolutely sure that the two accused had acted in concert, because if no common design was proved the jury could not convict both of the charge of murder. And if the jury was doubtful which of the two did the killing both had to be acquitted. Neither accused pleaded diminished responsibility.

The jury brought in a verdict of guilty of both accused; they were automatically sentenced to life imprisonment. An appeal to the Court of Criminal Appeal, 28/29.5.1963, was unsuccessful. That Court declared that where two people are both present in a house at the time that the killing took place that was evidence that the two acted in concert in killing the victim, sufficient for the jury to conclude that they did act in concert.

Joan McDonnell   William Webster

McDonnell (21), a kitchen-hand at a club, stabbed Webster (22), a waiter at the same club, in the back with a 26 in. meat knife. They had quarrelled over a bottle of wine that Webster had stolen, and for which another waiter was blamed. When McDonnell complained, he threatened to kill her and she stabbed him. They had been engaged for 3 years, and he had been violent to her on several occasions. She was pregnant by Webster, which in the circumstances caused some mental anxiety and depression.

At *Surrey Assizes, 13.3.1962, she was found not guilty of murder but guilty of manslaughter under section 2. Mr. Justice Lawton put her on probation for 3 years.*

Daniel Clyde McGowan   John Harvey

McGowan (52) was the bo'sun of the s.s. *Barrington Court*, in which Harvey (21) was serving. During the voyage, Harvey, a bully, had several fights and tried to become "the top dog". In Rangoon, he had an argument with McGowan over who should be nightwatchman and thus earn the extra pay. He was told to take his turn, whereupon he punched McGowan who drew a sheath-knife. Harvey rushed forward and the knife went into him. McGowan said: "I only drew it to frighten him. I never intended using it."

At the *Old Bailey, 25.10.1962, McGowan was found not guilty of murder or manslaughter. McGowan was discharged.*

[Authors' note: Although in this case the accused was acquitted, it is remarkable how seamen figure continually in the calendar of murder. The conditions of life in many merchant ships under which men have to perform exacting work in close proximity for weeks on end and the not infrequent problem of alcoholism produce a situation in which violence is seldom wholly absent. A ship's company represents the context in which the modified Durk-

heimian proposition obtains—that murder varies directly with the
strength of the relational system see Chapter III p. 283]

Marion Madge   Twin children

Mrs. Madge (25), a mother of four children, killed her twins (14
months) while they slept in their pram, and then tried to gas herself
in the kitchen.

At *Hampshire Assizes, 17.12.1962, she was found not guilty of
murder, but guilty of manslaughter under section 2. A hospital order
was made under section 60 of the Mental Health Act 1959.*

She was depressed by another pregnancy.

Roger Martin   Doris Martin

Martin (44), a technical manager in paper-making mills, killed
his wife (42) with an axe. He admitted hitting her 6 times.

At *Kent Assizes, 19.11.1962, he was found not guilty of murder,
but guilty of manslaughter under section 2. He was sent to prison for
3 years. He is serving his sentence in H.M. Prison, Grendon—the new
psychiatric prison.*

He had been worried about money and loved his wife so much
that he could not bear to think of her anguish of mind, so he
killed her in her sleep. The Brixton medical officer and another
doctor said he was suffering from acute depression. He had lost
his job after 13 years and as a result had money troubles. He was
in ill-health and neurotic. He thought he would hang for murder
and only afterwards learnt he would not. He attempted suicide in
prison.

James Martin Meaney (see: Michael Butler)

Gerald Lancaster Miller   Josephine Iona Miller

Miller (23), an unemployed diver's dresser, struck his wife (18)
with a hammer and then, when she was asleep in a chair, stabbed her.
She was $8\frac{1}{2}$ months pregnant. He went straight to the police and
told them of the killing.

At *Lancaster Assizes, 28.5.1962, Miller was found guilty of
murder but insane. He was ordered to be detained during H.M.P.*

Two doctors—their evidence was unchallenged—said Miller was
a schizophrenic and did not know his act was wrong. He killed her

to protect her because he loved her. He had previously been in a mental hospital. He had "a recurring disposition to kill".

Christopher Minter   Leslie Minter

Minter (15), a fitter's mate, shot his father (42), a dock worker. The father had threatened several times to kill the mother and the boy had protected her. Leslie Minter drank heavily.

At *Kent Assizes, 29.11.1962, he was found not guilty of capital murder but guilty of manslaughter under section 2. He was ordered by Mr. Justice Melford Stevenson to be detained in Rampton under section 60 of the Mental Health Act, 1959.*

He was illiterate and had "a kind of Sir Galahad complex".

[Authors' note: Rampton is a State mental institution for dangerous mental defectives.]

Joyce Mitchell   Timothy Mitchell

Mrs. Mitchell (36) strangled her son (15 months) while she was a patient in a mental hospital. The son was also mentally defective, and this fact contributed towards his death.

At *Nottingham Assizes, 6.12.1962, she was found not guilty of murder but guilty of manslaughter under section 2. Mr. Justice Elwes ordered her to be detained at Saxondale Mental Hospital.*

During the trial, the judge followed the practice of *Mr. Justice Lawton* in *R. v. Price* [*1963*] *2 Q.B.I.* of not allowing the prosecution to allege that the accused was guilty but insane when the defence raised the issue of diminished responsibility. See also *R. v. Nott (1958) 43 Cr. App.R. 8, and especially Duke (1961).*

John Moore   Mary Patricia Moore

Moore (25), an alloy-casting viewer, beat, battered and shook his daughter, Mary (3), to death. She was finally killed with a boxer's blow to the jaw. Moore said: "I did not mean to do it. I lost my temper and hit her with my belt". Mary had lived with grandparents and been only 27 weeks with the parents. Although Mary was a persistent bed-wetter, Moore was fond of the child.

At *Kent Assizes, 19.11.1962, Moore pleaded not guilty to murder but guilty of manslaughter. This was accepted by the prosecution. He was sentenced to 8 years' imprisonment.*

Alfred Edwin Musgrave (see: Ada Patricia McCusker)

John Anthony Nation   Marlene Nation

Nation (24) stabbed his wife, Marlene (22), with a pair of scissors in October 1961, on the day he finished a 9-month prison sentence for receiving. He told the police at once. He had suspected that she was associating with another man and "saw red" when she said that she was going away with him. The other man had just gone to prison himself.

At *Manchester Crown Court, 1.6.1962, Nation was found not guilty of murder, but guilty of manslaughter, presumably on the grounds of provocation. He was sent to prison for 3 years.*

While on remand he had fallen from scaffolding in prison and is now paralysed and confined to a wheelchair.

Winifred Newsome   Sidney Newsome

Mrs. Newsome had been divorced from her husband (35), but they had gone back to live together. He frequently hit her and had once broken her jaw. One day he got drunk and attacked her. She said: "He put the knife in my hand and dared me to stab him which I did." She was bruised at the time. She said: "What shall I do without him? I did not mean to kill him."

At *Leeds Assizes, 27.11.1962, she was found not guilty of either murder or manslaughter, and was discharged.*

The victim was described as a bully and a drunkard.

Patrick Joseph O'Leary   Frank Harrington

O'Leary (39), a homeless labourer, known as "Singer Dublin", attacked Harrington (32), another Irishman, with a broken bottle and inflicted 60 cuts on him. The two men and others were drinking cheap wine and methylated spirits on a bomb site.

At the *Old Bailey, 12.2.1962, O'Leary was found not guilty of murder but guilty of manslaughter. He was sentenced to 5 years' imprisonment.*

Dan Padgett   Mary Padgett

Padgett (50), a miner, killed his wife (38) at their home. They were a devoted couple and had been married for 18 years. Padgett said he had gone to bed one night and fallen asleep; the next thing he knew, he had woken up with his fingers down his wife's throat. She was dead from suffocation. He at once told the police that he had "done his wife in".

At *Leeds Assizes, 17.5.1962, he was found guilty but insane and detained during H.M.P.*

There was no apparent motive. The defence was one of automatism; medical evidence was also given of epilepsy and a lung-disease (pneumoconiosis), which for a time could starve the brain of oxygen, thereby rendering Padgett violent and unaware of what he was doing.

John William Paget   Lilian Paget

Paget (25), unemployed labourer, strangled his wife (21) with her stocking one evening in a field, when he had seen a man kiss her; "she had later said that if she hadn't been with me she would have been with another man". He at once told the police. The couple lived apart.

At *Durham Assizes, 16.10.1962, Paget was found not guilty of murder, but guilty of manslaughter. He was gaoled for 12 years.* The defence, which was accepted, was provocation.

Charles Benjamin Palmer   Mary Ruston

Palmer (58), a lorry driver, was the brother-in-law of his victim (50), in whose house he lived. She was a widow and he often talked of marrying her. She was found stabbed and strangled, and Palmer was unconscious in a gas-filled kitchen. When rescued he was violent and said he did not wish to live. He told the police that he thought the world of her, but could not remember much that happened. Her sons-in-law were against their marrying.

At the *Old Bailey, 22.6.1962, he was found unfit to plead and detained during H.M.P.*

Alfred Pascall   Ann Pascall

Pascall (72), a retired Ministry of Works employee, was constantly nagged by his wife (62). One day he killed her and went and told the police: "I have killed my wife in the kitchen with a chopper." He later said: "(she) had wanted me out of it for some time—she threatened to stick a knife in me . . . I saw red."

At the *Old Bailey, 14.11.1962, he was found insane and unfit to plead. He was ordered to be detained during H.M.P.*

Doctors said he suffered from severe depression with senile degeneracy. He was unstable and was considered a suicide risk. He had earlier had mental treatment and spent a week in a mental hospital. He had also taken an overdose of sleeping tablets.

Brian Phillips   Ethel Jones

Phillips (20), an electrician's mate, strangled Miss Jones (70), a music teacher, at her home. He then ransacked the house. He had been sent by his aunt to find her address for a Christmas card. He said: "I didn't mean to kill her."

At *Leeds Assizes, 19.3.1962, Phillips was found not guilty of capital murder, but guilty of non-capital murder. He was sentenced to life imprisonment.*

A psychiatrist said he was not responsible, having had a brain-storm. He probably did not know what he was doing. He "staged" the theft to cover up the murder.

Sheila Margaret Pickard   Marianne Pickard
                                                 Lynn Margaret Pickard

Pickard (29), wife of an Army captain, poured boiling water over her two children ($2\frac{1}{2}$ and $1\frac{1}{4}$) in the bath. They both died from the scalds. She demonstrated how she did it with a smile on her face. She told the police: "I was putting on a sort of act . . . I thought I was on T.V."

At *York Assizes, 26.10.1962, she was found insane and unfit to plead, and was ordered to be detained during H.M.P.*

She was a schizophrenic.

Henry John Potter   Violet Emily Potter

Potter (69), a retired tailor from Hinckley, had a quarrel with his wife (69), in which he battered her to death with an axe and then took sleeping pills. He was in hospital 4 days. Potter said he was more than sorry for what he did. He told police: "She was always on, always on. She would not leave me alone . . . It was getting on my mind . . . she called me everything . . . she nagged, nagged and nagged me. I couldn't stand it any longer." He said he struck her after she had snatched a tea-cloth out of his hand and said she would get a doctor and have him put away.

At *Birmingham Assizes, 27.3.1962, he was found not guilty of murder but guilty of manslaughter under section 2. He was gaoled for 8 years.*

Two doctors (unchallenged) said he was a psychopath. He had attempted suicide previously and been in a mental hospital. He had twice, in the last 10 years, received sentences of 5 years' imprisonment for attacking women.

Christopher Barry Price   Lena Phyllis Knight Limbrick Fisher

Price (30), a sawyer's mate, lodged at the house of Mrs. Fisher (34). She was found battered with a hammer, a carving knife and two table-knives. She had also been manually strangled. Price told the police: "Mrs. Fisher came into the kitchen to wash up. I had had wild turns before. All of a sudden I came over evil." He described the killing and concluded: "We had not been on bad terms."

At *Berkshire Assizes, 11.10.1962, he was found not guilty of murder, but guilty of manslaughter under section 2. Mr. Justice Lawton refused to allow the prosecution to allege that Price was insane. See [1963] 2 Q.B.I. The judge made a hospital order, under sections 60 and 65 of the Mental Health Act 1959, of unlimited duration. Compare R. v. Russell [1963] 3 All E.R. 603.*

Thomas William Price (See: Michael Butler)

Albert Henry Quigley   Patrick James Greene
John Henshaw

Quigley (18), a hod-carrier, and Henshaw (19), a lagger, attacked Greene, when all three were walking along the road. In the fight Greene fell into the culvert. Quigley hit Greene on the head with a stone. Items were taken from Greene's body, which was left battered in the culvert covered with stones. All three men had been drinking. Death was due to drowning.

At *Flintshire Assizes, 8.10.1962, Henshaw was acquitted of murder and discharged. No prima facie case had been made out against him. Quigley was found guilty of murder. Sentence: life imprisonment.*

John Patrick Quinlan   Michael Joseph Teahan

Quinlan (51), an Irish labourer, shared a room with his victim (15). The boy was found in his bed gassed. Quinlan was also in the room.

At the *Old Bailey, 22.6.1962, Quinlan was found not guilty of murder. He was, however, sentenced to 3 years' imprisonment for a serious offence against the boy.*

Anthony Regan   Florence Regan

Regan (41), a builder's labourer, stabbed his wife (39), and concealed her body in the house for 3 months, before his step-daughter became suspicious and told the police. His defence was that they had had a quarrel, she picked up the knife and was wounded in the struggle, whereupon he panicked and failed to report it.

At the *Old Bailey, 19.9.1962, he was found guilty of murder and sentenced to life imprisonment.* Charges of wounding and incest with his step-daughter (18) were not proceeded with. His love for the latter may well have been the motive.

[Authors' note: In 1950 Regan was acquitted of murdering a man (66) with a poker. In 1951 Regan received a sentence of 10 years' imprisonment for manslaughter of a woman (56), having been acquitted of murder.]

Stella Rich   Joseph Rich

Rich (41) killed her husband (44) one evening at home when he came in drunk. They were said to be normally a "devoted couple", but on this occasion she thought he was going to hit her. "I picked up the poker and hit him." The wound, near the nose, was apparently trivial. The husband had been violent on previous occasions.

At *Durham Assizes, 24.5.1962, she pleaded not guilty to murder but guilty of manslaughter. This was accepted and she was sentenced to 3 years' imprisonment.*

George Harry Roberts   Ann Roberts

Roberts (47), a male nurse, was due to see a psychiatrist. He stabbed his wife in their garden and then drank Dettol. He was saved, and told the police: "I don't understand a thing. I know we weren't happy. I took Dettol. She said she was going to leave me, that's all I remember."

At the *Old Bailey, 23.10.1962, he was found unfit to plead and detained during H.M.P.*

John George Robinson   Clive Jones

Robinson (33), a driver, cut the throat of Jones (9), a Wolf Cub, whom he invited down by the river. He admitted the offence and told the police: "I do not know what made me do it. I love kids." He had earlier bought a penknife.

At *Leeds Assizes, 24.10.1962, he was found guilty of murder and sentenced to life imprisonment.* Robinson had told a fellow-prisoner: "I had been drinking and if he had not struggled, I would not have done him in."

Ronald Leonard Rose   Marjorie Ann Oaten

Rose (33), a painter, had been living for 4 years with Mrs. Oaten, whom he had met when they were both patients in a mental hospital. They had a row over a broken window the previous day. The offence occurred when Rose was dozing in a chair and she hit him. "I hit her a couple of times. I must have gone mad. I might have hit her a hundred times." He was diagnosed as a depressive psychotic.

At *Kent Assizes, 18.7.1962, Rose was found not guilty of murder, but guilty of manslaughter under section 2. Mr. Justice Salmon ordered him to be detained in a mental hospital under the Mental Health Act 1959 with restrictions of unlimited duration.*

Rose appealed against his sentence, requesting that some time-limit be placed upon the restrictions on his discharge, on the ground that restrictions of unlimited duration were tantamount to a life sentence and this fact hindered his recovery (this plea was supported both by Dr. Brisby, principal medical officer at Brixton Prison, and Dr. Capoore, consultant psychiatrist at Bexley Heath Mental Hospital). The court held, however, that the detrimental effect on a mental health patient's recovery by the imposition of a section 65 order, unlimited in time, could not outweigh the primary and over-riding interest that the public should be protected (*The Guardian* Law Report, 2 July 1963).

[Authors' note: The Court of Criminal Appeal's insistence on the protection of the public, even where it meant a retarding of a mental health patient's recovery, is a reflection of the judicial attitude to the premature discharge by mental hospitals of patients committed by the criminal courts under section 60 of the Mental Health Act 1959 with no restriction upon discharge (see Nash (1961)).]

Michael Russell   Elizabeth Kane

Russell (33), a kitchen porter, met Mrs. Kane in a pub where they both drank heavily. She had recently separated from her husband and invited Russell home, where she undressed and asked him for £1. He told the police: "I wouldn't give it to her. She got hold of me and wouldn't let me go. I caught hold of her round the throat. I don't know what made me do it. I didn't mean to kill her". He went straight to the police. She was strangled with his belt.

At the *Old Bailey, 21.5.1962, he was found not guilty of murder but guilty of manslaughter under section 2. Mr. Justice Paull ordered him to be detained in a mental hospital. A restriction order of unlimited duration under section 65 of the Mental Health Act 1959.*

Russell was apparently illiterate.

Reginald James Rutherford   Robert Jenkins

Rutherford (17), a butcher's apprentice, was involved with six other youths in a street fight outside a Newcastle public house, in which a man, Jenkins, was stabbed to death and another man wounded. Rutherford said he had the knife to fit an ashtray into his car and he pulled it out in fright and stupidly used it.

At *Newcastle Assizes, 24.7.1962, he pleaded not guilty to murder and the prosecution offered no evidence. He was found guilty of wounding with intent, and of making an affray. Rutherford and the 6 others were each sentenced to 3 years' imprisonment.*

John Sharp   Doris Streeter

Sharp (39), a labourer, assaulted and battered to death Mrs. Streeter (43), with whom he was living. He had given her money to buy food, but she had spent it on drink.

At *Lancaster Assizes, 6.2.1962, he was found not guilty of murder but guilty of manslaughter under section 2. He was sentenced to 12 years' imprisonment by Mr. Justice Marshall.*

The prison doctor said Sharp had tried to hang himself in prison. He had an earlier head injury causing a post-traumatic personality. He was over-susceptible to alcohol. Sharp could remember little about the crime.

Walter Shaw   Janet Shaw

Shaw (40), unemployed, battered and strangled his daughter (20)

in a field near their home. He then went and told the police. The victim was the mother of two children.

At *Nottingham Assizes, 6.12.1962, he pleaded guilty to murder* in a trial lasting 40 seconds. *He was sentenced to life imprisonment.*

Mohinder Singh Benning   Swarn Singh
Phuman Singh
Pargan Singh

Mohinder Singh Benning (23), a welder, Phuman Singh (34), a labourer, and Pargan Singh (27), a scaffolder, were alleged to have gone to attack another Indian at his home, when Swarn Singh (34), a professional wrestler, came to the rescue and was fatally stabbed in the chest by Singh Benning. The latter said that Swarn Singh had drawn a knife first and hit him with a milk bottle.

At *Kent Assizes, 4.4.1962, Mr. Justice Winn directed the jury to acquit all three of murder. Mohinder Singh Benning was then found not guilty of manslaughter. All three were discharged.*

Phuman Singh (see: Mohinder Singh Benning)

Pargan Singh (see: Mohinder Singh Benning)

James Smith   Isabella Cross

Smith (26), a rubber moulder, entered the sweet shop of Mrs. Cross (57), for the purpose of stealing. There was a fight and Mrs. Cross was battered to death with mineral water bottles.

At *Liverpool Crown Court, 19.10.1962, he was found guilty of capital murder. He was sentenced to death.* He had denied having been near the shop.

The Court of Criminal Appeal, 5.11.1962, dismissed Smith's appeal. The Home Secretary, 26.11.1962, refused to reprieve him and Smith was executed at Strangeways Prison, Manchester 28.11.1962.

[Authors' note: This case conforms to the classic stereotype of the young male thug battering to death the matronly proprietor of a sweet shop. Classical as it may be, it is a rare type of killing.]

Saul Vboglo Sodje   John Francis Gordon

Sodje (23), a Nigerian, who worked as a kitchen hand in an

R.A.O.C. camp, had a fight with Gordon (43) over a piece of
bread and butter. Sodje pushed Gordon into a sterilising tank of
boiling water. He told police "Gordon slapped me across the
mouth. We started to fight: he slipped and fell into the sink."

At *Surrey Assizes, 13.11.1962, he was found not guilty of murder
but guilty of manslaughter "under extreme provocation". He was
sentenced to 3 years' imprisonment.*

The jury had recommended mercy.

Roslyn Anthony Edwin Steer   Audrey Steer

Steer (31) entered the kitchen where his family were having tea,
and at close range shot his mother in the back of the neck. His
father grabbed the gun, and soon after Steer walked hand-in-hand
down the drive with his sister to meet the police. He told the
police: "I had to do it, mate. She was trying to poison me." He had
once previously threatened his mother. He had previously received treatment as a mental in-patient.

At *Devon Assizes, 22.6.1962, he was found guilty but insane. He
was detained during H.M.P.*

Doctors said he was a paranoid schizophrenic and suffered from
persecution mania. He thought people were trying to poison him.
He did not know really what he was doing.

Joan Taylor   Lorraine Taylor
                                                       Sharon Taylor

Mrs. Taylor (23), a spinner, was found by her husband in a gas-
filled room at their home with the three children. One (2½) was
revived; Lorraine (3½) and Sharon (1½) were dead.

At *Manchester Crown Court, 20.11.1962, she was found not
guilty of murder but guilty of manslaughter under section 2.*

There had been domestic trouble about her general untidiness.
She had been married since 1958. At the time of the crime she was
again pregnant and was depressed by this, by money troubles and
the children's mischief. Doctors said she came within section 2.

*Mr. Justice Brabin made a hospital order under the Mental
Health Act 1959.* Treatment was expected to last 6-9 months.

Lionel George Taylor   George Taylor

Taylor (22), a married man, normally a "peaceful, mild and

gentle boy" shot his father at their home after a quarrel which was overheard by his wife in which the father slapped him. He said that he was full of rage and "burning with humiliation". Afterwards he saw his wife, who was expecting a baby, crying bitterly, and seeing her upset like that was the last straw.

At *Manchester Crown Court, 17.7.1962, he was found not guilty of capital murder (shooting) but guilty of manslaughter. Mr. Justice Nield sentenced him to 10 years' imprisonment.*

Michael Taylor   Leonard Riley

Taylor (15), a slaughterman's assistant, stabbed Riley (17) once in the heart during a fight. Riley attacked another man and Taylor went to the aid of his friend, Riley. He intended to "nick or prick" the other man who was getting the better of Riley. In fact, he missed the other man's arm and killed Riley. He later hid the knife in panic.

At *Manchester Crown Court, 23.7.1962, he was found not guilty of murder but guilty of manslaughter. He was ordered to be detained for 3 years under section 53(2) of the Children and Young Persons Act 1933.*

The jury clearly accepted that Taylor had no intention to do injury to either Riley or the other man.

Albert George Vivian Thomas   Dorothy May Thomas

Thomas (51), a wholesale newsagent, believed he was financially ruined, and decided to commit suicide. He was worried that his wife would not be able to cope without him, so he told her: "Sorry, my love, it's the only way", and hit her 6 times on the head with a hammer and strangled her with a dressing-gown cord. He then tried to kill himself, but was disturbed, so he hid her body under the bed. Next day, he took 300 aspirins, tried to drown himself and inhale exhaust fumes.

At *Derbyshire Assizes, 22.2.1962, he was found not guilty of murder, but guilty of manslaughter under section 2.*

Four doctors said he suffered from a reactive depression. Mr. Justice Howard said: "It is not necessary to pass a very long sentence. I take into account your character, the obvious state of your frantic mind and that there was no personal motive." Taking all this into account, the judge *sent Thomas to prison for 5 years* (our italics).

Graham Thomas   Henry Hoot

Thomas (25), an unemployed labourer, visited his girl-friend during working hours at the factory where she worked. While they were talking, Hoot (62), a supervisor, told her to return to work, whereupon Thomas lost his temper and hit him with a hammer. He was arrested in a pub and said: "What's all this caper? I'll finish my pint first." He later said: "I did not mean to kill him ... I panicked . . . I am very sorry ... I did not know him, but I thought he was going to grab me for trespass or something." Thomas had been drinking.

In 60 seconds at Carmarthen Assizes, 13.12.1962, he pleaded guilty to murder and was gaoled for life.

He had told his girl-friend that he contemplated suicide.

Michael Tilley   Maureen Tilley

Tilley (25), an electrician, was separated from his wife (23) who lived with her mother in the same street. They had had rows and he had removed their baby daughter to his flat. Despite his entreaties, his wife refused to give up her association with another man and return to him. When she finally wrote a note to this effect, he decided to kill her. She was strangled. He told the police at once: "If I can't have her, no one will."

At the Old Bailey, 24.5.1962, before Mr. Justice Paull, he was found not guilty of murder but guilty of manslaughter (presumably) under section 2. He was ordered to be detained in a mental hospital under sections 60 and 65 of the Mental Health Act 1959. A restriction order for 5 years was made.

Archibald Harley Niel Trew   Robert Percy Wallis

Trew (37), a poultry farmer, married with 2 children, had a blameless character, until one day he walked into a country bank with a loaded sawn-off shotgun and demanded money. The gun went off and killed the bankguard, Wallis (67).

At Hampshire Assizes, 21.3.1962, he was found not guilty of capital murder but guilty of manslaughter. He was sentenced to 10 years' imprisonment.

The offence was utterly out of character. Trew said that his business was failing and he was hopelessly in debt, so he decided to rob a bank. "I was a self-condemned man. I had not the slightest intention of firing." This was accepted by the jury.

George Emmanuel Tulloch   Wesley Spencer McCallum

Tulloch (30), a Jamaican labourer, was alleged to have stabbed McCallum (30) during a fight in the street. Tulloch claimed at his trial at *Bristol Assizes, 16.11.1962,* that he acted in self-defence, having been previously threatened. The prosecution in the final speech argued that it would be proper to bring in a verdict of manslaugher.

Tulloch was found not guilty of manslaughter and was discharged. On the direction of *Mr. Justice Melford Stevenson, he was formally acquitted of wounding 2 other men.* No evidence was offered on these counts.

Wonterus James Wilhelme Van Gestel   Thomas Crabtree

Van Gestel (19), a Dutch seaman, was alleged to have drunk a lot of gin with a companion on board his ship. There was a quarrel when the companion refused to drink any more and Van Gestel struck him and chased him ashore. A police officer later saw Van Gestel in the ship. Later Crabtree (75), a ship's watchman, was found battered beyond recognition. Blood was found on Van Gestel's boots and trousers. It was alleged that he kicked Crabtree, who died two days later.

At *Leeds Assizes, 10.4.1962, he pleaded not guilty to murder but guilty to manslaughter.* These pleas were accepted. *He was sentenced to 12 months' imprisonment.*

Wilfred Charles Vanstone   Thomas Harry Rice

Vanstone (53), a builder, weighed only 9½ stone. One night he was taking his dogs for a walk when Rice (43), weighing 17½ stone who had drunk 15 whiskies, drove by, stopped and attacked Vanstone. Vanstone drew his pocket knife "just to . . . frighten him off" and severed an artery. The judge called Rice "a powerful enraged drink-sodden bully".

At *Devon Assizes, 18.10.1962, Vanstone was found not guilty both of murder and manslaughter, and was discharged.*

Edward Carson Watters   Anthony Lennox Durrant

Watters (22), an Irish packer, lived in the same house as Durrant (5) and his West Indian parents. The boy visited Watters' room and started a fight. Watters said, "As I struggled some strange

feeling came over me and the next thing I knew he was dead."
Watters then hid him in the cellar. He had been strangled but no
sexual interference had occurred.

Before finally admitting the offence, he had alleged that he had
seen the child in the company of a coloured man. He later told the
police "I did not mean to harm the young lad at all."

At the *Old Bailey, 18.7.1962, he was found not guilty of murder
but guilty of manslaughter. He was gaoled for 18 months.*

Sher Newton Gratario Weller   Esmine Weller

Weller (33), a rubber worker, lived apart from his wife and had
threatened her before. She refused to return to live with him
although he still loved her, because she did not wish to give up
her association with another man; so he stabbed her.

At the *Old Bailey, 1.11.1962, he was found guilty of murder and
sentenced to life imprisonment.*

Christopher Whitfield   Edith Stuart

Whitfield (32), a labourer, was said by the prosecution to have
shot Mrs. Stuart (39), with a sawn-off shot gun when she remonstrated with him for attacking his mother. Whitfield said he was
sorry and had been carrying the gun to put it away when he went to
fetch his mother indoors. There was an argument and a struggle in
which the gun went off. He had no intention of hurting her. He had
a previous criminal record (including convictions for violence).

At *Newcastle Assizes, 21.11.1962, he was found not guilty of
capital murder (by shooting) but guilty of manslaughter. He was
sentenced to 12 years' imprisonment.*

Trevor William Whiting   Marlene Whiting

Whiting (23), a railwayman, and his wife (20) were temporarily
separated and each was living with another person. When the wife
said she had decided to leave him for good for the other man,
Whiting strangled her with his hands and her scarf.

At *Bristol Assizes, 6.3.1962, he was found not guilty of murder but
guilty of manslaughter on the grounds of provocation. He was sentenced to 5 years' imprisonment.*

George Dickens Williams   Ann James Williams

Williams (37), steel worker, was alleged to have strangled his mother (59) at their home with a dressing gown cord. He admitted to the police that he had killed her.

At *Flintshire Assizes, 6.7.1962, he was found not guilty of murder and was discharged.*

His defence was that he tied the cord round her neck in wild horse-play.

Norman Williams	Muriel Williams

Williams (47), a jobbing builder, stabbed his wife (44) to death in the street. He told the police that he was paying her 30/- a week under a court order and had just been told he owed a further £10 10s. 0d. "I went to meet my wife . . . to talk things over. I took the knife with me to show her that I meant business. She said something sharp and nasty to me and I lost my head."

At *Cumberland Assizes, 5.10.1962, he was found guilty of murder and sentenced to life imprisonment.*

Barry Anthony Wilson	Dean Patrick Mulligan

Wilson (21), unemployed, had been living for some months with Mrs. Mulligan, the mother of the victim (3). The child died from injuries to the liver and kidneys due to blows or kicks. Wilson told the police: "I punched him a few times. I killed him, I want to hang."

At *Leeds Assizes, 28.3.1962, he was found not guilty of murder but guilty of manslaughter. He was sentenced to 12 years' imprisonment.*

He had at least 2 previous convictions for violence. Defence was that there was no evidence that Wilson had caused the boy's injuries.

Colin Wilson	Frances Phillips

Wilson (27) had been lodging for 4 years with Mrs. Phillips (74) when he battered her to death. He then made a half-hearted attempt at suicide. He said that she was possessive and wanted him to sleep with her. He told the police: "I wanted to marry a young girl, but she wanted me to belong to her. She played on my nerves. She almost adopted the seeds of Nazism." Both were Jehovah's Witnesses.

At *Nottingham Assizes, 26.7.1962, he was found guilty but insane.*
The jury did not retire. *He was detained during H.M.P.*
He was apparently sexually perverted towards old women.

Sonia Wilson   Unnamed child

Miss Wilson (37), a former teacher and company director, was
indicted for the murder of an unnamed child between January 1947
and April 1962. However at *Derby Assizes, 24.10.1962, the indictment was held by Mr. Justice Widgery to be defective, and was
quashed.*

The facts were that 9 bodies were found at Wilson's home and
that she had been regularly seduced and blackmailed by a man for
15 years. She pleaded guilty to 9 charges of concealment of birth
and 8 of fraud, and was released at once. The man was convicted of
blackmail in July 1963.

John Albert Wood   Margaret Ann Wood

Wood (27), a ward orderly, stabbed his wife (22) 11 times.
They had married in October 1961 but were estranged. In May 1962
Mrs. Wood went to see Wood. While at his home she was killed.
Wood then absconded. He professed to be very much in love with
his wife and child, but admitted to there having been an argument
before the killing.

At *Birmingham Assizes, 19.7.1962, he was found guilty of murder
and sentenced to life imprisonment.*

A defence doctor, whose evidence was contradicted by two
prosecution doctors, said Wood came within the meaning of
diminished responsibility, having a severe reactive depression. The
*Court of Criminal Appeal, on 22.11.1962, refused Wood leave to
appeal.*

George William Woodall   Jessie Woodall

Woodall (38) killed his wife (33). He told the police: "I strangled
her because of her mental state."

At *Manchester Crown Court, 16.3.1962, he was found guilty of
murder but insane. He was ordered to be detained during H.M.P.*

David Owen Norman Wright   David John Fulton

Wright (18), a ship's galley boy, dragged Fulton (16) from the
cabin which they shared, and dropped him over the side of their

ship which was in dry dock. Wright admitted to homosexual acts with Fulton and said he panicked when Fulton started wheezing. He was also committed to Assizes on a charge of manslaughter of, and indecency with, Patrick Kelly (40), another shipmate. Wright said he had suffocated Kelly during homosexual practices.

At *Monmouth Assizes, 19.7.1962, Wright was found not guilty of murder but guilty of manslaughter under section 2.* Evidence was given that Wright was a homosexual and a psychopath, and had a split personality.

Mr. Justice Edmund Davies ordered him to be detained in a mental hospital under sections 60 and 65 of the Mental Health Act 1959 with a restriction for an unlimited duration. Mr. Justice Edmund Davies said ordinarily he would have passed a sentence of 20 years' imprisonment.

A 15 year-old boy   Noel Dowd

The accused (15), a sheet-metal worker, was standing outside a pub on a Saturday when 4 men started to push him about. In terror he drew his sheath-knife. Dowd (19) jumped on to it.

At the *Old Bailey, 26.1.1962, he was found not guilty of murder, but guilty of manslaughter. He was put on probation for 3 years.*

ESSAYS

CHAPTER I

HOMICIDE—A SOCIAL PHENOMENON

"AND CAIN said to Abel his brother: 'Let us go forth abroad.'
And when they were in the field, Cain rose up against his brother,
Abel, and slew him.

"And the Lord said to Cain: 'Where is thy brother Abel?' And
he answered: 'I know not. Am I my brother's keeper?'

"And he said to him: 'What hast thou done? The voice of thy
brother's blood crieth to me from the earth.

" 'Now, therefore, cursed shalt thou be upon the earth . . .' "

Thus, in the Book of Genesis, iv. 8-11, wanton murder is
dramatically defined as the most dreadful of crimes, a view which
has been upheld by the laws and customs of civilised societies
down the ages. The act of murder occupies a unique place in the
feelings of men in that it falls into a class of actions the results of
which are irreversible. Short of achieving the miraculous, the dead
cannot be raised to life again; the light has been put out. The
irrevocability of death itself is a psychological problem with which
man has wrestled since the beginning of time; it has given rise to an
infinite variety of complex philosophical and religious beliefs, many
of which have the function of preparing men for the only event in
their lives for which there is absolute certainty, and in turn of
consoling the bereaved in their loss. Around the notion of death a
whole series of institutional beliefs and practices have arisen
creating a sense of social balance in which the realisation of
mortality is incorporated into the fabric of human experience;
only thus is death made tolerable.

The act of murder disturbs this balance. It accelerates the inevitable in a way which profoundly unsettles the delicate equi-
librium which social institutional devices have achieved, and
arouses in individuals the most deep-seated unconscious fears and
anxieties. When a murder is accompanied by great violence or
sexual sadism these unconscious feelings may be even more deeply
disturbed, and the mildest and meekest of individuals are sometimes moved to advocate the most barbarously cruel penalties for
the offender.

271

Murder produces a sense of profound social shock—heightened in our own society by dissemination of the details through modern mass media. It can normally be relieved only by some highly dramatic act on the part of the community towards the offender. In days gone by this act was the public imposition of capital punishment; latterly, with the modification of the criminal law and the creation of a category of non-capital murder, the criminal trial and the dramatisation of its preliminaries may be gradually taking its place. Where the capital penalty remains, the trial and execution of the killer are regarded by the community as of such magnitude that the whole process may assume a public interest of monolithic proportions. Thus, for example, the long trial of James Hanratty was not merely a prosaic unravelling of the evidence tending to establish his guilt, but was a symbolic mobilisation of the morbid interests of a whole nation on a man's life and death struggle, milled out within a framework of its judicial process. Clearly, it is the special character of murder, the attendant sensationalism of the re-enactment of the killing with its actual risk of imitation, which wide advertisement brings in its trail, that gives murder its quint-essential quality—a crime apart.

Social theory which is of any consequence must at some stage be based upon facts, and unfortunately in the criminological field hard and reliable data are seldom easy to come by. This applies to the phenomenon of homicide no less than to other crimes. The starting point in any inquiry is the Criminal Statistics. But these statistics are importantly biased by what may be termed "the iceberg effect", the ratio of "crimes known to the police" to those which are unknown. The 'submerged' or unknown amount of crime, may in fact be greater than that which is actually visible. With offences like larceny this is almost certainly so, though whether the same is true of murder is not clear.

Because it is generally difficult to dispose of a corpse other than by socially accepted means it has long been assumed that the figure of murders known to the police represents fairly accurately the total volume of criminal homicide, but it has been suggested that because of medical slackness in certifying causes of death many murders may go undetected each year.[1] Thus people who die from overdoses of medicine or "natural causes" may sometimes also be murder victims. This was the case with the second and third husbands of Mrs. Mary Wilson who in fact poisoned them for the money in their Post Office Savings Accounts, although in both cases death certificates had been signed 'natural causes'.

What then are the factors influencing the official registration of murder? First and foremost comes the finding of a body. This is without doubt the most common source of discovery in killings which have taken place in the open, in public places, on commercial premises at night, and in killings where there have been attempts to hide the body away from the scene of the crime. Second, there are situations in which the offender cannot remove the body, nor even think what to do—the classic example being the domestic killing in which a man murders his wife and then gives himself up to the police. Third, there are situations in which individuals disappear or fail to appear.[2] Fourth, there are suspicious circumstances, for example when a woman like Mrs. Wilson (1958) has a series of husbands who appear to die with some curious frequency.

We do not know how many killers do in fact manage to dispose the bodies of their victims without trace. Recently a skeleton was discovered in a cave in South Wales which was identified as that of a woman who had disappeared in 1922. In 1961 a body of a man was found in a sludge tank in a disused gasworks with a newspaper in his pocket dated 1940. He may, or may not have been murdered. Donald Hume, the self-confessed killer of Suleman Setty, would have succeeded in his ingenious plan of distributing the dismembered corpse from an aeroplane over the Essex marshes had not one packet been fortuitously discovered by a wildfowler.

There is a considerable register of "missing persons" on the police files. Some who disappear have deliberately sought obscurity; they may wish to avoid making maintenance payments to their wives, or paying debts; they may be mentally ill, or, as is sometimes the case with young girls, they simply do not want to stay with their families because they cannot get on with them. Some of these may be, or become, the victims of murder, but we have no way of telling. Christie, we know, was in the habit of picking up women recently come to London to try their fortunes as prostitutes; the bodies of some of these unfortunate females remained undisturbed in cupboards and in the garden of 10 Rillington Place for ten years or more.

We have to be content with the data that are recorded, but even these are not wholly satisfactory. As far as the offenders are concerned, we know nothing of those who go undetected, though those, like Christie, who are caught eventually, are seldom distinct from those more readily apprehended. Much more serious is the problem of interpreting the statistics of murders known to the police—police-defined murders. The police make an entry for murder where there is a prima facie case for it having been committed, for example, if they find a dead woman who has been raped and strangled or the body of a night watchman battered about the head. If a body is found under "suspicious circumstances", it is thus treated, and recorded, as murder, fortified by a coroner's verdict. But things may turn out otherwise. The courts may reduce a charge of murder to a verdict of manslaughter, either because the element of intent was not present, or on account of the diminished responsibility of the accused. Less logical, but with good sense, juries often bring in legally indefensible verdicts, such as in the case of the Liège thalidomide baby, of acquittal or just culpable homicide. There is also the possibility that the courts may decide that although homicide had been committed it was not unlawful, i.e. that it was the result of a genuine accident. Moreover, in the process of making further inquiries into suspicious circumstances, what may look like a murder may not in fact have been murder at all. Thus the woman whose skeleton had been in a Welsh cave since 1922 was probably murdered by her lover (who died some years ago). But another skeleton discovered (with its wrists manacled) in the Cheddar Caves in 1962 turned out to be the remains of a man of eccentric habits who used to shackle himself up from time to time as a form of exhibitionism to get someone to release him. He did it once too often in a lonely spot and almost certainly starved to death.

The Criminal Statistics for a given year include all occurrences still on the record as murder at the date of going to press which is usually in March or April of the following year. These are all "police-defined murders" (P.D.M.). Where the courts try an offender during the year in question and return a verdict of manslaughter, the P.D.M. and manslaughter statistics are correspondingly adjusted. This also applies to cases in which persons are awaiting trial at the end of the year and who are found guilty of manslaughter in the period of the following year before the statistics go to press. But no account can be taken of modifications resulting from trial verdicts *after* the Criminal Statistics have gone to press, nor of variations of trial court verdicts by the Court of Criminal Appeal which may similarly have been delayed. But perhaps the most unsatisfactory aspect of the P.D.M. figure is that it takes no account of proceedings which have resulted in the discharge or acquittal of the accused. This is because a murder may have been committed but by someone else, or because the evidence offered by the prosecution was insufficient to convince the jury, although the police have little doubt, that the killing was the act of the accused. Thus Nash (1960) was acquitted of the murder of Cooney at the infamous Pen Club. A vital witness was intimidated and did not give evidence; Nash was merely found guilty of causing grievous bodily harm.

In some instances of course there may genuinely have been no murder but because it is a laborious process to distinguish between the acquittals of the truly innocent and the good fortune of the almost certainly guilty; the Criminal Statistics do not attempt to do so. The Home Office Research Unit in its recent study made a detailed analysis of acquittals and found that in the cases of a court acquittal in 1960 there was reason to believe the accused in half of these cases were truly innocent. If this is true as a general rule then the P.D.M. figure, even when adjusted by findings of manslaughter, may over-estimate the incidence of murder by as much as 5 per cent each year.[3]

Information from Criminal Statistics, besides being subject to both bias and a certain degree of error, is also somewhat scanty. The tables say something of the age and sex of the killers, whether the victims were under or over one year old, and indicate how the courts disposed of the accused. A brief commentary in the introduction to the statistics gives information about the ratio of suspects to victims, the numbers of suspects committing suicide before they are brought to trial, and about the operation of diminished responsibility. But since only about 100 of the 30,000 or so persons who are tried in the higher courts each year stand indicted for murder it might not be unreasonable for this section of the Criminal Statistics to be expanded; murder, after all, is commonly regarded as the most serious of all crimes. Thus we are left in total ignorance of some of the most basic information; we know nothing of the circumstances of the offence, whether the killings were sexual in nature, or the result of family quarrels or drunken brawls. Moreover, murder may be the one crime in which analysis is meaningless without data on the victim. A good deal of information is certainly on file at the Home Office, but there are clearly reasons for its non-publication which do not relate to trouble and expense alone.

Apart from sparing the relatives of the victim from further pain attendant upon publicity, there is a tendency for the role of the victim to have the overtones of innocence. In reality this may be far from the truth, and the phenomenon of "victim precipitation" is greatly in need of exploration. Setty, Donald Hume's victim, was a car dealer whose honesty was not above repute; Selwyn Cooney who died a violent death in the Pen Club was deeply enmeshed in the underworld of unsavoury "clubs". Some women may contribute to their own deaths by running the risks associated with prostitution, of which violent death is an occupational hazard, and the child victims of sexual killing may in fact be children in a stage of psycho-sexual development in which they deliberately involve themselves with men in a quasi-seductive role.[4]

NOTES

(1) J. D. J. Havard, *The Detection of Secret Homicide*, 1960. See also paper by Prof. C. J. Polson, President of the British Association of Forensic Medicine to an international conference of forensic specialists in London (*The Times* 17, April 1963), the subject of a leading article in that newspaper.

(2) See the case of James Camb who murdered a girl in a liner off West Africa in 1948. See R. v. Onufrejczyk [1955] 1 Q.B. 388 and R. v. Horry [1952] N.Z.L.R. 111.

(3) *Murder*, para. 10, p. 3.

(4) In a study of a delinquency area conducted by one of the authors (TM) it was discovered that certain little girls would approach men in a local park and actually offer to take down their knickers for sixpence. And *see* Chapter VII infra on "victimology" p. 321.

CHAPTER II

HOMICIDE—THE STATISTICAL PICTURE

ALTHOUGH MURDER is regarded as a serious crime in this country, it can hardly be said to be a serious social problem. As a form of violent death it is a comparative rarity; between 1900 and 1949 there were just under 7,500 murders 'known to the police' in England and Wales—only about 2,500 more than the average number of suicides and about 1,500 more than the average number of persons killed on the roads *in a single year*. And every year about three times as many people are killed by drunken drivers as are murdered. As a form of violent crime it is also rare, accounting for no more than 136 of the 11,519 crimes of violence against the person, and the 806,900 indictable crimes of all types committed in 1961. And of the 182,217 persons found guilty of indictable offences in that year only 56 (of the 124 persons who stood trial for murder)[1] had a verdict of guilty brought in against them. That a crime, which occupies such an insignificant part of the time of the police, the courts and the penal system, should nevertheless be regarded as the most serious of crimes would be absurd were it not for the special quality of murder and the character of the social reaction that criminal homicide provokes. It is noteworthy that since the passing of the Homicide Act and the limitation of the death sentence to special categories of killing, there is a general impression that public attendance at murder trials has fallen off appreciably and press coverage has become much more selective. The fact that the commonest punishment for murder is now life imprisonment has in one respect reduced the status of murder to that of other crimes punished by imprisonment. By and large, the community is not nearly so interested in murder trials which are no longer dramatised by the shadow of the gallows.

Murder in England and Wales is not only a rare phenomenon but one characterised by a stability which is most marked when comparisons are made with other types of serious crimes, especially violent crime. (See Table I over).

Although the actual number of murders fluctuates from year to year, the oscillations of the murder pendulum are remarkably

TABLE I

Murders known to the police per million of population

Annual	Averages
1900–09	4·4
1910–19	4·0
1920–29	3·8
1930–39	3·6
1940–49	4·4
1950–56	3·7
1957–60	4·1

Sources: *Annual Criminal Statistics* (England and Wales)

regular, even under the stress of wartime conditions. In 1931 there were 138 murders known to the police: in 1961 the corresponding figure was 136. In the intervening years the highest figure occurred in 1942 with 192 murders and the lowest in 1937 with 111 murders. When expressed as a *murder rate*, i.e. as related to the number of persons at risk in the population, the fluctuations appear as much less marked even than those of the crude figures. For the period 1900-1949 the murder rate was 3·9 per million,[2] with a standard deviation[3] of 0·45. In the sixty odd years since the beginning of the century the total volume of recorded crime of all types has increased enormously, and by over 300 per cent since 1930. Wounding, a serious crime of violence, had an average rate of 46·1 per million in the decade 1930-39, but by 1961 the rate had risen to 391·9 per million. That the incidence of murder should be so remarkably consistent while all other recorded crime, both serious and not so serious, has continuously and substantially increased, suggests that the aetiology of murder must be quite distinct from that of other crimes.

One factor which immediately suggests itself is the state of mind of the murderer. In no other crime is there such an incidence of suicide by the offender before he can be brought to trial. The Royal Commission on Capital Punishment[4] found that between 1900 and 1949 no fewer than 29·1 per cent of murder suspects committed suicide. For the period 1950-59 the corresponding figure is 33 per cent. While some people may argue that suicide on the part of a murderer is not necessarily proof of his mental illness or abnormality, the weight of clinical evidence about suicide in general suggests that a dramatic change in an individual's normal instinctual drives is a pre-condition of self-destruction.

Before the Homicide Act it might be argued that a man would prefer to kill himself rather than be hanged; suicide on the part of a non-capital murderer must, if this line of reasoning is to be pursued, be based on a preference for death rather than life imprisonment, a much less plausible explanation. Rather, from what we know of those offenders who do stand trial, morbid depression which can be simultaneously associated with both homicide and suicide is a recurrent feature. Bearing in mind the stringent tests of mental abnormality necessitated by the M'Naghten Rules (which were employed in forensic work before the Homicide Act 1957 and the Mental Health Act 1959), it is all the more remarkable that over the period 1900-49 as many as 21·4 per cent of persons brought to trial were found either unfit to plead or guilty but insane. Since 1957 the percentage of apprehended killers found unfit to plead or guilty but insane fell to 13 per cent. Those successfully pleading diminished responsibility formed an additional 14 per cent of the total number indicted for capital or non-capital murder. And by no means all of those who were unable to plead 'M'Naghten-madness' were executed; by the exercise of the Prerogative of Mercy some, though by no means all, of the mentally abnormal killers were reprieved after having been sentenced to death—principally to penal servitude for life, though in a few instances specifically to Broadmoor. During the decade 1950-59, 26·5 per cent of apprehended killers were found unfit to plead or guilty but insane. The introduction by the Homicide Act of the plea of diminished responsibility has made it more difficult to compare the incidence of mental abnormality and mental illness in the periods before and after 1957. The Home Office Research Unit found[5] that most of the cases of manslaughter on grounds of diminished responsibility would previously have resulted in verdicts either of murder (carrying the death penalty) or guilty but insane, and suggest that although now classified as manslaughter they should be treated for comparative purposes as murder.

A second factor which distinguishes murder from other crimes is the extent to which the killer and victim are related, or known to each other, in contrast to the situation in most other offences. (See Table II over).

These data, as well as those collected by the Home Office Research Unit and the study of Wolfgang in Philadelphia,[6] all indicate that homicidal violence is associated with close inter-

TABLE II
Murder-victim relationships
1957/60

	Capital Murder	Non-Capital Murder	All Murders
Per cent related	22·5	59·5	53·0
Per cent known	37·5	25·5	27·9
Per cent strangers	40·0	14·9	19·0
Total Number	81	385	456

Source: Press reports of trials 1957/1960

personal ties. In this country murder is overwhelmingly a domestic crime in which men kill their wives, mistresses and children, and women kill their children. Of the murder victims over the age of 16, 70 per cent are female, and of those females nearly half are killed by their legal husbands and a quarter by other relatives or lovers.[7] When considering victims under 16, again, about three quarters are killed by their parents or other relatives.[8] Our own analysis, as does the analysis made by the Gowers Commission, confirms that the commonest murders are that of a wife by her husband, a child by one of its parents or a woman by her lover. Between 1900 and 1949 of the 1,210 persons convicted, 224 had killed a wife or husband, lover or sweetheart, compared with only 161 who had killed in the course of robbery and 19 who had killed police or prison officers. Sir John Macdonnell, commenting on an analysis (given in the Criminal Statistics for 1905) of the motives of murderers convicted between 1885 and 1905, said: "I am inclined to think that this crime is not generally the crime of the so-called criminal classes, but in most cases rather an incident in miserable lives in which disputes, quarrels, angry words and blows are common. The short history of a large number of cases which have been examined might be summed up thus:—

"Domestic quarrels and brawls; much previous ill treatment, drinking, fighting, blows; a long course of brutality and continued absence of self-restraint. There is, however, a clearly marked class of murders, of *rare occurrence* [our italics] the motive of which is robbery, committed by habitual criminals and forming the climax, and usually the termination, of a career of crime."[9]

Bearing in mind that the physical violence to wives and children associated with drunkenness, which was characteristic of life among the poorer sections of society at the turn of the century, is now a mere shadow of its former self, and that in any case these 'miserable lives' which resulted in domestic quarrels probably had a considerable element of mental illness behind them, there is little in Sir John Macdonnell's view with which our own evidence collected since 1957 would lead us to disagree. Moreover, the 'clearly marked class' of murders committed by habitual criminals is still very much with us in a form so neatly delineated by the Homicide Act of 1957—those who murder in the course or furtherance of theft.

The Home Office Research Unit Report on Murder, published in 1961, cast some doubts, nevertheless, on the view, widely held by opponents of capital punishment, that murder is for the most part a solitary blot on a hitherto unblemished character. The Research Unit study found that the proportion of convicted murderers with criminal records has steadily increased, from 26 per cent in the period from 1 January 1955 to the enactment of the Homicide Act on 20 March 1957, to 36 per cent in the period from then until 31 December 1960. In both periods previous convictions were primarily for property offences and secondarily for offences of violence. But in the lower class milieu, from which such a large proportion of murderers are drawn, convictions for property offences are by no means uncommon, and violence in words and deeds is a commonplace expression of feeling. The increase in the proportion with previous convictions is probably associated closely with the increase in property crimes in general, of which the increase in capital murder is itself certainly a reflection.[10]

Seventy-nine per cent of the men convicted of capital murder until the end of 1960 (and 84 per cent of those executed) had previous convictions, while among those convicted of non-capital murder the proportion was 55 per cent.[11] It is vital, however, to consider the proportions of capital and non-capital murder. Among the 764 indictments from 21 March 1957 to 31 December 1962, 637 were for non-capital and only 127 for capital murder. Nearly all those convicted in capital cases with previous convictions had more than one conviction, usually for larceny and breaking and entering. In the non-capital category the proportion of offenders with records of violence and sex offences was somewhat higher than in the capital category. Vickers (1957) and Riley (1960) were typical of the capital murderer; Jones (1961) a fair example of a non-capital murderer with a record of violence and a sexual offence.

The proposition put forward half a century ago by Macdonnell, that murder is not a crime of the so-called 'criminal classes', may need some modification both in the light of modern knowledge about mental illness and the fact that the lower a person's status in the social hierarchy, the more likely he is to have a previous conviction for crime, generally property crime. On the other hand it is not clear whether the incidence of psychopathology as evidenced in sexual offences and violence against the person is increasing; statistically it would appear to be so. But even if there are among us more aggressive psychopaths (some of them manifesting their disorders in sexual offences) as well as more panic-stricken housebreakers (to swell the category of capital murder) none of these groups significantly alters the picture of murder as an act committed largely under the stress of emotion, or in consequence of mental illness, by those who are closely related to their victims. The increases in property and violent crime are, as it were, mere tributaries to swell the mainstream of murder whose waters are clouded by sickness, unhappiness and domestic strife. And so far as the murder rate is concerned, these additions have made little significant increase to the level of murder and only a marginal acceleration in the flow of persons indicted for it through the courts.

NOTES

(1) Criminal Statistics, 1961.

(2) In the United States, for example, the rate for 1958 was 47 per million of the population.

(3) The square root of the mean of the squares of the deviations of each yearly rate from their arithemetic mean.

(4) 1949-53, Appendix 3, Table 1, paragraph 298.

(5) *Murder*, p. 2.

(6) Marvin Wolfgang. *Patterns of Criminal Homicide*, 1958.

(7) *Murder* op. cit., p. 18 passim.

(8) Ibid.

(9) Quoted by the Gowers Commission. Report, p. 330.

(10) "The number of murders for robbery or financial gain rose from 6 a year to 12 a year after the Homicide Act, in spite of the fact that murder in the course or furtherance of theft is capital." *Murder*, op. cit., p. 41.

(11) This should not, however, obscure the fact that according to the Home Office Research Unit Report (Table 38, p. 35), during the period 1957 to December 31, 1960, 64·2 per cent of the total number of *male* offenders had no previous convictions.

CHAPTER III

HOMICIDE—SOME SOCIOLOGICAL STUDIES

OVER THE years there have been a number of important studies of homicide, though many of them have been handicapped by the inadequacies of available data. One feature which appears outstanding is the extent to which *homicide proper*—the killing of one person by another—and *suicide* seem to be linked phenomena homicide being an expression of the killer's own death wish.

As early as 1833 André Guerry in his *Essai sur la Statistique Morale de la France* noted an inverse relationship between the incidence of suicide and homicide in different regions of France. In the South, where violence against the person predominated over property crime, homicide appeared to be institutionalised though suicide was almost wholly absent. Suicide was the characteristic of the northern areas of the country. Even today one finds that homicide, institutionalised in the context of the blood feud, is the special characteristic of the underdeveloped areas of southern Europe, such as Sicily and the wilder parts of Calabria and Sardinia. This inverse relationship between homicide and suicide between the northern and southern countries of Europe was discussed by Emile Durkheim in his great work *Suicide*,[1] though in the present century the relationship has changed in the northern countries where suicide and homicide are no longer mutually exclusive. Thus the Finnish criminologist Verkko[2] found that Finland, Estonia and Latvia had high rates of both suicide and homicide. France had medium rates of both, while the United Kingdom had a low homicide rate but an average suicide rate. (In 1959 the P.D.M. figure was 135, compared with 5,253 suicides.) Verkko argued that both homicide and suicide stem from a common primary cause—alcohol. Durkheim on the other hand was concerned to show that both phenomena are related to prevailing conditions of the social structure, and particularly to what he termed *anomie,* a situation in which the individual is unable to perceive any of the norms of society, or where the norms themselves are confused.

Both Durkheim and Verkko reject the theory that suicide or homicide are forms of antagonism or aggression, either against the self or against others. Morselli, on the other hand, a member of the positivist school of Criminology, writing in the early 1880's argued that:

> "The criminal type blindly obeys his instincts and passions and because of the weakness of his mental structure commits homicide, whereas the non-criminal type in whom the sense of duty has been implanted destroys himself instead."

The aggression theory, however, has support from Hans von Hentig who in *The Criminal and his Victim*[3] reasoned that:

> "Murder and suicide are complementary phenomena: the total amount of available destructiveness is discharged in two psychologically similar but socially distinct *gestalten*."

The aggression theory is consistent with the Freudian theory of the 'death instinct'. The psychiatrist Karl Menninger put forward the view that suicide is in reality a form of psychological displacement.[4] The death instinct, he claims, contains three elements: a desire to kill, a desire to be killed and a desire to die. The desire (albeit at an unconscious level) to kill someone who has thwarted the individual is turned back upon the self; the suicide murders the introjected object and at the same time expiates his guilt. Thus, the ego is satisfied and the superego (conscience) is mollified by self-murder. This may explain why in this country about a third of all murder-suspects commit suicide before they are brought to trial and while others go with equanimity to the gallows. Capital punishment therefore may not only satisfy the demands of the community but also the psychic needs of the killer. Menninger goes to some length to point out that suicide is not in fact a spontaneous occurrence but the culmination of a series of circumstances which end in death. It is interesting that Wertham in his book *A Show of Violence*[5] makes precisely the same point about murder.

Durkheim's theory of suicide was that it varies inversely with the degree of social integration of the group to which the individual belongs.

Anomic suicide occurs where integration does not exist at all, *egoistic* suicide where integration is inadequate and *altruistic* suicide where integration is excessive—as for example in military élites where a breach of etiquette demands it. If homicide and suicide are actually the two sides of the same coin (the inversion problem), then homicide ought to vary positively with the degree of social integration experienced by the individual. There is some evidence for this in the proportions of killers and victims who are known or closely related to each other. Moreover under some social conditions individuals may be highly integrated into groups which, although not recognised as legitimate by the wider society, come into being for specific social purposes. In this context can be considered such things as the hoodlum executions of the American underworld, and the murders committed by 'terrorist' political organisations such as the Mau Mau, the Irish Republican Army, and more recently, the F.L.N. and the O.A.S. in Algeria and metropolitan France.

Possibly one of the most interesting of recent sociological studies was that published by Henry and Short in 1954 under the title *Suicide and Homicide*, in which they were concerned with the 'inversion' problem. Sociologists, they reasoned, must be concerned with murder and suicide because of their strong and persistent relationship with other social variables. Basing their work on American data[6] they analysed the incidence of homicide and suicide in terms of the business cycle. Suicides, they found, increased during economic depression, and fell during prosperity; homicide, on the other hand, appeared to fall during depressions and rose in times of prosperity. But by analysing the social status of suicides and killers they found that the suicidal response to economic depression diminished as position in the social hierarchy declined. At the same time the response of homicide to prosperity increased as the social status of killers progressively diminished.

It would seem then that what determines the choice between homicide and suicide is position in the social hierarchy. But social position may also be related to a form of social integration which depends upon the kind of external pressures bearing upon the individual. Durkheim had noted that people in subordinate social positions are subject to more external social constraints than those more highly placed in the status system. Lower class individuals are 'pushed around' by those in authority more than middle and upper class people; they are subject to external authority but never exercise it themselves. The more a man is 'pushed around' the easier it is for him to direct his aggression and hostility outwards; when his behaviour is the subject of stringent demands and expectations on the part of others, 'other directed' aggression can be rationalised and appear legitimate. In contrast, individuals of higher status find themselves less constrained by outside forces and grow up to believe that they, not others, are responsible for what happens in their lives. Hence when things go wrong there is a tendency to blame themselves and a sense of guilt turns aggression inwards against the self. Henry and Short thus subscribe to a theory which assumes that there is a relationship between aggression and frustration.[7] Where external pressures are strong by virtue of subordinate social status—or intense involvement in relationships with others—aggression turns outwards. Where external constraints are weak the self must bear responsibility for frustration. This theory goes some way towards explaining the predominantly low social status of persons indicted for murder and the frequency of murder among relations, lovers and mistresses. Marvin Wolfgang in his study of 588 cases of homicide in Philadelphia between 1948 and 1952[8] found that 90 per cent of both killers and victims were lower class,[9] a reflection of the fact that 73 per cent of the victims and 75 per cent of the killers were Negro, although Negroes constituted no more than 18 per cent of the population of the city. Only in 14 per cent of the cases were killer and victim unknown to each other, which led Wolfgang to consider the problem of victim precipitation, which he defined very narrowly as: "A situation in which the victim was the first to show and use a deadly weapon or strike a blow in altercation".

On this basis he found that victim precipitation occurred in 26 per cent of all murders and in these cases no fewer than 62 per cent of the victims had records of previous arrest by the police. One further fact which Wolfgang elicited that may be of relevance to the predominance of lower class Negro males among his 588 victims and 621 killers was the presence of alcohol. In $13 \cdot 5$ per cent of the cases both parties were under the influence of drink, in 9 per cent the victim was drunk and in 11 per cent the killer was inebriated.

It is perhaps worth considering the relevance of the data from the selection of studies which have been quoted—by no means a comprehensive survey of all the work that has been done[10]—to the problem of motivation. What was it that caused Cain to slay his brother Abel? We have already suggested that it is a hazardous process to infer motives from overt behaviour; we cannot normally open men's heads and plumb the depths of the human mind, although if pharmacological experiments could be conducted on convicted killers our knowledge might well be enlarged. Unfortunately for criminological science we either destroy our research material altogether by putting murderers to death or allow them to serve out their terms of life imprisonment without regarding them as especially worthy of interest.

Both Durkheim, and in his different way Menninger, would have us throw out the notion of motive altogether. Durkheim in particular wished to divorce objective social facts from ethical speculation; he did not consider that the individual had much influence over his ultimate destiny, this being decided for him by the collective forces of the society in which he lived. Consequently, like Menninger, he rejected popular explanations of suicide in terms of financial reverses, unrequited love and so forth. The term 'motive' has in fact two meanings, the reason for a particular action in the mind of the individual and the 'cause' assigned to that action by other members of society. The 'cause' may be no more than the most convenient social label which the community can apply.

What is more important is to isolate the social situations in which murder tends to occur, and examine the statistical regularities which exist independently of individual motivation. In this way it is possible to predict the general characteristics of situations in which homicide is likely to occur. Merely to count corpses or accused persons in the dock is not enough; we need to look at the constellation of all the relevant social facts which surround the act of murder, for homicide, whatever else it may be, involves a social relationship between killer and victim. It may even be called the most definitive of human relationships, but like all other social relations it must occur within the context of human culture. The social scientist, if he is true to the rules of sociological method laid down by Durkheim, one of the greatest masters of sociology, must devote his energies to exploring this aspect of culture. He cannot say with authority what society should do with its murderers; what he can do is provide the kind of facts which may push back the frontier of public ignorance and thereby facilitate an ethical discussion in which reason may have some chance of a hearing beside primitive emotion. Yet if we continue with execution as a method of dealing with even only a few of our capital murderers we deprive ourselves of the most vital material in any study of the nature of murder.

NOTES

(1) 1897.

(2) *Homicides and Suicides in Finland and their dependence on National Character, 1951.*

(3) 1948.

(4) *Man against himself*, 1938. (Reprinted Rupert Hart Davis, London, 1963.)

(5) 1949.

(6) It must of course be remembered that the United States has a high homicide rate; in 1958 it was 47 per million compared with 3·4 per million in England and Wales.

(7) Henry and Short, op. cit.

(8) 76 per cent of the victims and 82 per cent of the killers were male, Wolfgang, op. cit.

(9) A finding amply borne out by the U.K. data for 1957 onwards which are presented in this book.

(10) There are a number of studies of homicide in non-western societies which the interested reader might care to pursue, for example, Bohannan's *African Suicide and Homicide, 1960.* Verrier Elwin's classic *Maria Murder and Suicide, 1943* and A. L. Wood's "Crime and Aggression in Changing Ceylon" (Transactions of the American Philosophical Society. New Series. Vol. 51, Part 8, 1961).

CHAPTER IV

HOMICIDE—JUSTIFIABLE AND INEXCUSABLE

HOMICIDE CAN be defined as the killing of one human being by another human being. Yet the very simplicity of this definition conceals the degree of uncertainty in the law's attitude to the various kinds of homicide—an uncertainty which to some extent reflects the social attitudes. The categories of homicide elicit the whole spectrum of human emotions—ranging from outright condemnation (expressed in the form of the most violent retributive feelings) through numerous gradations of tolerance to genuine sympathy, approval and even, in times of war, active encouragement. Justifiable homicide includes not only the killing of the enemy in time of war but also judicial hanging, acts of self-defence[1] and acts committed in arresting a felon or suppressing a riot.

Necessity is generally thought not to be a defence. In the famous 19th century case of R. v. Dudley and Stevens[2] two of three shipwrecked men adrift in an open boat out in the Atlantic for 20 days, killed and ate a fourth, the ship's cabin boy, in order to keep themselves alive, after having been eight days without food, and five without water. They were found guilty of murder. Logic would demand, however, that in certain circumstances the choice between two evils might require the taking of human life. If a mountaineer loses his grip and so endangers the lives of others on the rope, would there not be a defence to one of those others deliberately cutting the rope rather than that all should perish? In the Dudley and Stevens case the cabin-boy was not directly endangering the lives of his shipwrecked mates, and rescue was not out of the question—as indeed it turned out. If the law were to regard necessity as a species of self-preservation—as it ought to—it would rank alongside the recognised plea of self-defence. At least if it were not regarded as a complete defence it should rank as only manslaughter. It is hard to understand why a man who is driven to killing as a result of acts of provocation from his victim commits manslaughter, whereas the person who kills to preserve his own life and the lives of others has no such defence to murder.

While it is true that the provocation must emanate from the victim, the law recognises chiefly that it is the effect of provocative acts on the mind of the killer which minimises the heinousness of the act of killing; the public reaction that the victim to some extent brought about his own death, while accurately symptomising the defence of provocation, is not the rationale of the law. Was the intention to kill in the case of Fantle (1958) or Holford (1963) any the more excusable than in the case of Dudley and Stevens?

Self-preservation (which falls short of self-defence because the killing is objectively disproportionate to the acts of the victim) is in fact recognised as a species of provocation where the act of killing is retaliatory. Since the law, in assessing the degree of the accused's criminal responsibility, is not concerned to measure the deserts of the victim, self-preservation, if subjectively tested, ought to reduce the crime to manslaughter. If the victim's acts operate to create fear and apprehension in the mind of the killer for his own life, surely his responsibility for the killing is diminished.

Necessity, self-defence and killing by misadventure, are really species of excusable homicide, in that the killing, but for the circumstances in which it is carried out, would be unjustifiable. The motive or reason for the killing will invariably shade off until the law regards the killing as unjustifiable—although with mitigating circumstances. That the law has recognised this can be seen by the creation of a number of crimes of homicide which carry pro-portionately less public opprobrium than either murder or man-slaughter. Indeed, in Norman times murder and manslaughter themselves were not distinguished; every homicide was felonious unless it was justified or excusable.

The labels which are attached to unjustifiable homicide are varied and the negative sanctions of disapproval corresponding to them are equally varied.

Even within the rubric of manslaughter, the sanction will vary according to the ground upon which manslaughter was maintain-able. The sentence of the court will vary accordingly whether the manslaughter was because of provocation or diminished re-sponsibility.[4] Outside of the two most culpable forms of homicide —murder and manslaughter—there are the offences of infanticide, child destruction and causing death by dangerous driving, as well as, before 1961, suicide.

A cursory glance at the data of murder indictments since 1957 quickly discloses the high proportion of child deaths at the hands of either or both the children's parents. Yet until 1922 child killing at the hands of a mother, while often arousing the deepest sympathy and understanding, remained the crime of murder. Infanticide— killing a newly-born child—had long been tolerated by the law, although not until 1922, was it made a separate crime equivalent to manslaughter. The law was in fact somewhat tardy in recognising both the special psychological and physiological elements in the offence and the existence of post-puerperal depression. The medical profession had long recognised the peculiar features of the crime and no woman had been executed in England for the murder of her child under the age of one year since 1849.[5] Until 1922 judges had solemnly to go through the ritual of donning the black cap and pronouncing the awesome words of the death sentence, knowing full well—as did everyone except probably the wretched accused—that the execution would not be carried out. The judges publicly declared their revulsion to intoning the death sentence in such nauseous circumstances. The 1922 Act provided that if a woman had wilfully caused the death of her 'newly-born' child, but at the time the balance of her mind had been disturbed by the effects of childbirth she committed only the crime of infanticide. The Act gave no definition of 'newly-born' and in 1938 the legislature once more intervened to provide a 12 months' limitation on the period in which a mother could claim mental derangement as a result of bearing her child.[6]

Allied to this crime is the crime of child destruction. The law of murder had always been confined to the unlawful killing of a person 'in being'. The killing of a child partially extruding from its mother's womb was, therefore, neither murder nor manslaughter. The umbilical cord did not need to have been severed, but the whole body of the child had to be brought into the world before the child was 'in being'. Thus in 1929 the Infant Life (Preservation) Act was passed by which it became the offence of child destruction wilfully to cause a child to die before it had an independent existence from its mother; the offence carries a maximum penalty of life imprisonment.

Another form of homicide which has failed to arouse the outright disapprobation of society is the killing on the roads. Until 1956 there was a crime generically known as motor manslaughter. While killing through the instrument of a motor car was equated with manslaughter and therefore carried the maximum sentence of life imprisonment, jurors were loth to convict—possibly on the basis that, as jurymen increasingly become car owners, they identify the situation of the accused as being closely akin to their own:—'there, but for the Grace of God, go I'. The Road Traffic Act[7] now imposes a maximum of five years' imprisonment for causing death by dangerous driving. If jurors are less unwilling to convict on this charge, their reluctance to acquit so readily has been fortified by the attitude of the judges who only on infrequent occasions impose any prison sentence. The massacre on the roads, compared with other killings, is barely condemned by the leniency of the law's sentences.

There remains for consideration the ancient crime of suicide. Until the Suicide Act 1961 *felo de se* and attempted suicide remained crimes. The change in the law came about in part as a result of humanitarian feelings and in part from a recognition that both attempted and successful suicides are the acts not of criminals but of the mentally ill. The social stigma, however, lingers on; many Christians still regard suicide as a sin and some of the mediaeval ecclesiastical sanctions regarding burial rites remain.

The process of reform was started by the Homicide Act 1957 itself. The survivor of a genuine suicide pact ceased, by virtue of section 4, to be guilty of murder but only of manslaughter for the killing of the other party to the pact. Such cases are comparatively rare and before 1957 the Home Office practice was to commute the death sentence passed on any survivor of a genuine suicide pact. Under the Suicide Act 1961 any aiding, abetting or counselling of someone who commits suicide remains a crime. Suicide plays in fact a large part in the crime of murder. If few cases of attempted mutual killing disclose a deliberate agreement between the parties, a large number of killers commit suicide shortly after killing the other party—usually a spouse and/or children—and many more make unsuccessful attempts both before and after arrest. The desire to die also remains prevalent among those charged with murder—the cases of Airey (1961), Bartley (1961) and Wilson (1962) are examples. As a psycho-social phenomenon, suicide and murder are linked in many instances. The killer's death wish is often fulfilled on himself as well as on his victim.

What of the remaining two types of unjustifiable homicide—murder and manslaughter? Unlike the types of homicide discussed above they are creatures of the Common Law and not of statute, and they have remained undefined by the legislature. The description of murder by Coke in the 17th century has remained for the best part of 250 years the lawyer's operational definition. The Royal Commission on Capital Punishment 1943-1953 quotes it in the following form:[8]

"When a man of sound memory[9] and of the age of discretion[10] unlawfully kills any reasonable[11] creature in being, and under the King's Peace,[12] with malice aforethought, either express or implied by law, the death taking place within a year and a day."[13]

The incessant controversy over the law of murder has centred on the phrase 'malice aforethought, either express or implied by law'; one could hardly conceive of a more misleading phrase, as this and the succeeding chapter will endeavour to show.

Basically, murder is distinguishable from manslaughter in that the latter is 'an unlawful killing' without 'malice aforethought' and for the purposes of the present discussion the distinguishing feature is the malice aforethought which is the intention to kill, although we shall observe how the crime of murder is not so strictly confined.[14]

Lawyers define criminal responsibility by the use of two Latin tags, the *actus reus*, which in murder is the act of killing a human being, and *mens rea* (the guilty intent). The guilty intent (or malice aforethought) can be the intention to kill the victim actually killed or it can relate to some other unlawful act in the course, or as a result, of which a killing takes place.

There are two aspects of the intents to kill which are the subject of current controversy and at present either blur the distinction between murder and other crimes of killing, or hamper the development of the law where mental illness is a feature of the crime. The former problem—which is more conveniently dealt with in the chapter on malice generally—has been authoritatively resolved by the House of Lords in a thoroughly unsatisfactory way; the latter remains largely unresolved and presents a stark challenge to the renowned adaptability of the Common Law.

At a trial for murder the accused's mental condition is at present relevant in one of three ways. The accused may be found insane and unfit to plead[15] or he may be found guilty but insane, which is in effect an acquittal[16]; in both these instances the result is that the accused are detained during Her Majesty's pleasure under

Part V of the Mental Health Act 1959; the third is the new defence of diminished responsibility. Both the former pleas are subject to the stringent M'Naghten rules crystallised by the Advisory Opinion of the Judges of England in the well-known case of Daniel M'Naghten.[17] (A person may be insane and unfit to plead other than on grounds of his mental instability. Insanity on arraignment may arise simply because the accused cannot understand the proceedings so as to defend himself.)

M'Naghten, an extreme delusional paranoic, was found not guilty on the grounds of insanity for the murder of Sir Robert Peel's secretary, William Drummond, whom he mistook for the Minister. Victorian society was outraged at the acquittal, particularly since members of the Royal family had themselves been the object of several attempts on their lives.[18]

The response of the Judges to the crucial question was:

"To establish a defence on the ground of insanity, it must be clearly proved that, at the time of committing of the act, the party accused was labouring under such defect of reason from a disease of mind as not to know the nature and quality of the act he was doing, or if he did know it . . . he did not know what he was doing was wrong."

The verbal exactitude of this right-wrong test has proved both legally deceptive and medically unacceptable. The report of the Royal Commission on Capital Punishment recognised from the legal point of view the practical flexibility of the test. When contested, the rules were applied strictly; but otherwise they were stretched or even ignored to meet the justice of the case.[19]

As Professor Sheldon Glueck has pointed out,[20] the tests of responsibility have had the rigidity of an Army cot and the flexibility of a procrustean bed. The test in fact embalms long outworn medical notions and is in any event too narrow a measure of responsibility. It takes no account of those mental disorders which manifest themselves in disturbances of an impulsive and transitory kind.

Despite a recommendation to the contrary by the Royal Commission on Capital Punishment,[21] the Homicide Act 1957 introduced the doctrine of diminished responsibility which has to some extent replaced the notion of guilty but insane.[22] This is partly because an accused favours the determinate sentence (more often passed in the case of manslaughter on the grounds of diminished responsibility) and because, both in cases of guilty but insane and diminished responsibility, the burden of proof is on the defence. Where the burden is on the defence it is lighter in terms of the medical evidence required to establish the plea. It is easier also to establish substantial impairment of mental condition than it is to prove M'Naghten-madness.

Yet little attempt has been made in England's courts to use the accused's mental state as defeating or destroying the *mens rea* (or intent) necessary for the prosecution to obtain a conviction. As Mr. Justice Stephen in *A History of the Criminal Law of England* (1877) observed,[23] 'the law . . . is that a man who by reason of mental disease is prevented from controlling his own conduct is not responsible for what he does'. The existence of any insane delusion, impulse, or other state which is commonly produced by madness is a fact relevant to the accused's ability to control his conduct.

The House of Lords only two years ago in a murder case from Northern Ireland[24] involving the increasingly common defence of 'automatism'[25]—in this case alleged to have been induced by psycho-motor epilepsy—underlined the requirement that the prosecution must prove both conscious awareness and voluntary control in a case where sufficient evidence of abnormal mental state has been introduced by the defence. The former Lord Chancellor, Viscount Kilmuir, said:

"Normally the presumption of mental capacity is sufficient to prove that [the accused] acted consciously and voluntarily, and the prosecution need go no further. But, if, after considering the evidence properly left to them by the judge, the jury are left in real doubt whether or not the accused acted in a state of automatism, it seems to me that on principle they should acquit because the necessary *mens rea*—if indeed the *actus reus*—has not been proved beyond reasonable doubt."

Lord Denning in his judgment added confusion to this perceptible change in the law (forced on the courts by modern medical science). He stated, without authority and with no word of approval from his fellow judges, 'the old notion that only the defence can raise the issue of insanity is now gone. The prosecution is entitled to raise it, and it is its duty to do so rather than allow a dangerous person to be at large' as a result of a possible acquittal.[26]

The English courts may find that modern psychiatric evidence will force upon them the development taking place in the United

States under the influence of the rule in Durham's case in 1954[27] when the court used these words:

"We find that as an exclusive criterion the right-wrong test is inadequate in that (a) it does not take sufficient account of psychic realities and scientific knowledge, and (b) it is based upon one symptom and so cannot validly be applied in all the circumstances. We find that the 'irresistible impulse' test is also inadequate in that it gives no recognition to mental illness, characterised by brooding and reflection and so relegates acts caused by such illness to the application of the inadequate right-wrong test. We conclude that a broader test should be applied."

The rule to be applied was stated simply: "that an accused is not criminally responsible if his unlawful act was the product of mental disease or mental defect". Disease is defined as a condition capable either of improvement or of deterioration; the term 'defect' is defined as a condition incapable of either improvement or deterioration, which might be consequential or the result of injury or the residual effect of a physical or mental disease.

The result of a finding of no criminal responsibility for an unlawful act due to mental illness would make it obligatory upon the courts to treat the person as a mental patient and not as a prisoner. At the moment the position is unsatisfactory. An accused who pleads to any charge, "I am perfectly normal but I had a sudden blackout at the time of the deed and did not know what happened", leaves the onus resting heavily on the prosecution to resolve any reasonable doubt the jury may have about the accused's story; failure by the jury to resolve the doubt leads to an outright acquittal. But if the accused's story is, "I have a long history of mental illness and that is why I had the blackout at the time of the deed", the onus is on the defence to prove either insanity or diminished responsibility.

This is not a hypothetical situation. The case of Sergeant Boshears, a U.S. airman, at Essex Assizes in 1961 dramatically depicts the problem. Sergeant Boshears was acquitted of murdering a young woman whom he had admittedly killed. He denied all knowledge of the killing, saying that he was suffering from amnesia, since he did it in his sleep; the jury accepted that plea. No medical evidence had been called by the defence and the Crown pathologist, Dr. Francis Camps, said that he had no special knowledge whether a man could strangle a woman in his sleep; as a matter of common sense he thought a man in a deep sleep would be incapable of movement and that a man in a light sleep—as sleep walkers are—would almost certainly be awakened by a slight stimulus such as produced by the victim's struggles. But he could not say killing while amnesic was impossible.[28]

Mr. Justice Glyn-Jones directed the jury that the burden of proof remained on the prosecution, and that even if the evidence raised in the jury's mind a doubt whether Boshears was telling the truth he was still entitled to be acquitted;[29] there were only two verdicts open to the jury—guilty or not guilty.[30]

The novelty of this plea of automatism or amnesia, both of which are symptoms of loss of control through mental abnormality, whether temporary or permanent, has this result.

If the jury finds the accused guilty the accused probably goes to prison instead of being treated as a mental patient;[31] if he is found not guilty, a person of a potentially dangerous disposition is let loose upon the community. The defect might be cured by a return to the law before Woolmington v. D.P.P. in 1935[32] which left it to the accused to bring forward and prove any circumstance of mitigation or defence. In Woolmington's case Viscount Sankey, the Lord Chancellor, said: "Throughout the web of the English Criminal Law one golden thread is always to be seen, that it is the duty of the prosecution to prove the prisoner's guilt . . . if, at the end of and on the whole of the case there is a reasonable doubt . . . as to whether the prisoner killed the deceased with a malicious intention, the prosecution has not made out the case and the prisoner is entitled to an acquittal."[33]

After Woolmington, in all cases except pleas of insanity and—since 1957—of diminished responsibility, the burden has been on the Crown. But even if the process were reversed—and it can be achieved only by the legislature—enough doubt might still exist in a jury's mind for the accused to escape conviction; but at least that likelihood is less great.

The answer surely is that amnesia, automatism or 'blackout' are manifestations of mental abnormality, whether temporary or permanent.[34] If the killing is done by a person in such a state of mind, the *mens rea* is lacking and the concept of criminal responsibility consequently inappropriate. The suggestion by Lord Denning in Bratty's case[35] that the verdict should be guilty but insane cannot be right either in the present state of the law or in any amended law. The Durham rule alone provides a satisfactory solution; the accused is found not guilty and a hospital order may be made if treatment is required; the accused is treated as if he were being considered for certification under the Mental Health legislation. Otherwise the accused should go free. The community should after all be merely concerned to ensure that the accused will not repeat his socially harmful act rather than be demanding a verdict in favour of criminal responsibility.

Repetition of the offence will either not occur or needs to be minimised or eradicated by hospital treatment. Imprisonment could be justified only if madness were accompanied by wickedness—by no means incompatible notions. But in such a case of mixed reasons for the criminal act, criminal responsibility would not be wholly displaced and would best be dealt with under the doctrine of diminished responsibility[36] which calls for a verdict of manslaughter—thus connoting criminal responsibility—while at the same time recognising that the responsibility is only partial.

NOTES

(1) In 1962 at the Old Bailey a young boy who had been invited back to the flat of a senior trade union official, was acquitted. The boy had killed the man with a decanter when he believed that the man, a homosexual, was about to assault him. He was acquitted of a charge of manslaughter.

(2) (1884) 14 Q.B.D. 273; see Donald McCormick, *Blood on the Sea* (Muller, 1962).

(3) Chisam (1962).

(4) The defences may not be mutually exclusive, but see R. v. Holford (1963) *The Times*, 30 March, 1963 and R. v. Walker (1963) *The Guardian* (Manchester edition), 6 April, 1963: a verdict of manslaughter on both grounds is surely illogical, since the defence of provocation presupposes a reasonable man driven to the act of killing, whereas unreasonableness is endemic in the defence of diminished responsibility.

(5) The Royal Commission on Capital Punishment, para. 155, p. 57. Since 1899 no mother has been executed for the murder of her child under the age of 12 months.

(6) Under section 178 of the New Zealand Crimes Act 1961 it is infanticide and not murder whenever a woman kills any of her children under the age of 10 if at the time of her offence the balance of her mind was disturbed by reason of her not having fully recovered from the effect of giving birth 'to that or any other child'.

(7) Section 1 of the Road Traffic Act 1960.

(8) Para. 72, page 25-26.

(9) Unfitness to plead, guilty but insane, and the doctrine of diminished responsibility are dealt with separately.

(10) The age of criminal responsibility was raised recently from 8 to 10, an attempt to raise it to 12 having failed; see section 16(1) of the Children and Young Persons Act 1963.

(11) Reasonable does not mean 'sane' but human.

(12) The inclusion of this phrase makes justifiable the killing of the King's enemies.

(13) The reason for this—now no longer applicable in view of modern medical knowledge—was that it was impossible after such a length of time to connect cause and effect.

(14) D.P.P. v. Smith [1961] A.C. 290.

(15) Section 2 of the Criminal Lunatics Act 1800 has in practice been extended to include persons who were not insane within the M'Naghten rules but who by reason of some physical or mental condition could not follow the proceedings at the trial and so properly defend themselves. Deaf mutes are the most common example. Loss of memory in itself does not render the accused 'insane' so that he could not be tried upon the indictment. See R. v. Podola [1960] 1 Q.B. 325. The Criminal Law Revision Committee on Criminal Procedure (Insanity) declined to recommend any change in the test for unfitness to plead.

(16) Trial of Lunatics Act 1883; see also Felstead v. R. [1914] A.C. 534, R. v. Duke [1963] 1 Q.B. 120 and Duke v. D.P.P. [1961] 1 W.L.R. 1434. The Criminal Law Revision Committee on Criminal Procedure (Insanity) recommended that the special verdict should be altered to "not guilty by reason of insanity", and that, although constituting an acquittal, the verdict should be subject to the accused's right of appeal.

(17) (1843) 10. ch. & Fin. 200.

(18) In one of her more witty moments Queen Victoria is alleged to have said she "did not believe that anyone could be insane who wanted to murder a Conservative Prime Minister"; she was less than in her most humorous mood when in 1883 she insisted upon the illogical verdict of 'guilty, but insane'. This followed the firing at the Queen by Roderick Maclean. He missed her but was prosecuted for high treason. He was found not guilty of treason because of his insanity. Both the Atkin Committee of 1922 and the Royal Commission on Capital Punishment recommended the abolition of the verdict 'guilty but insane'. The Criminal Law Revision Committee on Criminal Procedure (Insanity) produced a draft Bill changing the special verdict to "not guilty by reason [Sic] of insanity".

(19) P. 79-98, paras. 226-276.

(20) *Law and Psychiatry* (Tavistock Publications), p. 46.

(21) Para. 413, p. 144.

(22) The proportions in any of the years 1957-1962 are: roughly 25 per cent unfit to plead; 25 per cent guilty but insane; and 50 per cent diminished responsibility. These cases form approximately 45 per cent of the total number of persons standing trial on indictment for murder. See Appendix—Table D, p. 375.

(23) P. 167-168.

(24) Bratty v. Attorney-General for Northern Ireland [1963] A.C. 386.

(25) The problem was present, but was not dealt with, in the following cases: Horvath (1957), Littlestone (1958), Boshears (1961), Kirk (1961), Weston (1961), Padgett (1962) and Phillips (1962), but see Gnypiuk (1960) and Knight (1961).

(26) This is a pure obiter dictum. In R. v. Price [1963] 2 Q.B.I. at 17 Mr. Justice Lawton, after considering Lord Denning's dictum, decided precisely the reverse, and has been followed by Mr. Justice Elwes in Mitchell (1962). There is support for Lord Denning's view in the judgment of Mr. Justice (now Lord) Devlin in R. v. Kemp [1957] 1 Q.B. 390.

(27) Durham v. United States 214 F.2d 862 (D.C. Cir. 1954) before the U.S. Circuit Court of Appeal for the District of Columbia. The Durham Rule is not universally accepted. It is established only in the courts of Maine, New Hampshire and District of Columbia (the birthplace of the Durham rule). Some of the numerous decisions rejecting the Durham rule are conveniently collected in a case from New Jersey: State v. Lucas 30 N.J. 13 (1959), 152 A.2d 50, 67; see also the concurring opinion of the Chief Justice Weintraub in this case.

The Federal Courts have similarly felt themselves bound to reject the rule in the face of Supreme Court decisions adhering to the test of M'Naghten-madness (plus the doctrine of irresistible impulse). Some of these courts, even if they had felt free, would have declined to accept the Durham rule, largely because they see in the rule more difficulties than it solves. Academic support and criticisms are conveniently collected by Circuit Judge Barnes in his judgment in Sauer v. United States 41 F. 2d 640 (9th circuit, 1957) at p. 646, footnotes 14 and 15. Many of the cases are helpfully discussed by Judge Levin in United States v. Pollard 171 F. Supp. 474 (D.C. E.D. Michigan 1957).

There is some ground for suggesting that if and when the Durham rule comes before the U.S. Supreme Court it might be favourably received. The testimony of a former Justice of the Supreme Court, Felix Frankfurter, to the Royal Commission on Capital Punishment (p. 102) and an address by Justice William O. Douglas, 'The Durham Rule: A meeting ground for lawyers and psychiatrists' (1956) 41 Iowa Law Review 485 augur well for the proponents of the Durham rule. See the sanguine outlook of Sheldon Glueck for a favourable reception by the Supreme Court, *Law and Psychiatry*, at p. 113 ff.

(28) See Scots case of H.M. Advocate v. Fraser (1878) 4 Couper 70 where a father while asleep killed his child. He was dreaming that he was struggling with a wild beast. He was acquitted of manslaughter.

(29) The judge felt bound to apply the doctrine in Woolmington v. D.P.P. [1935] A.C. 462. It is known that many judges intensely dislike the Woolmington doctrine since it can be used so often to support the argument that in the end the burden always remains on the prosecution.

(30) Mr. Justice Glyn-Jones was supported by the House of Lords in Bratty v. Attorney-General for N. Ireland [1963] A.C. 386; see also the South African case of R. v. Ahmed 1959 (3), S.A. 776 where there was a similar result to Boshears. See also cases cited in Brett, *An Inquiry into Criminal Guilt*, p. 180.

(31) The court may, but, in the absence of a successful plea of diminished responsibility, is unlikely to make a hospital order under Section 60 of the Mental Health Act 1959; it is always open to the Home Secretary to transfer the person to hospital under section 72.

(32) See Foster's *Crown Law* (1762), p. 255.

(33) "Acquitted" was modified to read "benefit of the doubt" by the judgment of Viscount Simon, with Lord Sankey's concurrence, in Mancini v. D.P.P. [1942] A.C. 1.

(34) See a judgment of Mr. Justice Ramsbottom in R. v. Vermeulen 1954 (2) S.A. 231. See also an address by the Chief Justice of Australia, Sir Owen Dixon,

"A legacy of Hadfield, M'Naghten and Maclean" (1957) 31 Australian Law Journal 255.

(35) [1963] A.C. 386 at p. 410.

(36) In R. v. Holford (1963), *The Times*, March 30, this was accurately reflected. The accused was to some extent morally to blame but his crime was mitigated by successful pleas both of provocation and diminished responsibility due to mental depression; and see R. v. Walker (1963), *The Guardian*, 6 April 1963.

CHAPTER V

TOWARDS PARTIAL RESPONSIBILITY

ALLEVIATION OF the incidence of the death penalty—a prime consideration of the authors of the Homicide Act 1957—has been achieved largely by confining the death penalty to specific categories of murder. But the ostensible abolition of constructive malice, the widening of the defence of provocation and the system whereby the survivors of suicide pacts are now liable only to a charge of manslaughter, have all in their small way reduced the numbers of killers whose lives would otherwise have been at risk.

It might be expected that the other major change in the law in 1957—the introduction of the doctrine of diminished responsibility —would have had an even more marked effect on saving those otherwise guilty of murder from the gallows. In practice, this has not been so. The assumption that this defence of 'borderline' or 'partial' insanity[1] might merely be a liberalisation of the M'Naghten rules, and would therefore include a large number of persons who before 1957 would have been found M'Naghten-mad has equally not proved to be the case;[2] only a slightly smaller number of persons indicted for murder since 1957 have been found guilty but insane.

This would suggest that the diminished responsibility cases form a new group of mentally ill people who before 1957 would have been unable to satisfy the rigorous test of insanity and therefore would have been liable to suffer the death penalty. The fact is that a high proportion of those successfully pleading diminished responsibility were charged only with non-capital murder or, if charged with capital murder, would have had their offence reduced to non-capital murder or manslaughter on some ground other than diminished responsibility. Whereas the ratio of those found guilty of capital murder to those found guilty of non-capital murder since 1957 has been 1:4, the ratio of successful diminished responsibility cases, where, but for that defence, the accused would have been guilty of capital or non-capital murder, has been 1:7.

Even among the seventeen cases where diminished responsibility reduced the offence from capital murder to manslaughter (and by virtue of that defence alone were not liable to the death penalty) some at least, on the evidence of pre-1957 reprieve policy, would not have been hanged.[3]

It cannot be claimed, therefore, that this defence has made any significant social contribution to the lessening of the incidence of capital punishment (indeed some of these who were saved might have managed, in view of trends towards applying the insanity test less rigidly, to succeed on a plea of M'Naghten-madness[4]). If diminished responsibility, with its lighter burden of proof on the accused, could be successful, why should an accused risk failing to establish insanity? If one cannot refrain from expressing relief that the death penalty was obviated even in only a few such cases involving severe mental disturbance, a rationale of diminished responsibility cannot depend on any such emotional response. If the concept of diminished responsibility was conceived as an attempt to escape from the shackles of a mandatory penalty of death, it has not been an unqualified success.[5] It has, for example, in the cases where there was a charge of non-capital murder, freed the courts from the equally mandatory sentence of life imprisonment. Yet many judges have not accepted this new-found freedom quite so gleefully; the evidence is that life sentences, or determinate sentences of comparable length, have in practice, frequently been passed by the judges. More seriously, it has (as the Royal Commission warned) brought confusion to the jurisprudence of the criminal law.

Is there then another justification for this doctrine, which was not perceived by the legislature? The Royal Commission on Capital Punishment specifically did not advocate the introduction of this defence in the law of murder.[6] It thought that the concept raised fundamental issues of jurisprudence, and that so radical an amendment to the law of England would not be justified for the limited purpose of devising a special category of mitigating circumstances so as to avoid passing the death sentence where such circumstances existed. The Royal Commission assumed that the Scottish precedent for the doctrine was itself confined to the field of homicide, but, as Professor T. B. Smith observes,[7] this was probably erroneous. Nevertheless the Government did not heed the Commission's sound advice. The Homicide Act clearly intended that the doctrine of diminished responsibility should mitigate the rigours of the law[8].

The Home Secretary said that the defence was of little practical importance except where there was a fixed sentence, either of death or of life imprisonment. It was thus unsoundly based as a jurisprudential concept.

Is there in fact a place in the criminal law generally for a doctrine of partial responsibility in which the law recognises that the accused, while suffering from mental illness, has nevertheless consciously acted irresponsibly—that an anti-social act dubbed as a criminal offence betokens madness and badness at one and the same time? Or is its usefulness confined to the crimes with the ultimate penal sanction? A consultant psychiatrist once instanced to one of the authors the case of a schizophrenic detained in a mental hospital. When one day his pockets were empty (which he replenished during his days of freedom through ill-gotten gains) the patient absconded, only to be found committing an amateurish shop-breaking in the nearby town. Was this not an accurate manifestation of wickedness as well as madness? Thus in Wilkinson (1961) Mr. Justice Finnemore said of the accused, that she was not so mentally ill as to be irresponsible for her acts.

The experience of the doctrine of diminished responsibility in England has had at least one merit. The all-or-nothing choice between full guilt and complete innocence has been avoided. This intermediate verdict has not been merely an evasion from the duty of determining guilt or innocence. It has enhanced precision, recognising the admixture of blameworthiness and some exculpation in a situation where mental abnormality is either only transitory or not sufficiently serious to be solely the case of inducing anti-social behaviour. Psychopathy and schizophrenia are mental conditions symptomatic of this admixture. Hitherto the law has drawn too strong a line between sanity and insanity and did not accurately reflect the much less sharp distinction between the sick and the wicked. But if this is so there can be no logical reason for confining the defence of diminished responsibility to a charge of murder.

In Scotland the doctrine of diminished responsibility has been evolved by the judges, consonant with the development of medical science as accepted by the courts. Even today Scots judges are not shackled, as are their brethren in England, by the strict statutory formula of the Homicide Act 1957, although in fairness it must be said that in England the doctrine has been sensibly applied by the courts. Whereas in Scotland it has been restricted sufficiently to exclude psychopaths,[9] the English judges have not hesitated to rule that the doctrine embraces at least the aggressive psychopath.[10] The Scots have in this way—perhaps unwittingly—excluded those types of mental abnormality from the application of the doctrine, which would connote not just madness but varying degrees of criminal responsibility.

The cases in England since the Act have shown that, within the statutory formula, two distinct types of diminished responsibility have arisen. The first is where the concept of criminal responsibility, by reason of medically and socially recognised abnormal mental condition, calls either for a lesser grade of offence (which is the English solution) than that charged, or more accurately for an acquittal of criminal responsibility. The premeditation and deliberation associated with murder have been so vitiated by mental abnormality that the capacity of the killer to form the requisite elements of the supreme crime is absent. The accused is on the borderline of insanity although not actually M'Naghten-mad. It presupposes the absence of anything approaching full criminal responsibility.

The second type of partial responsibility refers to mental abnormality not sufficient to meet the extreme requirements of the tests of irresponsibility. This second type recognises that under the law, mental disease (or defect) does not necessarily relieve the accused from all responsibility. Here a second enquiry is called for; the court must decide whether the particular mentally disordered accused knew the physical nature of his act and knew substantially that it was wrong, in the sense that it was socially condemned behaviour. Such mental abnormalities as psychopathy, psychoneurosis, epilepsy, schizophrenia and incipient psychoses are mental conditions where this second inquiry is pertinent (the mercy killing although not necessarily associated with mental illness is usually included).

In these cases the law's distinction between responsibility and no responsibility is unrealistic and takes no account of modern psychiatric assessment of mental illness; it is equally inaccurate to relegate the crime to a lesser grade (from murder to manslaughter) while still retaining the notion of full criminal responsibility. For these kinds of mental illnesses the concept of partial responsibility is wholly apt. A review of a single year's cases since 1957 gives a clear indication of the two distinct types which fall generically under the single statutory formula of diminished responsibility.

11

If the doctrine of diminished responsibility were confined to the first type of case, that of depriving the accused of capacity to form the requisite elements of a criminal offence, one would expect the sentence to be uniformly a committal to a mental hospital. The fact that the courts have not considered every diminished responsibility case deserving of treatment in a mental institution reflects the judicial view that many of the cases merited punishment by imprisonment.[11] This would be particularly true since Part V of the Mental Health Act 1959 came into force on 1 November 1960—in addition to the existing provision whereby an accused could be put on probation on condition only that mental treatment in hospital was undergone for no more than 12 months. In a parliamentary answer in the House of Lords on 1 May 1963[12] the Minister of State, Home Office stated that up till the end of March 1963 of 91 persons found guilty of manslaughter in cases in which the only, or the principal, defence to a charge of murder was diminished responsibility, hospital orders had been made in respect of 42 people. In our study in the two years (1961 and 1962) 31 hospital orders were made in 73 such cases. In six of the other 49 cases from 1 November 1960 until the end of March 1963 the Secretary of State issued a transfer direction under section 72 of the Mental Health Act.[13] There is a distinct cleavage in judicial attitude towards section 2 defences. Some judges appear to accept that, other than in exceptional cases, a hospital order should normally follow conviction for manslaughter under section 2. Others regard it merely as another species of manslaughter and to be treated accordingly.

So far the Court of Criminal Appeal has given no clear indication of its policy, except to say that judges have a wide discretion in the matter and, other than in exceptional circumstances, the court should make a hospital order where no punishment is intended. In Morris (1960) the Court of Criminal Appeal upheld a sentence of life imprisonment in a case of mercy killing. In Bailey (1961) it allowed an appeal on the grounds that the jury was bound to accept uncontradicted medical evidence of diminished responsibility but the court did not disturb the sentence of life imprisonment of an epileptic. In James (1961) the court substituted a hospital order, with a restriction order of unlimited duration, for a sentence of 3 years' imprisonment on a woman suffering from extreme melancholia after she had already been transferred by the Home Secretary to a mental hospital; the court said that it did not think the accused merited punishment. In McCrorey and Clarke (1962) both accused succeeded on appeal under section 2, both being sentenced to life imprisonment—McCrorey's alone was reduced from death.[14]

The courts in fact have not yet fashioned any sentencing policy for those convicted of manslaughter on the grounds of diminished responsibility. Their difficulty lies in the fact that the legislature meant the defence to be equated with ordinary manslaughter where the mental abnormality fell short—but only a little short—of M'Naghten madness. In practice juries have sensibly brought in verdicts under section 2 in all kinds of mental abnormality—from those cases where the disease of the mind removed any reasonable imposition of criminal responsibility to those cases where responsibility was impaired by mental illness manifested in particularly aggressive forms.

The trouble has been that both types of case under section 2 have indiscriminately been regarded along with provocation as an example of extenuating circumstances. The defence of provocation does not normally depend on medical evidence but usually derives its validity from the behaviour of the victim precipitating his own death to some lesser or greater extent. The reverse is in fact the truth of diminished responsibility; it depends entirely on medical evidence and is dissociated from any contact of the victim with his mentally sick killer. The English law attempts to equate the two situations by classifying them, for different reasons, as manslaughter.

The theory is that there is in 'essence no, or substantially no difference between the effect on Othello's mind of Iago's intrigue, and the effect on Othello's mind of Desdemona's confession of adultery.[15] But this example is to compare like with like within only a narrow framework. If Othello were suffering from melancholia fanned by the intrigue of Iago, then it was his mental condition which impaired his responsibility. In cases of provocation the defence presupposes a mind undiseased and reacting as the reasonable man would to such provocative acts or words.[16]

The fact is that provocation, like necessity and self-defence, is a species of criminal act with extenuating circumstances produced by the environmental conditions to which the reasonable man is subjected. Diminished responsibility is essentially a notion of impaired mental equipment quite unrelated to the accused's environmental factors. The effect of mental disease can either reflect insanity or partial impairment of responsibility varying according to the nature of the disease. It is high time that English jurisprudence formulated the doctrine of diminished responsibility in the light of these theoretical considerations and without preconceived ideas or attempts merely to mitigate the rigours of a once excessively severe law. If the Victorian innovation of the verdict of guilty but insane was illogical, and ought to be removed, there is room for a much more rational verdict of guilty but with partial responsibility.

NOTES

(1) R. v. Spriggs [1958] 1 Q.B. 270 at p. 275 per Lord Goddard C.J. and R. v. Byrne [1960] 2 Q.B. 396 at p. 404 per Lord Parker C.J. Approved by the Judicial Committee of the Privy Council in Rose v. The Queen [1961] A.C. 496 at pp. 507-8.

(2) Mr. Montgomery Hyde, M.P., in 1956 thought that it would mean practically the end of the M'Naghten rules, H.C. Hansard Volume 560, Col. 1236. The Attorney-General (at Col. 1254-5) thought that, although it would not mean the end of the M'Naghten rules, not many accused would put forward a defence of insanity.

(3) Dunbar (1957); Lawrence, Marples, Matheson, Perkins and Pike (1958); Dolby, Gilsenan and King (1959); Barclay (1960); Samuel and Sims (1961); Golder, Blanks, Gregoriou, McCrorey and Martin (1962). Of these Golder, Lawrence and Marples would certainly have been reprieved while Perkins, Dolby and Gilsenan might have been reprieved. McMenemy (1961) did not plead diminished responsibility.

(4) Matheson (1958); Sims (1961); Dolby (1959); Perkins (1958) whose case resembled that of Straffen's: he was on the first occasion found guilty but insane.

(5) Cf. "Diminished Responsibility; A Layman's View" by Barbara Wootton (1960), 76 L.Q.R. 224 at pp. 235-6.

(6) Para. 413, p. 144.

(7) "Studies, Critical and Comparative" (1962), p. 241.

(8) H.C. Hansard, Vol. 560, Col. 1153-1156.

(9) H.M. Advocate v. Callaher, 1946 J.C.108. See also the case of Burnett (1963), reported in The Scotsman, 24, 25 and 26 July 1963.

(10) R. v. Byrne [1960] 2 Q.B. 396 is the classic example. In a parliamentary answer on 6 May 1963, the Minister of State, Home Office (H.L. Hansard, Vol. 249, Col. 543-4) stated that up to the end of March 1963, hospital orders, under section 60 of the Mental Health Act 1959, had been made in respect of 307 psychopaths and 163 suffering from mental illness or subnormality. In 90 of these cases restriction orders under section 65 had been made. Cf. Table M, p. 385 infra.

(11) See particularly Edgington, Geis, Sims, Wilkinson (1961), Billings and Sharp (1962)—to cite but a few examples.

(12) H.L. Hansard, Vol. 249, Col. 174-5, question asked by Lady Wootton.

(13) In the first two months of the operation of Part V of the Mental Health Act 1959 the courts seemed wholly unaware of its application. There were eight cases of successful pleas of diminished responsibility—Barrett, Hanlon, Lecointe, Morris, Rodney, Twells, Ward and Wiggins. In the case of the first three named the accused were transferred to mental hospitals under section 72 of the Act after having been sentenced to 7 years' imprisonment, life imprisonment and ten years' imprisonment respectively.

(13a) R. v. Morris [1961] 2 Q.B. 237.

(14) In R. v. Abbott [1963] 2 W.L.R. 1011 it never occurred to anyone that a hospital order was a possible alternative.

(15) See T. B. Smith, op. cit., p. 251.

(16) In Bedder v. D.P.P. [1954] 1 W.L.R. 1119 the House of Lords reaffirmed the principle that a man's infirmity of body or affliction of mind is not a material fact in applying the test of provocation which is the effect of acts—and, since section 3 of the Homicide Act 1957, of words—upon the mind of a reasonable and normal man. See also Mancini v. D.P.P. [1942] A.C. 1.

CHAPTER VI

MALICE—CONSTRUCTIVE, IMPLIED OR OTHERWISE

SOME CRIMES are inherently difficult to define. Any offence containing the element of fraud provides, for example, peculiar difficulties for the legislator, primarily because the consummated act—the deprivation of the person's property—does not readily afford a criterion for judging the criminal intent of the accused.[1] Although most of us can recognise fraud when we see it, we find it difficult to define.

No such difficulties need arise in the case of the crime of crimes; any such difficulties that do occur are the product of a society which seeks, in its legal definition, to reflect the variable motives surrounding the taking of human life. The Select Committee of the House of Commons, which reported against proceeding with the Homicide Law Amendment Bill of 1874—on the ground that it would be a mistake to codify the law of homicide—nevertheless earnestly recommended that attention be paid to the imperfect state of the law of murder. The Committee added:[2]

> "If there is any case in which the law should speak plainly, without sophism or evasion, it is where life is at stake; and it is on this very occasion that the law is most evasive and most sophistical."

A century of case law—with a helping hand from the legislature in 1957—has done nothing to dispel the charge either of evasiveness or sophistry. Rather the reverse; when Parliament announced—as it did in section 1 of the Homicide Act 1957—that the doctrine of constructive malice was abolished—the House of Lords simply came along and, in some commentators' views,[3] revived the doctrine. If it did not restore the doctrine to its full vigour at least it did so in a manner that has aroused legal academic—and, for once, even professional—opinion to a pitch of intensity that calls for a cleaner sweep from Parliament. The law of murder in England remains, in fact, positively obscurantist in the face of a clear need for leadership of public opinion.

The act of killing evokes such emotive utterances that reason about the crime of unjustifiable killing is consistently lacking. This is partly due to the public's willingness to label those who kill unjustifiably as murderers, with all the overtones that that labelling evokes.

If a man intends to kill another—and does so—he undoubtedly commits the crime of murder in the absence of the special mitigating circumstances giving rise to established defences. But is that man a murderer? The analysis of murder in our society demonstrates that it is a one-man one-time offence. It is a crime apart, in that well over half of those convicted of murder have no criminal record and are unlikely ever to commit another serious offence.[4] Yet the public labels these people as murderers. Macbeth was certainly a murderer; but was Othello?

Because a man is found in the divorce courts to have committed adultery, do we automatically damn him as an adulterer? He might well have been thought to be an adulterer in the days when adultery was a criminal offence. It is only because killing another human being is regarded as so heinous that we tend to heighten the quality of the act by condemning it so volubly. In this way we are guilty of mis-labelling the offence, and by doing so we minimise the effectiveness of those killings which are without question murders. By declaring that Gypsy Jim Smith (1960) was guilty of murder when he dislodged a police constable off the bonnet of his car into the street, we lessen the public opprobrium for the cases of murder. Minimising of guilt by association (as with guilt by association itself) is a reality in the minds of the public.

The ending of life—particularly its shortening in such a dramatic way—is so socially cathartic that society feels it must damn the act with all the verbal armoury at its command. Society regards the act of unjustified killing as so abhorrent that the single particular act of killing is equated with every other unjustifiable killing, and marked 'murder'. The Royal Commission concluded[5] that the quest for defining degrees of murder was chimerical and had to be abandoned. This was due entirely to the fact that in attempting to categorise murder the Commission was always testing its attempts against the penalty that would be meted out. But the substantive law is not concerned with the penalty attaching to the crime;[6] it is concerned in reflecting the measure of public opprobrium for the crime. Once punishment is excluded from the consideration of definition of the crime, the degrees of murder are clearly demarcated. Murder can safely be left to the case of an intention by the killer to kill the particular victim. It matters not that this might include a mercy killing and leave out of account the violent death in the course of a robbery where the killer could not have had the intention to kill the particular victim. Society can exact its retribution proportionately if need be, without tampering with the essential moral weight it attaches to the sanctity of human life.

The mercy killer will receive a light sentence, the robber who kills (but fortuitously escapes the gallows) will be locked away for many years simply because his crime betokens repetition. At the same time the law preserves its air of generality—murder is simply the intention to kill; any other unjustifiable homicide is manslaughter.

The law in a civilised community, governed as it should be more by the power of reasoning than by public emotion, is increasingly driven to recognising a clearer distinction between murder and manslaughter. Even though the intention to kill is the primary distinguishing feature of the two crimes, it is not always so. A successful plea of provocation or of diminished responsibility does not involve the killer in having one jot less intention to kill; the law merely recognises that the intention to kill is mitigated to some degree because of the circumstances in which that intention is formed. As if to compensate for this concession to the moral judgment of the community that such killings are manslaughter and not murder, English law includes in this classification of murder acts of killing which result other than from the intention to kill a defined victim. A whole series of fictions have been produced by the law whereby killings are labelled murders.

'Killing with malice aforethought' was never more of a misleading phrase than as reflected in the doctrine of constructive malice. The modern doctrine was simply that in a killing in the course of a violent felony the 'malice aforethought' was the *mens rea* required for committing that other felony. Originally the rule was even wider. Coke thought killing in the course of any unlawful act was murder. Foster, however, limited it to felonies and modern decisions of the Courts have reflected that limitation,[7] although in R. v. Stone,[8] killing in the course of an attempted rape was held to be murder although attempted rape is only a misdemeanour.

The classic instance of a form of constructive malice is the killing in the course of robbery by a number of persons. If all the robbers set out to commit their crime with the intent, if necessary, to use violence all are guilty of murder even if only one of them actually does the killing.[9] The only change in the Homicide Act was that only the person who by his own act caused the death of the victim is guilty of capital murder; the others are guilty of non-capital murder. The intention of the person causing death to kill is communicated to all those who are engaged on the common purpose to rob with violence even though none of the others would have at the crucial moment committed the act of killing. Here the constructive malice is employed together with a transferred *actus reus*.

Section 1 of the Homicide Act 1957, in cumbrous parliamentary language, says that "where a person kills another in the course or furtherance of some other offence, the killing shall not amount to murder . . ." Had the legislature stopped there, all would have been well. But the section goes on to qualify it by saying it is not murder "unless done with the same malice aforethought (express or implied) as is required for a killing to amount to murder when not done in the course or furtherance of another offence".

The layman may justifiably boggle at that cascade of legal language; he is not alone, for lawyers have had cause to question this saving clause. The phrase did not, as we have seen, sweep away all the other types of 'malice aforethought' which proliferated through the law of murder. In one of the first cases after the Homicide Act, R. v. Vickers,[11] it was apparent that the law had not abolished the form of malice consisting of an intent to inflict grievous bodily harm. To avoid flatly contradicting Parliament, the Court of Criminal Appeal had to say that this was 'implied' and not 'constructive' malice, which is almost a juggling with words. An intention to kill is not genuinely 'implied' if the Court is satisfied that no intention existed. Even under the recognised constructive malice doctrine the intention was 'constructive' because there was an intention to commit a felony—which incidentally, would include an intention to cause grievous bodily harm. In reality all forms of malice that do not include an intention to kill are constructive.[12]

One wonders whether the courts are going to revive the transferred malice—the intention to shoot at A but killing B—or the universal malice—the intention to kill someone not caring whom—or the imputed malice—the killing where there has been an intention to resist by violence a lawful arrest. These are not fanciful suggestions since the House of Lords only recently held[13] it was murder where the act of the accused was of such recklessness that although there might have been no specific intention on his part either to kill or to cause grievous bodily harm, a reasonable man—the lawyers' "reasonable man"—might have foreseen that death was likely to result. Murder has become possible where death is accidental simply because the act of the accused is the *causa causans* of the death.

Gypsy Jim Smith was stopped by a policeman on traffic point duty who suggested that the accused, whom he knew quite well, had stolen property in his car. He told the accused to pull in at the kerb-side while the constable walked beside the car. Then the accused suddenly accelerated; the policeman began running and although there was no running board, he clung on until some 130 yards up the road when he was shaken off by the tortuous path taken by the car. The policeman fell in the face of an oncoming bubble car, as a result of which he suffered a crushed skull, causing death. Had there been no other traffic the constable would almost certainly not have been killed. His fall from the car was intended by the accused; his death was accidental. The accused was nevertheless convicted of murder by the jury; the Court of Criminal Appeal reduced the offence to manslaughter, but the Law Lords, to widespread consternation among lawyers, restored the verdict of murder. They laid down three prerequisites in the offence to constitute murder:

1. The accused must intend to do something unlawful to someone;
2. The unlawful act—the throwing off of the policeman—must be of such a kind that grievous bodily harm or death is the natural and probable result; and
3. the act must result in death.

It is the second prerequisite that has caused the trouble. The accused stoutly maintained that he never intended to kill; indeed he was appalled at the death of someone he knew and apparently liked. How then could the accused be said to have intended to kill? The court imputed, constructed, implied—the choice matters not—such an intention because it said that it did not matter that the accused did not intend his victim's death; it was murder if an ordinary man would have foreseen the likelihood of really serious harm (which was not sufficiently serious to involve the foreseeable likelihood of death). The objective test—reached through those miraculous eyes of the law's reasonable man—and not a subjective test of the accused's own intent, was the relevant test.

Although other common law jurisdictions in the Commonwealth have all weaned the law away from the objective test,[14] England seems destined to be shackled with an outmoded and unfortunate doctrine. (It is almost as if the judges themselves have regretted their own decision, since, in a case of attempted murder, R. v. Grimwood,[15] the Court of Criminal Appeal said that the subjective and not the objective test applied.)

The House of Lords leaned significantly upon the concept of the reasonable man without defining that figure of legal mythology in terms of objective and readily identifiable characteristics.

Half a century of Freud and the work of social and clinical psychologists over the last 25 years have cast serious doubts on the reality of the man who travels daily on the Clapham omnibus oblivious to his exalted status accorded by the legal fraternity. Beneath the surface of the 'reasonable man' may lurk a whole range of repressed feelings which in a moment of stress may be released with terrifying results.[16] The lawyers have signally failed to emulate the economists who abandoned, as of doubtful utility, the concept of 'economic man'.

It is somewhat the same with the problem of intent. It is a hazardous enterprise sometimes to infer a man's intentions from his overt actions, if only because a common phenomenon may be the result of different patterns of motivation. If it were not so, it would be difficult to explain why so many manufacturers of consumer goods engage in complicated psychological investigations as to why people buy or do not buy their products, or have initially inexplicable resistances to purchasing new ones.

Yet the law is wedded to the hackneyed phrase, trotted out on every conceivable occasion, that a man must be taken to intend the natural consequences of his act, even though he does not desire those consequences, if he has foreseen them. Although the legal maxim is usually ascribed as a presumption, it is frequently taken as axiomatic. No less a great social document than the report of the Gowers Commission utters this shibboleth.[17] Perhaps the classic ignorance of lawyers on the intention of human beings appears in a recent worthwhile book by Professor P. J. Fitzgerald of Leeds University on *Criminal Law and Punishment*.[18] Writing on the new doctrine of diminished responsibility, Professor Fitzgerald has this to say: "The sort of evidence which is likely to substantiate a defence of diminished responsibility is evidence that the act was performed in circumstances where the agent has nothing to gain and everything to lose from his performance. This would be some evidence of abnormality *since generally human beings do not act in a manner directly contrary to their own interests*." (Our italics.) The lawyer's reasonable man seems devoid of all the human impulses and psychological factors that govern the behaviour of man in society.

But even if the law, in deploying the test of the reasonable man, has hit on a simple workable test, is it right that criminal responsibility should be measured in this way? It is true that in a majority of cases there is little difference in the result from applying either a subjective or objective test. Where it is found that the accused 'ought to have foreseen' the natural consequences of his act it could usually be shown that he 'must have foreseen' and therefore by inference 'did foresee'. But the adoption of the subjective test means that in those instances where the Crown fails to prove that the accused 'did foresee' the consequence of his act, whether his lack of foresight was due to stupidity, ignorance, or negligence, the accused will escape criminal liability. It would be of no avail to show that although the accused did not foresee the consequences of his act, as a reasonable man he should, or ought to, have foreseen them.

The subjective test is right both in moral and ethical terms. If a man is stupid, is it right to penalise him because his intelligence does not measure up to the standards of the mythical reasonable man? This would be particularly relevant in cases of minority groups. The lack of comprehension by, say, a Cypriot of the English language might prevent him foreseeing the consequences of his act, prompted by something said to him, which his fellow English citizen would obviously foresee. It cannot in any event be right to put a premium upon unintelligence.

The reverse side of the coin of the objective test is equally unfortunate. If the highly intelligent man's acts are tested according to the acts of a reasonable man, something may be foreseen by the intelligent man that the ordinary average rider on the Clapham omnibus might not foresee. An intelligent man might then be acquitted of a charge although he personally, because of his perspicacity, could have foreseen the consequences of his act.

The subjective test restores a proper balance as between differing citizens faced with similar situations. The more unintelligent, superstitious and lacking in foresight the accused is, the more difficult it will be to establish his guilt of a crime. The premium is then on intelligence; the greater the gifts the individual is endowed with or possesses, the greater the responsibility he has for the way in which he conducts himself.

The objective test of intent is used by the Royal Commission to recommend that, apart from the abolition of constructive malice, the English law of murder should not be altered. It regarded the limited definition of murder as simply an intent to kill as 'defective and inadequate' whether considered from a logical point of view or as a means of distinguishing these heinous cases that deserve punishment of death. We can ignore the latter because definitions can never take into account heinousness or punishment consequent upon conviction, for to do so is to argue either from the particular to the general or to involve oneself in a circular argument.

The Royal Commission contented itself with commending the reasoning of two 19th century Commissions. The Commissioners on the Criminal Law in their fourth report in 1839[19] said that there was "no difference in point of legal distinction whether death results from a direct intention to kill or from wilfully doing an act of which death is the probable consequence". The Royal Commission then, parrot-like, repeated the hallowed phrase about a man contemplating the probable consequences of his own act. It concluded, more rationally, that "it is the wilful exposure of life to peril that constitutes the crime". If 'wilful' constitutes the 'malice aforethought' of the traditional definition, it does so only by a form of constructive malice.

In 1843 the Criminal Code Bill Commission[20] said that the principle, that in certain circumstances murder can be committed although there was an absence of an actual intention to cause death, ought to be maintained. The Commission could find no distinction between a man "who shoots another through the head expressly meaning to kill him, a man who strikes another a violent blow with a sword, careless whether he dies of it or not, and a man who, intending for some object of his own, to stop the passage of a railway train, contrives an explosion of gunpowder or dynamite under the engine, hoping indeed that death may not be caused, but determined to effect his purpose whether it is so caused or not".

The differences do, however, exist. The intention necessary to constitute the crime of murder is all important—so important indeed that, to include as murder heinous killings which do not exhibit intentions to kill, the law has had to construct a series of fictions to impute the necessary intention.

There seems in fact great merit in treating the crime of murder as simply the intention to kill; to do otherwise devalues the currency of the offence. It is simply because in the heyday of capital punishment for killings it was necessary to inflict the death penalty on killings brought about as a result of intention to commit violent felonies other than those resulting in death, that the law of murder was defined with such amplitude. But the use of fiction in the law of murder has by no means disappeared.

In all the cases cited by the Criminal Code Bill Commission the jury in each case might well infer from conduct that there was an intention to kill. If a man is so careless about others' lives it is a logical step to say that he intends that they should die. Intent is not so positive an act that it must be transposed by a real desire for loss of life; it is enough if it is wholly indifferent to the maintenance of life.

Intention should not be confused with motive, the latter alone reflecting an element of wish-fulfilment, whereas intention is neutral so far as desire is concerned. Intention indicates that a man is consciously shaping his conduct so as to bring about a certain event; whereas motive indicates the reason why he desires that event, and therefore why he pursue the selective course of conduct so as to achieve it. Another way of stating the point is to regard motive as the ulterior intention—the intention with which an intentional act is done. If A intentionally poisons B's whisky with the intention of killing him, the latter intention constitutes the motive. Motive is expressed in the criminal law as "with intent to"—for example, housebreaking with intent to commit a felony.

The real object of a definition of murder, limited to an intention to kill, would be to remove from the category of murder those cases where death occurs—one almost says, fortuitously—accidentally. If A, while stealing from a store, is interrupted and picks up the first piece of wood he can find to hit his interruptor, the death that ensues should not be murder. If asked what his intention was the killer would say that it was merely to prevent the detection of his crime of theft and he hit hard enough to incapacitate his victim only temporarily.[21] If the jury believes that that was his intention, there is no reason why the killing should be murder. The instrument—the manner in which it is acquired and used—will to a great extent determine the intention of the user to kill. There is a world of difference between the killing by shooting—with a weapon not normally ready to hand—and a killing by the use of a bread-knife—readily available in every household. Juries already, even under the present law, do exercise their right to draw inferences from the acts committed. Even where, for example, a gun is fired at the victim, a jury has been known to bring in a verdict of man-slaughter (other than on grounds of provocation or diminished responsibility) even though the weapon used was so potentially lethal that it would be hard to imagine how a jury could accept an accused's story that he did not intend to kill. Manslaughter, with the whole spectrum of punishment available, will sufficiently meet the case where the jury cannot be certain of the accused's intention to kill. In such cases of doubt the accused is not a 'murderer', and should not be dubbed so by the law.

NOTES

(1) Fisher v. Raven [1963] 2 W.L.R. 1137.

(2) 1874 [315] IX-471, p. v.

(3) Glanville Williams, "Constructive Malice Revived", (1960) 23 M.L.R. 605.

(4) This is confirmed by the Royal Commission on Capital Punishment, para. 617, p. 216. Indeed those serving life sentences for various forms of criminal homicide form a relatively large proportion of long term 'star' prisoners.

(5) Para. 534, p. 189

(6) See Chapter VIII, Capitalised Murder, infra.

(7) At one time the rule was applied to abortion, but now a jury is directed to bring in a verdict of manslaughter. In abortion, however, the violence done is to a *willing* victim.

(8) [1937] 3 All E.R. 920.

(9) See the case of Forsyth, Harris, Lutt and Darby (1960); and the Mitcham Co-op murder case: R. v. Thatcher and others (1963), *The Times*, 2 April 1963.

(10) Section 5(2).

(11) [1957] 2 Q.B. 664.

(12) As Lord (then Sir Patrick) Devlin said, [1954] Crim.L.R. 668, "I take an intent to be constructive when there is imputed to a man a state of mind other than his actual state of mind."

(13) D.P.P. v. Smith [1961] A.C. 290.

(14) High Court of Australia: R. v. Smythe (1957) 98 C.L.R. 163 and Parker v. The Queen (*The Times* Law Report, 12 June 1963), Manitoba Court of Appeal:

R. v. Malinik [1951] 1 W.W.R. (N.S.) 561; the Appellate Division of the Supreme Court of South Africa: R. v. Nsele 1955 (2) S.A. 145.

(15) [1962] 2 Q.B. 621.

(16) See Emmanuel Miller, "Delinquent Traits in Normal Persons", Brit. J. Delinq. X. 3 Jan. 1960.

(17) Para. 472-3, pp. 162-163.

(18) Clarendon Law Series, O.U.P. (1962), p. 141.

(19) 1839 [168] XIX—235 pp. XX, XXIV

(20) p. 24.

(21) On the second reading of the Homicide Bill in the Commons on 15 November 1956, Mr. Charles Fletcher-Cooke M.P. (later for some time a joint Under-Secretary at the Home Office) supported this view, H. C. Hansard, Vol. 560, Col. 1231. He instanced the case he had had, while at the Bar, of a young man who went into a tobacconist's shop and held up the tobacconist with an unloaded revolver. The tobacconist called the young man's bluff and leapt over the counter. The young man hit him on the head with the butt end of the revolver and ran out of the shop in a panic without robbing the till. The tobacconist had been hit on a sensitive spot and choked as a result of an internal haemorrhage. The young man was convicted of murder and, despite the jury's recommendation to mercy, he was hanged. The jury obviously felt that there had been no intention to kill.

CHAPTER VII

VICTIMOLOGY

NOT EVERY crime need have a victim, but in those which do there often exists an especially interesting quality; the nature of the relationship between criminal and victim. More than this; just as the commission of a crime is no isolated, idiosyncratic act, but the culmination of a process in which many factors are at work, so for the most part there are few genuinely random victims of crime. The householder who is the victim of burglary has, as often as not, paid no heed to the state of his locks, left windows unfastened, or has gone away and advertised his absence by omitting to cancel the milk. The motorist who leaves a camera or briefcase on the seat in full view is asking to have them stolen. But victims may go beyond carelessness. The man who has had more liquor than he can take lies in the arms of a prostitute and may lose his wallet if it has not already been emptied by paying exorbitant sums for drinks in the shady 'club' where he picked her up. Victims may suffer as a consequence of their own cupidity and foolishly entrust money to 'confidence men' who assure them that some financial venture (beyond the reach of the Inland Revenue) is about to produce a fantastic profit. And some women approaching middle age and anxious about their sexual attractiveness are not infrequently the victims of unscrupulous Don Juans who fleece them of their money as well as their modesty. People who are careless about their goods, who are prepared to penetrate the Rialto of the half-world of prostitutes, 'club' owners and criminal lay-abouts, whose greed or whose vanity craves satisfaction, may all fall victim to crimes of one sort or another.

But how much of this applies to murder? Few people, it might be argued, die simply because they have been careless, promiscuous, avaricious or vain. And while it is relatively easy to say that a man has lost his belongings through his own fault, it is much more difficult to say that a man has lost his life through his own fault. For one of the more permanent qualities attributed to the victims of murder is that of innocence. Even a cursory reading of the thumb-nail sketches of homicide printed in this book will show that this is often misplaced generosity, for some of the victims might well have been capable of killing on their own account, while others so goaded their killers either by provocation in words or deeds, or by incessant nagging that they directly precipitated their own deaths.

One factor emerges very clearly from these homicide cases, and that is that the area of heterosexual relationships is one exceptionally fraught with potential violence whether within the marriage or outside it. Relationships between men and women outside marriage are likely to focus on overtly sexual issues which bring in their train deeply charged emotions concerning exclusive rights of possession, and anxieties about unfaithfulness. Love and hate in psycho-analytic theory are juxtaposed and often intertwined, so that an individual can both love and kill the object of his desire if the normal expression of his feelings is deflected by jealousy. Desdemona, had she been unloved by Othello, might have lived.

There are several cases, too, where murder occurred immediately after, or even during sexual intercourse, instances where true sadism—the infliction of pain upon the love object—occurred, accompanied by masochism—a desire to be hurt by the love object —on the part of the victim. Such complementary sadism and masochism has been observed among animals and is not uncommon among the human species. Within marriage, the frame of reference for the victim-killer relationship is not exclusively sexual. For although sexual infidelity is frequently an apparently precipitating factor, other tensions between husbands and wives may build up. The pattern of neurotic interaction in marriage is frequently such that, although the relationship may be characterised by continuous conflict, participation in it satisfies the unconscious psychological needs of the partners, and neither has the wish to alter the situation. But, where the effect of conflict is not integrative but erosive, things are very different. Hostility may take a variety of forms—refusal by the wife to co-operate in getting a divorce, pestering or molesting the wife after or during the divorce, or the physical violence of murder. But because the act of murder in most human beings involves the mobilisation of intense feeling it is more *possible* in relationships which by their very intimacy produce an intensity of emotion.

Vulnerability exists, not only in emotional proximity, but in certain practical circumstances. Many of these, unlike the circumstances of love and marriage, in no way involve a common psychological bond between killer and victim but are essentially situational hazards. Thus the prostitute whose client is unknown to her, may be murdered simply because she represents a readily accessible sexual object to her killer, to whom anonymity in his victim may be important. More commonly prostitutes are the only women prepared to co-operate in the sado-masochistic sexual perversions which form, for the killer, an integral part of the homicidal drive. While understandably little sympathy attaches in the public mind to the prostitute victim of homicide, the same is not true of other victims of 'sexual' murders, particularly when they are young. Where certain young children are concerned 'innocence' is probably a misplaced term, for while little girls cannot be classed directly with adult prostitutes, by no means all of them are lacking in sexual curiosity. It is invariably a drive they but dimly perceive, but one which may draw them into situations where they may become the victims of crime.

Children who take lifts from strangers generally do so either because their parents have exercised little responsibility in instructing them or in direct defiance of parental injunction; in either case there is a situational factor at work. Similarly women who ask for lifts late at night run a risk of being sexually assaulted, largely because the drivers who give lifts to women in such circumstances know that a woman asking for a ride is likely to be of 'easy virtue'; if she is not, it is often the worse for her, as the sad stories regularly recounted in one Sunday newspaper bear testimony.

Leaving aside those situations in which the victim is likely to be drawn into the homicidal situation, partly in consequence of some special feature of personality or adjustment, there are others in which the instinctive behaviour of the victim triggers off the act of killing. The commonest of these is undoubtedly in the typical capital murder—murder in the course or furtherance of theft. The housebreaker is disturbed by the householder (or nightwatchman), who attempts to arrest him, and in panic the housebreaker hits out, often with some vase, ornament or movable object, killing the citizen who is attempting to defend his property. The law, as often as not, assumes that the killer intended to do grievous bodily harm, and is therefore guilty of murder. In reality this is seldom the case; the housebreaker is normally in a state of great tension and some regularly urinate on the premises, which fact is sometimes recorded on their criminal record cards as a useful piece of information for future detective work. Some householders on the other hand, especially women, attempt to defend their property with quite exceptional vigour, frequently screaming loudly. Such behaviour is likely to trigger off a violent attempt to silence the victim on the part of the intruder who himself is tense and fearful, and the violence of such panic reaction may well result in death. The ferocity of resistance on the part of women householders may be connected with the fact that housebreaking is not unlike forcible rape in the way the victims speak of it.[1] The use of the word 'outrage' is common, and as a woman whose home had been burgled said to one of the present writers, "what is so awful is the thought of that man being in my bedroom". Although the severity of injuries sustained by these victims is often appalling (e.g. Riley 1960) they are not inconsistent with the behaviour of an offender whose panic has destroyed all control and reduced him to the level of a cornered animal. The law, however, while not averse in the quieter atmosphere of the courtroom to applying such descriptions to the killers, is seldom moved to consider 'animal' responses in their situational context when the question of the formation of criminal intent is under discussion.

'Pleas of panic' in such circumstances are seldom if ever accepted by the law as provocation, although initial violence on the part of the victim can amount to such. Costas Panayi (1960), a Birmingham café proprietor, in protecting his wife and his premises from a group of young hoodlums, stabbed two of them with a knife lying on the counter. Although these youths had caused trouble before, and were intending to do damage again, the court took a serious view of the crime and sentenced Panayi to 4 years' imprisonment. Chisam (1962), a middle-aged garage owner, fired a gun into the air to drive away some youths annoying him late at night by playing a transistor radio loudly outside his house. The youths forced their way into the house and assaulted Chisam who picked up a swordstick, injuring two and killing a third. His appeal on the grounds of self-defence against conviction of manslaughter under section 2 of the Homicide Act 1957 was rejected by the Court of Criminal Appeal. He was sentenced to life imprisonment. However in Vanstone's case (1962) the court took a different view. Vanstone, a small man of 53, was attacked by Rice a local farmer who, having drunk 15 whiskies, stopped Vanstone while the latter was taking his dog for a walk. Vanstone drew his pocket knife and severed an

artery in his 18 stone attacker whom the trial judge called a
'powerful drink-sodden bully'. Vanstone was acquitted of both
murder and manslaughter, and discharged.

What is perhaps most important in any discussion of 'victimology' is to distinguish between the legal and the psycho-social
aspects of the relationship between victim and killer. The law, both
in respect of provocation and self-defence, utilises definite criteria in
assessing responsibility, and in awarding penalties it does not regard even legally defined provocation as cancelling out liability for
punishment, although the severity of such punishment varies from
case to case and court to court. Nor, contrary to what many people
believe, does the law give the citizen *carte blanche* to defend himself or his property with any degree of force he chooses to employ.[2]
But in examining the social and psychological aspects of the victim-
killer relationship it is abundantly clear that homicide 'out of the
blue', in which the victim is struck down without reacting in any
way, is exceptionally rare. Almost invariably there are words or
actions (frequently recognised by the law as legitimate, and wholly
approved by the community at large) which provoke the killer into
the use of force or—in the instance of attempted rape—into still
greater force. If householders kept calm, and women passively
accepted unwanted interference—counsels of perfection, it is true—
they might avoid more disastrous consequences.

But clearly, to expect this is to ask a great deal of human nature.
Householders are after all no more likely to keep a cool head in the
context of criminal activity than are their assailants. That these
reactions and counter-reactions exist is an inescapable fact, and
they ought not to be ignored when 'innocence' and 'guilt' are under
either judicial scrutiny or public discussion. As George Meredith
wrote:

> . . . . I see no sin:
> The wrong is mixed. In tragic life, God wot,
> No villain need be! Passions spin the plot:
> We are betrayed by what is false within.[3]

326   A CALENDAR OF MURDER

NOTES

(1) The tremendous physical resistance of some victims of rape may indeed provoke the additional force which brings about their death. Such instances were not uncommon in wartime: see, for example, the cases of William Collins (21), a merchant seaman hanged at Durham in 1942 for the murder of a young W.A.A.F.; Charles Raymond (23), a Canadian soldier hanged at Wandsworth in 1943, who mortally injured a 22 year-old W.A.A.F. while raping her; Terence Casey (22), a private soldier, also hanged at Wandsworth in the same year for strangling a woman of 45 while attempting rape; Ernest Kemp (24), a gunner, hanged at Wandsworth in 1944 after raping a W.A.A.F. of 21; John Davidson (18), a private soldier, hanged at Walton in 1944 for strangling a woman of 27 during attempted rape; and Horace Gordon (28), a Canadian private, hanged at Wandsworth in 1945 for stabbing a girl of 18 during rape. All, except Gordon, killed by the use of bodily force during the sexual act.

(2) He may use only such force as is necessary for him to exercise his legal rights. See Hodgson (1959).

(3) From *Modern Love*, XLIII.

CHAPTER VIII

CAPITALISED MURDER

THE FACT and legal quality of murder are one thing; the penalty for murder is quite another thing. Yet if the present public perturbation over the Homicide Act 1957 is directed at the penalty for murder this dichotomy is not fully recognised; emotions about the sanction for murder, perhaps inevitably, spill over to the facts and legal consequences of the widely varying degrees of moral responsibility for killings. The law is, after all, concerned with abstractions, and is not able to concern itself with the particular case. The law can provide for every situation involving the infinite complexities of human behaviour only by stating a rule. The rule is then applied by the courts to the particular situation. In the case of murder, the selection of those which carry the death penalty—a mandatory sentence—immediately involves a consideration of the penal treatment—if the judicial killing can ever be regarded as 'treatment'—in terms of the facts and legal consequences of the killing. Yet if this is so, it is still necessary to recognise the dichotomy.

Anyone coming fresh to the Homicide Act 1957—to be precise, section 5 of the Act which deals exclusively with the penalty—would be struck immediately by how interwoven are the problems of criminal responsibility and of the punishment meted out by the law. The fact that the court's sentence is mandatory is enough to mark out the crime of murder as failing to reflect the dichotomy of criminal justice. And the public's desire to impose the death sentence only for certain murders reflects, in the absence of a wise discretion to commute the death sentence in individual cases, the inability to separate the crime from the appropriate treatment or punishment. There is a fundamental fallacy in the view that it is either expedient or right to fix a sentence according to the classification of the criminal act regardless of the responsibility of the individual criminal. The legislature in 1957—in spite of the clearest possible direction from the Royal Commission—attempted to grade murders, thereby judging the twin, but distinct, problems of crime and punishment.[1]

Part of the confusion comes from a looseness in thinking. Motive or reason for the crime of murder is of no real concern to the lawyer; he is interested in them only as factual evidence tending to show that the accused is the killer and that he intended to kill.

The legal quality of the act of murder, in which intention to kill (or some fictitious intention) is the key component, is relevant to punishment only to the extent that it may disclose a particular motive. The Home Office itself in its memorandum to the Royal Commission[2] declared that "there are not in fact two classes of murders but an infinite variety of offences which shade off by degrees from the most atrocious to the most excusable". The law in its general way hives off a large number of killings and classifies them as manslaughter. But within the categories of murder and manslaughter the law makes no attempt to measure the heinousness of the particular criminal offence. For manslaughter it recognises the breadth of public tolerance by leaving the sentencing body with the widest possible discretion—from absolute discharge to life imprisonment. Yet if the law does that for manslaughter it is odd that there is such impervious rigidity in the penalty prescribed for murder; in fact, of course, the rigidity is loosened by the executive powers of the Home Secretary to release any person serving a life sentence (either as a result of the death sentence being commuted or because of the fixed penalty at law) at any time. The operation of the death penalty—if tolerable at all —is tolerable only where someone or some body has an absolute discretion to commute the sentence in any particular case.

No one can define in advance that certain categories of murder are more or less deserving of the law's ultimate sanction. The Royal Commission recommended that the trial jury should be empowered to substitute a life sentence since this was the only way of correcting the rigidity of the present law.[3] The major defect of this scheme is that under the English system the trial court may be in possession of very little background information about the convicted man.[4]

Yet we should not be too harsh on the legislature. It sought (whatever the practical effect was to be) to mitigate considerably the incidence of the death penalty by introducing the doctrine of diminished responsibility and by declaring certain categories of murder non-capital.[5] By establishing these two distinct categories of murder, the legislature has also provided sociologists with a unique opportunity of examining the phenomenon of murder in closer detail.

It is frequently said that in passing the Homicide Act the government attempted to do what the Royal Commission declared to be chimerical: confine the death penalty to the more heinous murders.[6] While it is true that the Royal Commission sought and failed to classify murders so as to confine the death penalty to the more heinous[7] it was certainly not unaware of classifications of murder based on the need to maintain law and order by making those murders most inimical to public order subject to the death penalty.[8]

And it seemed to anticipate the view of Lord Goddard, then Lord Chief Justice, that the distinction between capital and non-capital murders was not founded on any rational principle and would lead to many anomalies and inconsistencies. The categories of capital murder were a "mere hotch-potch consisting of those which were thought to arouse the greatest public apprehension or abhorrence". It is significant that during the passage of the Criminal Justice Bill in 1948 a not dissimilar suggestion had been made for distinguishing between capital and non-capital murder; significantly, the capital category was to include murders involving sexual offences and murder by the systematic administration of poison.

The Royal Commision rightly thought that the 1948 venture, abandoned in favour of a full scale inquiry into other possible ways of limiting capital punishment, could not be rationally supported. "Any attempt" it concluded, "to formulate degrees of murder by this method would, we believe, be open to objections similar to those raised against the compromise clause [the clause in the 1948 Bill] and we are driven to the conclusion that it is impracticable to find a solution of the problem along these lines"[9].

Yet the Conservative Government in 1956, with the two notable excisions from the 1948 categories, adopted the classification formulated by the Labour Government. The Home Secretary (Major Gwilym Lloyd George, now Lord Tenby) elaborated the rationale of the new definition of capital punishment.[10] There were two basic themes dictating the definitions: the Government's prime duty to maintain law and order, and the recognition of the real fear in the public's mind that the removal of the ultimate sanction would lead to increased violence. Those murders involving the greater amount of public violence, and so inimical to public order, and murders most likely to arouse fear in the minds of the public at risk as victims were singled out for capital classification. It was on these grounds that crimes involving sexual offences and murders for poisoning were omitted. Instead there were four types of murders which ultimately formed sections 5 and 6 of the Homicide Act 1957.[11] There were (a) murders by professional criminals—represented by the formula of murder "done in the course or furtherance of theft" and murder "by shooting or causing an explosion";[12] (b) murders of agents of law and order—policeman, prison officers and those assisting in the performance of their duties;[13] (c) murders by shooting or by the use of explosives, which are crimes supposedly most associated with particularly dangerous and indiscriminate activity, and are usually associated with gang warfare;[14] and (d) murderers who make a habit of their crime.[15]

Much of the public opprobrium heaped on the Homicide Act for the way in which it has operated in practice would be allayed if the public recognised that heinousness was never intended as the criterion for the selection of the capital crime. Yet if the inimical nature of the particular form of murder was the legislature's yardstick it can hardly be said to have proved any the more successful in producing a just or even socially valuable distinction between the two classes.

Those who have in fact suffered the death penalty have not always fitted neatly into the categories devised. How was it possible to justify the execution of Bernard Walden (1959), the mentally sick Technical College lecturer, who shot a young secretary in the office and her student boy friend. Three condemned men—Stokes (1958), Constantine (1960) and Harris (1960)—were hardly professional criminals, having indulged in only petty crimes of hitherto non-violent character. Again, the case of Niemasz (1961), although involving shooting, was essentially a domestic crime. And, paradoxically, one of the two killings committed by Niemasz within seconds of the other was non-capital because Niemasz used only the butt of the rifle instead of firing it; Edwin Bush (1961) who murdered a woman in a curio shop off the Charing Cross Road, was deserving of sympathy because of an unhappy inheritance and an appalling childhood; the gallows seemed singularly inappropriate to his case. And had Smith (1961) not been reprieved (because his appeal in the Court of Criminal Appeal was successful, although reversed by the House of Lords) would he have been executed because he killed a policeman? Of the killers of policemen, only

Henry King (1959) escaped the gallows by a successful defence of diminished responsibility.[16] And what of Vickers (1957), who had only one recorded previous conviction—for larceny at the age of eleven? His execution was hotly opposed, also on the grounds that he was guilty of murder only because the doctrine of constructive malice, abolished under the Act, was let in by a side-door. His intention to do grievous bodily harm—the Crown pathologist said the blows on the 72 year-old spinster were "moderately severe to slight"—was enough to provide the "malice aforethought".

The record of the Act, on the basis of those few who suffered the death penalty, is unimpressive. Since it is impossible to tell how many and which of the non-capital murderers would have experienced the hangman's noose had the 1957 Act not become law, there is little purpose in speculating. Some would have been more obvious candidates than others—some like Matheson (1958), Byrne (1960) and Dowdall (1960), all of whom successfully pleaded diminished responsibility, would, on past evidence of the Home Secretary's failure to exercise the prerogative of mercy, probably have been hanged.

Suffice it to say, much public misgiving has been felt over the comparative injustices. A was executed but B, whose crime happened to be non-capital, survived.

But this is to introduce subjective elements of heinousness and abhorrence, and those two notions were ostensibly disavowed by the authors of the 1957 Act. How many of the non-capital murders were symptomatic of lawlessness and gross public disorder, and therefore should have fallen within the categories of capital murder under the rationale of the Homicide Act? We will take one year's cases—1960, Coyne, Hamilton, Reid, Smith A. J., Soltysiak, Szabo, Todd. These cases reveal the fact—one would have thought, blindingly obvious to the architects of the 1957 Act—that murders most injurious to public order can be and are committed with offensive weapons (excluding firearms) other than in the course or furtherance of theft. Uncontrolled behaviour is just as inimical to public welfare as are crimes committed for gain in the course of a fight or in a fit of jealousy or hatred. And so we come full circle. While the Homicide Act abjures the element of moral wickedness to justify the retention of murder for those crimes, heinousness creeps back as a justification for the execution of one murderer and not another. The Gordian knot of capital punishment was thus unloosed in 1957; it has become so entangled since then as to require its final and irreversible cutting.

The topic of capital punishment cannot be left without a word about its deterrent effect. Deterrence was in fact one of the Government's props to its thesis for retaining the death penalty for those murders which cause the greatest public anxiety. It was said that in certain types of murder the deterrent effect of the death penalty was likely to be more powerful than in other crimes. The professional criminal, the Home Secretary at the time of the Homicide Bill[17] said, "who had so much to gain by murder, rarely commits it because . . . he does count the cost, and thinks it too high." Other criminals carrying offensive weapons, it is frequently claimed, are deterred from lethal violence. Many people fear that if the deterrence of the death penalty, which is said to restrain criminals from carrying weapons, is removed they will be exposed to attack by men who will have little to lose from adding murder to their appalling criminal records.

These views prompt certain questions. Are offensive weapon-carrying criminals deterred by the death penalty any more—and if so, how much more—than by the threat of lengthy imprisonment? If capital punishment is not the unique deterrent claimed for it—in order to justify the retention of the death sentence—is the public fear still reasonable? If it is not reasonable, ought the legislators still to retain the gallows merely to satisfy the groundless fears of its citizens?

Deterrence in the form of the death penalty can, by definition, have no relevance to the particular accused. It can have an effect only upon any future potential killer. While in certain circumstances the prospect of the death sentence can have a generally deterrent effect on potential offenders, whether any sentence of a court, or the knowledge that death is the only penalty that can be meted out, deters is much less certain; and on any rational calculation, it will depend on an examination of the attitude of those supposed by the law to be deterred rather than on any objective criteria.

Lady Wootton, in an unpublished lecture in 1962,[18] claimed that there were four factors on which the deterrent effect of any sentence depends. The four are: 1. The risk of the individual's being found out, as subjectively estimated by the offender, which may be greater or less than the actual risk objectively determined; 2. Knowledge of the penalty to be inflicted by a court with variable modes of penalty available to it (where there is no mandatory sentence); 3. The severity of the penalty to be inflicted; and 4. The reward—again subjectively estimated—of escaping detection.

If one disregards the undetected homicides—as one has to do, because they represent the unfathomable 'iceberg' element in criminal statistics—the detection rate of homicide is high. In 1960, for example, the rate of those convicted of a homicidal crime to the number of 'murders' known to the police was 75 per cent, and this excludes killers who committed suicide before trial. It is not unreasonable to assume that potential killers are aware—so far as the problem ever crosses their minds—that the detection rate is high. But all the evidence of the cases shows that few killers plan their crime sufficiently for them to be presumed to have taken into account the detection rate. Indeed, in the cases of murder following a rape it is generally assumed that the killing is committed for the very reason that it will remove all evidence of the rape. This is a typical lawyers' inference of motive from the subjective evidence. Studies of the psychopathology of sexual violence would suggest that both the acts of coitus and the killing represent a psychic unity and indeed the rapist may achieve orgasm only during the act of killing itself.

Knowledge of the penalty to be inflicted by the court must be present to the potential killer's mind. Even if one supposes that a potential killer is unaware of the defences available to him—the pleas of insanity and diminished responsibility, self-defence, provocation—there is still the distinction between hanging for capital murder and life imprisonment for non-capital murder. The opponents of any categories or degrees of murder might justifiably point to the confusing result of the law's distinction upon the deterrent effect of the death penalty has upon the potential killer's mind.

A number of cases since the Homicide Act have shown that accused killers are often quite unaware of the types of murder which carry the death penalty. In the case of Theakstone (1959), the accused, after killing three relatives with a knife, was told by a policeman to put it away. He replied, "I have got to swing, so keep away from me." This interpretation of the law was wrong since the three murders were committed on the same occasion. In Seller (1959) the accused, who had expressed a desire to die, committed a non-capital murder. Only as an afterthought he told the police that the motive was theft, since this was the only way he could 'commit suicide'. If he had known the law he would have made sure that he stole something while killing his victim. In Riley (1960) the accused clearly was unaware of the law since only his confession that he "wanted some money"—which could have meant that he wished to borrow money from the victim whom he knew and from whom he had borrowed before—brought him within the category of capital murder. If he had known the law he would never have admitted to anything which could possibly have constituted theft unless he wanted to die as Seller (1959) did; there was absolutely no evidence, other than his confession of theft. In Wilson (1962) the accused, after killing his 3 year-old son, said, "I punched him—I killed him. I want to hang." If he knew the law he would have known that he could not have been hanged; it is fairly clear that by saying "want" he was saying that he did not want to be reprieved, whereas he had not even committed a capital offence. In Bartley (1961) the accused said, "I would like to hang", whereas if he had known the law he would have known that he could not hang. In Martin (1962) just as in Cox (1962) the accused said that he thought he would hang for killing his wife in her sleep with an axe. In the case of Tomlinson (1960) the accused planned to kill so that he should be executed but he carried out only a non-capital murder.

The two other factors on which the deterrent effect on any sentence depends—the severity of the penalty to be inflicted and the reward, subjectively estimated, of escaping detection—are not strictly relevant to capital murder. In the case of the professional killing in the course of robbery a large sum of money might induce an assessment of the penalty and the reward. But since most killings in the course of theft are for petty amounts (never more than a few hundred pounds and often only for quite a small sum) there is strong evidence to suggest that the severity of the penalty is not present in the potential killer's mind.

To what extent is it true that it is fear of the consequential penalty that prevents anybody from committing murder? Ignorance of the law generally is widespread, and, as we have seen, there is just as much ignorance (or total unawareness) of the murders that carry the death penalty. Again, the importance of the risk of detection as a factor in general deterrence is often emphasised, while insufficient attention is paid to the important distinction between the objective and the subjective risks of detection. The subjective estimate of the risk diverges from the objective estimate. High though the objective estimate of risk of detection may be in homicide, there is reason to believe that in murder—where there is also a high rate of mental instability—the subjective estimate is quite low.

The subjective estimate is a complicated product compounded of temperament, mood and knowledgeability. Timid persons may tend to over-estimate the likelihood of conviction, and they are not, we think, normally the stuff of potential murderers. (It is of course true that under extreme stress or after continuous pressure or humiliation even the meekest of worms may turn; such aggression as they have being introverted until the point is reached beyond which no more can be tolerated, and the aggression bursting destructively outwards (Drummond 1961).) Bolder spirits, the so-called 'professional criminal' and possibly non-professional criminals (the persistent and intermittent petty thieves), err on the side of underestimating the risk of detection. The very fact of being in the criminal world makes them think that they, of all people, know how to beat the policeman at the game of 'cops and robbers'.

And, finally, the risk estimate of anyone committing offences in a mood of passion—which is true of a large number of people charged with homicide—is liable to be reduced to zero.

NOTES

(1) A quip among lawyers is to call the 1957 Act the 'Reggie-cide' Act, since Sir Reginald Manningham-Buller (then Attorney-General, now Lord Dilhorne, the Lord Chancellor) was one of the main architects of this compromise legislation.

(2) Cited by Mr. Anthony Greenwood M.P. in the 2nd Reading debate on the Homicide Bill on 15 November 1956, Hansard, H.C., Vol. 560, Col. 1170.

(3) Para. 595, p. 208.

(4) One of us has had occasion to elaborate on this theme arising out of the Hanratty case.

(5) Roughly the annual number of executions has been reduced to a third. There are now on average 4 executions a year compared with 12 in the years immediately preceding 1957 (apart from the period of 18 months between 1955 and 1957 when the death sentence was in practice suspended).

(6) Sydney Silverman M.P. in an appendix to *Reflections on Hanging* by Arthur Koestler (Macmillan 1957), p. 213, cited uncritically by J. E. Hall Williams in an appendix to *The Crusade against Capital Punishment in Great Britain* by Elizabeth Tuttle (Stevens 1961), p. 1496.

(7) Para. 534, p. 189.

(8) Para. 493, p. 171 where proposals under the 1948 Criminal Justice Bill were discussed.

(9) Para. 504, p. 176.

(10) Hansard, H.C., Vol. 506, Col. 1146, 1149, 1150 and 1258.

(11) See Appendix, infra.

(12) Section 5(1)(a), Homicide Act 1957.

(13) Section 5(1)(c), (d) and (e), ibid.

(14) Section 5(1)(b), ibid.

(15) Section 6, ibid.

(16) The others, besides Smith, were Marwood (1959) and Podola (1959).

(17) Hansard, H.C., Vol. 506, Col. 1146.

(18) "Sociological Aspects of Crime and Criminal Law", delivered at Bedford College, University of London, 27 February 1962.

CHAPTER IX

HOW LONG IS 'LIFE'?

A MAJOR OBSTACLE to the final abolition of capital punishment is the disquiet among the public—however irrationally founded—that the substitute sentence of 'life imprisonment' is grossly inadequate to protect the public and does not reflect the public opprobrium for the crime. A more extreme view is that the penalty of life imprisonment for murder is not nearly severe enough and is in practice an 'empty formula'.[1]

The fear is that if capital punishment were abolished those murderers who would before 1957 have been executed, will now serve in prison no more than the so-called nine years—a period of incarceration that is considered inadequate both from the point of view of retribution and of reformation. But the figure of nine years reflects the policy of the Home Office in pre-1957 cases, and only in those cases where there were some mitigating circumstances. The very fact of a person before 1957 having been reprieved at all connotes some substantial mitigating circumstance.

The period of nine years was not in any sense a mathematical average but the most common period served by a murderer who merited release on licence because of his personal circumstances and the mitigating factors of his crime. Release after 9 years corresponds to a sentence of 14 years' imprisonment—with a full one-third remission, release comes after 9 1/3rd years—which is the maximum determinate sentence fixed by statute.[2]: the 42 years imprisonment on George Blake and the 18 years passed on John Vassall breached this traditional maximum by producing a compound of three consecutive sentences. Only since 1948 when the courts could pass sentences of preventive detention up to 14 years—which carried a possible lesser remission of 1/6th—could a prisoner serve more than 12 years. And, since earlier this year the remission period on a sentence of preventive detention is to be equated with that applicable to simple imprisonment, that former distinction has gone.

In practice, the period of detention served by murderers is very much longer than that served for any other offence, and will

337

inevitably be longer under post-1957 conditions. In 1959 for example, apart from 44 sentences of life imprisonment for murder or manslaughter, only six sentences of imprisonment for more than 10 years were imposed—one for manslaughter, one for felonious wounding, one for burglary and three for robbery. Two of these were life sentences, the other four were determinate sentences on which ordinary remission could be earned.

The Home Office policy of releasing on licence those serving life sentences is limited exclusively to pre-1957 Act cases.

If there have been any releases of persons convicted since the Homicide Act 1957[3] they will have been persons who would similarly have been released in pre-1957 conditions because of the special mitigating factors about their crime. The policy hitherto has been that there is little need to imprison a person convicted of murder for more than 15 years; exceptionally a longer period may be justified. The test always has been whether the prisoner could be released, once he has served a term of imprisonment consonant with the gravity of his particular offence, without danger to the public. The Royal Commission on Capital Punishment[4] concluded that there was no reason for any general increase in the period served at that time in order that the deterrent effect of the life sentence should not be weakened. The Commissioners were convinced that any convicted murderers whom it would be unsafe to release were likely to be in the category of the mentally ill, for whom special provisions for detention are made. Society's reprobation of the most heinous crimes would always be adequately satisfied so long as those convicted of the more serious murders served longer sentences than other criminals—with the notable and understandable exception of spies.

Experience in Britain and in the countries releasing from prison on parole or licence those serving life sentences, is that they rarely commit any other crime. Out of the 76 released in the five years 1955-60, only two were subsequently convicted of offences of violence. Of 11 persons detained during Her Majesty's Pleasure (having been under 18 at the time of the offence) and subsequently released during the same period, two had been convicted of a crime of violence.

These figures bear out the view of the Royal Commission which stated that the evidence from abolitionist countries showed that those released who committed further crimes of violence were rare and those who became useful citizens were common.[5] In Britain, during a period from 1928-48, 112 out of 174 life sentence prisoners were released. Only five of them have been convicted of any serious offence and only one of them of murder. (This was the case of Walter Rowland about whose second crime there are grave doubts; another man (Ware) who was serving a prison sentence confessed to the murder but then withdrew it before the Jolly tribunal set up to inquire into the case. Ware in fact committed another murder some years later.)[6]

Of the 76 cases during the period, 1955-60, the following table indicates the length of term served:—

TABLE III

Time served by prisoners sentenced to life imprisonment for murder

Less than 1 year		.	.	1
Released after	1 year	.	.	2
,,	,,	2 years	. .	2
,,	,,	3 years	. .	1
,,	,,	4 years	. .	1
,,	,,	5 years	. .	3
,,	,,	6 years	. .	2
,,	,,	7 years	. .	6
,,	,,	8 years	. .	16
,,	,,	9 years	. .	26
,,	,,	10 years	. .	10
,,	,,	11 years	. .	5
Up to 20 years		.	.	1

Source: Answer to Parliamentary question in House of Lords, March 1961

The persons released after 1, 2 and 6 years were all women. There was one woman among the three released after 5 years and one among the six released after 7 years. The bulk of those serving life imprisonment served between 7 and 11 years imprisonment.

The figures for the years 1909-49 quoted by the Royal Commission[7] indicated a similar period of imprisonment, although a higher proportion of prisoners were released after 11 years; but no one was detained after 20 years in prison and only a few served more than 15 years. The Royal Commission endorsed the view of Sir Alexander Paterson to the Select Committee in 1930 that "whatever means of education, stimulation and recreation may be employed, however you may seek to ring the changes on handicraft and literature, skittles or chess or ping-pong, despite the most devoted voluntary workers, it requires a superhuman to survive 20 years of imprisonment with character and soul intact . . . I gravely doubt whether an average man can serve more than 10 continuous years in prison without deterioration". The Royal Commission thought that this risk of deterioration of the human personality was not such that the community ought to shrink from contemplating a 20 year sentence for a dangerous criminal—this would particularly be true in the case of aggressive psychopaths, the final remission of their aggressive proclivities coming only in later middle-age. As the Home Office in its evidence aptly concluded, even if the cage were more commodious and comfortable it would still remain a cage.[8]

Far too little attention has been given by abolitionists to the problem of alternatives to capital punishment. Most of the concerted thought on the problem has come from the unconvinced or lukewarm abolitionists, such as the present Lord Chief Justice. Lord Parker has aired the widespread view—not confined to the legal profession—that the death penalty should be abolished on condition that the judges would be free to pass sentences of 25, 30 or even more years of imprisonment.

Among penal reformers there is a natural repugnance to the notion that a court, determining the issue of a person's guilt of murder, should be free to fix a sentence of such duration which would inevitably be immutable in the hands of penal administrators.

Even if determinate sentences bulk large in the sentencing policy of the courts they do so within fairly restricted limits as to time, and the trend in penal practice is towards indeterminate sentencing.[9]

Sentencing may not ideally be a function to be performed by the judiciary. But it is idle for penal reformers to kick against the pricks and demand that judges yield their powers of sentencing. While it is true that most judges express inadequacy in deciding the proper sentence—implementation of the Streatfeild committee's recommendation should reduce this real sense of uneasiness at the lack of material necessary for sound sentencing—they are loth to hand it over. For the foreseeable future the judges in Britain will remain the prime sentencers. If this is to be so—and we think that it can scarcely be gainsaid—it is penologically dangerous if the judiciary ever has the feeling that its function as sentencers will be subverted by penal administrators.

If life imprisonment remains mandatory for all murders, the judges must be guaranteed that 'life' is not 'just an empty formula'.

Judges are not unsympathetic to the proper claims of the indeterminate sentence. Very often life sentences are imposed by the judges where there is a discretion—as in all cases of manslaughter where life imprisonment is the maximum sentence—simply because the judges recognise that the indeterminate sentence is more appropriate to the needs of the criminal. And they have every confidence that the administrators will release the prisoner only when it is both right and safe to do so.

For the legislature to provide a mandatory sentence of life imprisonment for any crime is to reduce to zero the element of judicial election in sentencing. Even in the case of the death sentence the judges do influence the exercise of the prerogative by the Home Secretary asking the trial judge's advice on the question of a reprieve. In the case of infanticide before the Act of 1922 the judges rebelled at the nauseating task of passing sentence of death—a real 'empty formula'. The judges have not by a long way become perfervid abolitionists, but many more today than in the past would welcome the departure of the death penalty. They are, however, sensitive to their role in determining the country's sentencing policy for those convicted of murder.

It is odd that, in a penal system which has given its judges the greatest breadth of discretion in sentencing, for the gravest crimes all discretion has been taken away from the courts.[10] This is the more surprising when one realises that degrees of sanity and insanity shade off into one another by imperceptible gradations. If ever the penal treatment should fit the criminal, to the exclusion of any tariff system applicable to the crime, it is in the case of murder.

The Mental Health Act 1959[11] provides a useful precedent for a combined administrative-judicial sentencing function that could profitably be used in sentencing all those convicted under the Homicide Act. Where a judge is satisfied that a person convicted of a criminal offence needs mental treatment he can make a hospital order, whereupon he effectively commits the person to the care of the authorities of a mental institution. If the court is fearful that early release would be fraught with risks for the community it is empowered to make a restriction order for a limited or unlimited period of time. Thus in the case of Sowle (1961) Mr. Justice Melford Stevenson placed a 40 year restriction on the release of the accused. The effect of such an order is to deprive the patient and his family of the right to apply for the patient's discharge or, if necessary, to argue for discharge before a mental health review tribunal. The Secretary of State is given the sole discretion to say when the patient may be released; a potent factor in the Minister's mind will be the judge's restriction order.[12] On the whole the judge does not need to specify the time limit of the restriction order,[13] since the mere existence of the restriction order operates as a caveat on the Minister's exercise of the power to release the patient.

In the cases of those convicted of murder the sentence should remain the obligatory one of life imprisonment. Psychologically there is merit in retaining a life sentence (as an automatic sentence) for the most serious crime, even if 'life' in practice means something other than detention for the rest of the prisoner's natural life. In all those cases where there are—in the eyes of the court—mitigating factors, the life sentence would be passed without more ado.[14] The prisoner will be treated as in the past; he can expect release within the time range of 7-11 years.

Where there are no apparent mitigating circumstances the judge could have a discretion. Just as under the Mental Health Act, the judges would have the power to make a restriction order for a limited or unlimited period. If a limitation period is stated, then once that period is served the Home Secretary's power to release on licence[15] would be unfettered. Where the restriction is unlimited or where the limitation period has not yet run out, the power to release on licence would be circumscribed.

Any ministerial decision, that it would be in the public interest for a person serving a life sentence to be released, should be subject to review by a Parole Board, consisting of a departmental official, the trial judge (or permanent representative of the judiciary), a psychiatrist, a probation officer and a lawyer.

Any release on licence in these cases would be the responsibility of the Parole Board. After ten years in prison, the person serving a life sentence (including those not subject to restriction) would, without the initiative of the Home Office, have the right to come before the Parole Board and put his case for release. His case would thereafter, apart from references to the Parole Board by the Home Office, be required to be considered quinquennially, except where the trial court's restriction order was for a period in excess of ten years. The right to ask the Parole Board for release would be taken away to the extent that a restriction order as to time was in force.

Thus, a restriction order for 20 years would deprive the offender of his right to come to the Parole Board for 20 years. Any move for the prisoner's release earlier than 20 years could be initiated only by the Home Secretary and be subject to approval by the Parole Board.

Where the Parole Board was required to review a decision of the Home Secretary to release a prisoner before the expiry of the restriction order, the decision of the Board should be unanimous. We believe that this provision should exist, since what is proposed to be done administratively conflicts with what has already been done judicially. We anticipate of course that it would be very rare for the Board to dissent from the Home Office view, simply because release before the expiry of a restriction order would be proposed only in quite exceptional circumstances. Where, however, the restriction is of unlimited duration the Parole Board should be free to confirm or reject by a simple majority the Home Secretary's proposal to release.

After the expiry of any restriction order the prisoner would fall into the same category, for purposes of release by order of the Home Secretary, as other prisoners serving sentences of life imprisonment with no restriction orders attached. Where the prisoner is exercising his right to apply for his discharge, either by virtue of the restriction order having lapsed or because he has already served at least 10 years of an unrestricted life sentence, the decision of the Parole Board should be by a simple majority. Any release, either by the Home Secretary or by the Board, should be subject to the same conditions as now apply to released persons—there should always be the ultimate provision for recall.

The establishment of any such Parole Board must be recognised as impinging upon the doctrine of ministerial responsibility. Under the present system the Home Secretary is always liable to questioning in Parliament about the proposal to release any prisoner before he has completed the sentence of the court.[16]

Such discussion, although theoretically in the public interest, is in practice likely to do no more than attract morbid curiosity through sensational treatment in the press (where the crime had been notorious), the general effect of which would be merely to retard rather than facilitate the rehabilitation of the prisoner. In practice this is well recognised by responsible Parliamentarians who quite properly forgo a natural inclination to probe such actions on the part of a Minister. Therefore, the proposal to set up a Parole Board would not to any discernible extent alter the present practice. We would, however, go a stage further, and suggest that the proceedings of the Board, while being wholly private, should not preclude the right of the prisoner or his family to be both present and legally represented. So far as surviving relatives of the victim are concerned, we believe that the possibility for misguided or vindictive opposition to release is such that there should be no provision for their attendance or representation; we think that such interests as they may quite properly have in the matter can be adequately protected by the Home Office view on the Board. The fact that it is necessary to consider possible rights of the victim's relatives before the Parole Board is indicative yet again of the absence of any scheme for compensation to the victims of crimes of violence. This is particularly relevant in the case of relatives of the victims of homicide.

NOTES

(1) See the letter of 12 June 1961 from Mr. Edward Gardner, Q.C., M.P., to the Home Secretary; the letter and official reply are printed below, pp. 369-73.

(2) Where the statute prescribes a maximum of life imprisonment the court can, and occasionally does, pass a sentence of more than 14 years; see e.g. Matheson (1958) and Sims (1961).

(3) Very sensibly, the Home Office does not reveal the time of any such release see footnote 15, infra.

(4) Para. 649, p. 228.

(5) Para. 651, p. 229.

(6) The case is fully recorded by Paget, Silverman and Hollis, *Hanged—and Innocent?* London, 1953.

(7) Appendix 3 (Statistical tables), Table 12, pp. 316-7.

(8) The least sanguine about the thought of prolonged detention was Mr. Charles Cunningham from the Scottish Home Office—now Sir Charles Cunningham, Permanent Under-Secretary at the Home Office.

(9) Almost 60 per cent of persons convicted of indictable offences, by virtue of being under 21, are (with certain minor exceptions) eligible for an indeterminate period of corrective detention or Borstal training.

(10) This does not apply to those crimes commonly called "murder" but are in fact manslaughter; and in those cases the disparity in sentencing is very marked, even between comparable cases.

(11) Sections 60 and 65 of the Act.

(12) R. v. Higginbotham [1961] 1 W.L.R. 1277 at pp. 1282-3.

(13) This seems to have been the view of Mr. Justice Lawton in Blanks (1962).

(14) A jury's recommendation to mercy ought to operate as a brake upon any discretion on the judge's power to restrict release.

(15) Section 27 of the Prison Act 1952.

(16) On 6 February 1963, Col. Marcus Lipton M.P.—it would seem, in order to ask a wholly unrelated supplementary question concerning the release of an IRA prisoner—questioned Mr. Henry Brooke about his reasons for proposing to release Christopher Craig in May 1963 (information which had leaked into the popular press).

APPENDICES

CHAPTER 11

An Act to make for England and Wales (and for courts-martial wherever sitting) amendments of the law relating to homicide and the trial and punishment of murder, and for Scotland amendments of the law relating to the trial and punishment of murder and attempts to murder.

[21st March, 1957]

BE it enacted by the Queen's most Excellent Majesty, by and with the advice and consent of the Lords Spiritual and Temporal, and Commons, in this present Parliament assembled, and by the authority of the same, as follows:—

PART I

AMENDMENTS OF LAW OF ENGLAND AND WALES
AS TO FACT OF MURDER

Abolition of 'constructive malice'

1.—(1) Where a person kills another in the course or furtherance of some other offence, the killing shall not amount to murder unless done with the same malice aforethought (express or implied) as is required for a killing to amount to murder when not done in the course or furtherance of another offence.

(2) For the purposes of the foregoing subsection, a killing done in the course or for the purpose of resisting an officer of justice, or of resisting or avoiding or preventing a lawful arrest, or of effecting or assisting an escape or rescue from legal custody, shall

be treated as a killing in the course or furtherance of an offence.

Persons suffering from diminished responsibility

2.—(1) Where a person kills or is a party to the killing of another, he shall not be convicted of murder if he was suffering from such abnormality of mind (whether arising from a condition of arrested or retarded development of mind or any inherent causes or induced by disease or injury) as substantially impaired his mental responsibility for his acts and omissions in doing or being a party to the killing.

(2) On a charge of murder, it shall be for the defence to prove that the person charged is by virtue of this section not liable to be convicted of murder.

(3) A person who but for this section would be liable, whether as principal or as accessory, to be convicted of murder shall be liable instead to be convicted of manslaughter.

(4) The fact that one party to a killing is by virtue of this section not liable to be convicted of murder shall not affect the question whether the killing amounted to murder in the case of any other party to it.

Provocation

3. Where on a charge of murder there is evidence on which the jury can find that the person charged was provoked (whether by things done or by things said or by both together) to lose his self-control, the question whether the provocation was enough to make a reasonable man do as he did shall be left to be determined by the jury; and in determining that question the jury shall take into account everything both done and said according to the effect which, in their opinion, it would have on a reasonable man.

Suicide pacts

4.—(1) It shall be manslaughter, and shall not be murder, for a person acting in pursuance of a suicide pact between him and another to kill the other or be a party to the other [killing himself or]* being killed by a third person.

(2) Where it is shown that a person charged with the murder of another killed the other or was a party to his [killing himself or]* being killed, it shall be for the defence to prove that the person

* These words were removed by their repeal in the Second Schedule to the Suicide Act 1961.

charged was acting in pursuance of a suicide pact between him and the other.

(3) For the purposes of this section 'suicide pact' means a common agreement between two or more persons having for its object the death of all of them, whether or not each is to take his own life, but nothing done by a person who enters into a suicide pact shall be treated as done by him in pursuance of the pact unless it is done while he has the settled intention of dying in pursuance of the pact.

PART II
LIABILITY TO DEATH PENALTY

Death penalty for certain murders

5.—(1) Subject to subsection (2) of this section, the following murders shall be capital murders, that is to say,—

(a) any murder done in the course or furtherance of theft;

(b) any murder by shooting or by causing an explosion;

(c) any murder done in the course or for the purpose of resisting or avoiding or preventing a lawful arrest, or of affecting or assisting an escape or rescue from legal custody;

(d) any murder of a police officer acting in the execution of his duty or of a person assisting a police officer so acting;

(e) in the case of a person who was a prisoner at the time when he did or was a party to the murder, any murder of a prison officer acting in the execution of his duty or of a person assisting a prison officer so acting.

(2) If, in the case of any murder falling within the foregoing subsection, two or more persons are guilty of the murder, it shall be capital murder in the case of any of them who by his own act caused the death of, or inflicted or attempted to inflict grievous bodily harm on, the person murdered, or who himself used force on that person in the course of furtherance of an attack on him; but the murder shall not be capital murder in the case of any other of the persons guilty of it.

(3) Where it is alleged that a person accused of murder is guilty of capital murder, the offence shall be charged as capital murder in the indictment, and if a person charged with capital murder is

convicted thereof, he shall be liable to the same punishment for the murder as heretofore.

(4) In this Act 'capital murder' means capital murder within subsections (1) and (2) of this section.

(5) In this section—

(a) 'police officer' means a constable who is a member of a police force or a special constable appointed under any Act of Parliament, and 'police force' has the same meaning as in section thirty of the Police Pensions Act, 1921 (as amended by the Police Act, 1946) or, as regards Scotland, the same meaning as in section forty of the Police (Scotland) Act, 1956;

(b) 'prison' means any institution for which rules may be made under the Prison Act, 1952, or the Prisons (Scotland) Act, 1952, and any establishment under the control of the Admiralty or the Secretary of State where persons may be required to serve sentences of imprisonment or detention passed under the Naval Discipline Act, the Army Act, 1955, or the Air Force Act, 1955;

(c) 'prison officer' includes any member of the staff of a prison;

(d) 'prisoner' means a person who is undergoing imprisonment or detention in a prison, whether under sentence or not, or who, while liable to imprisonment or detention in a prison, is unlawfully at large;

(e) 'theft' includes any offence which involves stealing or is done with intent to steal.

Death penalty for repeated murders

6.—(1) A person convicted of murder shall be liable to the same punishment as heretofore, if before conviction of that murder he has, whether before or after the commencement of this Act, been convicted of another murder done on a different occasion (both murders having been done in Great Britain).

(2) Where a person is charged with the murder of two or more persons, no rule of practice shall prevent the murders being charged in the same indictment or (unless separate trials are desirable in the interests of justice) prevent them being tried together; and where a person is convicted of two murders tried

together (but done on different occasions), subsection (1) of this section shall apply as if one conviction had preceded the other.

Abolition of the death penalty for other murders

7. No person shall be liable to suffer death for murder in any case not falling within section five or six of this Act.

Courts-martial

8.—(1) The foregoing provisions of this Part of this Act shall not have effect in relation to courts-martial, but a person convicted by a court-martial of murder (or of an offence corresponding thereto under section seventy of the Army Act, 1955, or of the Air Force Act, 1955) shall not be liable to suffer death, unless he is charged with and convicted of committing the offence under circumstances which, if he had committed it in England, would make him guilty of capital murder.

(2) An accused so charged before a court-martial under the Naval Discipline Act may, on failure of proof of the offence having been committed under such circumstances as aforesaid, be found guilty of the murder as not having been committed under such circumstances.

Punishment for murders not punishable with death, and other consequential provisions

9.—(1) Where a court (including a court-martial) is precluded by this Part of this Act from passing sentence of death, the sentence shall be one of imprisonment for life.

(2) Accordingly paragraph (*a*) of subsection (3) of section seventy of the Army Act, 1955, and of the Air Force Act, 1955, and the first paragraph of section forty-five of the Naval Discipline Act, shall each be amended by the addition, at the end of the paragraph, of the words "or, in a case of murder not falling within section eight of the Homicide Act, 1957, imprisonment for life".

(3) In section fifty-three of the Children and Young Persons Act, 1933, and in section fifty-seven of the Children and Young Persons (Scotland) Act, 1937, there shall be substituted for sub-section (1)—

"(1) Sentence of death shall not be pronounced on or recorded against a person convicted of an offence who appears to the court to have been under the age of eighteen years at the time the offence was committed, nor shall any such person be sentenced to imprisonment for life under section nine of the Homicide Act, 1957; but in lieu thereof the court shall (notwithstanding anything in this or any other Act) sentence him to be detained during Her Majesty's pleasure, and if so sentenced he shall be liable to be detained in such place and under such conditions as the Secretary of State may direct."

(4) The provisions of the First Schedule to this Act shall have effect with respect to procedural and other matters arising out of sections five to seven of this Act, and with respect to the convictions which may be taken into account under section six.

PART III

AMENDMENTS AS TO FORM AND EXECUTION OF DEATH SENTENCE IN ENGLAND AND WALES

Form of sentence of death for murder

10. Where by virtue of section five or six of this Act a person convicted of murder is sentenced to death, the form of the sentence shall be to the effect only that he is to "suffer death in the manner authorised by law".

Notice of execution

11.—(1) Sections seven and ten of the Capital Punishment Amendment Act, 1868, shall cease to have effect, in so far as they require provision to be made for the purpose of making known without the prison walls the fact that execution of sentence of death for murder is taking place, or require any document relating to such an execution to be exhibited on or near the prison.

(2) Where sentence of death for murder is to be executed in accordance with that Act, it shall be the duty of the Secretary of State, as early as he conveniently can, to publish in such manner as he thinks fit the time and place fixed for the execution.

(3) Where sentence of death for murder has been executed in accordance with that Act, it shall be the duty of the Secretary of State, as early as he conveniently can, to publish in such manner as he thinks fit the fact that the execution has taken place, and to cause to be published in the London Gazette a copy of the coroner's inquisition required by the Act.

Avoidance of double executions

12. Where two or more persons sentenced to death for murder are confined in the same prison, the Secretary of State may, with a view to avoiding the execution of more than one such sentence in that prison on the same day, direct that any of those persons shall be removed to and confined in some other prison specified in the direction; and the sentence on that person may lawfully be executed in the prison so specified, and the sheriff charged with the execution shall for that purpose have the same jurisdiction in that prison and over the officers of it, and be subject to the same responsibilities and duties in it, as though the prison were that in which the sentence would have been executed but for the direction.

PART IV makes special provisions for Scotland.

PART V

COMMENCEMENT, ETC.

Past offences

16. This Act shall not have effect in relation to any offence, where an indictment for that offence has been signed or, in Scotland, has been served before the date of the commencement of this Act, or, as the case may be, a court-martial for the trial of that offence has been ordered or convened before that date; but (subject to that) this Act shall have effect in relation to offences committed wholly or partly before that date as it applies in relation to offences committed after that date.

Short title, repeal and extent

17.—(1) This Act may be cited as the Homicide Act, 1957.

(2) The enactments specified in the Second Schedule to this Act are hereby repealed to the extent specified in the third column of that Schedule.

(3) This Act, except as regards courts-martial, shall not extend to Northern Ireland.

SCHEDULES

FIRST SCHEDULE

SUPPLEMENTARY PROVISIONS AS TO PROCEDURE, APPEALS, ETC.

PART I
ENGLAND AND WALES

1.—(1) On an indictment charging a person with capital murder, he may be found not guilty of capital murder but guilty of murder.

(2) Capital murder shall be treated as a distinct offence from murder for the purposes of any appeal against conviction; but where on an appeal against conviction of capital murder the court substitute a verdict of guilty of murder for the verdict of guilty of capital murder, the court shall nevertheless confirm the sentence of death if the sentence is warranted by section six of this Act.

(3) Subject to the foregoing sub-paragraphs, capital murder shall not be treated as a different offence from murder for any purpose.

2.—(1) Where a person is convicted of murder, he shall not by virtue of section six of this Act be sentenced to death by reason of a previous conviction of another murder done in Great Britain on a different occasion, unless—

    (a) at least three days before the trial notice is given to him and to the clerk of assize that it is intended to prove the previous conviction; and

    (b) before he is sentenced, his previous conviction of the other murder, and the fact that the murders were done in Great Britain on different occasions, are admitted by him or found by the verdict of a jury:

Provided that head (a) of this sub-paragraph shall not apply where he is convicted of both murders at the same assizes (or before the same court of assize held by virtue of a special commission).

(2) The said jury shall be the trial jury, that is to say the jury to whom he was given in charge to be tried for the murder for which the sentence is in question, and the members of the jury need not be re-sworn:

Provided that—

    (*a*) if any member of the trial jury, either before or after the conviction, dies or is discharged by the court as being through illness incapable of continuing to act or for any other cause, the inquiry under this paragraph shall proceed without him; and

    (*b*) where there is no trial jury, a jury shall be constituted as if to try whether or not he was fit to plead, and shall be sworn in such manner as the court may direct.

(3) Where a person is sentenced to death by virtue of a verdict given by a jury in proceedings under this paragraph, he shall have the like right of appeal under the Criminal Appeal Act, 1907, against the sentence of appeal were against a conviction involving sentence of death:

Provided that he shall not by virtue of this sub-paragraph have a right of appeal against a sentence passed on a conviction of capital murder, unless he appeals against that conviction.

(4) On any such appeal against sentence, the court shall have the same powers as to allowing or dismissing the appeal as on an appeal against a conviction; and where the court allow the appeal, and it appears to the court that having regard to the decision on the appeal the sentence is not warranted in law, the court shall quash the sentence and pass the appropriate sentence in substitution for it.

(5) The proviso to section thirteen of the Criminal Law Act, 1827 (which provides that a pardon of a felony shall not affect the punishment on a subsequent conviction for felony), so far as it relates to free pardons, shall not apply for the purposes of section six of this Act.

3.—(1) Where a person is sentenced to death on being convicted of murder after a previous conviction of murder, and afterwards the previous conviction is set aside on appeal, he may thereupon (or at any time not later than ten days thereafter) apply to the Court of Criminal Appeal to set aside the sentence of death on the ground that it is no longer warranted in law having regard to the decision on the appeal; and the court if satisfied that the sentence is no longer warranted in law shall set it aside and pass the appropriate sentence in substitution for it.

(2) Where a person is sentenced to death as aforesaid, then (unless he is so sentenced on being convicted of capital murder)

the sentence shall not in any case be executed so long as the previous conviction can be set aside on appeal.

(3) No application to extend the time for giving notice of appeal or of an application for leave to appeal against a person's conviction of murder shall be entertained if he has been sentenced to death on a later conviction of murder and the time for giving notice of appeal against the later conviction has expired.

4.—(1) Where a person is convicted of two murders tried together, he shall not by reason thereof be sentenced to death by virtue of section six of this Act, unless before he is sentenced the fact that the murders were done in Great Britain on different occasions is admitted by him or found by the verdict of a jury: and sub-paragraphs (2) to (4) of paragraph 2 of this Schedule shall apply for the purposes of this paragraph as they apply for the purposes of that paragraph.

(2) Where sentence of death is passed on a person convicted of two murders tried together, it shall be treated as passed in respect of each of the convictions; but if one of the convictions is and the other is not set aside on appeal, the court deciding the appeal, unless satisfied that the sentence remains warranted in law in respect of the other conviction, shall set the sentence aside and pass the appropriate sentence in substitution for it.

5. The power to make rules of court conferred by section eighteen of the Criminal Appeal Act, 1907, shall include power to make rules for the purpose of carrying into effect this Schedule, so far as relates to appeals and applications to the Court of Criminal Appeal.

6. This Part of this Schedule shall extend to England and Wales only, but references therein to a previous or later conviction include a conviction in Scotland.

PART II of the Schedule deals with Scotland.

SECOND SCHEDULE

REPEALS

Session and Chapter	Short Title	Extent of Repeal
24 & 25 Vict. c. 100.	The Offences against the Person Act, 1861.	Sections two and three.
11 & 12 Geo. 6 c. 58.	The Criminal Justice Act, 1948.	Section sixteen.
12, 13 & 14 Geo. 6. c. 94.	The Criminal Justice (Scotland) Act, 1949.	Section seventeen.

Table of Statutes referred to in this Act

Short Title	Session and Chapter
Criminal Law Act, 1827	7 & 8 Geo. 4. c. 28.
Criminal Law (Scotland) Act, 1829....	10 Geo. 4. c. 38.
Criminal Law (Scotland) Act, 1830....	11 Geo. 4 & 1 Will. 4. c. 37.
Naval Discipline Act	29 & 30 Vict. c. 109.
Capital Punishment Amendment Act, 1868....	31 & 32 Vict. c. 24.
Criminal Appeal Act, 1907	7 Edw. 7. c. 23.
Police Pensions Act, 1921	11 & 12 Geo. 5. c. 31.
Criminal Appeal (Scotland) Act, 1926	16 & 17 Geo. 5. c. 15.
Children and Young Persons Act, 1933....	23 & 24 Geo. 5. c. 12.
Children and Young Persons (Scotland) Act, 1937	1 Edw. 8. & 1 Geo. 6. c. 37.
Police Act, 1946	9 & 10 Geo. 6. c. 46.
Criminal Justice (Scotland) Act, 1949	12, 13 & 14 Geo. 6. c. 94.
Prison Act, 1952	15 & 16 Geo. 6 & 1 Eliz. 2. c. 52.
Prisons (Scotland) Act, 1952	15 & 16 Geo. 6. & 1 Eliz. 2. c. 61.
Army Act, 1955	3 & 4 Eliz. 2. c. 18.
Air Force Act, 1955	3 & 4 Eliz. 2. c. 19.
Police (Scotland) Act, 1956	4 & 5 Eliz. 2. c. 26.

SECTION 4 OF THE CRIMINAL JUSTICE ACT 1948

4. *Probation orders requiring treatment for mental condition:—*

(1) Where the court is satisfied, on the evidence of a duly qualified medical practitioner, [approved for the purposes of section 28 of the Mental Health Act 1959, that the mental condition of an offender is such as requires and may be susceptible to treatment, but is not such as to warrant his detention in pursuance of a hospital order under Part V of that Act.*] the court may, if it makes a probation order, include therein a requirement that the offender shall submit, for such period not extending beyond twelve months from the date of the order as may be specified therein, to treatment by or under the direction of a duly qualified medical practitioner with a view to the improvement of the offender's mental condition.

(2) The treatment required by any such order shall be such one of the following kinds of treatment as may be specified in the order, that is to say:

[(*a*) treatment as a resident patient in a hospital or mental nursing home within the meaning of the Mental Health Act 1959, not being a special hospital within the meaning of that Act*]

(*b*) treatment as a non-resident patient at such institution or place as may be specified in the order; or

(*c*) treatment by or under the direction of such duly qualified medical practitioners as may be specified in the order.

but except as aforesaid the nature of the treatment shall not be specified in the order.

(3) A court shall not make a probation order containing such a requirement as aforesaid unless it is satisfied that arrangements have been made for the treatment intended to be specified in the order, and, if the offender is to be treated as a resident patient as aforesaid, for his reception.

(4) While the probationer is under treatment as a resident patient in pursuance of a requirement of the probation order, the probation officer responsible for his supervision shall carry out the supervision to such extent only as may be necessary for the purpose of the discharge or amendment of the order.

(5) Where the medical practitioner by whom or under whose direction a probationer is being treated for his mental condition

*As amended by the Mental Health Act 1959, Schedule VII.

in pursuance of a probation order is of opinion that part of the treatment can be better or more conveniently given in or at an institution or place in or at which the treatment of the probationer will be given or under the direction of a duly qualified medical practitioner, he may, with the consent of the probationer, make arrangements for him to be treated accordingly; and the arrangements may provide for the probationer to receive part of his treatment as a resident patient in an institution or place notwithstanding that the institution or place is not one which could have been specified in that behalf in the probation order.

(6) Where any such arrangements as are mentioned in the last foregoing subsection are made for the treatment of a probationer;

    (a) the medical practitioner by whom the arrangements are made shall give notice in writing to the probation officer responsible for the supervision of the probationer, specifying the institution or place in or at which the treatment is to be carried out; and

    (b) the treatment provided for by the arrangements shall be deemed to be treatment to which he is required to submit in pursuance of the probation order.

(7) Subject as hereinafter provided, a report in writing as to the mental condition of any person purporting to be signed by a duly qualified medical practitioner experienced in the diagnosis of mental disorders may be received in evidence for the purposes of subsection (1) of this Section without proof of the signature, qualifications or experience of the practitioner;

Provided that such a report shall not be so received unless the person to whom it relates consents or, where that person is under 17 years of age, unless his parent or guardian consents or no parent or guardian can be found.

(8) Where a person of whose mental condition evidence is received for the purposes of subsection (1) of this section (or, where that person is under 17 years of age, this parent or guardian) desires to call rebutting evidence, the court shall not make a probation order in his case containing any such requirement as is authorised by this section unless he, or his parent or guardian, as the case may be, has been afforded an opportunity of calling such evidence.

(9) Except as provided by this section, a court shall not make a probation order requiring a probationer to submit to treatment for his mental condition.

SECTION 60 OF THE MENTAL HEALTH ACT 1959

60. *Powers of courts to order hospital admission or guardianship*

(1) Where a person is convicted before a court of assize or quarter sessions of an offence, other than an offence the sentence for which is fixed by law, or is convicted by a magistrates' court of an offence punishable on summary conviction with imprisonment, and the following conditions are satisfied, that is to say:—

    (*a*) the court is satisfied, on the written or oral evidence of two medical practitioners (complying with the provisions of section 62 of this Act):—

        (i) that the offender is suffering from mental illness, psychopathic disorder, subnormality or severe subnormality; and

        (ii) that the mental disorder is of a nature or degree which warrants the detention of the patient in a hospital for medical treatment, or the reception of the patient into guardianship under this Act; and

    (*b*) the court is of opinion, having regard to all the circumstances including the nature of the offence and the character and antecedents of the offender, and to the other available methods of dealing with him, that the most suitable method of disposing of the case is by means of an order under this section;

the court may by order authorise his admission to and detention in such hospital as may be specified in the order or, as the case may be, place him under the guardianship of a local health authority, or of such other person approved by a local health authority as may be so specified.

(2) Where a person is charged before a magistrates' court with any act or omission as an offence and the court would have power, on convicting him of that offence, to make an order under subsection (1) of this section in his case as being a person suffering from mental illness or severe abnormality, then, if the court is satisfied that the accused did the act or made the omission charged, the court may, if it thinks fit, make such an order without convicting him.

(3) An order for the admission of an offender to a hospital (in this Part of this Act referred to as a hospital order) shall not be made under this section unless the court is satisfied that arrangements have been made for the admission of the offender to that

hospital in the event of such an order being made by the court, and for his admission thereto within a period of 28 days beginning with the date of the making of such an order.

(4) An order placing an offender under the guardianship of a local health authority or of any other person (in this part of this Act referred to as a guardianship order) shall not be made under this section unless the court is satisfied that that authority or person is willing to receive the offender into guardianship.

(5) A hospital order or guardianship order shall specify the form or forms of mental disorder referred to in paragraph (*a*) of sub-section (1) of this section from which, upon the evidence taken into account under that paragraph, the offender is found by the court to be suffering; and no such order shall be made unless the offender is described by each of the practitioners whose evidence is taken into account as aforesaid as suffering from the same one of those forms of mental disorder, whether or not he is also described by either of them as suffering from another of those forms.

(6) Where an order is made under this Section, the court shall not pass sentence of imprisonment or impose a fine or make a probation order in respect of the offence, but may make any other order which the court has power to make apart from this section; and for the purposes of this subsection 'sentence of imprisonment' includes any sentence or order for detention, including an order sending an offender to an approved school.

SECTION 65 OF THE MENTAL HEALTH ACT 1959

65. *Power of higher courts to restrict discharge from hospital*

(1) Where a hospital order is made in respect of an offender by a court of assize or quarter sessions, and it appears to the court, having regard to the nature of the offence the antecedents of the offender and the risk of his committing further offences if set at large, that it is necessary for the protection of the public so to do, the court may, subject to the provisions of this section, further order that the offender shall be subject to the special restrictions set out in this section, either without limit of time or during such period as may be specified in the order.

(2) An order under this Section (in this Act referred to as an order restricting discharge) shall not be made in the case of any person unless at least one of the medical practitioners whose evidence

is taken into account by the court under paragraph (*a*) of subsection (1) of Section 60 of this Act has given evidence orally before the court.

(3) The special restrictions applicable to a patient in respect of whom an order restricting discharge is in force are as follows, that is to say:

(*a*) None of the provisions of Part IV of this Act relating to the duration renewal and expiration of authority for the detention of patients shall apply, and the patient shall continue to be liable to be detained by virtue of the relevant hospital order until he is duly discharged under the said Part IV or absolutely discharged under the next following section.

(*b*) no application shall be made to a Mental Health Review Tribunal in respect of the patient under Section 63 of this Act or under any provisions of the said Part IV.

(*c*) The following powers shall be exercisable only with the consent of the Secretary of State, that is to say:

(i) power to grant leave of absence to the patient under Section 39 of this Act;

(ii) power to transfer the patient in pursuance of regulations under section 41 of this Act; and

(iii) power to order the discharge of the patient under section 47 of this Act;

and if leave of absence is granted under the said Section 39 the power to recall the patient under that Section shall be vested in the Secretary of State as well as the responsible medical officer; and

(*d*) the power of the Secretary of State to recall the patient under the said section 39, and the power to take the patient into custody and return him under section 40 of this Act, may be exercised at any time and in relation to any such patient the provisions of the said Part IV described in the first column of the Third Schedule to this Act shall have effect subject to the exceptions and modification set out in the third column of that Schedule in lieu of those set out in the second column of that Schedule.

(4) A hospital order shall not cease to have effect under subsection (5) of Section 63 of this Act if an order restricting the discharge of the patient is in force at the material time.

(5) Where an order restricting the discharge of a patient ceases to have effect while the relevant hospital order continues in force, the provisions of section 63 of this Act and the Third Schedule to this Act, shall apply to the patient as if he had been admitted to the hospital in pursuance of a hospital order (without an order restricting his discharge) made on the date on which the order restricting his discharge ceased to have effect.

Section 72 of the Mental Health Act 1959

72. *Removal to hospital of persons serving sentences of imprisonment etc.*

(1) If in the case of a person serving a sentence of imprisonment the Secretary of State is satisfied, by reports from at least two medical practitioners (complying with the provisions of this section)

- (a)   that the said person is suffering from mental illness, psychopathic disorder, subnormality or severe subnormality; and
- (b)   that the mental disorder is of a nature or degree which warrants the detention of the patient in a hospital for medical treatment

the Secretary of State may, if he is of opinion having regard to the public interest and all the circumstances that it is expedient so to do by warrant direct that that person be removed to and detained in such hospital (not being a mental nursing home) as may be specified in the direction.

(2) A direction under this section (in this Act referred to as a transfer direction) shall cease to have effect at the expiration of the period of 14 days beginning with the date on which it is given unless within that period the person with respect to whom it was given has been received into the hospital specified therein.

(3) A transfer direction with respect to any person shall have the like effect as a hospital order made in his case.

(4) Of the medical practitioners whose reports are taken into account under subsection (1) of this section, at least one shall be a practitioner approved for the purposes of section 28 of this Act by a local health authority as having special experience in the diagnosis or treatment of mental disorders.

(5) A transfer direction shall specify the form or forms of mental disorder referred to in paragraph (a) of subsection (1) of this section from which, upon the reports taken into account under that subsection, the patient is found by the Secretary of State to be suffering;

and no such direction shall be given unless the patient is described in each of those reports as suffering from the same one of those forms, whether or not he is also described in either of them as suffering from another of those forms.

(6) References in this section to a person serving a sentence of imprisonment include references:

(*a*) to a person detained in pursuance of any sentence or order for detention made by a court in criminal proceedings, or made or having effect as if made in any proceedings under the Children and Young Persons Act, 1933 (other than an order under any enactment to which section 71 of this Act applies or an order for detention in a remand home under section 54 or in a place of safety under section 67 of the said Act of 1933);

(*b*) to a person committed to custody under subsection (3) of section 91 of the Magistrates' Courts Act, 1952 (which relates to persons who fail to comply with an order to enter into recognisances to keep the peace or be of good behaviour); and

(*c*) to a person committed by a court to a prison or other institution to which the Prison Act, 1952 applies in default of payment of any sum adjudged to be paid on his conviction.

THE SUICIDE ACT 1961

1. *Suicide to cease to be a crime.* The rule of law whereby it is a crime for a person to commit suicide is hereby abrogated.

2. *Criminal liability for complicity in another's suicide*

(1) A person who aids, abets, counsels or procures the suicide of another, or an attempt by another to commit suicide, shall be liable on conviction on indictment to imprisonment for a term not exceeding 14 years.

(2) If on the trial of an indictment for murder or manslaughter it is proved that the accused aided, abetted, counselled or procured the suicide of the person in question, the jury may find him guilty of that offence.

(3) The enactments mentioned in the first column of the First Schedule to this Act shall have effect subject to the amendments provided for in the second column (which preserve in relation to

offences under this section the previous operation of those enactments in relation to murder or manslaughter).

(4) an indictment for an offence under this section shall not be triable by a court of quarter sessions; and (subject to sections 13 and 40 of the Children and Young Persons Act, 1933 as applied by subsection (3) above) no proceedings shall be instituted for an offence under this section except by or with the consent of the Director of Public Prosecutions.

3. *Short title, repeal and extent*

(1) This Act may be cited as the Suicide Act, 1961.

(2) The enactments mentioned in the Second Schedule to this Act are hereby repealed to the extent specified in the third column of the Schedule.

(3) This Act shall extend to England and Wales only, except as regards the amendments made by Part II of the First Schedule and except that the Interments (felo de se) Act, 1882 shall be repealed also for the Channel Islands.

SECTION 53 OF THE CHILDREN AND YOUNG PERSONS ACT 1933

53. *Punishment of certain grave crimes*

(1) Sentence of death shall not be pronounced on or recorded against a person convicted of an offence if it appears to the court that at the time when the offence was committed he was under the age of eighteen years; but in lieu thereof the court shall sentence him to be detained during His Majesty's pleasure; and if so sentenced he shall be liable to be detained in such place and under such conditions as the Secretary of State may direct.*

(2) Where a child or young person is convicted on indictment of [any offence punishable in the case of an adult with imprisonment for fourteen years or more, not being an offence the sentence for which is enforced by law]† and the court is of opinion that none of the other methods in which the case may legally be dealt with is suitable, the court may sentence the offender to be detained for such period [not exceeding the maximum term of imprisonment with which the offence is punishable in the case of an adult]‡, as

*This sub-section has now been replaced by section 9(3) of the Homicide Act 1957 (see supra, p. 353).

†As amended by section 2(1) of the Criminal Justice Act 1961.

‡Added to, or amended by, the Fourth Schedule to the Criminal Justice Act 1961.

may be specified in the sentence; and, where such a sentence has been passed the child or young person shall, during that period, be liable to be detained in such place and on such conditions as the Secretary of State may direct.

(3) A person detained pursuant to the directions of the Secretary of State under this section shall, while so detained, be deemed to be in legal custody.

(4) Any person so detained as aforesaid may, at any time, be discharged by the Secretary of State on licence.

Such a licence may be in such form and may contain such conditions as the Secretary of State may direct, and may at any time, [by notice in writing]* be revoked or varied by the Secretary of State. Where a licence has been revoked the person to whom the licence related shall return [shall, if at large, be deemed unlawfully at large].*

*Added to, or amended by, the Fourth Schedule to the Criminal Justice Act 1961.

CORRESPONDENCE
ON LIFE SENTENCES FOR MURDER

Life imprisonment for murder; an exchange of letters between Mr. R. A. Butler, the Home Secretary, and Mr. Edward Gardner, Q.C., M.P.

June 12th 1961

Dear Home Secretary,

May I invite your urgent attention to the motion, No. 121, on the Order Paper, which has now been signed by more than fifty Conservative Members of Parliament? This, I believe, reflects the loss of confidence by most people in the country in the present punishment of 'life imprisonment' for non-capital murder and shows a strong desire that the Government should "take immediate steps to introduce legislation to ensure that a sentence of life imprisonment for this crime shall be for a period of not less than twenty-five years, unless a Court in its discretion orders otherwise".

The Homicide Act of 1957 distinguished non-capital murder from all other crimes by expressly limiting punishment to an indeterminate sentence 'imprisonment for life'. In theory this is 'the most rigorous sentence of imprisonment known to the law'; in practice it is an empty formula. This dangerously debases both the deterrent and punitive value of the only sentence upon which the community can now rely for protection from sadistic, sexual and other murderers. Under the Homicide Act their methods of killing can allow them to escape the death sentence.

The average term of imprisonment served by a prisoner sentenced to life imprisonment has recently been about nine years (for murders committed before 1957). In future, one understands 'life imprisonment' is likely to be prolonged to an average of about twelve years. It may be argued that the average includes longer (and shorter) periods of imprisonment but the weakness of an indeterminate sentence is not its ultimate length or brevity but its *uncertainty*. What has a killer to fear if he can kill believing that if he is caught and convicted he may spend less time in prison than a thief?

13

Among the reasons for the present dissatisfaction with the working of the Homicide Act are:

(i) It seems incredible that, when Parliament replaced the death penalty by life imprisonment in 1957, it can have intended to bring about the present illogical consequences.

(ii) Murder has always been 'the gravest of all crimes' for which the community has always exacted 'the severest of all penalties'.

(iii) Though the deterrent effect of the death penalty may be debatable, no one can doubt the deterrent value of a long term of imprisonment.

(iv) There is a strong and growing anxiety in the country that the Homicide Act does not give the community the protection which it has the right to expect.

(v) But where a murderer may deserve compassion, for instance in the case of a mercy-killing, a trial Court should have discretion to impose a lenient sentence.

I know that I write expressing views that are widely held and that there are many people who would be grateful for your answer.

Yours sincerely,

(SGD.) EDWARD GARDNER

4th July 1961

Dear Gardner,

You wrote on 12th June drawing my attention to the motion on the Order Paper on the subject of life imprisonment for murder and seeking my views. You will not expect me to deal in detail with the proposals for legislation contained in the motion. It may, however, be helpful if I say something about the existing policy in relation to the release of prisoners serving life sentences, since the terms of the motion suggest that there may be some misunderstanding on this matter.

Dealing first with the pre-Homicide Act cases, it is true that for life sentence prisoners released in recent years the period of detention served in an average case has been about nine years. This is not a mathematical average. It is the period served in a case in which there were some mitigating features which justified a reprieve, where there were no compassionate circumstances calling for specially early release and where the Home Secretary has been satisfied, on the basis of full reports on the circumstances of the offence and on the prisoner, including reports on his conduct in prison and his mental condition, that he could be released without danger to the public at the end of that period. Where there have been specially mitigating or compassionate circumstances the period of detention has been shorter. On the other hand, there have been many cases in which it has been thought right to detain a prisoner for more than nine years. The important point is that no prisoner serving a life sentence is released unless the Home Secretary is satisfied that there is unlikely to be a risk of his repeating his offence or being a danger to the public. One person released during the last five years had been detained for 20 years, and among the life sentence prisoners now detained are two who have served 16 years and two who have served 13 years. A further point I should make is that life sentence prisoners are always released on licence and can be recalled to prison at any time if this is thought to be desirable. Successive Home Secretaries have not hesitated to use this power in the interests of public safety.

The passing of the Homicide Act created a new situation. Prisoners who are now sentenced to life imprisonment for non-capital murder include some whose crimes present no mitigating features, and who, before the Act, would have been executed. It is to be expected that many of these prisoners will have to be detained for periods much longer than has been found necessary, save in the most exceptional circumstances, in the past, where there have usually been extenuating circumstances to justify a reprieve. In an extreme case it may be necessary to detain a prisoner until he dies. It is obviously quite impossible, when the Act has been in operation for only just over four years and the only prisoners released have been those for whom some exceptional compassionate grounds for early release existed, to predict what the average period of detention will be in the future. I do not know the origin of the figure of twelve years to which you refer; it certainly does not derive from anything that I have said on this subject.

You say that the weakness of an indeterminate sentence is its uncertainty. I do not believe that this is so. Prisoners do not know until about a year before they are due to be discharged how long they will have to serve, and experience has shown that this uncertainty is, for most prisoners, the worst feature of their detention. As regards deterrence, the Royal Commission on Capital Punishment saw no reason to conclude that any general increase in the periods served was necessary to ensure the deterrent effect of the life sentence. Nine years—the period recently served, in an average case, by a man whose sentence was commuted to life imprisonment before the Homicide Act—is the equivalent, with one third remission of a sentence of imprisonment of nearly fourteen years. Moreover, as I have already said, many prisoners sentenced to life imprisonment under the Homicide Act are likely to be detained for more—some for much more—than nine years. It is therefore not correct to say that a man who commits a murder will spend less time in prison than a thief. Indeed, it is clear that the period of detention served by murderers in recent years, and still more the period which they are likely to serve in future, is very much longer than that served for any offence of theft, or indeed, save in most exceptional cases, for any other offence not involving homicide. (In 1959, for example, apart from 44 sentences of life imprisonment for murder or manslaughter, only six sentences of imprisonment for more than 10 years were imposed—one for manslaughter, one for felonious wounding, one for burglary and three for robbery. Two of these were life sentences; the other four were determinate sentences, on which remission can be earned.)

As regards your proposal to make a life sentence one of not less than twenty-five years, unless a court in its discretion orders otherwise, it seems likely that in practice the twenty-five years' sentence would become the exception rather than the rule, since the great majority of murders are not of the kind which understandably give rise to especial public anxiety and concern, and which have no doubt prompted your motion, but are murders committed by relatives, often in circumstances which allow a compassionate view to be taken.

I should have no objection to our arranging for this letter to be published. Indeed I would welcome any steps which might help to remove some of the misapprehensions which I believe to exist on this subject.

I am sending a copy of this letter to Bingham, who has also written me about the motion.

Yours ever,

(SGD.) R. A. BUTLER

Edward Gardner, Esq., Q.C., M.P.

STATISTICAL AND OTHER TABLES

TABLE A

Murders known to the police*

Annual Averages

	1930–39	1940–49	1950–54	1955–56	1957	1958	1959	1960	1961	1962
Number .	131	167	141	148	166	137	149	153	147	159
Number per million of population .	3·6	4·4	3·7	3·7	4·2	3·4	3·7	3·8	3·6	3·9

Source: *Annual Criminal Statistics*, England and Wales

* Since the Act, and specifically since 1958, those homicides subsequently defined by the courts as manslaughter under section 2 are excluded from the final total of murders (see Table D).

TABLE B

Suspects who commit suicide

	1957	1958	1959	1960	1961	1962
Suspects*	105	103	115	131	117	129
Suicides	39	38	35	39	33	45

Source: *Criminal Statistics, England and Wales, 1957-62*

*Suspects include all those proceeded against on charges of murder but excludes persons at whose trials the murder charge was reduced to ordinary manslaughter or other less common case of unintentional killing.

TABLE C

Murder Indictments

				Capital	Non-capital	Total
Male .	.	.	.	121	548	669
Female	.	.	.	6	89	95
Total .	.	.	.	127	637	764

Source: *Criminal Statistics, England and Wales, 1957-62*, and Home Office information.

Table D

Verdicts of courts in cases of those indicted with capital and non-capital murder

Source: *Criminal Statistics and Press Reports of Trials, 1957–1962*

	1957*	1958	1959	1960	1961	1962	Total
1. Guilty of capital murder	5(7)	8	6	9	7	3	38
2. Guilty of non-capital murder	22(28)	20	37	31	40	24	174
3. Guilty but insane	3(4)	8	15	15	7	9	57
4. Unfit to plead	14(19)	11	11	8	11	11	66
5. Guilty of manslaughter	17(23)	17	15	19	33	28	129
6. Guilty of manslaughter under Section 2 (diminished responsibility)	12(16)	26	21	25	40	36	160
7. Guilty of manslaughter under Section 3 (provocation)	8(11)	8	5	6	—	8	35
8. Guilty of manslaughter under Section 4 (suicide pacts)	—	1	—	—	—	—	1
9. Not guilty and acquitted	11(15)	15	9	26	16	19	96
10. Infanticide	—	—	2	—	1	—	3
11. Concealment of birth	—	1	—	1	—	—	2
12. Guilty of wilful neglect	2(3)	—	—	—	—	—	2
13. Attempted murder	—	—	—	—	1	—	1
Totals	94(126)	115	121	140	156	138	764

* Figures for 1957 from March 21. Figures in brackets represent an annual estimate.

Table E

Age of persons indicted for murder 1957–1962

	under 14	15–24	25–34	35–44	45–54	55–64	65 and over	all ages
Capital murder	1	56	43	11	9	5	2	127
Non-capital murder . .	3	175	204	130	71	27	27	637
Total	4	231	247	141	80	32	29	764

Source: Home Office information.

TABLE F

Killers related to their victims, March 1957—December 1962

Killer	Victim	No. of persons charged
Husband . . .	Wife	132
Father . . .	Child	52
Mother. . .	Child	56
Lover . . .	Mistress	47
Miscellaneous blood relationship . .	(including in-laws, cousins, siblings. . . .	32
Son . . .	Mother	25
Wife . . .	Husband	24
Son . . .	Father (including step-father)	13
Fiancé(e) or ex-fiancé(e) .	Fiancé(e) or ex-fiancé(e) .	10
Mistress . .	Lover	3
Daughter . .	Father	1
Daughter . .	Mother	1
		396*

*The disparity in the total number of killers 'related' to their victims in this table and Table J occurs because some parents kill their spouse and child at the same time.

Source: Press Reports, 1957-62. See also Table J.

TABLE G

Sex of Victims

	Capital	Non-Capital	Total
Male	76	266	342
Female . . .	49	350	399
Total . . .	125	616	741*

Source: *Press reports of Trials, 1957-62.*

*One victim may suffer at the hands of more than one killer; hence the figure of victims is less than those indicted for murder.

TABLE H

March 1957–1962. Number of victims, by age at time of offence.

Age (years)	1957 Mar. 21– Dec. 31	1958	1959	1960	1961	1962	Total
Up to and including 5	15	18	11	16	14	18	92
6–14	5	5	8	12	11	5	46
15–24	15	17	20	23	33	24	132
25–34	18	13	22	22	30	15	120
35–44	9	12	17	15	15	18	86
45–54	13	19	14	17	8	8	79
55–64	6	9	11	10	13	9	58
65–74	9	8	11	7	6	14	55
75 and over	2	6	7	4	6	3	28
Not reported	4	7	3	3	11	17	47
All ages combined	96	114	124	129	147	131	741

Source: Press reports, 1957–62

TABLE J

Connection between Killer and Victim

March 1957–1962. Relationship of victim to person indicted for capital or non-capital murder.

Relationship	1957 Mar. 21–Dec. 21			1958			1959			1960			1961			1962			All years combined		
	Cap.	N/C	Total	Cap.	N/C	Total	Cap.	N/C	Total	Cap.	N/C	Total	Cap.	N/C	Total	Cap.	N/C	Total	Cap.	N/C	Total
'Related'	3	50	53	8	52	60	6	58	64	1	62	63	6	69	75	5	66	71	29	357	386‡
'Known'	5	22	27	8	26	34	6	21	27	11	29	40	8	30	38	9	26	35	47	154	201
'Strangers'	3	12	15	6	13	19	10	19	29	13	12	25	8	26	34	8	17	25	48	99	147
'Related' to one person 'known' to the other	—	—	—	—	1	1	—	1	1	—	—	—	—	—	—	—	2	2	—	2	2
Not reported	—	1	1	—	—	—	1	2	3	—	1	1	—	—	—	—	—	—	1	4	5
Total	11	85	96	22	92	114	23	101	124*	25	104	129	22	125	147	22	111	133	125	616	741†

† On two occasions one person was the victim of 2 people formally charged—one charged with capital, the other with non-capital murder.
* There is always a slightly less number of victims than killers.
Definitions:
   (i) 'Related' also includes mistress and lover; and fiancé(e).
   (ii) 'Known' also includes boy/girl friends; ex fiancé(e)s; relatives of mistress/lover.
   (iii) 'Strangers' also includes persons met for the first time just prior to the offence.
‡ Cf. Table F.

Source: Press reports, 1957–62

TABLE K

Sentences of Life Imprisonment under the Homicide Act 1957†

Killers convicted of:	Capital murder but reprieved and sentences commuted to life imprisonment	Non-capital murder	Manslaughter	Manslaughter* on grounds of diminished responsibility	Total
1957	3	20	1	4	28
1958	3§	19	—	11	33
1959	1	32	2	7	42
1960	3	32	—	11	46
1961	1	38	—	13	52
1962	—	23‡	1	9	33
Totals	11	164	4	55	234

† Does not include those under the age of 18 who are ordered to be detained at the discretion of the Home Secretary.
* These cases may include persons who since their trial have been transferred, under section 72 of the Mental Health Act 1959 to Broadmoor or other State mental institution.
§ Including one person who has since died.
‡ including one person against whom an order recommending deportation was made under the Commonwealth Immigration Act 1962.

Source: Press reports, 1957-62

TABLE L

Successful pleas of diminished responsibility since 1 November 1960 when Part V of the Mental Health Act 1959 came into force

Name	Sentence H.O.=Hospital Order; length of any restriction order under section 65 of the Mental Health Act 1959 is shown in brackets. Number of years indicates ordinary imprisonment	Trial judge and, where applicable, the C.C.A. or other disposal
1960		
Barrett	7 years	Pearson J.—transferred to Broadmoor and later repatriated to Jamaica.
Hanlon	Life	Winn J.—transferred to Broadmoor.
Lecointe	10 years	Winn J.—transferred to Broadmoor.
Morris	Life	Austin-Jones J. (C.C.A.—Parker L.C.J., Ashworth and Lawton JJ.)
Rodney	5 years	Pearson J.
Twells	Life	Havers J.
Ward	10 years	Winn J.
Wiggins	4 years	Salmon J.
1961		
Abernethy	Life	Austin Jones J.
Airey	Life	Fenton Atkinson J.
Bailey	Life	Hinchcliffe J (C.C.A.—Parker L.C.J., Ashworth and Veale JJ.)
Bryant	H.O. (12 months)	Elwes J.
Collop	Life	Havers J.
Dean	3 years' probation	Veale J.
Dovaston	H.O.	Finnemore J.
Edgington	15 years	Sachs J.
Faulkner	Life	Stable J.
Geis	15 years	Streatfeild J.—transferred to Broadmoor
Gooch	H.O.	Thesiger J.
Grist	H.O. (5 years)	Howard J.

TABLE L—*continued*

Name	Sentence H.O. = Hospital Order; length of any restriction order under section 65 of the Mental Health Act 1959 is shown in brackets. Number of years indicates ordinary imprisonment.	Trial judge and, where applicable, the C.C.A. or other disposal
Hill	Life	Fenton Atkinson J.
James	3 years	Austin Jones J. (C.C.A. —Slade, Glyn-Jones and Thompson JJ.)
James	H.O.	Elwes J.
Jones	12 months	Sachs J.
Jowett	Life	Nield J.
Kinley	Life	Winn J.
Kneller	H.O. (12 months)	Hinchcliffe J.
Nash	H.O.	Lawton J.
Nickells	3 years	Glyn-Jones J.
Nixon	10 years	Streatfeild J.
Pachy	3 years	Howard J. (C.C.A.— Parker L.C.J., Ashworth and Veale JJ.)
Pateman	H.O.	Finnemore J.
Peck	Life	Veale J.
Perkins	H.O. (12 months)	Pilcher J.
Pillinger	H.O.	Fenton Atkinson J.
Poynton	Life	Thesiger J. (C.C.A.— Finnemore, Havers and Melford Stevenson JJ.)
Prescott	Life	Nield J.
Rainbow	H.O.	Elwes J.
Sims	21 years	Finnemore J.—transferred to Broadmoor
Smith	H.O. (unlimited)	Edmund Davies J.
Sowle	H.O. (40 years)	Melford Stevenson J.
Squires	3 years	Fenton Atkinson J.
Stock	H.O. (unlimited)	Barry J.
Sweary	Life	Streatfeild J.
Warnock	Absolute discharge	Slade J.
Wibberley	H.O. (unlimited)	Glyn-Jones J.
Wilkinson	3 years	Finnemore J.

TABLE L—*continued*

Name	Sentence H.O. = Hospital Order; length of any restriction order under section 65 of the Mental Health Act 1959 is shown in brackets. Number of years indicates ordinary imprisonment.	Trial judge and, where applicable, the C.C.A. or other disposal
1962		
Abbott	H.M.P.	Hinchcliffe J. (changed to detention for life by C.C.A.—Parker L.C.J., Ashworth and Winn JJ.)
Armstrong	Life	Veale J.
Arno	H.O. (unlimited)	Paull J.
Barker	H.O. (1 year)	Melford Stevenson J.
Billings	12 years	Howard J.
Birch	H.O. (unlimited)	Finnemore J.
Blanks	H.O. (unlimited)	Lawton J.
Chisam	Life	Lyell J. (C.C.A.—Parker L.C.J., Streatfeild and Megaw JJ.)
Clarke	Life	Havers J. (C.C.A.—Parker L.C.J., Gorman and Fenton Atkinson JJ.)
Coupland	2 years' probation	Havers J.
Eastwood	Life	Phillimore J.
Flynn	Life	Phillimore J.
Gibson	H.O.	Veale J.
Golder	H.O.	Hinchcliffe J.
Gregoriou	Life	Roskill J.
Harland	2 years	Melford Stevenson J.
Harvey	H.O.	Glyn-Jones J.
Hebden	H.O.	Parker L.C.J.
Heron	Life	Roskill J.
King	H.O. (unlimited)	Veale J.
Lister	H.O.	Salmon J.
McCrorey	Life	Lyell J. (reduced from death sentence by C.C.A.—Parker L.C.J., Streatfeild and Megaw JJ.)

TABLE L—*continued*

Name	Sentence H.O.=Hospital Order; length of any restriction order under section 65 of the Mental Health Act 1959 is shown in brackets. Number of years indicates ordinary imprisonment.	Trial judge and, where applicable, the C.C.A. or other disposal
McDonnell	3 years' probation	Lawton J.
Madge	H.O.	Glyn-Jones J.
Martin	3 years	Melford Stevenson J.
Minter	H.O.	Melford Stevenson J.
Mitchell	H.O.	Elwes J.
Potter	8 years	Howard J.
Price	H.O. (unlimited)	Lawton J.
Rose	H.O. (unlimited)	Salmon J. (C.C.A.—Parker L.C.J., Widgery and Stephenson JJ.)
Russell	H.O. (unlimited)	Paull J.
Sharp	12 years	Marshall J.
Taylor	H.O.	Brabin J.
Thomas	5 years	Howard J.
Tilley	H.O. (5 years)	Paull J.
Wright	H.O. (unlimited)	Edmund Davies J.

TABLE M

Sentences of Persons Convicted under section 2 of the Homicide Act 1957

| | HOSPITAL ORDERS[1] | | | | | | | | | | |
	Without any restrictions on discharge	With restrictions of unlimited duration	With restrictions of up to 9 years	With restrictions of more than 9 years	Absolute discharge	Probation with or without condition	Life imprisonment	Imprisonment of less than 3 years	Imprisonment of 3–9 years	Imprisonment of more than 9 years	Totals
1957	—	—	—	—	—	1	4	—	2	5[4]	12
1958	—	—	—	—	—	2[2]	11	4	6	3[4]	26
1959	—	—	—	—	—	1	7	2	10	1	21
1960	—	—	—	—	—	2	11	5	5	3[5]	25
1961	7	2	5	1	1	1	13	6	—	4	40
1962	10	7	2	—	—	2	9[3]	2	2	2	36
Totals	17	9	7	1	1	9	55	19	25	18	160

1. Part V of the Mental Health Act 1959, came into force on 1 November 1960.
2. Includes one person sent to Approved School
3. Includes one infant detained for life under section 53(2) of the Children and Young Persons Act 1933.
4. Includes one person in each year who were transferred to Broadmoor following sentences of 12 years' and 15 years' imprisonment respectively.
5. Includes one person detained for 10 years under section 53(2) of the Children and Young Persons Act 1933.

Source: Press reports, 1957-62

SELECTED BIBLIOGRAPHY

Bohannan, P.: African Suicide and Homicide (Princeton University Press 1960).

Brett, P.: An Inquiry into Criminal Guilt (Stevens, 1963).

Christoph, James B.: Capital Punishment and British Politics (Allen & Unwin, 1962).

Criminal Law Revision Committee on Criminal Procedure (Insanity), 1963, (H.M.S.O. Cmnd. 2149).

Departmental Committee on Insanity and Crime, 1922–23 (H.M.S.O. Cmd. 2005).

Durkheim, Emile: Suicide (1897). English trans. Routledge 1952.

Elwin, Verrier: Maria Murder and Suicide (O.U.P., 1943).

Glueck, Sheldon: Law and Psychiatry (Tavistock Publications, 1963).

Gowers, Sir Ernest: A Life for a Life? (Chatto and Windus, 1956).

Hart, H. L. A.: Punishment and Elimination of Responsibility (The Athlone Press, 1962).

Havard, J. D. J.: The Detection of Secret Homicide (Macmillan, 1960).

von Hentig, Hans: The Criminal and his Victim (Yale University Press, 1948).

Kenny, Courtenay: Outlines of Criminal Law, 18th edition, edited by J. W. C. Turner (C.U.P., 1962).

Koestler, Arthur and Rolph, C. H.: Hanged by the Neck (Penguin Special, 1961).

McCormick, Donald: Blood on the Sea (Muller, 1962).

MacDermott, Lord: Murder in 1963 (Presidential address to the Holdsworth Club 1962-1963, delivered at the University of Birmingham).

Macdonald, J. M.: The Murderer and his Victim (Thomas, 1961).

Menninger, K. A.: Man against Himself (Hart-Davis, 1963).

Murder, A Home Office Research Unit Report (H.M.S.O., 1961).

Neustatter, W. Lindesay: The Mind of the Murderer (Christopher Johnson, 1957).

Paget, Silverman & Hollis: Hanged—and Innocent? (London, 1953).

Reinhardt, J. M.: The Psychology of Strange Killers (Charles C. Thomas, Springfield, Illinois, 1962).

Royal Commission on Capital Punishment, 1949-1953 (H.M.S.O., 1953, Cmd. 8932).

Tuttle, Elizabeth: The Crusade against Capital Punishment in Great Britain (Stevens, 1961).

Pollack, O.: The Criminality of Women (University of Pennsylvania Press, 1950).

Sargant, W.: Battle for the Mind (Heinemann, 1957).

Wertham, F.: A Show of Violence (Doubleday, 1949).

Williams, Glanville: The Working of the Homicide Act (Howard League for Penal Reform, 1961).

Wolfgang, Marvin E.: Patterns in Criminal Homicide (Oxford University Press, 1958).

Wootton, Lady [Barbara]: Social Science and Social Pathology (Allen & Unwin, 1959).

Zilboorg, Gregory: The Psychology of the Criminal Act and Punishment (Harcourt, Brace, 1954).

INDEX

GENERAL INDEX

INDEX OF CASES CITED

INDEX OF NAMES

N.B. Names of accused persons are printed in italics. Those convicted of, and executed for, capital murder are marked †. Other names are of victims, judges, authors and others.

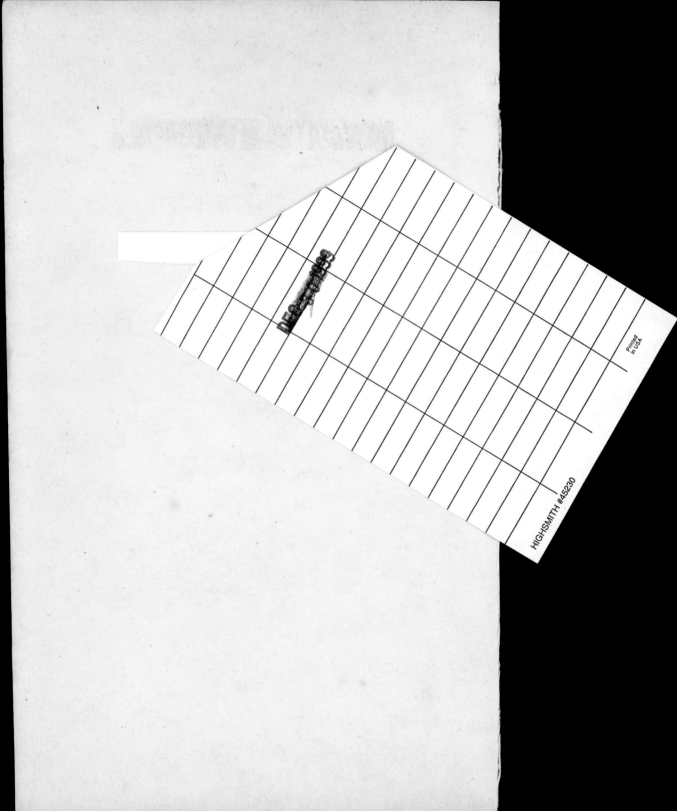